The
MUSICIAN'S
HANDBOOK

REVISED EDITION

A Practical Guide to Understanding the Music Business

1. Pursuing a Career in the Music Business
2. Types of Business Relationships
3. Key Players in Your Career
4. Sources of Revenue

BOBBY BORG

BILLBOARD BOOKS
AN IMPRINT OF WATSON-GUPTILL PUBLICATIONS/NEW YORK

Editor: John A. Foster
Designer: Leah Lococo Ltd
Production Director: Alyn Evans

First published in 2008 by Billboard Books,
an imprint of Watson-Guptill Publications,
Nielsen Business Media, a division of The Nielsen Company
770 Broadway, New York, NY 10003
www.watsonguptill.com

Library of Congress Cataloging-in-Publication Data

Borg, Bobby.

The musician's handbook : a practical guide to understanding the music business / by Bobby Borg.

p. cm.

ISBN-13: 978-0-8230-9970-2

ISBN-10: 0-8230-9970-9

1. Music trade. I. Title.

ML3790.B68 2008

780.2373—dc22

2007031178

Printed in the United States

First printing, 2008

1 2 3 4 5 6 7 / 14 13 12 11 10 09 08

ACKNOWLEDGMENTS

Thanks to my Family: Dad, Mom, Chris, Pete, Joe, Wendy, Jonathan, and Michael.

Thanks to Billboard: Victoria Craven (editorial director), John Foster (editor), Nicole Miller (senior publicist), Andrea Glickson (director of publicity), Bob Nirkind (former executive editor), Alyn Evans and Sal Destro (production), and Leah Lococo (designer), and to all those behind the scenes.

Thanks to my technical advisors, consultants, focus group members, proofreaders, close friends, and to those directly involved in the 2008 revision of this book: Dina LaPolt (LaPolt Law P.C.), Burgundy Morgan, ESQ, Steven Winogradsky, ESQ, Shawna Hilleary, ESQ (Artist Law Group), Virginnie Parant, ESQ (Artist Law Group), Joe Sofio, ESQ (law office of Joseph M. Sofio), Jeff Cohen, ESQ (Millen, White, Zelano, and Branigan), Gerry Bryant (secretary of The Board of Directors of California Lawyers for the Arts), Michael Eames (president, PEN Music Group, Inc.), Ernie Petito (Warner/Chappell), Neil J. Gillis (president, North America and Global Head Creative), Ted Lowe (Choicetracks, Inc.), James Leech (writer/public relations, SESAC), Kyle Staggs (vice president of business and legal affairs, BugMusic), Ed Pierson (vice president of legal affairs, Warner/Chappell Music), Ryan D Kuper (founder, Redemption Records/Balance Entertainment), Britt Draska (consultant & director of royalties, Lakeshore Entertainment Group), Brian Perera (president, Cleopatra Records), Rob "Blasko" Nicholson (Mercenary Management), Nancy Meyer (Bates Meyer, Inc), John Hartmann (former manager of Eagles and others), Jake Versluis (Verse Management Corp.), Mike Gormerly (L.A. Personal Development), Robert Shahnazarian, JR. (producer of Killers, Incubus, John Legend, and others), Jeff Weber (Weberworks Entertainment Group), Geza X (producer of Black Flag and others), Claris Sayadian Dodge (Studio Expresso, Inc), Samm Brown III (award-winning record producer and songwriter), John Charlillo (producer), Andrew Frances (consultant), Moses Avalon (consultant), Chris Opperman (consultant), Andreas Wettstein (former vice president of new media, Warner Bros. Records), Randall Kennedy (head of marketing & sales, ARTizen Music Group), Michael Lavine (Levine Communications Office), Jeff Hinkle (Gudvi, Sussman & Oppenheim), George Fernandez (certified public accountant), Chris Fletcher (Coast to Coast Music Promotion & Booking), Ian Copeland (Frontier Booking International), Michael Laskow (CEO of TAXI), Ken Blaustein (director of A&R, Virgin Records), Dick Gabriel (AFM), Stefanie Taub (national manager of Sound Recordings/West Coast AFTRA), Bob Fierro (president, Zebra Marketing), Jimi Yamagishi (Songwriter's Network), Kenny Kerner (Musician's Institute), Pascale Helm (UCLA Extension), Mike Inez (Alice In Chains), Randy Castillo (Ozzy Osbourne), Rob Danson, Steven Rosen, Marty Ogilive, Jared Jackson, Pam Moseberry, Nard Berrings, Karyn Bryant, James Marcey, Girl Named Jaen, Francine Uyetake, and Gail Hickman,

Thanks to the educational institutions that use this book, my Crash Course panelists, and to those from whom I have obtained invaluable advice throughout the years. You know who you are. For a more complete list, see www.bobbyborg.com.

Table of
Contents

Preface

Welcome back! For several years, *The Musician's Handbook* has benefited songwriters, bands, producers, bookers, managers, start-up record labels, and countless others who are interested in a successful career in the new music industry. The book is used at top educational institutions around the country, discussed at major conventions and songwriter's camps, and reviewed in international publications online and in print. And now, the benefits of *The Musician's Handbook* live on!

What's new? With thirteen revised and updated chapters covering nearly every aspect of the music industry, including publishing, live performing and touring, merchandising, recording royalties and advances, managers, producers, agents, attorneys, solo artists, band memberships, contract employees, independent contractors, and more, I feel like this is practically a new book! New updates and features include the following:

+ New royalty rates and structures for the digital age
+ New How To tips for both the independent and do-it-yourself musician
+ Hundreds of new strategies for pursuing and succeeding in today's music business
+ New stories paralleling current events and industry happenings
+ New interviews with top industry professionals discussing new business models and future forecasts
+ Hundreds of new industry contacts, addresses, and URLs
+ Secret passwords to additional information, updates, and special perks at my website: bobbyborg.com

What makes this book unique? *The Musician's Handbook* is the layman's guide to the music industry. It's written by me, a professional musician, for musicians, providing invaluable tips that only someone who has been in the trenches himself (from reharsal rooms to recording studios, from tour buses to concert stages) could reveal to those looking to pursue a career in the music business. Furthermore, numerous music industry professionals offer invaluable wisdom, real-life anecdotes, and one-on-one interviews which give *The Musician's Handbook* a broad perspective and universal appeal. Serving as a music business consultant and educator at top institutions for several years, I focus on topics that musicians want and need to know. However, this book is not only for musicians; fledgling attorneys, personal managers, producers, and many others in the music business can gain an invaluable perspective on this fascinating industry. *The Musician's Handbook* is a solid, concise, entertaining, and easy-to-read introduction to the

The Musician's Handbook investigates the realities behind the glamorous fantasy world of the music business that is often portrayed in the media. The book is designed to help you understand the ins and outs of the music industry. At times it will seem harsh, but the more aware you are of the potential obstacles in your path, the better prepared you will be to overcome them. Whether you're out on the road or just getting ready to cut your first record, it pays to be armed with as much ammunition as possible. Perhaps this quote from *The Art of War*, a classic work of military strategy and Eastern philosophy popular among music industry executives, will help illustrate my point:

"Know the ground, know the weather; your victory will then be total."
—SUN TZU, THE ART OF WAR

How to use this book. Although the best way to fully appreciate this book is to read it from front to back so that you don't miss a single beat, *The Musician's Handbook* is also designed so that each chapter can be understood and followed on its own, allowing you to refer to individual chapters as they relate to your personal career. Therefore, you can get exactly what you want, when you need it. And for those of you who are really on the fast track, *The Musician's Handbook* is full of boxed anecdotes and sidebars that relate to important aspects of the text, making it easy to flip through and read interesting stories and facts. Every attempt has been made to keep the information as current as possible, but since the music business is fast and ever changing—especially in the face of emerging technologies and the Internet—I encourage readers to keep up with the weekly trade magazines, websites, and my webpage.

The Musician's Handbook will provide you with a strong foundation in the music business, but every business situation you encounter will be unique. Therefore, I strongly recommend that you always consider the advice of an appropriate business professional.

Keep in mind that the music business is not always easy to understand, and that it will require some patience and work to do so. But remember, a journey of a thousand miles begins with a single step. The information presented here is only as good as your desire to comprehend and use it.

With talent, preparation, and a lot of luck, you can have an extremely rewarding career—creatively and financially—in music. I hope this book will be a valuable tool that helps you achieve your professional goals. Now, let's get to it!

CHAPTER 1

Important Tips
to Consider on Your
Path to Success

"The music business is a cruel and shallow money trench;
a long plastic hallway where thieves and pimps run free, and
good men die like dogs. There's also a negative side."
—HUNTER S. THOMPSON

Let there be no mistake—pursuing a career in the music industry is not easy, nor is it for the thin-skinned. The truth is that all the successful artists and bands you see glamorized on television or in magazine articles represent only a minuscule percentage of all the bands in, or trying to break into, the music business today. Even after getting signed to a recording agreement, there are still no guarantees for success. As estimated by the Recording Industry Association of America (RIAA), 90 percent of all bands released by traditional labels fail to turn a profit. As a result, new bands are usually dropped from their record contracts and are never heard from again.

Knowing these odds, why would anyone in their right mind continue to pursue a career in the music business? The love of playing music and the success stories of renowned artists inspire plenty of people to try. Hey, why can't you be one of the lucky ones who achieve tremendous success or at least makes ends meet doing what you love as an independent musician, artist, or songwriter? You're talented, you're smart, and you're reading this book to better understand the inner workings of the music industry. That's more than the majority of musicians out there can say. You've already got a lot going in your favor!

Although there are no rules or guidelines that can guarantee a prosperous and long-lasting career in the music business, in this chapter, I highlight some important issues and tips you should consider as you pursue your path to success. Regardless of whether you're a musician, a songwriter trying to place your music in film or TV, or a solo artist or band member promoting your own CD or trying to get a record deal, these tips apply to you!

ANALYZE YOUR CAREER MOTIVATIONS AND GOALS

Understand what truly motivates you. Do you want to be successful at all costs, simply cash in and be wealthy? Or would you rather be respected artistically, make a long-lasting contribution to the world of music, and settle for a modest living? As you know, success and wealth do not always go hand in hand with respect. Are you pursuing a career in music for the fame, fun, and wild lifestyle it may bring you? Or are you pursuing this career because of the spiritual satisfaction it brings, and there is nothing else in life you would rather do?

Ultimately, your answers to these questions are going to affect the career decisions you make. For that reason, you need to be totally honest with yourself about your goals. Having said that, it's also extremely important to interpret the goals of the people and organizations with whom you may become professionally involved. What motivates them? Do you truly respect and like them, and do they in return truly respect and like you? Do you really want to do business with these people? Tour manager/agent/promoter Chris Arnstein calls this approach to self-awareness the "decision-making tree." Your decisions (or branches) should be based on the core (or root) of who you truly are as a person. If you haven't thought about your real motivation for pursuing music professionally, now is a good time to do so.

DEVELOP A REALISTIC OUTLOOK BY IGNORING THE MEDIA HYPE

Don't be blinded by media hype or glamor. It's no secret that the expensive houses, the cars, the yachts, the beautiful women and handsome men, and the large screaming audiences that you see in the videos for most new bands are actually rented or hired for the video. When you're signed to a record company, these expenses (which have been known to cost hundreds to thousands of dollars) are all charged against your future earnings. The majority of artists are never able to pay these back; these artists are usually dropped by their labels. Singer Johnny Rzeznik of the band Goo Goo Dolls says, "Record companies sell the dream. They never talk about the struggle." It's important for you to completely understand the realities of the music business beyond the fantasy world portrayed by the media. Are you willing to give it your all, work odd jobs just to pay for your rehearsal studio and to record your own CD, book your own gigs, pay to play, promote your music 24/7 on the Internet and all over your own hometown, hit the road in a passenger van, sleep five in a cramped hotel room, and take rejection after rejection for a crack at the big time? Even then, your break may never come. Most successful artists have lived and breathed music with no thoughts of ever turning back. Is this the path for you?

MAKE REALISTIC CAREER DECISIONS BY EDUCATING YOURSELF FIRST

Understand how the music industry works behind the scenes. Learn the business inside and out so that you can make realistic and educated business decisions rather than decisions based on dreams. Read music trade magazines such as *Billboard.* Read books on the music business such as Don Passman's *All You Need To Know about the Music Business*; M. William Krasilovsky, Sidney Shemel, Jonathan Feinstein, and John M. Gross's *This Business of Music*; Peter Thrall's *What They'll Never Tell You about the Music Business*; and Richard Schulenberg's *Legal Aspects of the Music Industry*, as well as biographies of popular artists such as *The Dirt,* which chronicles Mötley Crüe's rise and fall. Check out the VH1 video series *Behind the Music* for a dose of reality television. Take a music industry course offered at a nearby college: New York University (NYU), Berklee College of Music in Boston, and the University of California at Los Angeles (UCLA) offer excellent classes. Pay a music business consultant to meet with you and discuss your career (you can contact me at www.bobbyborg.com if you'd like). Speak to fellow artists who have more experience than you and who have been in the trenches themselves. Make sure you're willing to make the major sacrifices and take the risks necessary to pursue your goals. The life of a musician is not an easy one. As Billy Mitchell says in his book *The Gigging Musician*, "The music business is a living thing, a beautiful yet vicious animal that sometimes eats its young. It is important that you know what [the business] is . . . and who you are."

COME TO TERMS WITH THE ECONOMIC REALITIES OF THE MUSIC BUSINESS

Understand that there are far easier ways to make money than being in the music business. The truth is that most musicians get involved in the business simply because of their love of music—not for the love of money. In fact, for most musicians, music is akin to a fever that never goes away. It's an addiction—a need to express oneself. Those musicians who are in the business only to become wealthy are fooling themselves. Sure, there are exceptions to every rule, but the majority of bands never reach financial security, even after being signed. Make sure you're playing music because there's nothing else that you'd rather do. *You've got to love it*. If you can make a lot of money doing it, then that's icing on the cake. When a Los Angeles DJ at KROQ asked the British band Coldplay what they attributed their success in the music business to, they quickly responded, "Not caring about fame and fortune. Whatever comes our way is only gravy."

OVERCOME AGE DISCRIMINATION IN THE MUSIC BUSINESS

Although age can be a sensitive subject for most musicians, you should know that there's a general prejudice against aging in the commercial music industry: The industry views music as a youth-oriented business. The feeling is that a musician's life expectancy in the pop, rock, R&B, and rap genres parallels that of an athlete's career span in the sports world. As you approach the age of thirty-five, your chances of succeeding have significantly diminished. That fact is somewhat paradoxical, since musicians' skills tend only to improve with age and experience, but most record companies rely heavily on youth, vitality, and sex appeal to sell albums. Most record labels also prefer signing younger acts that, if successful, can bring them a return on their initial investment for several years to come. A record company is a business just like any other, and the bottom line comes first and foremost.

So, does all this mean that unsigned artists nearing their mid-thirties should throw in the towel and abandon their life dreams if they still haven't found success with the MTV generation? Of course not! The professional artist who takes care of his or her health and image can get away with looking, acting, and seeming much younger than he or she actually is. And, of course, there's always the rare exception to the rule whereby an older, more "adult" artist breaks all the barriers and is signed strictly on the virtue of his or her musical talent and songwriting abilities—bravo! But even if you're one of the lucky artists who gets that big break, only the most creative and business-minded artist can still appeal to younger audiences both musically and physically as he or she approaches the ages of fifty or sixty. Do I agree with this type of thinking? NO! But, the music business has consistently maintained this age bias.

So, what's the whole point of this discussion? Although age is not something you think about in the entertainment business when you're in your teens or twenties, age and image in the commercial marketplace are very real issues for musicians in their "middle years." Therefore, unless you want to go on a personal crusade to change the status quo (and some artists do—hats off to them), it's advisable to look at your career reasonably and have the foresight to set realistic goals for yourself. For instance, if you are older, and are considering your career status, age, and image, it might be prudent to focus on a genre of music whose audience has a more sophisticated demographic profile or to seek a recording deal with a smaller, less commercial, independent record label, or to simply resort to a do-it-yourself (DIY) approach—a situation in which you can make all of your own business decisions and not let the record companies dictate what you can and cannot do and how old you have to be to do it! Taking this one step further, some musicians find more purpose in doing "behind the scenes" work—composing for other artists, for film and television, and even for video games; there's big money there! To be sure, doing such work is not about abandoning your original dreams or succumbing to this age prejudice; it's about looking at age and image in the music business realistically and learning how to continually reinvent and brand yourself over time to find your appropriate audience.

REALIZE YOUR DREAMS BY VISUALIZING THEM FIRST

In the early 1990s, in a small club called the Button South in Fort Lauderdale, Florida, I witnessed Marilyn Manson gaze out into the audience and say, "One day I'm going to be a pop star who shocks the world." He truly believed this, and over many years, with one successful album and tour after another, he proved himself right.

Visualize your dreams. As the old saying goes, "A picture is worth a thousand words." If you can hold a picture of success in your mind and keep it focused by having faith in yourself, your subconscious can bring it to pass. In his best-selling book *The Power of Your Subconscious Mind,* author Joseph Murphy calls this the "mental-movie method." In his words, "[If I] act as though I am . . . I will be."

PREPARE FOR THE LONG HAUL BY BECOMING FINANCIALLY SOUND

There are countless stories about people who move to the "big city" and give themselves six months to "make it." Needless to say, that is a completely unrealistic plan. Most of these people end up either returning home broke or living on a friend's couch feeling helpless. Be prepared (both financially and mentally) to spend years pursuing your goals. Find ways to live comfortably while working toward your dream. If you do, you'll be in a better position to make connections with important people without appearing desperate. Success won't happen overnight. Billy Mitchell sums things up once again: "Too many of us think that the world of music is a magic-carpet ride, from the garage to superstardom. It ain't. It's blood, sweat, and tears—and then you still might not get the gig." Learn to be simultaneously persistent and patient.

EXPECT THE WORST TO HAPPEN SO THAT THE WORST WON'T SEEM SO BAD

David Geffen, a music industry mogul, once said jokingly, "There's your plan, and there's God's plan—and yours doesn't matter." Realize you can't control everything that happens in your life. Focus on the positive, but remember the old saying: "Shit happens!" Bands fall apart, CDs sell poorly, industry reps fail to show for showcase performances, names get misspelled on venue marquees and in magazines, music journalists write unfavorable reviews, and people will try to rip you off. Such events are an inevitable part of pursuing a career in music and an aspect that's certainly not for the thin-skinned. Expect to be knocked down, but learn how to get up quickly and see the lesson in every negative experience. To survive in the music business, you must be resilient. As Jon Kabat-Zinn says in his book *Wherever You Go, There You Are,* "You can't stop the waves, but you can surely learn to surf."

LEARN HOW TO OVERCOME REJECTION BY NOT TAKING IT PERSONALLY

Don't take the music business too personally. Don't abandon your dreams every time you receive a rejection letter or a door shuts in your face. Most successful artists knocked on doors and created their own opportunities for years before finally getting their big break. Even then, if a record company fails to promote your band and suddenly drops you, keep the fact that it's strictly business in mind. Companies are interested in one thing: an immediate return on their investments. No matter how talented you think you are, the music business is about profit and the bottom line. After all, this is show business: If there's no business, there's no show.

ENJOY THE JOURNEY BY LEARNING TO LIGHTEN UP

I once heard a great expression: "Be happy now, for you're a long time dead." Working hard toward achieving your goals is extremely important, but it's equally important to learn not to take yourself too seriously. Have a little fun in your endeavors. Lighten up! Smile! You'll project a much more confident and positive attitude. You'll be less stressed-out and more approachable. This is the entertainment industry—how can you expect to entertain others if you can't entertain yourself? Don't waste valuable energy being hateful, envious, or jealous of others' successes, and never associate with those who can infect you with negativity. Stay positive! Believe that one day you, too, will get your big break. Just keep in mind that a record contract is not the key to happiness; it's the beginning of a long journey—and for many artists, it's the beginning of a long nightmare. There are no guarantees in the music business, no matter how hard you work, so learn to enjoy the ride each and every day. You'll be healthier mentally and much happier.

LET GO OF YOUR FEARS AND LEARN HOW TO GO FOR IT

According to Danny Sugerman and Jerry Hopkins' book *No One Here Gets Out Alive,* Jim Morrison once asked, "If your life was a movie, would anyone want to watch it?" The answer is up to you. Many artists claim they want exciting and extremely successful careers, yet they never take the serious steps and make the real commitment necessary to realize their goals. Unfortunately, a half-assed approach just doesn't cut it in the music business. If you have what it takes—if you're realistic, smart, and talented—then what's holding you back from giving your career your best shot? Perhaps it's the fear of moving to the big city, the fear of rejection, or the fear of going broke. Regardless of your reasons, understand that your fears are just that—fears. They can be overcome.

By learning to replace your negative thoughts with more positive ones, you will have won half the battle already. You'll be armed with the determination that's necessary to forge ahead in this competitive business. You'll have the mental clarity to devise a logical plan of attack. What's the worst that can happen, anyway? You might fall short of getting what you want. But you'll at least

According to boxer Mike Tyson, "Fear is like fire. It can either cook for you or it can burn you." Make it cook for you.

know you gave your career your best shot. As the saying goes, "When you reach for the stars, you may not quite get one, but you won't come up with a handful of mud either." Singer/songwriter Jewel suffered through one full-time job after another before she finally decided to move into her van and devote 100 percent of her time to her musical career. She supposedly ate fruit off trees at times just to survive. She began playing local coffeehouses and was eventually signed to Atlantic Records. Her record *Pieces of You* was released in 1995 and took fourteen months to break, but it became a best seller with the hit song "Who Will Save Your Soul."

KNOW YOUR LIMITATIONS AND EXPLOIT YOUR STRENGTHS

The three most significant benefits of knowing your limitations and exploiting your strengths are as follows. First, you will be able to concentrate on improving your weaknesses (for example, instead of pretending to know everything about the music business, you'll read this book and others like it and acquire some useful knowledge). Second, you'll learn to surround yourself with people who can help minimize your limitations (e.g., you'll choose your band members wisely and know when to step back and let them shine). And finally, knowing your limitations and exploiting your strengths allows you to focus, capitalize on, and build on your best attributes (you'll exploit your best physical characteristics when defining your visual image, write songs to show off your strongest vocal range, or use your sense of humor or ability to dance to produce stage routines that get the audience engaged and excited every time). Drummer Kenwood Dennard, who has performed with Sting and Dizzy Gillespie, says, "Find your forte and excel. No one is going to judge you for what they don't see; they're going to judge you for what is presented before them." This brings to mind the old expression, "It's not how much you have, it's how you use what you've got." Or, in the unforgettable words of the late James Brown, "You gotta use whatcha got ta get jus what ya want."

AC/DC knew that they were not musical geniuses, but they capitalized on their abilities to use the same three chords to write one successful record after another. And because the members of the band No Doubt knew that their fans most identified with the charismatic and beautiful Gwen Stefani, the band enjoyed several years of success by letting go of their egos and doing their part of providing well-crafted songs and tight performances.

By knowing your limitations and exploiting your strengths, you'll not only put your best foot forward 100 percent of the time, but you will also know when to step back and allow others to shine in areas where you're lacking.

LOCATE YOURSELF IN THE MOST OPPORTUNE CITY TO SUCCEED

Where is the best place to live and pursue your musical career anyway? Is it Los Angeles? New York? Nashville? Your very own hometown? Living in one of the larger cities in the country will present you with more opportunities to meet other musicians and will make you more accessible, for instance, to record company executives who may be interested in signing your band. On the other hand, there's more competition in larger cities, and you may get lost in the sauce. You may be able to create a big enough wave in your small town to entice the record companies to come to you. Record company representatives and scouts check local music papers, surf the Web for MP3 files, and review college radio play lists. If your band is really good and you've built up a strong buzz, the record companies will find you regardless of where you are.

PROTECT YOURSELF FROM THE START BY GETTING EVERYTHING IN WRITING

Always get the terms and conditions of all business agreements in writing and keep a signed and dated copy of them in your files. This will clarify the expectations of each party and provide protection in case there's a dispute; people often forget what they promise. Even between friends, a written agreement is an essential tool for establishing a professional relationship. Although you may initially question this point, you'll see its importance illustrated in several real-life examples throughout this book.

> As the old adage says, "An oral agreement isn't worth the paper it's written on." Believe it!

By law, an agreement should consist of three basic requirements: offer, consideration, and acceptance. When an offer is made with mutual consideration (i.e., when there's a benefit for both parties, such as a service in return for a fee) and the said offer is accepted, then a contract is formed. An agreement doesn't necessarily have to be in writing, but if a dispute occurs, clear and convincing written evidence produces a firm account of the truth.

> The more involved a business transaction, such as the signing of a recording agreement, the more necessary it is to retain an experienced entertainment attorney to make sure your rights and interests are protected. Attorneys are covered in detail in Chapter 5.

Sometimes the people with whom you're doing business (employers, bands, managers, etc.) may respond unfavorably to your requests for a written agreement. Or, they'll present you with an agreement and then be unwilling to negotiate the terms. This type of behavior will offer insight into what you can ultimately expect from the relationship. In these predicaments, it's especially important that you have a clear understanding of your objectives and goals and of what you will and will not give up.

> The music business is very complex and confusing, but learn to trust your gut instincts. If a situation doesn't feel right from the beginning, it probably isn't. This principle of trusting your snap judgment is outlined in Malcolm Gladwell's powerful book *Blink*.

PAY YOUR DUES, BUT USE YOUR HEAD

Paying your dues means paying the price for your lack of professional experience. The price is your time and hard work, which sometimes ends with little or no compensation. However, keep in mind that the more experience you gain, the more valuable a commodity you become. Whether you're in a band that's playing local clubs for free or a musician who's performing on demo recordings for pennies, the day will come when you're justly compensated. It's not always what you earn but what you learn that matters.

Warning: There are many people in the business who will attempt to take advantage of your inexperience. Welcome to the "school of hard knocks," or as some call it, "the new kid" treatment. Stay focused! Use the relationships you develop as stepping stones toward your professional goals. But draw the line if you feel that the outcome may have a negative impact on your career, or if you generally feel that you're being ripped off!

DELIVER THE GOODS BY KNOWING YOUR CRAFT, AND THEN SOME

Know your craft and be prepared to deliver the goods. Whether you play an instrument, write songs, or sing in a band, take the time to become as proficient as possible. At first glance, the music business appears to be glamorous and fun, but most successful artists have sweat blood and tears in the course of honing their professional skills. This is especially true of successful songwriters! Songwriting, probably the most important skill to have in this industry, requires tremendous amounts of time and effort to master. Be sure to check out books like John Braheny's *The Craft and Business of Songwriting* and Jason Blume's *This Business of Songwriting*, and to attend as many classes and seminars on the subject as possible. Also, work at developing your communication and networking skills as well. Become a better writer and speaker, develop your telephone and computer skills, and learn to have a sense of humor. Your physical presentation is also very important; make your health and diet a priority. Become a well-rounded and well-balanced person. As Dan Kimpel says in his book *Networking in the Music Business*, "Once you've opened up some doors, you need something amazing to shove inside." But with that said, know when "enough is enough." Understand that pushing yourself to be too perfect can be as damaging as not pushing yourself at all. This is not to be taken lightly.

WHAT MAKES A SONG A HIT? Songwriting is probably the single most important skill for artists to master. But what makes a hit? Ralph Murphy, vice president of ASCAP in Nashville, conducted research in conjunction with Belmont University on eighteen #1 hits and found the following common characteristics:

1. Style/Genre: pop or country
2. Subject: romantic, sad/heartfelt, or humorous
3. Lyric: tells a clear story and/or relates a strong opinion
4. Person/Tense: in first person (I/me/my) or second person (you/your)
5. Melody: linear melody (very few chord changes) in the verse, growing to a soaring melody (significant chord changes) in the chorus
6. Structure: verse, chorus, verse, chorus, bridge, chorus, out
7. Tempo: mid- to up-tempo
8. Time signature: 4/4 time
9. Introduction: up to 13 seconds long, but no longer
10. Authorship: co-written between the artist and another professional songwriter

GET AHEAD BY ADOPTING A SALES APPROACH

Many musicians overuse the excuse that they're all about the music and not about the sale. Wrong! Nobody is going to invest their time or energy in your career if you're not willing to invest a little time and energy into it yourself. This is especially true at the beginning of your career. Read sales and negotiation books such as *Zig Ziglar's Secrets of Closing the Sale* and *How to Master the Art of Selling* by Tom Hopkins. Selling doesn't have to be sleazy or deceptive. As long as you're honest and your intentions are pure, it's simply a way of letting people know what you have to offer. Even after you're signed, most artists don't realize that they still have to continue selling themselves. Your success is not left entirely in the record company's hands! It's a team effort. You'll have to meet with radio station personnel and participate in interviews so that they'll play your single. Schmooze with retail buyers at record stores so that they'll stock your record. Try to get gigs opening for more well-known bands with enthusiastic fans to develop a strong following of your own. Let your live audience know where it can purchase your record. (Many musicians actually feel they're "selling out" by doing this.) Meet with fans after your live performances to sign autographs, and participate in Internet chat rooms to collect fan names for your promotional street teams. The list goes on . . . In the words of Andy Gould, who has managed Linkin Park, Jurassic 5, and Rob Zombie, "A band's idea of working can't be smoking pot and doing groupies." Simply put, if you expect to get ahead, you must be willing to work hard at selling yourself.

GET THINGS DONE BY DOING WHAT YOU SAY

The best musicians in the world aren't worth a damn if they're unreliable. It's amazing how many musicians are passive when it comes to business. Many find it difficult to follow through in a timely manner with simple business matters such as returning a phone call or showing up to a rehearsal on time. This may be due to the general artistic nature of musicians or simply a lack of motivation. They tend to talk about what they're going to do but never do it. In what may seem to be a truism, respected music publicist Laurie Gorman says, "The key to success is simply doing what you say you're going to do." Or, to put it another way, as hockey legend Wayne Gretzky once said, "One hundred percent of all the shots you don't take are guaranteed not to go in." It may appear that most musicians lead a carefree and laid-back life, but those who are the most successful had a clear vision of their goals and have worked extremely hard to achieve them.

DEFINE YOUR MUSICAL CATEGORY AND IDENTIFY YOUR AUDIENCE

Author Jeffrey P. Fisher, in his book *Ruthless Self-Promotion in the Music Industry*, says, "The world is not your market." This is an extremely important point. Many artists lose their focus by trying to reach everyone at once. They define their music in broad terms like "modern alternative, indie-punk rock with a hip-hop and quasi-Latin flair," and they claim their audience includes "everyone from ages four to eighty" (from their young niece to their grandparents). It's admirable for artists to want to cover all musical categories and reach people of all ages, but this isn't the most prudent business approach—it doesn't lend to a focused marketing campaign, nor does it make sense economically. Instead, you must work toward defining your musical category in one clear word (alternative, pop, R&B, etc.), know where it fits on store shelves and online sites, and understand what radio shows and formats it is most appropriate for. Furthermore, you must understand what age group, race, and gender your music is most appealing to and know what fashions, websites, and lifestyles your demographic fans gravitate toward. All this will help you to maximize your promotional efforts and dollars and help you to better meet the wants and needs of your target fans.

Defining your market is not an issue of "labeling" or "pigeonholing" yourself, nor does it mean giving in to the mainstream corporate mentality. Artists such as Elvis Presley, Prince, Madonna, Michael Jackson, David Bowie, Lenny Kravitz, and Marilyn Manson are all unique in their own way, but they had a clear understanding of where their music fit in the marketplace and of who their target audience was. With this understanding, they established a very consistent package, or "brand," from album covers, logos, photographs and videos to merchandising and live performances. Branding is vital to the overall success of any artist. It gives consumers something substantial to latch onto and identify with. In the words of Jeffrey Jampol (personal manager for Tal Bachman), "No one really cares about just the soap in a box, but the brand name *Tide* is worth millions."

Rather than grumbling about why your music has to be labeled and why it has to fit into specific categories, take a course on marketing at your local college and research the answers. Check out books like *This Business of Music Marketing and Promotion* by Tad Lathrop and Jim Pettigrew Jr. and *Ogilvy on Advertising,* written by advertising mogul David Ogilvy. You'll realize that even the major labels, with all their manpower and deep budgets, must target specific demographic markets because it's just not economically practical to do anything else. It can cost millions of dollars trying to break one artist into a very specific market, and yet there are still no guarantees for success. In fact, nine out of ten records released by most labels are unsuccessful by commercial standards.

Keep in mind that creating music is an art, but getting it heard is a very strategic and serious business. It may take some time to figure out what your identity or niche market is, but you should at least start giving it some serious thought today.

KNOW WHEN TO A USE A PRESS KIT AND WHAT IT SHOULD INCLUDE

When CDs, biographies, one-sheets, photographs, and press clippings are assembled in one package or folder, they are commonly known as a physical press kit, or more simply, a "press kit." While these two terms are relatively familiar to most artists and bands, you'd be surprised at the number of persons who still have difficulty understanding when and when not to use the press kit and knowing the finer details of what a press kit should include.

When and When Not to Use a Press Kit

Press kits are most useful when you are trying to get exposure (interviews, stories, and reviews) in newspapers, magazines, and Internet sites. They are also helpful when trying to get booked in a club or other live performance venue. A press kit may even entice an attorney or personal manager into representing you.

On the other hand, sending out your press kit to every record label or music publisher you find in a resource book is not a very practical method for furthering your career. The reality is that out of the thousands of "unsolicited packages" that record companies and publishers receive in the mail each year containing press kits, perhaps one band will get discovered. There are tremendous odds against obtaining a record contract this way. In fact, your package will most likely end up in a wastebasket without anyone ever reviewing it. Although frustrating, it is the harsh reality.

Another misconception is that a press kit will lead you to a great audition and gig. Many musicians waste their time, energy, and money sitting at home sending unsolicited packages to management companies with hopes they might get a call for the next big audition. Perhaps a far more effective approach to getting a big gig would be to just get out, be heard, make friends, and personally hand out business cards directing folks to your website, where more detailed information can be retrieved. Keep in mind that the majority of all the work you receive will be based on personal relationships that you form and nurture over the years.

What a Press Kit Should Include

Now that some of the misconceptions about when, and when not, to use press kits are out of the way, let's discuss the finer points of what a press kit should include.

Compact Disc

Your press kit should contain either a full-length CD or a three-song demo that highlights your most memorable material—*be sure to put your very best song first*. Although there are some exceptions depending on whom you are sending your press kit to, if you include too many songs or if you include songs that are too diverse in style, you may send the message that you're not sure what it is you do.

The production of your CD should be as high in quality as you can afford. The key is not to leave anything to the imagination of your intended audience. Fortunately, digital equipment has enabled musicians to cut "broadcast quality" demos in their own homes (with a little skill, of course). If you don't own your own recording gear, chances are that you have a friend who has home equipment and may be willing to help. Just be sure that both the CD and the CD packaging are clearly marked with the song titles and your contact information.

Biography

Your press kit should also include a biography (or bio). A bio can come in a variety of lengths but should be no longer than one page (about 500 words). Be sure to give a professional appearance by including your name and logo centered at the top of the page, along with your address, e-mail, and website. Avoid using a lot of flowery adjectives and big words, and focus on being as informative as possible. Indicate the date your band formed and the city in which you reside. Clearly identify the style of your music and "like" bands (i.e., the bands you sound most like). List the members of the band and the instruments they play. If there's a unique story about how your band formed or about the various members in your group, include it—this gives writers at newspapers and magazines a special twist or hook when writing about your band. Also list all of your band's accomplishments (number of CDs sold, radio stations that have played your music, etc.). If you have any flattering quotes from important industry people, include them here as well—but don't overdo it. Including fifteen quotes from people no one knows is pointless. Conclude your bio by stating what you plan to do next to further your career (recording your new release, planning a tour, etc.). This shows you're proactive and not waiting for anyone to help. At the bottom of the page, restate your contact info. Check out other bands' bios on the Web and see what their approaches are. If you're not an experienced writer, finding someone skilled to write your bio is a good idea. If you can find someone with influence, such as a local radio personality or journalist, all the better.

Photograph

A picture of your band should also be included in your press kit. People will not only want to hear and read about you, but they'll want to see what you look like. It ties your whole package together. While it's no longer necessary to include a glossy 8 x 10 photo of your band in your press kit (though it doesn't hurt to have one), you'll at least need to drag a small JPEG of your photo onto your bio page or "one-sheet" (one-sheets will be discussed in a moment). You might also include a burned disc containing the photo in your press kit or let the recipients know where they can download it from the Internet. Just make sure that the style and composition of your picture is consistent with your music—if you're in a hard rock band, then you must look hard rock. If you're not sure what image you want to portray, review magazines like *Rolling Stone* to see what other bands are doing and/or *Details* to investigate current fashion trends. And though I'm sure you have a lot of buddies running around with digital cameras claiming to be expert photographers, I highly recommend hiring a professional who has experience working with musicians. *You only have one chance to make a good first impression.*

One-Sheet

A one-sheet is literally one-sheet of paper that combines your bio and photo. A typical style for a one-sheet includes your picture aligned to the left of the page, key information about your career in bullet points to the right, brief biographical information below the photo, and your contact information. If you have a bar code on your CD packaging, a one-sheet often includes this as well. A one-sheet can either be used together with, or in lieu of, your bio.

Tear Sheets

our press kit can also include clippings, known as "tear sheets," from newspapers and magazines you've collected over the months. Clippings help prove that you're established and not just another fly-by-night operation. Again, don't overuse them. Use the best reviews and articles, and highlight the most interesting paragraphs or quotes.

Merchandising Items

Personalized key chains, CD case openers, stickers, buttons, and other merchandising items can be included in your press kit to serve as continual reminders of your band to the recipients. But be conservative in what you send. Overstuffing your press kits with a lot of "extras" increases your postage and handling costs, and it may even send the message that you're more about flash. Remember, when it comes right down to it, your music is what's most important.

Cover Letter

An important part of the press kit—and usually the first thing that prospective magazine editors, journalists, and publicists read—is the cover letter. When clearly written, the cover letter addresses who you are, what you do, and what you want—all in just a few short paragraphs. It's a good idea to

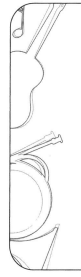

ONLINE VS. PHYSICAL PRESS: WHAT YOU NEED TO KNOW In today's digital age, the physical press kit still has its place; but establishing an online presence is quickly becoming far more important. Many publicists and bookers prefer going to a website where they can listen to your MP3s and view your photos with the click of a mouse—it beats receiving a package they have to store somewhere or otherwise throw out. And if a publicist needs your picture, he or she often asks that it be sent electronically. There are a number of free community sites like MySpace (www.myspace.com) and Tagworld (www.tagworld.com) where you can create a personal profile and even upload a music video for public viewing. Companies like Sonic Bids (www.sonicbids.com) specialize in building electronic (online) press kits and in providing gigging and other opportunities. The idea is to be prepared for whatever someone asks of you. Having both physical and online materials ready to be viewed will serve in your best interest.

close with a mention about when you will be checking back (this somewhat keeps the ball in your court). Be sure to include all of your contact information here as well.

To ensure your press package arrives intact, put all of your materials in a padded envelope. You might also consider sending it FedEx or overnight delivery to give the perception of importance. Call the person you're soliciting to inform him or her that your package is on the way and follow up in a few weeks with another call for feedback. Be realistic, though. Keep in mind that editors at magazines, just like people at record and publishing companies, receive hundreds of packages per week. Your package could easily be left unopened in a pile for several weeks or months before it's opened, so be patient, and never get mad. If you work hard enough at getting your name out there, eventually you'll succeed.

APPRECIATE THE VALUE OF MAKING CONNECTIONS

Networking is an important part of establishing a career in the music industry. A lot really does depend on whom you know—and who knows you! Put yourself in situations in which you can meet others who are already doing what you want to do, are working toward similar goals, or are in positions that can further your career. Some of the people around you right now who are pursuing a career in music will one day be successful. Learn to recognize those who are talented, intelligent, and ambitious and create your own "clique of the future." Rather than consuming all your energy trying to break into established and seemingly impenetrable cliques, get in on the ground floor and work at creating your own. The majority of the work you do will be based on word-of-mouth recommendations and the personal relationships that you form over the years. Surround yourself with happy, positive people who have goals similar to yours. Jam sessions, adult education classes, college courses, music conventions, songwriting workshops, and networking groups are great places to make new connections. For a great read, check out Dale Carnegie's best-selling book *How to Win Friends and Influence People.*

MIDEM (www.midem), SXSW (www.sxsw.com), CMJ (www.cmj), the West Coast Songwriter's Conference (www.westcoast songwriters.org), and the Durango Song Expo (www.durango song.com) are a few music conventions worth checking out. See the Music Business Registry (www.musicregistry.com) for a complete listing. ASCAP (www.ascap.com), BMI (www.bmi.com), and SESAC (www.sesac.com) are performing rights organizations that hold songwriter's workshops. NARIP (www.narip.com) is a networking group founded in Los Angeles. Also check out Just Plain Folks (www.just plainfolks.com).

HELP YOURSELF BY HELPING OTHERS

Surround yourself with as many people as possible who may be able to help you; also, surround yourself with people whom you may be able to help as well. As the old proverb goes, one hand washes the other. If you're able to find opportunities to offer something to others, there's a good chance they'll return the favor in the future. In *Zig Ziglar's Secrets of Closing the Sale,* he suggests that learning how to give people what they want is important in the business world. Whether it's putting together a band for a well-paying gig that you booked, hooking someone up with a gig on a recording session, turning someone on to a band that's looking for musicians, or reviewing a band's live performance for a music paper or website, helping others is a good way to nurture relationships and open doors.

NURTURE NEW CAREER OPPORTUNITIES WHILE YOU'RE ALREADY ON THE JOB

The best time to find work is when you're already working. It's only natural for younger musicians to believe that their current musical relationships will exist indefinitely—and they very well might. However, many of the most successful groups are composed of musicians who were originally with other established bands. Gary Cherone (who had a short stint with Van Halen) was originally the vocalist for the once successful rock group Extreme, who opened for Van Halen. Mike Inez (Alice in Chains) originally played bass with the legendary singer Ozzy Osbourne when Alice in Chains was his opening act. Dave Navarro worked with Jane's Addiction before joining the Red Hot Chili Peppers and later forming The Panic Channel. Matt Sorum worked with The Cult before joining Guns N' Roses and moving on to join Velvet Revolver. Kirk Hammett and Jason Newsted played with Exodus and Flotsam & Jetsam (respectively) before joining forces with Metallica. Newsted then left Metallica to join Ozzy Osbourne before joining Rock Star Supernova. And the list goes on . . . If you're currently an employee of a group or even a member of a band, use your situation to make as many new connections as you possibly can. People will have the opportunity to see you perform in situations where you feel confident and comfortable. Remember, networking does not have to feel deceptive or dishonest. Putting all your eggs in one basket can often backfire—a mixed metaphor never made more sense. The music business is very fickle. Tours are canceled, record releases are postponed, and bands are suddenly dumped. That's the reality! In the words of Miyamoto Musashi in *The Book of Five Rings*: "The best time to prepare for adversity is when all appears calm."

A BIRD IN HAND IS WORTH TWO IN THE BUSH A musician, who was working with a very successful singer/songwriter, was growing tired of his life on the road. When he heard of an audition to be part of the house band for a television talk show, he jumped at the opportunity. But to make the audition, the musician had to back out of a prior obligation to the singer/songwriter. As it turns out, the musician not only failed to get the television gig, but he was also fired from the singer/songwriter's band for being unreliable. The moral of the story: It's important to take advantage of every opportunity to make connections and find work, but not at the expense of your current situation. If you make a commitment to an employer or band, you must honor it first or suffer the consequences. While networking is important, maintaining the highest professional standard should be your top priority.

CLIMB THROUGH BACK WINDOWS WHEN FRONT DOORS AREN'T OPENING

If doors aren't opening, then climb through back windows. As the old saying goes, the definition of insanity is doing the same thing over and over and expecting different results. For instance, instead of trying to put your CD directly into the hands of higher-ups who are unapproachable and standoffish, get to know them personally in more casual settings. Jeff "Skunk" Baxter of the Doobie Brothers and Steely Dan say, "It doesn't matter whether you're driving an equipment truck or sweeping studio floors; get yourself into the music business any way you can." You may find that working as an intern for a management or publishing company or recording studio or writing for a local music magazine provides great opportunities to make connections. You'll have the opportunity to get to know people more naturally than you will in situations that make you appear desperate and needy. Whatever it is you're trying to accomplish, consider a variety of approaches to achieving your goals. It's important to be tenacious and not to abandon your initial plan of attack, but banging your head against the same stone wall is pointless. (For listings of available jobs in the music business, try logging onto www.entertainmentjobs.com or www.velvetrope.com.)

KNOW WHO'S WHO IN THE MUSIC BUSINESS BY KEEPING UP-TO-DATE WITH THE TRADES

Stay up-to-date on who the power brokers in the business are. How are you supposed to network and meet people in the business if you don't know who's running the business in the first place? *Billboard* magazine (www.billboard.com) regularly provides information about the movers and shakers in the industry. Read the liner notes of CD booklets and find out who's producing and managing the most successful artists. You'll be more knowledgeable and you'll appear informed and on top of your game when networking and conversing with other people in the business. It also helps to stay on top of which records are at the top ten of the *Billboard* record charts, which songs are the most downloaded on iTunes (www.itunes.com), and which songs are the most popular master tones or "mobile tones" for cell phones. When you walk into retail stores, what type of promotion do you see for the artist? Did you hear the artist on college radio stations before hearing him or her on commercial stations? Did the band tour before its record came out? How well did the tour do? Keep your ears and eyes open for the hottest independent acts as well. Are they getting a lot of attention on sites like MySpace (www.myspace.com) and YouTube (www.youtube.com)? Are they aligned with any corporate sponsors? Are they charting in College Music Journal (www.cmj.com)? All of this information will make you more knowledgeable about how the music business is run—and who's running it.

Check out these periodicals: *Music Connection* (www.musicconnection.com), *Music Row* (www.musicrow.com), *Hits* (www.hitsmagazine.com), *CMJ New Music Report* (www.cmj.com), and *Pollstar* (www.pollstar.com). MusicDish e-Journal (www.musicdish.com) is an online journal loaded with articles on the music business that is worth checking out.

KEEP YOUR OPTIONS OPEN BY DROPPING YOUR ATTITUDE

Although most of us hate to admit it, musicians can have a tendency to be somewhat aloof and rude, even to those in the business. Let's face it, it takes a lot of attitude to get on stage and be a performer, and some people just don't know how to turn themselves off. Realize that you never know who may be in a position to help you one day. An unknown musician at a jam session may become the hottest and most well-connected session player. An intern at a recording studio may be the next big producer or engineer. An opening act could go on to sell millions of records. A stage tech might someday become a successful manager. A writer from a local fanzine may one day write for *Rolling Stone*. These people can all serve as valuable connections to you one day. Understand that the music community represents only a small percentage of the entire working world. If you stay in the business long enough, you'll start to see the same people over and over again. Learn to treat others in all facets of the business as your comrades rather than your subordinates, competition, or adversaries. Look at the big picture. You'll open

THERE WILL BE ROTTENNESS. The Sex Pistols were signed by EMI in 1976, but they were soon dropped after a series of outrageous events. First, according to a 1977 *Rolling Stone* article, vocalist Johnny Rotten declared himself an antichrist who "wanted to destroy everything." The BBC radio network didn't find this funny and refused to play the Pistols' single. Then, the band publicly insulted an interviewer on the British *Today* show, calling him a "dirty fucker" and a "fuckin' rotter." The Pistols were asked to apologize, but they refused. Next, the band was involved in an incident at Heathrow Airport in which they allegedly vomited on a number of female passengers. After public pressure mounted, the Pistols were dropped from EMI. On March 10th, 1977, the band was picked up by A&M Records, only to be dropped one week later. Apparently, the Pistols vandalized several offices at the A&M headquarters and were involved in a bar fight with the head of programming for the BBC. A&M was also under a great deal of pressure from distributors, disc jockeys, and A&M's own employees to drop the band. So A&M let the group go. The Pistols received yet another shock when Virgin signed the band a few months later. The Pistols eventually broke up, but on February 24, 2006, they were officially inducted into the Rock and Roll Hall of Fame—to no one's surprise, they refused to attend the induction, calling the museum a "piss stain." Not many bands today would get as many chances as they did. Johnny Rotten sums up the Pistols' attitude in his typically arrogant, simple style, "We were right thick cunts, we were."

doors down the road that you never imagined entering.

If you're fortunate enough to have a successful career in the music business, have some understanding that your success is not single-handed. Whether you're the hottest local band around or a group that just signed a recording agreement, remember that there are a number of people behind the scenes who are just as responsible for your success as you are. Make a conscious effort to be pleasant with everyone, because no one in this business owes you anything. Don't learn this lesson the hard way! If you flaunt your attitude to a club booker, you may never be asked to play at his or her club again. If you fail to appreciate your fans, they may stop coming to your shows. If you're impatient with a music journalist whom you want to review your CD, you may never get in his or her magazine. If you piss off the music director at a college radio station, you may not get your CD played. If you're rude to people at your record company, they may spend their time and energy on someone who appreciates their hard work. Being an artist may make you feel special, but don't fool yourself into believing that the world revolves around you. This brings to mind the old adage, "The people you see on the way up are the same people you see on the way down." Very few artists stay on top forever. Get the point?

KEEP BRIDGES INTACT BY KNOWING WHEN TO WALK AWAY GRACEFULLY

Don't burn bridges. Whether you're in a band you're unhappy with or working a gig that's getting you nowhere, if a relationship doesn't feel right from the start, trust your instincts and know how to walk away before it gets worse. Tom Collins, the former manager for Aerosmith, says, "Always take the high road." The music business consists of a very small community of people, and you cannot afford to have negative energy circulating. This is important! Only fight the battles that are really worth fighting.

LOOK TO FORM RELATIONSHIPS AND NOT JUST BUSINESS DEALS

Deals come and go. Once any deal is signed, you want to be assured that you're going to have a productive and ongoing relationship with the parties involved. Will your phone calls be returned promptly, or will you feel like you're being avoided? Will the other party communicate openly with you or lie and string you along? When the going gets tough, will the other party stand by you and see things through? Legendary R&B singer Barry White once advised, "Regardless of the business deals offered, don't jump at the first one just because it's available. Make sure it also feels right. Listen to your gut."

CREATE YOUR OWN DESTINY BY BEING PROACTIVE

The late Ian Copeland, founder of Frontier Booking International (FBI) and talent agent to the Police, Sting, and No Doubt, once said, "Doors were usually closed to newcomers in the industry. We decided to stop beating on them and create new ones."

It's not enough to simply give someone a business card or demo tape and then sit back and expect to gain employment or procure a record or publishing deal. No one's going to hand you success on a silver platter. You need to take more control of your career and create your own destiny. Whether you're an individual musician, a songwriter, a solo artist or a member of a band, *attract the attention of those who can help you by first helping yourself!*

Be a Proactive Musician

If you're a musician who wants to be known as a great player rather than just a band member or if you want to perform with successful artists on lots of recordings, then get out there and be heard! Don't wait for the phone to ring. Try starting your own band first, which will give you the opportunity to showcase your individual style and let people know what you do best and most comfortably. Attend local jam sessions to find other musicians whose personalities and abilities you admire and then perform together everywhere you can. Eventually, more successful musicians and bands will begin to notice you, and they may even ask you to play on their records or tours. Get to know the producers and managers of these acts. Your reputation and opportunities can grow from there. When Guns N' Roses was looking for a replacement drummer, guitarist Slash happened to attend a concert at which drummer Matt Sorum was performing. Because Slash liked Sorum's heavy, solid style, Slash offered Sorum the gig without auditioning thousands of candidates. Sorum worked hard at putting himself in situations in which he could shine. As a result, he got a great job with Guns N' Roses, one of the biggest rock bands in the world at that time.

Be a Proactive Songwriter

If you're a songwriter (not an artist/performer) who wants to get a publishing deal and get your music placed with successful artists and in television commercials and films, you can start by contacting some of the more popular bands in your area to see if they would be interested in performing one of your songs or co-writing one with you. If the group ends up getting a record deal, bingo, you're in business! Some writers even go so far as to develop their own artists, writing and producing songs for them and helping them get signed to a recording contract. It's a long-term approach, but you have to start somewhere. In addition you can try contacting the film departments at local colleges to make your music available for student films. The film may go on to win an award, or the student may even go on to become a successful director one day—and you'll be one of the first people he or she calls. Or, try contacting some of your local radio stations to see if they're interested in using your material for advertising spots. Start with the smaller radio stations and work your way up.

Also, try contacting a few of the many "music libraries" that exist (organizations that help place songs in video games, corporate video presentations, elevators, and for on-hold calls) such as Master Source (www.mastersource.com), RipTide Music (www.riptidemusic.com), or Opus1Music Library (www.opus1-musiclibrary.com). See if they would be interested in using your material. Another viable option to further your career is to try services such as Taxi (www.taxi.com) or Pump Audio (www.pumpaudio.com), which generally serve as screeners for industry professionals who are looking for material. Keep your eyes open as well for the number of songwriting workshops and competitions offered by performing rights societies such as American Society of Composers, Authors and Publishers (ASCAP) at www.ascap.com; Broadcast Music, Inc. (BMI) at www.bmi.com; or SESAC at www.sesac.com as a way to gain exposure, earn a few bucks, and improve your songwriting skills. Other organizations to check out include the Songwriter's Guild of America (SGA) at www.songwritersguild.com, the Association of Independent Music Publishers (AIMP) at www.aimp.org, and Nashville Songwriters Association International (NSAI) at www.nashvillesongwriters.com. The opportunities to take charge of your career are endless. For over eight thousand more places to promote your music, try checking out the *Indie Bible* at www.indiebible.com.

Be a Proactive Solo Artist or Band

If you're a solo artist or part of a band that wants to get a record deal, cut your own record first! Digital technology has greatly reduced studio costs and has made home-recording equipment cheaper and more practical to own. CD manufacturing has also become more affordable. You can sell your CDs at live performances or over the Internet (the Internet provides a number of marketing opportunities through online stores and MP3 sites). Book your own live shows and tours, submit your music to college radio stations, generate press in local papers and on the Internet, and align with local and national product sponsors. Create a buzz! Build a following. You'll be surprised by how many people you'll attract in the industry once you set the wheels in motion. Everybody likes a winner, and they will want to be part of your success by associating themselves with you.

"I didn't start out with dreams of rock stardom. I started out with the gratification of playing music for people. Just being happy where you are is a necessary ingredient for going the SLOW way." —ANI DIFRANCO

Note: DiFranco started her own label, and at one point sales of her albums were known to have reached thirty-thousand copies per month.

Gangsta rapper Master P also started his own label, No Limit, with a small inheritance he received from his grandfather. Releasing his own recordings, as well as the recordings of groups he signed, Master P created a mini-empire in seven short years without the support of a major record label, commercial radio, or MTV. The band Clap Your Hands Say Yeah rose to prominence by saturating Internet blogs. Notwithstanding the plethora of offers they receive from major labels, they still continue to release their own recordings as of this writing. In yet another classic example, both Guns N' Roses and Mötley Crüe were selling out at Los Angeles clubs before Tom Zutaut, an A&R representative at Geffen Records, discovered and then signed the bands. As Jayceon Teylor (better known as "The Game") said, "Ain't nobody gonna do for you what you can do for yourself—so get off your ass and make it happen."

Remember that hope is simply not a strategy. Take charge of your destiny, put together a game plan, and work toward becoming a success on your own. This might seem like a daunting task, but don't be overwhelmed. Focus on creating little sparks that can grow into one enormous blaze. Industry people are attracted to artists and bands that help themselves first. So don't wait till tomorrow for something you can do today. Get working right now!

BUILD CAREER AWARENESS BY EXPANDING YOUR INTERNET PRESENCE

Most of you are already up to speed on the vast opportunities the Internet provides; but in case you've missed out on something, let's take a quick look at some of the ways you can be more proactive about your career by promoting yourself over the Web:

Personal Websites

Creating a personal website is probably one of the best investments you can make toward promoting yourself. Andreas Wettstein, former vice president of new media at Warner Bros. Records says, "It's your center of the universe where you want to drive all of your fans and provide information." Be sure your site is loaded with features, including lyrics, bios, press and lifestyle photographs, testimonials from fans, current performance schedules, journals that document your weekly activities, links to helpful websites and resources, and a means to collect the e-mail addresses of visitors. Also include samples of your songs and those that are available as ring tones, merchandise, CDs for sale, and video clips. To see what other bands are doing and get even more ideas, check out popular

OPTIMIZING FOR THE WEB: James Marcey of Mean Man (www.meanman.com), a company specializing in website design, reminds us that an important part of your Internet marketing strategy is to register your personal website address or URL (Universal Resource Locator) with various search engines. Otherwise, you won't show up in search results when people try to find you (assuming, that is, you're promoting your ass off and people want to find you). Log on to search engines like Google (www.google.com) and register your URL to its database; just look for "submit your site" or something similar, and it will ask for your URL and description. It's that simple—and the best part is that it's FREE. For more information on registering and optimizing for Google, see www.google.com/technology.

You can raise your ranking within search results by having reciprocal links on other websites. One way to do this is by checking out WebRing (www.webring.com), a site that allows you to join or start your own community of people all linked together by their sites. Also check out the Indie Link Exchange (www.indielinkexchange.com), a site with over five hundred musicians who wish to exchange links with other music-related sites.

sites like Radiohead's (www.radiohead.com) and Dream Theater's (www.dreamtheater.net). Wettstein also suggests, "Just be sure to design a site that is consistent with your genre of music and that is simple and easy to navigate." To take care of all your personal website needs, it's a worthy investment to look into affordable Web hosting services like Host Baby (www.hostbaby.com), Nimbit (www.nimbit.com), and Band Zoogle (www.bandzoogle.com).

Social Networking Sites

Establishing profiles on community sites like MySpace (www.myspace.com), Pure Volume (www.purevolume.com), and Facebook (www.facebook.com) is another good way to expand your Internet presence. These sites all have something different to offer, from letting you post photos, videos, and MP3s, to starting and managing your own blogs, selling your CDs, and adding ring tones of your music for sale. And the best part about these sites is that they're free. Wettstein believes, "There's no excuse these days not to have a presence on the Web—no matter what your budget. Just be sure to allocate one location that has your main site or headquarters to draw back fans. Create a strong presence on the Web, but don't spread yourself too thin."

E-mail Lists

You can also build "quality" e-mail lists (not "quantity" lists) by personally asking audiences at live shows—and any other opportune place—to give you their e-mail addresses. Provide an incentive in return, such as a chance to win a free copy of your CD or a T-shirt. Make sure each person that signs your e-mail list really wants to receive your news (the last thing you want is to spend hours typing in the e-mail addresses of people who later want to be taken off your list). Also, make sure that each person writes his or her e-mail clearly (this will help limit the number of bounce-backs you get). And to help manage your personal e-mail list as it builds into thousands of names, check out iFanz (www.ifanz.com), a service that can pinpoint your messages to specific zip codes and individual fans celebrating birthdays. In addition, check out Group Mail (www.group-mail.com), an e-mail management software product that is both easy to use and affordable.

Newsletters

Starting a newsletter is another good way to supply your growing fan base with concise and regular information about your career. *But don't just hype yourself!* Add interesting music business headlines, trivia, and articles to make your newsletter more informative and useful. Use catchy and tight headers in the subject line that grab your fans' attention and entice them to read on. Also, avoid large blocks of text or graphics that make your newsletter difficult to download. Instead, include brief announcements with links to your site where further information and pictures can be obtained. To help you create e-mail newsletters and announcements that get immediate and measurable results, Wettstein suggests you check out Constant Contact (www.constantcontact.com) and Bronto (www.bronto.com).

Review Sites

Submit your music for reviews in e-zines, fan sites, and other organizations that feature independent artists of your genre. Be sure to examine the tone of the reviewers (some are extra critical, while others are friendly) and make a detailed list of the sites you feel are appropriate. You can check out Pitchfork Media (www.pitchforkmedia.com), Absolute Punk (www.absolutepunk.net), CD Reviews (www.cdreviews.com), Indie Music Review (www.indie-music.com), and Muse's Muse (www.muses muse.com) for starters. Paula Gould, former director of PR for Tag World (www.tagworld.com), adds, "Don't forget blogs [i.e., Web journals] as a source for getting reviews." She continues, "Most journalists, in addition to writing for specific magazines or sites, have blogs that allow them to elaborate on items of interest without having the restrictions of editorial space." Blogs like Music for Robots (www.music.for-robots.com) and Coke Machine Glow (www.cokemachineglow.com) are worth checking out, but conduct your own search and see what you find.

Forums, Discussion Groups, and Blogs

You can also tap into the Web community by leaving comments in forums such as Velvet Rope (www.velvetrope.com) and by joining, or starting your own, discussion groups like Yahoo! Groups (www.yahoogroups.com). Try starting your own Web journal, or blog, through sites like Blogger (www.blogger.com), Xanga (www.xanga.com), and Live Journal (www.livejournal.com). Dave Jackson, founder and CEO of the Musician's Cooler (www.musicianscooler.com), has noticed that "Fans seem to flock to blogs—especially when you keep them updated with tales from your gigs and happenings backstage. Blogs really help create a tight bond with your audience because they make your fans feel more like a part of your world." Whether you're targeting community sites, forums, Yahoo! groups, or blogs, you can discover hundreds of new leads just by typing your "like" bands into your favorite search engine and clicking away.

Online Retailers

You might also consider working with online retailers like CD Baby (www.cdbaby.com), the largest seller of independent CDs on the Web, as well. CD Baby can help sell both your physical CD and downloads of your music through sites like iTunes (www.itunes.com), Napster (www.napster.com), and Rhapsody (www.real.com/rhapsody). Furthermore, CD Baby can get your music into over 2,400 traditional retail music stores across America, including Borders (www.borders.com), Best Buy (www.bestbuy.com), Hot Topic, (www.hottopic.com), and Trans World Entertainment stores (www.twec.com). Check out services like CafePress (www.cafepress.com), The Orchard (www.theorchard.com), and Amazon.com's Advantage program (www.amazon.com) as well.

Podcasts

You can make your music available for podcasts (shows that can be downloaded and played on the popular Apple iPod players) by checking out sites like Podsafe Music Network (http://music.pod show.com). This site makes your music available to podcasters who are looking for music for their shows. For a complete directory of podcasts, see iPodder (www.ipodder.org). And for those of you who are really proactive, you might even start your own podcast show. David Jackson invites you to obtain a free tutorial called "Promoting Your Band through Podcasting" (www.promotingwithpodcast ing.com). Also check out Go Daddy (www.godaddy.com), a site that offers a "Quick Podcast" service that enables you to publish and manage your own podcast.

Videocasts

Getting your video played or "videocasted" by uploading your videocast (assuming you have one) to sites like Blip TV (www.bliptv.com), imusicflow (imusicflow.com), Get Your Flow (www.getyour

flow.com), YouTube (www.youtube.com), and Google Video (http://video.google.com) are a great way to reach fans all over the Internet that are out of your territory and unable to see you perform live.

Web Radio Stations

You can also start your own Web radio station. But first, let's be clear that I'm specifically referring to starting a Web radio station to play your original music and recordings for which you are the sole copyright owner. Check out Internet radio broadcasting software like Pirate Radio (www.pirate radio.com), which is both easy to set up and inexpensive. All it requires is a Windows-based desktop PC, an Internet connection, and, of course, a great deal of your time getting people to tune in. As they say, you can't save souls in an empty church. Also, check out services like Live 365 (www.live365.com) and SHOUTcast (www.shoutcast.com), both of which can help to get you broadcasted and, perhaps, in turn, gain a little bit of exposure.

The ideas presented here are just the tip of the iceberg of what you can do on the Internet, but they provide a good place to start. For more ideas or to brush up on some terms you may be unfamiliar with, check out Peter Spellman's book *The Musician's Internet* or David Kushner's *Music Online for Dummies*. Don't wait till tomorrow to check out all these sites. *Take advantage of all of them right now!* And keep your eyes open for new opportunities launching every day.

INCREASE YOUR ODDS OF GETTING SIGNED BY UNDERSTANDING MORE ABOUT A&R

In an age in which technology makes it possible for artists to thrive independently, many artists still dream about getting signed to a recording agreement with a record label. But few know anything about record companies, their personnel, how they discover new talent, what they look for in an artist, and where and when they look to find it. You might just find that the first step to getting a record deal is to take a do-it-yourself approach to your career. A discussion of A&R personnel within a record company can easily take up hundreds of pages, but here's a brief overview.

Who Are A&R Reps?

Artists and repertoire representatives, commonly called A&R reps, are record company personnel whose job is to discover new talent and develop their musicians' careers. Because A&R reps are primarily obligated to make money for the record label, some reps often follow trends, look for "sure things," or wait to see what reps at other labels are pursuing. Usually, A&R reps do not like to be approached by fledging artists, nor do they accept unsolicited materials through the mail. Contrary to popular belief, once they find a potential artist, A&R reps do not have "signing power." Instead, they have the difficult task of getting the approval from the label's presidents—and getting approval is often the hardest part of the job! The average life span of an A&R rep at a label is three years.

What Do A&R Reps Look for in New Talent?

A&R reps look for artists who have a potential hit song, signature sound, marketable image, long-term career potential (i.e., youthfulness and adaptability), and a great live show.

A&R reps prefer business-minded bands that achieve a great deal on their own first. Artists who press and sell their own recordings, perform live, build a strong fan base, design their own websites, establish a strong Web presence, and have a very clear vision of their goals are far more attractive to A&R reps than artists who don't. Musicians who know everything, from what sort of image they want to how they want their album cover artwork and videos to appear, make an A&R rep's job much easier. A&R rep Ken Blaustein at Virgin Records (who signed My Chemical Romance and The Used) says, "The DIY mentality is alive and well, as it's always been, but now it's even more important because labels are looking for both great songs they can market and established brands they can help accentuate."

A&R reps also look for artists who have a strong work ethic. They may consider questions such as, Will the members of the band continue to work hard at creating their own breaks once they get signed, or will they rely entirely on their label to do everything? Will they have the endurance to tour relentlessly, or will they burn out quickly? Do they have spouses, kids, substantial bills, and other domestic responsibilities that may inhibit the pursuit of their goals? Simply put, record labels look for the path of least resistance to ensure that they'll make a profit from their investments.

Where Do A&R Reps Look for New Talent?

A&R reps discover new bands through independent record labels, listening to college radio stations, keeping an eye on the College Music Journal's (www.cmj.com) music charts, searching the bins of mom-and-pop record stores, attending local club performances, reading reviews in local and national magazines, attending annual music conventions and conferences like SXSW (www.sxsw.com), surfing the Internet for MP3 music files, checking out the buzz on social networking sites like MySpace (www.myspace.com) and YouTube (www.youtube.com), reading blogs and forums, and keeping a watchful eye on reports issued by marketing information companies like Nielson SoundScan (an information service that reports album sales figures by tracking registered bar codes). They also rely on referrals made from established bands, record label scouts, friends and relatives of industry executives, reputable producers, club promoters, managers, attorneys, and publishing companies.

When Do A&R Reps Sign New Talent?

Pinpointing the exact time of year that A&R representatives are most likely to sign new talent is difficult; however, one thing is certain: There are usually not many signings during the fourth quarter of the year (October through December). During this period, most companies' financial budgets for new projects have likely been accounted for or depleted. Additionally, being that it's the holiday season, most companies are focusing on pushing their major artists, whose new albums are usually timed for release right before the holiday shopping season. Of course, there are exceptions to the aforementioned; it's possible for a really hot band in the middle of a bidding war to get signed in the fourth quarter, but generally October through December is not a good time for new bands.

Remember, A&R reps don't like to be approached directly by fledging artists, nor do they accept unsolicited press kits and other material in the mail. Although, as I've said before, there are exceptions to every rule, a rep's philosophy is that when you're truly ready to get to a recording agreement, he or she will find you! So be realistic about the music biz and your career goals, learn to be more proactive about your career, and don't get frustrated if your career doesn't take off the way you dreamed it would. Blaustein advises, "Remember that being a successful recording artist is not a given right, it is a privilege! Just keep doing what you do, and if you're lucky enough to get your big break, know that 'staying on top' takes a lot more work than just riding around on tour busses, having fun, and doing groupies. Nothing is ever a given in this biz."

BE PRACTICAL ABOUT MONEY BY KEEPING IT AND MAKING IT GROW

When you make money in the music business, learn how to save it and make it grow. There are far too many musicians who sell millions of records yet end up penniless. In 1991, *Forbes* magazine estimated rapper MC Hammer's worth at $33 million. Today, as a result of living a carelessly lavish lifestyle (he toured with sixty performers, employed an entourage of a hundred friends, drove seventeen exotic cars, and owned a mansion worth $14 million), he's penniless and doing commercials for a credit repair company. Certainly, he wasn't watching and respecting his money. What

To learn more about money, read best-selling books like *Think and Grow Rich* by Napoleon Hill and magazines like *Business Week, Entrepreneur, Smart Money, Money*, and the *Wall Street Journal*.

a shame! On the flip side, most super wealthy people, like Donald Trump, swear they are extremely conservative with money despite their conspicuous consumption. I believe it! It's about respecting money and knowing what you can and cannot get away with. Like Donald Trump says in his book *How to Get Rich*, "I still turn off the lights in every room I leave and I look for deals on shaving cream when shopping at Duane Reade." Just get smart and save and invest your money wisely! It doesn't take much to get started, so even if you have very few funds, speak with a successful financial planner. The money you invest today could be the money you depend on tomorrow.

ADAPT TO CHANGE BY DIVERSIFYING YOURSELF NOW

Broaden your career opportunities to increase your earning potential and "staying power" in the business. It was Charles Darwin who once said, "It is not the strongest of species that tend to survive; it is those that are most adaptable to change." Work on song/lyric writing, singing, playing multiple instruments, production, and engineering. Dave Grohl, drummer for the grunge-rock sensation Nirvana, was able to transform his career after Kurt Cobain (Nirvana's lead singer/songwriter) took his own life in 1994. Grohl formed a new band in 1995, the Foo Fighters, and assumed the role of vocalist, guitarist, and songwriter. The Foo Fighters entered the *Billboard* charts at No. 24 with their first album and have enjoyed a successful career ever since with several studio albums, a string of hits, and numerous Grammy nominations. If Dave hadn't been prepared, he could easily have been at the end of his musical career. Way back in the sixteenth century, Niccolo Machiavelli said it this way in his famous book *The Prince*: "One who adapts his policy to the times prospers."

Develop a backup plan through related music business opportunities such as artist relations, management, Internet-related careers, video production, record production, building your own studio, music publicity, musical equipment design and manufacturing, instruction, or starting your own label (to name a few). You may not think that you'll need something to fall back on, but you never know. Very few musicians and bands are able to sustain long-term careers as performers. Veteran session guitarist Steve Lukather puts it best: "You can only be the number one session cat for so long." Lukather has now moved on to producing records. Even the group Korn, with two platinum records to their credit and no sign of their careers slowing down, took precautionary steps by starting their own record label, Elementree Records, distributed by Reprise/Warner, in 1997. The majority of the group's members had families to support and could not risk relying solely on the success of their next CD. They also didn't want to spend as much time out on the road and away from their families as they had in the past. People grow up and their lives change—and so do dreams. The band Orgy, Elementree's first signing, sold over 500,000 copies with their release *Candyass*. Since then, Elementree signed such acts as Videodrone, rapper Marz, and Deadsy. Needless to say, Korn made a smart move!

STAY ON TRACK WITHOUT BURNING OUT MENTALLY OR PHYSICALLY

Take precautions against both physical and mental burnout. Fast food, lack of sleep, and stress can all contribute to physical burnout. It's important to make every effort to stay as healthy as possible, especially while out on the road. You'd be surprised at the number of artists' tours that have been cut short while they were hospitalized for exhaustion. Manager Tom Atensio warns, "When your record is in the top ten you're like an athlete. You get up in the morning, do morning shows, spend the afternoon doing press, you go to sound checks, do phoners, go to dinner with the record company, perform your show, and then hang out with retail buyers. If you're feeble and weak, eventually you'll crack." Pay attention to your health! This goes for artists of all levels—from the majors to those on the independent and DIY level.

You must also be careful to avoid mental burnout, which is far more serious and permanent than physical burnout, often resulting from suffering one rejection and disappointment after the other. The best way to combat mental burnout is to remember why you got into the music business in the first place—for the love of playing music. As musician/author/poet Henry Rollins says, "Music is the master, and we are only there to serve it. It's going to be fun, but it's also going to be a lot of work. Stick to the reason you got into it in the first place. You wanted to play music, right? So you won't mind playing in front of a few people as long as you get to play, right? Good. Also, know that all the greats played through all kinds of highs and lows and ebbs and tides. If you're a player, then play!"

MAINTAIN CONTROL IN THE FACE OF DRUGS AND ALCOHOL

Drugs and alcohol are a big part of music culture and have led to the downfall of many successful artists and bands. What might begin as casual partying can end up spiraling out of control. Keep yourself and your band members in check! Mike McCready of Pearl Jam was nearly fired at the apex of the group's career due to his drinking. Steven Adler of Guns N' Roses was booted out of his band for his drug abuse. Scott Weiland of Stone Temple Pilots jeopardized the continued existence of his band after being jailed on drug possession charges. And in a far more tragic example, Layne Staley of Alice in Chains thrust his band into a long hiatus because of his addiction to heroin; the band has never fully recovered. Even worse, Layne Staley finally died in 2002 of an overdose. Blind Melon's career also ended when singer Shannon Hoon died of an overdose.

If you think that you're developing a serious problem with drugs or alcohol, both Alcoholics Anonymous (AA) and Narcotics Anonymous (NA) offer free meetings in a city near you. Check your local yellow pages.

Finding solutions to these problems is clearly beyond the scope of this book, but one thing's for sure—you're not going to find answers to your problems by indulging in extreme behavior. As illustrated above, the problems only worsen. If this advice means nothing to you, at least consider your professional responsibilities to the other members of your band, as well your professional responsibilities to the people who have invested a lot of time and money in your career. Keep in mind that record labels, and others in the industry, are less tolerant today of artists who have drug and alcohol problems than they were in the past. With other talent waiting in line to take your place, record companies simply don't have the time to waste on your personal issues. The Brian Jones Town Massacre was an L.A. band that blew a record showcase with Capital Records when the singer, fueled by his drug habit, started fist fighting with his guitarists on stage (check out the shocking and sad documentary *Dig* if you can still find it). You can't afford something like this to happen to you!

REMEMBER THAT FINDING YOUR PASSION IS A BLESSING WITHIN ITSELF

It's also important to remember the reason why you became a musician in the first place. Don't let the challenges of the music business get you down. If you started playing because you truly love music, then you shouldn't mind working through both the ups and downs. Always remember that finding your true passion in life—something most people fail to do—is a true blessing within itself. Be grateful.

Q & A WITH PUBLICIST MICHAEL LEVINE

Los Angeles PR firm Levine Communications Office (LCO) has represented many diverse celebrities, such as Michael Jackson, Michael J. Fox, Prince, Kareem Adbul-Jabbar, Ozzy Osbourne, and Demi Moore. Michael Levine has also provided unpaid media counsel to three U.S. presidents: Ronald Reagan, Bill Clinton, and George W. Bush. Levine is the author of seventeen books, including the best-selling *Guerrilla PR*, and he lectures at universities and corporations on the topic of success and efficiency, which he discusses here.

Q: What are the most common attributes of the super successful?
M.L: I've found the super successful possess three qualities I call the "Three Magic O's": 1. Obsession, 2. Optimism, 3. Obligation.

Q: Obsession?
M.L: Super-successful people are OBSESSED! Obsession is not ambition. Obsession is a burning maniacal rage as if their lives depended on it.

Michael Jordan did not play basketball by telling his teammates, "Guys, look, we have a challenging and important game tonight. If we win, we win; if we lose, we lose. Let's have a good time and just see what happens." On the contrary, Jordon played basketball as if his life depended on it. Bill Clinton ran for president as if his life depended on it.

If I were to ask the readers of this book to perform a specific task, like selling a thousand units of their CD in a week's time, they might tell me that it is impossible given their circumstances—and this might very well be true. However, if I were to reach into my pocket, pull out a Colt .45 revolver, stick it down their throats, and tell them to sell the CDs, I guarantee that some way and somehow they'd get the job done. Why? Because now their lives would depend on it! I've found that all super-successful people possess a burning maniacal rage to succeed at all costs, as if their lives depended on it.

Q: Optimism?
M.L: The super-successful believe that if you work really, really hard for a long, long period of time, tomorrow could be better than today. They have this paradoxical sense that while the game is not

easy and while the game is not fair, the game is winnable—as long as you have enough focused intensity. Make no mistake, optimism, or more specifically, "perpetual optimism," is a force multiplier. General Colin Powell spoke of perpetual optimism. What he was saying, I believe, was that if you took ten men and saturated them with optimism, those ten men could fight with the force of fifty. If you took the same ten men and saturated them with negativity, they couldn't fight with the force of two. Remember, the game is absolutely winnable if you truly believe it to be.

Q: Obligation?

M.L: Super-successful people have a sense of responsibility and are never flakey. *Flakey* is another word for *loser*. When they said they were going to do something, they did, and they did it on time. And on the rare occasions when they didn't complete an assignment, they blamed only themselves—not the weather and not the state of the entertainment industry. They made themselves 100 percent responsible and were never victims. They were obligated to keeping their word primarily to themselves. They created very specific and measurable goals. For instance, they didn't just say that they were going to lose some weight in next year. They said they were going to lose fourteen pounds, increase upper-body strength, and build stamina all by July 9th.

So with the third magic O, I always give people a voluntary homework assignment. This is a homework assignment that everyone reading this book can do in the next twenty-four hours. And if they do it I will promise with 100 percent certainty that it will change their lives instantly, radically, and permanently. They must make a commitment to "fire their flakey friends." That's right, they must fire their flakey friends, band members, or whomever. I'm serious. Get rid of them all. And the reason they must fire their flakey friends is because nothing will interfere more profoundly with their capacity to reach their full potential as human beings as much as inhaling the secondhand fumes of flakiness. Remember, flakes are losers. Successful people don't associate themselves with losers, and neither should you!

Q: Any motivational, management, or leadership books you'd recommend?

M.L: *The Mailroom* by David Ranson is a great book for anyone serious about making it in the entertainment business, particularly in Hollywood. *The Operator,* by Thomas King, is a fascinating book about record mogul David Geffen and how raging ambition is often as valuable as talent—sometimes more so—in determining success. Finally, I believe I've made some solid contributions to the ideas of marketing, PR, and business in my book *Guerilla PR* and *Broken Windows, Broken Business.* Anyone who wants to look them up can go to my website at www.mlavineonline.com.

Q: Is there a Michael Levine's "must do" list to pursuing a successful career?

M.L: I'll give your readers ten concise and essential tips:

1. Recognize that if your goals are not written, they are not goals; they are just dreams. Create a solid game plan and keep it in a place where you can refer to it regularly.
2. Realize that your product is important, but not as important as your marketing. You better be prepared to promote your ass off!
3. Remember that it's not what you know; it's whom you know, and who wants to know you.

4. Nurture strong relationships by frequenting specific events (mixers, seminars, and classes) where good, inspired people congregate.

5. Create mastermind alliances or partnerships with friends who truly share the same life aspirations as you.

6. Be willing to join an internship program with a successful company and work for free to experience how the industry works on the inside. You might have to be enrolled as a student in an entertainment program to do this. But in any case, you can always volunteer at annual conventions or other events to learn the ropes.

7. Find a mentor, a trusted counselor or guide, who believes in you. Do this by first identifying a person who is in a place that you want to be in twenty years. Second, figure out how this person will benefit from mentoring you—you better bake him an apple pie, run his errands, or hang out with him at a ball game. Whatever the fuck it is, you better be equally prepared to give to the mentor.

8. Get out of your own fucking narcissistic self-involvement. Most creative people are suffering from an acute case of narcissism—it's all about their dreams, their careers, and their wealth. Enough! Get interested in others and in the world around you. It will make you a richer, finer, kinder, more interesting artist and human being.

9. Don't be afraid to take chances and go for it! Fear plays an enormous role in the underachievement of human beings.

10. Be good at what you do, and love it! You absolutely have to love it. Because, when the going gets tough, the love for your craft is what gets you through.

CHAPTER 2

Band Membership

"If we do not hang together, we will surely hang separately."
—NATHAN HALE

Being a member of a band is not much different from being a member of a professional sports team: You're part of a group of individuals united in the pursuit of a common goal, each person playing a unique and integral part in achieving a dream. The motto—at least in theory—is, "All for one, and one for all."

But unlike the sports world, where professional teams expect young athletes to meet extremely high standards before drafting them, young bands often form simply because the members are friends who share musical tastes. This common denominator is unfortunately not enough to create a successful band. Personality differences, as well as opposing views of how business and legal matters should be handled, eventually rear their ugly heads. The result: The band calls it quits, or a member is unfairly kicked out, or the group suffers setbacks due to its revolving lineup, or its members get entangled in an ongoing legal battle with one another. It happens all the time! And as you'll learn in Chapter 2, this fate can be avoided if a band establishes strong criteria for choosing its members and it drafts a band membership agreement. A band must all be on the same page and ready to work as a unit. To illustrate my point, according to the book *"What'd I Say?": The Atlantic Story, 50 Years of Music,* one of the inspirational slogans written on the walls of the band Rush's studio read, "Individually, we are an ass, but together we are a genius." Although playing music is supposed to be fun, a serious band is a business just like any other, and it should never be regarded as anything less.

CRITERIA FOR CHOOSING BAND MEMBERS

At first, when everyone in a band is excited and eager to get things rolling, character flaws and differences of opinion are often overlooked; but if problems are ignored, with the intention of dealing with them later, they always come back to bite you in the you-know-what. For this reason, it is crucial to consider both the personalities and goals of the people with whom you're about to get involved. Do this by using a personality questionnaire and a timeline of goals.

The Personality Questionnaire

A personality questionnaire is an informal interview you set up with the intention of spotting under-lying problems among band members and determining if you should proceed together in the music business. Include whatever issues you feel are crucial to the long-term success of the band—from loyalty to addiction. I do not recommend presenting these questions to potential band members the moment you meet, but after you've jammed together and are considering the possibility of moving the relationship forward. Below are some questions you might want to include in your interview:

+ If in three years the band is still unsigned, do you see yourself remaining a member?
+ How do you feel about holding part-time (instead of full-time) jobs in order to keep your schedule flexible?
+ If the band should decide it was necessary, would you relocate to another city?
+ How important is band rehearsal in relation to your own social schedule?
+ If the band should decide private lessons and individual practice time is what you need to get to the next level, would you be cool with this?
+ How open would you be to experimenting with—and changing—your visual image?
+ Do you drink, smoke, or do any drugs?
+ Do you have a problem with drinking, smoking, or doing any drugs?
+ Could you drop everything to go out on the road for several weeks at a time?
+ Could you handle traveling cross-country in a small passenger van and sleeping in one hotel room with three other band members—for little or no money?
+ If your significant other asked you to choose between staying in the relationship or in the band, what decision would you make?
+ If you could be in the ultimate band, would the band be your own solo project?

Although the above questionnaire might seem rather intense and even scare off potential band members, trust that it will only scare off those musicians with whom you should never partner. Remember, no matter how similar a potential member's tastes in music may be or how cool he or she may look, if there are different and conflicting personalities, problems will eventually occur. The last thing you want is to fire someone, have someone quit, or have the band break up after spending several months, or years, building it from the ground up. Needless to say, this would be a horrible waste of time! Trust me, I'm speaking from experience.

Timeline of Goals

Another method to ensure your band is composed of the *right* members is to put together—and agree on—a timeline of goals. This timeline identifies specific goals a band intends to achieve over a specific period of time (usually six months to a year). Furthermore, it helps to identify any problems certain members might have with commitment, dedication, and career strategy. Without uncovering these problems from the start, a band is quite likely to fail. Here's an example of what a timeline of goals might look like over a period of a year:

Months 1–3

✦ Rent a rehearsal studio and meet four times a week.

✦ Write twenty songs and hone the band's sound and direction.

✦ Demo the best compositions and get feedback.

✦ Define the band's image and meet with a fashion consultant.

Months 4–6

✦ Complete band press kit, including a professionally shot photo.

✦ Hire a webmaster to build a professional website.

✦ Book live performances and create a buzz locally before expanding into other territories.

✦ Assign promotional responsibilities to each member.

Months 7–9

✦ Hire songwriting coach and/or find producer.

✦ Pay to record best songs professionally.

✦ Manufacture CDs and band merchandise.

✦ Sell CDs/merchandise at shows and on personal and community websites.

Months 10–12

✦ Attend and showcase at networking conferences and conventions.

✦ Enter songwriting competitions.

✦ Contact music libraries and song pluggers (those who can help get your music in films or TV).

✦ Hire a music business consultant to access career direction.

FOUR CAPTAINS ON A SINKING SHIP A band that formed in California consisted of two members from New York and two members from Florida. After investing a full year of time in the group, one of its members decided the band should move to New York because this was where his wife needed to be for her career. Another member wanted to stick to what he believed was the original plan of staying in California. The other two members suggested the band should move to their homeland of Florida simply because they hated California and orange juice was cheaper (I'm not kidding). As it turns out, the entire band moved to Florida, but shortly thereafter they broke up after one member reneged on his agreement and moved to New York anyway. What a headache! If the nature and or character of these musicians had been exposed from the beginning, the members might have realized they had no business being in a band together in the first place. This story is hardly an isolated incident.

Remember, the point of this is to ensure that a band shares similar goals and strategies and that all members are in agreement regarding the time in which they intend to accomplish these goals. Surely, new opportunities will present themselves and the goals will evolve, but they will at least be derived from a core principle on which all agreed.

BAND MEMBERSHIP AGREEMENTS

Once all of your members are in place and everyone seems to share similar goals and their attitudes are in check, you need a written agreement defining the terms of your business and legal relationship. This document, called a "band membership agreement," compels a band to deal with important issues before they become problems. The terms of the agreement should include language stipulating the following:

- ✦ How income, such as that earned from record royalties, music publishing, concert money, and merchandising will be divided
- ✦ How the band will make decisions (for example, by unanimous or majority vote)
- ✦ When or if members will be required to put money back into the band for investments or expenses
- ✦ What happens to a member's share of assets acquired by the group (such as equipment) when he or she quits or is voted out of the band
- ✦ Who owns or controls the rights to the band name and its continued use

ATTORNEYS COST MONEY, AND SO DO BAND MEMBERSHIPS—OR DO THEY? A common excuse bands give for not putting together a preliminary band membership agreement is that they simply don't have the money for the attorney's fees in the early stages of their career. Although it's best to have an attorney draft such an agreement, there are a number of resources, like Nolo Legal Resources (www.nolo.com) and Legal Zoom (www.legalzoom.com), that provide adequate form agreements. A helpful book that you may want to check out is *Music Law: How to Run Your Band's Business*, by attorney Richard Stim. Attorney Jeff Cohen says, "As long as all the parties are capable of understanding the various clauses, I'm not against them using form agreements or even drafting a deal memo on a plain sheet of paper. A band can later take this to an attorney when they have money."

Another excuse bands have for not putting together a preliminary membership agreement is that it's not necessary at the beginning stages of their careers when they're not making money. The rationale is, "Any percentage of zero is still zero." However, if the band has any aspirations toward one day procuring a record or publishing deal, their short-sightedness may end up causing serious problems later. Some members may have different ideas about how their business should be handled, leaving other members feeling as though they're getting the short end of the stick.

- ✦ What the guidelines are for hiring and firing band members
- ✦ What services will be expected of each member in the band
- ✦ How disputes will be resolved (in a court of law or outside the courts)
- ✦ What kind of vote (unanimous or majority) can amend the agreement terms
- ✦ Whether the negligence of one member legally affect the others

While an agreement won't stop a band from breaking up or running into conflicts, it will help define the individual beliefs, desires, and perspectives of the members from the start. Without a written agreement, should a serious argument ensue regarding control or profits, state partnership laws might dictate the outcome for you. That's right! You see, as soon as two or more people (such as a band) come together and are willing to share in the profits and losses of their business, they are already recognized as a legal partnership. State partnership laws vary, but if a band does not have a written agreement that stipulates anything to the contrary, all members may be presumed to have (1) an equal right to the profits and financial losses of the band, (2) an equal say in making decisions, (3) the right to use the band name should they decide to leave the group, and (4) liability for the other member's negligence while conducting business. The list goes on. Though most groups are usually fair in wanting to share in the profits and losses equally, sometimes members will want to break up the relationship based on their individual feelings. The earlier these issues can be addressed in a written agreement, the better off all involved will be in the long run.

So whether you're in a band that's just forming, or you're in a band that's already hot on the independent scene and on the verge of signing your first record deal, if you don't have a band membership agreement, then schedule a meeting and come up with one today. An attorney is recommended, but one is not always necessary in the early stages of your career, as long as you understand all of the agreement terms. Read the interview with attorney Jeff Cohen at the end of this chapter for a brief review of the contractual terms found in band membership agreements, such as voting members' rights to a band name, fictitious name statements (aka DBAs), trademark issues, and business entities.

Key Members and Minority Partners

Members of a band do not always agree to share equally concerning control over their business or profits. Sometimes one member may feel he or she deserves more compensation than the others because he or she does the bulk of the work. Sometimes the founder, the lead singer, or the main songwriter are the only members who own the rights to the band name or who control the vote and have the final word in making business decisions. In fact, should the band progress to signing with a record company, the label may even view these individuals as the group's "key members," those most important to the functioning of the band. In some instances, a non-key member or "minority partner" may not even be signed to the initial recording agreement. If you're not a signatory, the benefit is that you can walk away without any financial or recording obligation to the record company. As a minority partner you have the freedom to leave and start your own group. Keep in mind, though, that this doesn't negate any internal agreement you may have with the band itself. For example, there may be a clause in your band membership agreement that says you have the right to quit the band if you're unhappy, but not in the middle of a tour when the band can incur a loss as a result.

Potential Revenue Sources and Group Percentage Shares

Every band and its members should understand the various sources of revenue that may become available to them and, more important, include a description in their band agreement of the way that money will be divided among the members. Why is this so important? In the words of Mick Jagger, "There is nothing like money to break up the band." Ain't that the truth! We've all heard stories about bands hitting it big and one member driving a Mercedes and the others driving beat-up station wagons. Needless to say, you don't want this to happen to you.

> Your individual interests and the band's interests may not always coincide. Therefore, unless the group is dividing the profits and control over business matters equally, seeking the advice of your own entertainment attorney is worth a small investment to ensure that your interests are protected. You can get inexpensive legal advice by contacting your local office of the Volunteer Lawyers for the Arts.

During the early stages of a band's career, when they are paying their dues and trying to take in any amount of money they can, there usually isn't much left over once their expenses are covered; and in the event that there is a profit, the monies are usually invested back into the group or divided equally among the members.

However, once the band signs with a record label or publishing company, business matters will become much more sophisticated, their career track will move at a faster pace, and the revenue pie is not only split among band members but also among other business entities (and sometimes even owned and controlled by other people). Furthermore, once a band has been signed to a label, additional revenue sources may include record advances, recording fees, record royalties (including digital and master tone royalties), master use licenses, audio/video DVD royalties, interactive webcasting royalties, noninteractive webcasting royalties, live performance monies, merchandising revenues (e.g., income from the sale of T-shirts and hats), and music publishing royalties. I will briefly describe these revenue sources now. (Note that revenue sources are covered in detail in chapters 11–14.)

Record Advances

In recording contracts, most record advances are structured as "recording funds." The recording fund covers all recording expenses and any monies that are paid to the band in the form of an "artist advance." For instance, if you're a new rock band signed to a major label, such as—at the time of this writing—Sony/BMG, Warner, Universal, or EMI, the recording fund is negotiated on many variables, but let's say it is $250,000 under a traditional deal structure. From this fund, $200,000 may be budgeted toward the "recording cost budget" of an album and submitted by the producer to the record company for approval. Recording costs can include the producer's advance, studio costs, equipment rentals and accessories, techs, transportation, hotels, and per diems (costs per day). The remaining $50,000 from the recording fund may be budgeted as an artist advance and split among band members; but once the other members of your team, such as your attorney, personal manager, and business manager, receive their commission from the advance—as well as any other income entitled to them—and after taxes are deducted, there is very little money left over from the advance to be split among the members of the band. (Chapter 10 covers recording advances in greater detail.)

Recording Fees

Recording fees are usually factored into a band's recording budget and are the union minimum scale wages to which each musician is entitled for recording an album. The record company may advance these monies to you at the time of your signing, so that you have some personal money with which to pay your expenses while preparing to record, or it may pay these monies over the course of the recording process. Most record companies are affiliated with the American Federation of Musicians (AFM) and the American Federation of Television and Radio Artists (AFTRA) and therefore must report all recording sessions to their local branch under an agreement called the "collective bargaining agreement." The record company is required to pay the band a wage at union minimum scale and to make additional contributions on your behalf to union pension and welfare funds. Although it's your option, the record company will ask each band member to affiliate with the union before recording an album; consequently, dues should also be factored into the recording budget. (For more information on unions, see Chapter 3.)

Record Royalties

Record royalties are percentages (also called "points") that the record company pays to you for the sale of your record. A common royalty rate for a new rock band under a traditional deal structure, for instance, is anywhere from 13 to 16 percent; however, what it actually amounts to in cents depends on a number of factors, such as at what price, in what configuration, and in what country the record sells and by what means the record company calculates its royalties and takes certain deductions (which I'll address in detail in Chapter 10). After deducting anywhere from 3 to 5 percent from the rate for the record producer, the band divides the remaining points accordingly.

For example, let's say that a band receives a 14 percent record royalty rate. After subtracting 4 percent for the record producer's share, the band would have a *net royalty rate* of 10 percent. If the group consists of four members and they are dividing the percentages equally, each member would be allotted a royalty of 2.5 percent of the sale of their record. Keep in mind, though, that before receiving even a penny in record royalties, the band *must sell* enough albums to recoup (earn back) *all* the record company's recording and other recoupable expenses. Ninety percent of all bands fail to do this!

Digital Download Royalties

Digital download royalties are royalties of the sale of your music sold as digital downloads on music-download sites like iTunes (www.itunes.com). They are paid at the same royalty rate as record royalties described above. What this actually amounts to in pennies is discussed in Chapter 10. Like record royalties, the amount you receive would go toward recouping all recording and other recoupable expenses before you can split the money accordingly among each band member.

Master Tone Royalties

Master tone royalties (aka mobile ring tones) for the sale of your music used on cell phones are also the same as your record royalty rate. Ring tones are single sales. (I'm sure whole albums will be downloaded onto phones in the very near future.) Like record royalties and digital downloads, a penny breakdown of what you receive for mobile tones is discussed in Chapter 10. And of course, master tone royalties also go toward the recoupment of your advances.

Master Use Licenses (Film, TV, Video Games)

When a record company licenses the recorded masters of your music in film, television, video games, and even advertisements, it will pay you 50 percent of the monies it receives. Attorney Dina LaPolt explains, "Let's say the record company licenses a track from your recording to Paramount Pictures in connection with a new Denzel Washington movie throughout the universe. If the record company receives a $20,000 master fee for this license, and the recording agreement allocates the band 50% of net receipts for third-party licenses, the band receives $10,000 and splits it accordingly." And as noted in Donald Passman's book *All You Need to Know About the Music Business*, sometimes the label may take what's called a "special markets division" fee off the top (before calculating your percentage) for all its efforts in trying to push your record in areas such as film and TV. In any case, provided that the record company has recouped your recording and other expenses, the band may decide to split the remaining money equally.

Audiovisual DVD Royalties

Music videos, like the ones you see on MTV and VHI, are produced for one primary reason: promotion! However, as a band becomes more visible (and I hope you will one day), a record company may also manufacture an audiovisual DVD in any or all of the following formats: (1) a compilation of individual video clips with other artists or of one solo artist (like *Metallica: The Videos 1989–2004*), (2) documentaries (like *Metallica: Some Kind of Monster*), and (3) live concert videos (like *Metallica with the San Francisco Symphony*).

A common royalty rate for sales of your DVD can be anywhere from 10 to 20 percent of the wholesale price. If your video(s) is part of a compilation with other bands, then you will get paid on a prorated amount of your royalty, depending on the number of clips you have on the DVD. So if a band has a 15 percent royalty rate and one video on a ten-song DVD, the band would receive a royalty of 1/10 of 15 percent, or 1.5 percent of the wholesale price.

Video production costs are extremely expensive: It can cost from $75,000 to $350,000 to produce a single high-quality promotional video (Limp Bizkit spent $3 million for just one of its videos). The expenses have to be paid back to the record company from sales of the audiovisual DVDs *before* you ever see a penny. To make matters worse, once all the video expenses have been recouped, your audiovisual DVD royalties are then used to repay all record expenses that have not been recouped, and vice versa for the record royalties (i.e., once record expenses are recouped from record royalties, record royalties are then used to repay unrecouped audiovisual DVD expenses). **Note:** Typically, only 50 percent of video expenses are charged against record royalties.

Should a band be lucky enough to make a profit from audiovisual DVDs, then the profits may divided among bands members equally. However, for reasons stated above, unless you sell loads of records and DVDs, you probably won't make a penny. So why did I bother discussing video, you might ask? Because all artists crave them; having been in videos myself, I can say that the process of filming was one of the most exciting things I've ever done in my life so far.

Interactive Webcasting Royalties

When record companies license the master recordings of your CD or video to "interactive subscription services" (i.e., services through which consumers can stream on-demand and create personalized radio stations) like Yahoo! (music.yahoo.com), AOL (music.aol.com), and MSN (www.music.msn.com), the record company will collect a fee (about a penny per stream at the time

WANT THE REAL DEAL? Did you know that a major label may sign an average of twenty bands a year, while it really only has enough manpower and money to market six effectively? Understand that when you get signed to a label, you are essentially in direct competition with other groups on your label for marketing money. The record company may lose money by signing several bands a year, but it makes up for its loss with the few bands that become successful—the hits pay for the stiffs. Keep in mind that the spins you get on commercial radio stations, the visibility your CD receives in major outlets, the prominent positioning you obtain on key websites, and the top-grossing tours on which you provide support to a headliner, all depend on how excited the label is about you as a product and the amount of money, time, and effort the record company puts into marketing and promoting you. You can help ensure a label will be excited about you by first prescribing to a do-it-yourself philosophy and generating a buzz through social networking sites, podcasts, blogs, college radio, local press, strategic alliances with other bands, local and corporate sponsorships, live performances, festival tours, film and TV licensing, and any other outlet that might exist today. The more work that you do on your own and the more work you continue to do, perhaps on an independent label after that, the better chance you have at getting interest from a powerful label and gaining the full-court push you deserve.

of this writing) and pays you a split of these earnings. "The split is treated like other licenses and is about half," says attorney Dina LaPolt. "It's all money that goes into the big pot" toward paying off your recording fund and all other advances by the record company. Once recouped, the band may split these monies among them equally.

Noninteractive Webcasting Royalties

When master recordings on which you are a "featured" artist (i.e., the recording artist for purposes here) are broadcast on noninteractive Internet sites (i.e., those sites that do not allow the consumer to pick songs as they wish, make set lists, etc.), a webcasting royalty is due. Noninteractive sites include everything from terrestrial radio stations and fan-based stations that broadcast online to satellite subscription services like XM (www.xm.com) and Sirius (www.sirus.com) to subscription services like MusicChoice (www.musicchoice.com) via satellite transmission on digital cable television like Dish Network (www.dishnetwork.com) and DirecTV (www.directtv.com). Webcasting royalties are collected and paid out to you directly by two different agencies: Sound Exchange (www.soundexchange.com) and Royalty Logic (www.royaltylogic.com). Fifty percent of these monies are paid to the owner of the sound recordings (i.e., the record label), 5 percent is paid to the unions AFM (www.afm.com) and AFTRA (www.aftra.com) for session players, and the other 45 percent is paid proportionately to each member of the band (that's you). Just be sure to register with either Sound Exchange or Royalty Logic before your record is released. Note: Keep in mind that if you are a do-it-yourself artist that owns his or her masters, you will also receive another 50 percent, as you will be considered the "label." Also, payment for broadcasts on terrestrial radio may one day apply as well, so stay tuned.

Live Performance Monies

Usually after a band has finished recording its CD, the personal manager and talent agent come together to arrange live performances and tours. With a record in hand, a band can simultaneously establish its name in the press, on the radio and Internet, and in retail stores across the country. Newer groups with a record deal can command nightly fees in the range of $250 to $600 (maybe more) as the opening act in clubs. Considering the tremendous overhead incurred from "hitting the road," there's usually little, if any, money left to split between the band members. In fact, most bands usually return home from a tour *owing* money! This debt may initially be paid by the record company in the form of "tour support" (additional funds up to, say, $50,000), but every penny must be paid back by the band; tour support is 100 percent recoupable from your record sales.

As part of the total expenses and budget for a tour, the band may pay each member a weekly salary and a daily allowance (called a per diem) for food. Most bands usually decide to pay its members the same amount since each member is essentially doing the same job. No matter, since this money is usually available by way of tour support only, it, too, has to be paid back to the record company and is usually deducted from your future record royalties. Keep in mind that the main purpose of touring for most new bands is not to make a direct profit but to build a fan base, sell merchandise, and sell records. Detailed information on touring will be provided in Chapter 12.

Merchandising Revenue

When signing a recording agreement, your record label may want try to secure your exclusive merchandising rights (i.e., the rights to your name and image on T-shirts, hats, stickers, etc.). This is especially true when you are a new artist signing with a small, independent label, when you have little or no negotiating power when dealing with a major label, or when you sign a deal with a major record company, or "multimedia entertainment group," using a new and evolving business model that acquires all your revenue streams (see Chapter 10 for more on this). Traditionally, your record company will then license your merchandising rights to a third-party merchandising company to manufacture product and oversee sales. The merchandiser then pays the record company a merchandising royalty, and the label in turn splits it with the artist 50/50. Virginie L. Parant notes, "Ideally, the label will have its own merchandising arm, which will ensure a more cost-effective exploitation and will (somewhat) justify you to agreeing to such an arrangement."

If you're able to secure your merchandising rights upon signing a record deal, you can handle your merchandising independently by using a printer to manufacture product and, as you start to play larger venues, enter into a merchandising deal directly with a merchandising company (assuming the merchandiser wants you and believes it can get money from signing you, of course). The merchandiser pays you a royalty ranging from 25 to 35 percent of the gross sales and then advances a sum of money that is 100 percent recoupable from future earnings. The advance is based on fancy calculations called "per cap figures," but no matter what the advance amount—$100,000 let's say—new bands typically use these funds to subsidize their touring expenses. If all expenses are

"Multimedia entertainment group" is a term many record companies are using lately, and, coincidently, they are arranging new deals called multimedia, or 360 deals, in which they acquire a number of revenue streams like touring, merchandising, and publishing. Since the label now shares in these areas and acts in more of a management capacity, it can affect how you're paid.

paid and there are merchandising monies to be divided, the band may split these monies equally. (Merchandising is covered in detail in Chapter 13.)

Music Publishing Royalties

The way music publishing royalties from a song are divided among band members is usually different from the other sources of income discussed in this chapter. This is because the songwriting process can be an individual effort, or it can be a collaborative effort involving any combination of band members. A successful song can earn hundreds of thousands of dollars long after the band has parted ways. If you haven't been paying attention before, you had better start now.

Under copyright law, when two or more people collaborate on writing a song and each writer contributes either musically, lyrically, or in both ways, the ownership split is "pro rata" (equal), unless there is a written agreement between the writers that stipulates otherwise. A "musical contribution" is the song's melody or any original riff or groove that becomes an integral hook to the song—for example, the bass line by John Deacon in Queen's "Another One Bites the Dust," or John Bonham's drum intro to Led Zeppelin's "Rock and Roll."

When groups spend hours together in rehearsal, experimenting with song arrangements, tempos, and instrumentation, a certain percentage of the credits may initially be divided among all members, allotting a larger share of the copyright ownership to the actual author(s) of the song. For instance, one group composed of four members allotted 12.5 percent of every song to each member in the band. The remaining 50 percent per song went to the member(s) who contributed to the music and/or lyrics.

Often, when it is each member's unique performance that shapes the band's signature sound, the band simply divides all of the composition credits equally. For example, guitarist Stone Gossard and vocalist Eddie Vedder wrote most of Pearl Jam's songs, yet the band originally split the ownership in its compositions equally—each member (five in total) received 20 percent of the copyright. However, as the group became more successful and vocalist Eddie Vedder was recognized as the "star," essentially becoming the only irreplaceable member of the group, the band wanted to keep him happy. The group allotted 36 percent of each song to Vedder and 16 percent to each of the other three members of the band. In any case, division shares in your songs must be communicated to the record company before the release of your record.

When you share in a percentage of the rights to songs, you are entitled to a variety of incomes in proportion to your ownership shares. The main types or sources of income are as follows.

Mechanical Royalties Your record company pays you a licensing fee, or mechanical royalty, for the use of your songs on a record (CDs, downloads, etc.). I like to think of mechanicals as "special royalties," because unlike record royalties, they are typically not used by the record company for recouping recording costs. In the United States, mechanical royalties are based on a statutory penny rate per composition per CD made and distributed. This fee is subject to periodic changes (it was 2 cents back in 1978 and rose over the years to 9.1 cents in 2006), so your best bet is to check online for updates by logging on to the Copyright Office (www.copyright.gov). Mechanical royalties are one of the more immediate sources of income related to record sales (hence my title "special royalties"). Statements are sent out to you either four times yearly or semiannually, depending on the record company and the terms of your contract. (Mechanicals are covered in detail in Chapter 11.)

Performance Royalties Virtually any public venue that performs your music is required to obtain a license and pay a fee or performance royalty. Public venues include radio stations and television networks, cable stations (such as HBO, MTV, and VH1), satellite networks, colleges and universities, nightclubs, Internet websites, and mobile carriers. The amount you receive is difficult to nail down, but one thing is for sure: To collect anything, you must first become a member/affiliate with one of the major performing rights organizations and register your songs and percentage shares with them. The three U.S. societies include the American Society of Composers, Authors and Publishers (ASCAP), Broadcast Music Incorporated (BMI), and what was formerly known as the Society of European Stage Authors and Composers, today known as SESAC.

Synchronization Fees When motion picture companies, television broadcast stations, video game developers, and any other company who wishes to synch (i.e., match your music with a visual images), a synchronization fee is required. Unlike mechanical royalties, there are no statutory fees for the use of your compositions in these types of reproduction. Synch fees are completely negotiable and are based on a number of factors that will be discussed in detail in Chapter 11. **Note:** If you are a DIY artist, and the actual sound recording of your song is being licensed, you are also entitled to a master use fee.

> Should you get synch fees for promotional music videos like on MTV? Technically, yes, as a video is a reproduction of music and visual images. However, the record company will stipulate language in its contracts that it has the free rights of licensing fees in video since they are mostly used for promotional proposes.

Print Royalties When print companies are authorized to reproduce your music in sheet music and music books, a print royalty is paid on sales. While we'll discuss the payment methods in Chapter 11, just remember that unless you have a hit song, it's not likely your songs will ever make it to print or that you'll see a dime.

Electronic Transmissions Music downloads on sites like iTunes, ring tone sales with carriers like Verizon, "Interactive" streaming audio and video with services like Yahoo! (http://music.yahoo.com), and "noninteractive" streaming (i.e., webcasting) with sites like MusicChoice (www.musicchoice.com) are not new types of income but rather sources that encompass the various incomes previously discussed. Many of these rates are still being negotiated, so be sure to see Chapter 11.

Foreign Subpublishing Foreign subpublishing is another source of income you may receive when your music is published overseas. It's not a type of income but rather encompasses the various incomes already discussed. See Chapter 11 for more on this.

Publishing Advances If a publishing agreement is signed with a music publishing company, an organization that specializes in exploiting your musical compositions and generating the various types of royalty incomes discussed above, a specified percentage of these royalties will be designated between you ("the writer") *and* the publishing company ("the publisher"). The publisher typically offers an advance, recoupable from future song earnings, that should be divided among the songwriters in proportion to their individual shares. As you might have guessed, publishing companies and deals are discussed in detail in Chapter 11.

Q & A WITH ATTORNEY JEFF COHEN

Jeff Cohen is a partner in the law firm Millen, White, Zelano, and Branigan, where he heads the firm's trademark, copyright, and entertainment practice. In this interview, Jeff discusses important terms of band membership agreements, as well as the basics of setting up shop as a band: fictitious name statements (aka, DBAs), band names and trademarks, and business entities (partnerships, corporations, and LLCs).

Q: Besides income, what are the key terms to include in membership agreements?
J.C.: I see you already covered income shares in detail earlier. An agreement should also include issues such as voting, the obligations of individual members, the grounds on which a member can be fired, amendment of agreement terms, whether disputes will be resolved in mediation or arbitration, perhaps an indemnification clause, and ownership in a band's name.

Q: What's a fair system of voting?
J.C.: There are essentially two methods a band can use to vote on important issues: a unanimous vote and a majority vote.

A unanimous vote, which is obviously where everyone must agree on the same issue, should be used on more significant issues, such as hiring a personal manager.

A majority vote, which is where a proportionally higher number of people agree on an issue, should be used on less important but peripheral issues, such as expenditures or making decisions about merchandise. Majority votes work well when you have an odd number of people in a band; however, when you have an even number of people, the question is, what do you do if there's a deadlock vote? The answer is to appoint an objective third party, such as a personal manager, to be the tiebreaker.

Q: Is it important to add the obligations of individual members in the band agreement?
J.C.: I do believe it's helpful to define the services that each member will provide to the band in your agreement. On this note, you might even want to indicate which of these terms, if not fulfilled, serve as grounds for firing a member.

Q: Firing a member: Can't we all just get along?
J.C.: Sadly, no! A band should indicate the parameters of when one can be fired from the band, as well as the procedure in which the person accused of misconduct can potentially cure a problem. The later language is stipulated in what is known as a "cure provision." Remember, you can't just willy-nilly dump someone.

A cure provision essentially grants a person the chance to correct his or her mistakes within a limited period of time—usually within thirty-five to forty-five days. For instance, if thirty-five days have passed since your drummer was rightly given a written notice to enter a detox center for a substance abuse and he failed to do so, his agreement with the band can be terminated if the terms have been stated as such. Or, if thirty-five days have passed since a member was given notice that he must show up for rehearsals in connection with a tour and he failed to oblige, his agreement with the band can be terminated—if, once again, the original terms stated as such.

Q: Is an amendment clause in a band agreement important?

J.C.: The method by which a band can change the terms of its own agreement is certainly important. An amendment clause typically stipulates what type of vote, unanimous or majority, it will take to change the terms of a band agreement. To change more significant terms, a unanimous vote might apply. To change less significant terms, a majority vote might be sufficient. Keep in mind that without an amendment clause in your agreement, should an argument come up, state partnership laws will say it takes a unanimous vote to change all terms.

Q: Should a mediation or arbitration clause be added to the band agreement when resolving disputes?

J.C.: Certainly a band can consider inserting a clause in its agreement indicating how disputes will be resolved. Mediation or arbitration can be a smart alternative to going to trial and incurring delays and substantial legal expenses. Mediation means having an appointed third party, such as an attorney, brought in to help a band resolve its disputes. Arbitration is similar to mediation, only the appointed third party decides on the outcome of the dispute.

Q: Is an indemnification clause necessary in a band agreement?

J.C.: Under state partnership law, each member is liable for the other members' negligence while conducting business. If one member gets into a fight with a bar owner and is sued, the partnerships' assets as well as the personal assets of each member in the band are at risk. An indemnification clause can be included in your band membership agreement saying that if certain behavior is considered to be damaging or negligent to the band, then that person stands independent and the band is not responsible for their actions.

While an indemnification clause is useful, there's a downside. Should an offending member cause some third party to sue the band and that party is successful, *all members of the band will still have to pay out according to the terms of the settlement.* The members will then have to turn to the offending band member and request he or she pay them back. The problem is that the band member you have to collect the money from will probably be bankrupt himself.

So is it really a solution? It is more useful than not, but keep in mind that none of this would be an issue if a band were incorporated [which will be discussed later], because only the assets of the corporation could be grabbed, not the personal assets of each member.

Q: Can you discuss the ownership of a band's name?

J.C.: A band name is essentially a trademark. More on this later, but you should at least know that ownership in a trademark is strengthened by its usage in commerce, and not on who thought it up before joining the band. Therefore, if a member comes into a band with a name that he intends to keep, it behooves him to make sure that the band agreement represents that it's really his asset—that he's only loaning the band the name and at no time is the band entitled to assert any rights of ownership.

In most band agreements, however, what usually happens is that the group holds the band's name, and therefore none of the departing members have permission to utilize it. Should the entire group fall apart, any member requesting the name would be able to use it as long as all of the departed members gave permission and signed off on it. It's entirely contract dependent, though.

If you have no band agreement, the partnership laws of the state may prevail allowing each member, even departed members, the right to use it. It's possible that each departed member of a band can simultaneously use the band name on his or her own. The issue, however, may come down to a messy and expensive lawsuit as to which member is defrauding the public, the argument being that one or two key members are the identity of the group, and anyone else using it is defrauding the public. Needless to say, this can still cost thousands of dollars to prove in a court of law.

Q: What do we need to know about trademark registration?
J.C: There are a number of things: Why should one file for registration, when should you file, what do you need to do to register, and what happens after you file for registration.

Q: Why register for a federal trademark?
J.C: First let me say that as soon as a band publicly performs live, sells CDs, or commercially exploits its name by some other means, it already has a trademark. The rights, however, are limited to the "geographical area in which the name is being used." That being said, the purpose of registering with the federal government is to provide a band with "nationwide protection."

Q: When should one register for a trademark?
J.C: I'd suggest a new band spend its money on other things until they are sure its name is going to be exploited at the national level, such as when they are getting a lot of exposure and selling product on the Internet or preparing to sign a record deal.

Q: How should one register? Conduct a trademark search or file forms?
J.C: As soon as a band comes up with its name, the members should all conduct a limited search to make sure that no one else is using it. As a band becomes more established, an even more extensive search can be conducted. Here's a few ways to conduct a search:

- ✦ Use a popular search engine like Google to search community sites and blogs.
- ✦ Look through local music publications that provide lists of unsigned groups.
- ✦ Search record store shelves.
- ✦ Use handy resources like the *Billboard International Touring Directory*, which lists hundreds of touring bands.
- ✦ Utilize the United States Patent and Trademark office's website (www.uspto.gov). Note that here you can search for bands already registered at the federal level but not at the state level. The problem with this is that you cannot find the bands that have not yet registered and have limited rights to the small geographical area where they've played or sold material.
- ✦ Use a professional trademark searching company, or an attorney who is well versed in the area of trademarks. This, of course, can be extremely costly.

After making sure your name is free to use, you'll need to fill out and sign a trademark application form available at the United States Patent and Trademark office's (USPTO) website (www.uspto.gov). Furthermore, you'll need to submit a drawing of your logo, send advertisements and other proof (or "specimens") that you are exploiting the name in interstate commerce (across state lines), pay a fee of several hundred dollars (fees are subject to change but are approximately $335), and send in a self-addressed stamped envelope to eventually receive a tracking number of your registration. Make a copy of your originals for your files before sending them to the Commissioner of Trademarks, at 2900 Crystal Drive, Arlington, Virginia 22203-513.

The patent office will first check the availability of the name and post your mark in the U.S. official *Gazette*, offering anyone the opportunity to challenge your registration. Assuming there are no problems, expect the entire registration period to take up to one year.

Q: After trademark registration, must you keep the name active or renew it?
J.C: Yes. These are usually the two important issues to deal with: keeping a name active and renewing your trademark.

To keep the name active, you must continue to use it. If you discontinue to use your name for a period of three years, be aware that it could constitute abandonment of your band name. Assuming you won't let that happen and your band is still going strong after the fifth year of trademark registration, it is highly recommended to file a legal document confirming its continued use. This document is called an "affidavit of incontestability," which essentially ensures that if anyone were to come out of the woodwork and claim they were using the name before you, they'll have a real difficult time winning in a court of law (if it even went that far). Furthermore, the "affidavit of incontestability" is commonly filed together with an "affidavit of use." The affidavit of use is filed after five years to continue to maintain a valid federal registration. If this affidavit is not filed, your trademark registration is abandoned.

To renew your trademark, you must contact the Commissioner of Trademarks every ten years. The renewal process consists of an affidavit of continuing use and a filed renewal application. The failure to file both forms will result in cancellation of your registration.

Note that all forms can be filed electronically over the Internet at the USPTO website (www.uspto.gov), but it's probably a good idea to let an attorney handle it. Trade-marks are a complex and confusing area of the music business, and you want to make sure you handle your band name with care.

Q: Are fictitious business names, or DBAs, mandatory?

J.C.: The most important time to file a DBA (doing business as), also called an FBN (fictional business name), is when you're receiving payment under a fictitious name. In other words, if a club owner is writing checks out to your band's name rather than to the name of an individual in the band, you need to file a DBA. A DBA shows proof that you're an authorized representative of the band. Without proof, you cannot walk into a bank and cash the check.

Q: Which business entity is best: partnership, corporation, S corporation, or LLC?

J.C.: There's no absolute answer to which business entity works best for every band. I'd say for baby bands, forming a partnership works fine in the beginning. As the band begins to make money and wants to protect their assets, forming an LLC may be the next step. Later, to take advantage of certain tax breaks while continuing to limit their liabilities, a band may look into forming the classic C or S corporation. An attorney or accountant is always advised to help a band decide what's best for them.

Q: Can you discuss partnerships?

J.C.: When two or more people come together to conduct business and they share in the profits and losses of that business, a partnership is essentially formed. So for many of your readers, their band is already a partnership. A partnership requires minimal setup: While putting together a band membership agreement is strongly recommended, an oral agreement will suffice. So overall, a partnership is relatively easy to run. For tax purposes, the partnership's profits and losses flow through to the individual members in a prorated share and are filed on the partner's individual returns. The downside, however, is that a partnership has unlimited personal liability. This means that if one partner is sued by another party, each partner's personal assets can be at risk. If the band is in the genre of music where there's a lot of energy and there's a high possibility for serious injuries in the mosh pit, then a partnership can be a potential disaster.

Q: What are the benefits, procedures, and costs of a corporation?

J.C.: The benefit of forming a corporation is that it is treated as a separate legal entity. This means that your personal assets are not at risk. Corporations are also entitled to certain tax fringe benefits for expenses that partnerships are not.

Setting up a corporation requires you to file articles of incorporation (also called articles of association) as well as SS4 forms to get a taxpayer ID number. This is the number that allows you to open a bank account. Then you need to put together bylaws or "rules" for how your company will be run. Bylaws might contain issues like who owns the band name, what happens if a member leaves, and what shares each individual has in the company. The day-to-day business matters are handled by officers who are elected by a board of directors, who are in turn elected by the shareholders (all of whom can be the same persons).

The fees for setting up corporations are different in every state. In California, it costs approximately $100 for the initial paper-

If you decide on filing for a corporation, it is *extremely* important that you, your agent, or your attorney follow through and file the annual report each year before the deadline, which is generally around April or May in most states. Not filing this report can result in the loss of your status as a corporation and cause you to be personally liable (called "piercing the corporate veil") should you be defeated in any lawsuits filed against you.

BUSINESS ENTITIES AT A GLANCE

Sole Proprietor

What: Business owned by one person

Formation: No formalities required

Liability: Unlimited (personal assets at risk)

Ownership: By sole proprietor

Management: By sole proprietor

Taxation: Filed on personal tax returns

Governed by: Business plan

Partnership

What: When two or more persons engage in common business,
a partnership is presumed by law

Formation: No requirement (written agreement recommended)

Liability: Unlimited (personal assets at risk)

Ownership: By the partners as the partners decide

Management: By the partners

Taxation: Filed on personal tax returns

Governed by: Understanding of the partners (partnership agreement recommended)

Corporation

What: A separate legal entity (which could consist of one or more people)

Formation: Filing articles of incorporation with state

Liability: Limited liability up to value of assets of the corporation

Ownership: By shareholders

Management: Shareholders elect directors who elect officers to manage

Taxation: Two levels: corporate taxes and shareholder taxes

Governed by: Bylaws

LLC (Limited Liability Company)

What: An entity with limited liability but fewer formalities than a corporation

Formation: Filing articles of organization with the secretary of state

Liability: Limited liability protection in amount you personally invested

Ownership: By members

Management: By members, unless officers are elected

Taxation: On personal returns, or on two levels: LLC and personal

Governed by: An operating agreement

S Corporation

What: A separate legal entity with thirty-five or fewer shareholders

Formation: Filing articles of incorporation with state

Liability: Limited liability protection in amount you personally invested

Ownership: By shareholders

Management: Shareholders elect directors who elect officers to manage

Taxation: On personal returns, or on two levels: corporate and personal

Governed by: Bylaws

Note: Chart provided with the assistance of Burgundy Morgan, Esq. BurgundyMorgan@aol.com.

work with an annual payment of $800. Keep in mind that you also have fees for your attorney and/or accountant, whom you will likely hire to assist you at this stage. There may also be fees for local business licenses and permits.

For tax purposes, a corporation is subject to double taxation whereby both the corporation and shareholders are taxed separately. Running a corporation requires a number of formalities and paperwork (such as keeping minutes for company meetings and annual meeting filings) and is therefore far more difficult to run than a partnership.

Q: How do C corporations compare to S corporations?

J.C.: An S corporation provides similar benefits as a classic C corporation in that it affords the shareholders a shield from personal liability and offers certain tax fringe benefits for expenses (though more restrictive than the corporation—talk to your accountant).

Like a C corporation, setting up an S corp requires filing articles of incorporation, getting taxpayer ID numbers, and putting together bylaws for how your company will be run. The day-to-day business matters are handled by officers who are elected by a board of directors who are elected by the shareholders.

For tax purposes, the profit or loss of the business can either be handled like a corporation where the corporation and shareholders are taxed separately, or it can pass through to the shareholders' personal tax returns and taxed only once—based on that shareholder's pro rata share ownership percentage. This is definitely a huge advantage and attraction for smaller businesses.

However, just like a C corporation, running an S corporation requires a lot of formalities and paperwork and can therefore be difficult to run. There are also restrictions to the maximum number of shareholders an S corp can have, but being in the tens, this probably won't be an issue for most of those reading this book.

> Attorney Burgundy Morgan notes that the good news about forming a business entity is that you can always change; so you are not limited. You can move, for instance, from an LLC or S corp to a C corp. However, she does suggest that young bands always speak with an attorney or accountant first to help you determine what entity is best for your needs.

Q: Can you discuss LLCs?

J.C.: An LLC, a limited liability company, is rather a new concept in comparison with the other business entities we've discussed. Like both the C and S corporations, an LLC limits the liabilities that someone suing you can grab; however, the downside is that it may not afford you the same tax fringe benefits.

Setting up an LLC is similar to setting up a C or S [corporation] in that you must file articles of organization and get taxpayer ID numbers. However, the good news is that establishing a simple operating agreement can run it. The day-to-day business matters can also be conducted by the member/owners or by officers who are elected to manage.

For tax purposes, just like an S corp, the profit and loss of an LLC can be handled two ways: either double taxed, whereby the LLC and the members are taxed, or it can pass through to the individual members and be filed on their personal tax returns. Again, this is definitely an advantage for smaller businesses.

The real good news about running an LLC is that unlike the S or C corporation, it provides for far less formalities and paperwork and therefore is easier to operate.

BAND MEMBERSHIP AGREEMENTS: KEY POINTS IN REVIEW

✦ **Voting:** How will the members vote on key issues—by unanimous or majority vote? Depending on the seriousness of the matter, such as the hiring and firing of members, different issues can require a different vote. In case of a deadlock, one person can be appointed as the tie-breaker.

✦ **Division of income:** How will the profits and losses be split between band members? Although most bands usually split income equally (at least in the beginning), sometimes the main songwriters or founders of the band are allotted a larger share.

✦ **Purchases:** What vote will permit the band to make equipment purchases? As an example, an investment under $250 may require a majority vote, while a purchase of over $500 may require a unanimous vote.

✦ **Investments and debts:** What happens to the assets acquired as a group when one member departs or is terminated? Usually, all debts need to be resolved immediately. For equipment already owned, the band may buy out the departed member's share.

✦ **Band name:** In the event that a member is fired or quits, or in the event that the band breaks up, who has the right to use the band name? Usually a band will agree that any departing or terminated member has no right to use the name. In case the band breaks up, and one member wants to use the name, everyone must sign off on it.

✦ **Hiring and firing:** Hiring a manager may require a unanimous vote. Firing a band member may require a majority vote. A band may also want to stipulate the conditions under which a band member may be terminated—for instance, not fulfilling his or her obligations to the band.

✦ **Obligations:** A band may want to list what is expected of each member in the band, such as first priority over outside work and showing up to rehearsals.

✦ **Quitting:** A member may be able to leave if he or she is unhappy, as long as it is not in the middle of a tour or in other situations in which the band may incur a loss as a result.

✦ **Departed members' rights to profits:** A departed member will continue to earn his or her share of income on work in which he or she was involved but not on new work by the band.

✦ **Amendment of agreement:** What kind of vote can change the terms of the agreement? Usually a band will choose a majority vote.

✦ **Arbitration or mediation:** How will disputes be settled? Rather than incurring excessive fees in the courts, a band may choose mediation or arbitration as a more practical alternative.

✦ **Indemnification clause:** If certain behavior is considered to be damaging or negligent to the band, then that person stands independent and the band is not responsible for their actions.

✦ **Term:** The term of the agreement may be for one to two years.

✦ **Signature and date:** All members must sign and date the agreement.

CHAPTER 3

Contract Employment or
Self-Employment

"It's only rock 'n' roll. Is it really?"
—BILL WYMAN (ROLLING STONES)

We've all heard those famous stories about young musicians who watched the Beatles perform on *The Ed Sullivan Show* and from that point forward wanted to be in a band just like John, Paul, George, and Ringo. But what almost every aspiring musician comes to realize is that being in a band is not easy. It requires years of hard work and sacrifice, and even after that, there are no guarantees of a big payoff. This is one of the reasons many musicians resort to hiring out their services in return for a sure and immediate paycheck. Musicians who choose to do such work are contract employees or self-employed performers.

Generally speaking, the term "contract employee" refers to anyone who agrees to work on a long-term, continuing relationship under a set of conditions usually specified by a contract; such situations include working with a regularly touring and recording act or with a house band for a national television show, such as *Conan O'Brien* or *Saturday Night Live*. A self-employed performer, or independent contractor, is essentially anyone who makes his or her services available for hire for shorter-term relationships. For instance, after a musician finishes performing one gig for which he or she has been hired as an independent contractor, such as overdubbing a solo on another musician's record or sitting in with a band for one night at a local club, he or she moves on to the next job. This requires a bit more hustling for work than being a contract employee, but as long as the phone keeps ringing, independent contractors do just fine.

Keep in mind that the distinction between contract employees and independent contractors is not always so black and white; the distinction is really only important when you are dealing with business issues such as taxes and workers' compensation insurance. But we'll get to those issues in more detail later in this chapter.

The most important thing to grasp is that whether you're a contract employee or an independent contractor, *you're in the business of you!* You have no claim in the organizations for which you work, no share in the band's future royalties (except in less common relationships called "percentage involvements," which are discussed later in this chapter), and for that matter, no real job security. You're simply hired to perform a service for a set fee. For this reason, it's your responsibility to understand your rights as a working musician and to make sure you're compensated fairly for each and every gig you perform. "What rights and fair treatment?" you might ask. "Aren't all musicians just happy to be working, regardless of what they're being paid and how they're being treated?" After all, getting "that gig" is no easy task, and the last thing you want to do is create waves, right? You may feel this way early in your career, while you're still paying your dues, but if you ever expect music to be your livelihood, then eventually you'll have to adopt a more professional outlook.

HOW TO BE A "WORKING" MUSICIAN: TIPS ON GETTING THE GIG

- ✦ Learn to play as many different styles possible, but have one style you play best.
- ✦ Learn to sight-read music.
- ✦ Work on your sound and on maintaining your gear and road cases.
- ✦ Become visually appealing.
- ✦ Develop a happy, warm personality.
- ✦ Volunteer to play on as many sessions as possible, such as on indie artists' records, film, or TV, with which a local producer may be involved.
- ✦ Sit in frequently at open mikes and jams.
- ✦ Make your services known through free magazine listings, Web message boards, and your local branch of the union (AFM or AFTRA).
- ✦ Get involved with performing at your church (you never know who is part of your parish).
- ✦ Take lessons with an actively gigging teacher and impress the hell out of him or her (he or she might need a sub one day).
- ✦ Form your own band that features the style of music you play best and get out there and be heard.
- ✦ Consider working with older artists, those who may not currently be in the spotlight but with whom you can gain valuable experience.
- ✦ Consider becoming a road technician for the artist or band whom you'd like to hire you one day.
- ✦ Make friends with tons of other musicians, bands, roadies, club promoters, producers, managers, talent agents, attorneys, equipment manufacturers, photographers, journalists, actors, models, and others in the business.
- ✦ Always be professional, never be late for a gig, and play your ass off every night.
- ✦ Always remember why you started playing—for the fun and the love of music.

UNIONS PROTECTING ACTIVE MUSICIANS

Many aspiring artists don't even know that musicians' unions exist, let alone what they actually do. You should know that both the American Federation of Musicians (AFM) and the American Federation of Radio and Television Artists (AFTRA) were specifically established to secure and enforce fair wages and good working conditions for musicians. Additionally, the AFM and AFTRA provide a variety of benefits packages as well as health and retirement funds to their members. Although the music business may often seem like the Wild West, with no apparent guidelines, regulations, or support for musicians, these unions may offer some hope. Regardless of whether becoming a union member makes sense at this point in your career, you'll find the information provided here extremely useful. Note that rates and terms are subject to change.

> Contact the AFM at (800) 762-3444 or at www.afm.org.

The American Federation of Musicians

Founded in 1897, the American Federation of Musicians is one of the oldest entertainment labor organizations in existence today. Like any other labor union, the AFM is based on the idea that through "strength in numbers," or as they put it, "collective empowerment," musicians will have a stronger voice in the workplace. The AFM is 100,000 members strong and includes artists from every field of musical endeavor. Bruce Springsteen is an AFM member, as are the guys in Bon Jovi; Paul Shaffer and the whole CBS Orchestra; Kevin Eubanks and *The Tonight Show* band; Metallica; and Aerosmith. The list of famous AFM members could fill this book.

The AFM has 250 branch offices, called "locals," in cities throughout the United States and Canada. These include the Professional Musicians Union Local 47 of Los Angeles and the Associated Musicians Local 802 of Greater New York City. Since each local is run autonomously, the benefits they offer may fluctuate slightly from branch to branch, depending on its membership strength. The following information outlines the major benefits of joining the union, requirements for joining and receiving certain benefits, and considerations as to why joining the union may not be right for you. There's a lot of information to digest here, but keep in mind that a representative at your local is always available to answer any questions that you may have.

Major Union Benefits

Although the AFM provides a variety of benefits to its members, the most significant of them is the bargaining they do with thousands of employers—record companies, broadcasting and cable companies, motion pictures companies, theaters, symphony managements, circuses, and theme parks—to establish fair wages, good working conditions, and fringe benefits for their members. The union enforces these rules and regulations and collects payment defaults by the employer when necessary. Some of the specific situations unions regulate include the following:

✦ Live performances, including performance rehearsals, cartage (the cost of transporting your equipment), travel expenses (such as air travel and hotels), travel time (the time it takes to go back and fourth from each gig), personal mileage on your vehicle (when using your own car or van to get back and forth to gigs), per diems (daily allowances for food), and holiday payment scales (for performing on New Year's Eve and other holidays)

- Recording sessions, including major label recording sessions and some smaller label sessions, as well as live concert recordings
- Television and radio performances, including all commercial advertisements
- Videotaping, including live concert performances, promotional video shoots such as for MTV and VH1, and performances on live television such as *The Tonight Show*, *Conan O'Brien*, *Saturday Night Live*, and *Late Night with David Letterman*
- Motion picture performances, including on-camera appearances (for instance, the filming of a bar or concert scene in a movie) and off-camera appearances (for instance, a studio recording for a movie soundtrack)

The union also provides health care and retirement benefits for qualifying members. Through the union's health care programs, you will receive medical and hospital benefits (subject to availability at your local branch). If you've ever been sick or injured and incurred costly hospital bills, then you know how important insurance is. Your local may also provide dental plans and prescription drug benefits for qualifying members. And though retirement may seem like a long way off, it's comforting to know that money will be waiting for you—even if you're no longer working in the music business.

UNION TO THE RESCUE A group of ska musicians from Los Angeles who had only been in the union around three months played a New Year's Eve gig in Florida and drove there to do it. The group received a bad check for the show, and their van broke down in Texas on the way home. They got in touch with the AFM, who was able to pursue their claim, help them get their van fixed, and coordinate the whole mess through Local 23 in San Antonio, Texas. Although the band had to endure a lecture from the union about their poor business practices, they seemed to actually welcome it—after all, they were no longer stranded thousands of miles from home. The promoter subsequently settled up on the bad check, by the way. The AFM pursues claims less dramatic than this all over the country every day.

In another instance, an artist who performed with her band on *Late Night with David Letterman* believed that since her musicians were being paid by Letterman's television production company via the union, she wasn't responsible for paying them for the job as well. She was wrong; under the Collective Bargaining Agreement for Video Taping, the AFM stipulates that musicians shall receive payment when taped for television appearances. This fee is in addition to the standard wage musicians should receive from their employer for a live performance. As it turned out, all of the musicians in the artist's band were paid. **Note:** Musicians are also paid "reuse" payments for reruns of a taped performance. The AFM monitors, collects, and pays musicians for these uses.

Other Union Benefits

Now that you have a good idea of some of the major benefits you will receive from joining the AFM, let's take a look at some of the other benefits you will get:

+ The AFM will closely monitor all of the recordings on which you perform and collect residuals if they're used in film, television, and commercials. These payments are called "new use" payments.
+ Members will be encouraged to sign up for the sound recording special fund payments—an additional payment issued to you based on a percentage (ranging from 20 to 60 percent) of scale dollars you earn on *AFM covered* recording sessions on which you perform the prior year; sessions for which you will continue to be paid for the next five years. For instance, if you participate in only one recording session in 2009, from the year 2009 to 2014 you will receive monies from the special payment fund.

Indie artists releasing their own CDs on their own labels can affiliate with the AFM record under union agreements and receive all the benefits, like the special payment funds.

The special payment fund is made available through annual contributions by record companies and paid out by the union. **Note:** Although the SPF is a benefit in alliance with the union, *you do not need to be a member to receive these monies.* For more information, call the SPF hotline at 1-866-711-Fund.

+ Members will also be encouraged to register with an organization called Sound Exchange (www.soundexchange.com), for which AFTRA (see page 68 later in this chapter) sits on the board. Sound Exchange licenses the public performances of sound recordings on noninteractive digital channels like the Internet, satellite, and cable TV. If you're a "featured performer" (i.e., a musician who is prominently featured in print in connection to a phonograph recording and/or a group signed to a recording agreement), and/or if you own your master recordings, Sound Exchange will distribute licensing royalties *directly to you*. **Note:** Although Sound Exchange is a benefit in alliance with the union, you *do not need to be a member to receive the monies*—although you must be a member of Sound Exchange.

A "featured artist" is either a musician prominently featured in print with a connection to a phonograph recording or a musical group who is signed to a recording agreement. A non-featured artist is a musician who performs on a recording that fits neither of the descriptions above.

+ If you are a "nonfeatured" performer on recordings that are broadcast on noninteractive digital channels like the Internet, satellite, and cable TV, you will receive licensing fees that are first collected by Sound Exchange and then distributed through the AFM under something called the AFTRA/AFM Property Rights Trust Fund (www.raroyalties.org), for which the AFM sits on the board. **Note:** You do not need to be a member of AFM

Small claims court, an inexpensive and quick way to settle disputes (the rules are simple, costs are low and often waived, and attorneys are usually not present) is yet another way to deal with that employer "who does you wrong." You can only sue up to a certain amount per case in one year (in California, one claim cannot exceed $5,000). Contact your county superior court for detailed information, to obtain the proper forms, and to ultimately "get your day in court."

to collect these monies, but you must be registered to the Property Rights Trust Fund.

✦ Your name will be registered in the union's job referral database (called GoPro), potentially leading you to new employment opportunities.

✦ The AFM provides limited legal supervision and career development to its members.

✦ If you have problems on the road, or if you have questions about contracts or what you should be paid, the AFM provides 24-hour telephone assistance.

✦ AFM members have access to discounted recording and rehearsal studios.

✦ Insurance for theft and damage to your instruments is also provided through membership in the AFM.

✦ You'll receive travel discounts, health club discounts, credit card options, loan programs, mortgage programs, and more.

✦ The AFM also offers you a subscription to their monthly newspaper, *International Musician*, which will keep you up-to-date on all the industry happenings.

Requirements for Membership

To receive all of the AFM benefits discussed, it's now time to discuss some of the qualifications you'll need to meet. Note that the rates discussed below are subject to change and vary from one local to another.

✦ To become a member, you must pay a one-time initiation membership fee of about $85 and a yearly fee of approximately $200.

✦ Members are required to work "union gigs" only. A union gig means that the person or organization for which you work must be a signatory to the union. Your employer is required to pay you at least the minimum scale wages. Your employer must also report all of the gigs in which you work to the union and make an additional contribution toward your pension and health care fund.

✦ To qualify for a pension, your employer's contributions (typically between 10 and 12 percent of the union's suggested minimum scales) must total $3,000 each year for five years. You can begin collecting early retirement benefits at age fifty-five, or you can wait and collect higher benefits at the full retirement age of sixty-five.

✦ To qualify for health care, your employer's contributions must reach a minimum dollar amount, usually within six-month periods (from April to September and October to March). Since contributions and health benefits vary considerably depending on the job performed and on your local union, contact your local branch office for specific details.

✦ You are required to pay union dues of approximately 2.5 percent of the suggested minimum scale for live performances, 4 percent of the suggested minimum wage for recording sessions, and up to 12 percent for new use fees payments. Contact your branch office for local rates.

✦ You are encouraged to attend monthly local meetings to discuss current union events, to meet other union members, and to offer input for future policy development.

> Contact the AFM's nationwide pension department at 1-800-833-8065.

Is Joining AFM Right for You?

Now that you have a good idea of what the AFM provides and what some of the member requirements are, you can decide if joining is right for you. Keep in mind that the union is most beneficial when you're working union gigs often. This is how you'll qualify for the major benefits, such as the health care and pension funds, and receive the union's assistance in collecting payment defaults. However, keep the following in mind:

✦ Not all employers are union affiliated, nor are they willing to comply with union requirements. The union's strengths lie mostly in major venue performances, major label recordings, and television, theater, orchestral, Broadway shows, and motion picture work. Freelance drummer Kenwood Dennard adds, "I was a union member, but I changed my status from 'active member' to 'inactive member.' This way I can maintain a good relationship with them without having to pay dues. I became an inactive member because I wasn't doing enough of the gigs the AFM specializes in to fully benefit. I was doing more small club work in the jazz and pop gigs idiom."

✦ It is not considered "good standing" to accept any nonunion gig. Although the union is known occasionally to turn a blind eye and allow you to perform nonunion gigs, they may still require you to pay dues for the job performed. Unions are known to review performance listings in local magazines in order to police members who are not complying with this rule. Members that are not in good standing may be subject to expulsion.

✦ The musician's job referral database, made available through the union, has been appraised by many musicians as not being very effective. The competition among members to get the gigs that are offered is fierce, and unless you're calling your local union office 24/7, there aren't too many gigs that will come your way.

Regardless of whether you feel that it's time to become a member of the AFM, be sure at least to talk to a representative at your local branch. Mark Heter, former head of the Division of Touring, Theatres, Booking Agent Agreements and Immigration Matters for the American Federation of Musicians in New York City, gave these final words:

Membership is a participatory experience. AFM membership goes beyond paying dues and being taken care of by the union. By joining, you become a vital part of the union itself and acquire the empowerment to make positive changes in your own life. Membership is a commitment, not only for the member's personal benefit but toward the betterment of everyone else in the union to make things better for musicians. There is spiritual and personal satisfaction to be found by becoming engaged in the labor movement. The union is here to serve you.

The American Federation of Radio and Television Artists

The 70,000-member American Federation of Radio and Television Artists (AFTRA) has been representing singers, actors,

Contact AFTRA at (323) 634-8100 or www.aftra.com.

MEMBER OR NOT, HERE THEY COME! A contract musician touring with a pop/rock group and earning a weekly salary for his performances encountered a situation in which the group was scheduled to record a live performance for release on phonorecord. The group was not willing to negotiate an additional fee for this recording; the employer felt that the employee's salary covered an unlimited number of services to be determined at their discretion. However, union law provides that all location recordings shall be reported to the AFM prior to such recordings and that each musician shall receive a rate for each day the recording takes place. Although neither the musician, the band, nor the independent record company (to which the group was signed) were union signatories, the major record label that handled the distribution of the recording was a union signatory. As a result, the independent record label was covered under the major label's agreement, and the musician eventually received compensation with a union representative's assistance. Needless to say, the musician thereafter became a union member.

announcers, and news broadcasters in sound recordings, radio and television programs, and commercials since 1937. AFTRA's headquarters is located in Los Angeles, with thirty-five branch offices located in major cities throughout the United States. Since some benefits may vary slightly from local to local, it's always wise to contact a local branch near you.

Major Union Benefits

AFTRA negotiates with employers to provide fair wages, professional working conditions, and benefits for vocalists in sound recordings, radio and television programs, and commercials. AFTRA enforces recognition of these standards and collects payment defaults and original earnings on behalf of its members. AFTRA also works hard to promote legislation that benefits recording artists on the federal and state levels.

In addition, AFTRA offers one of the best health and retirement plans in the business, and depending on your eligibility, it will pay up to $1 million dollars in medical bills and hospital expenses. Through AFTRA's health plan, you may also be eligible for confidential mental health and substance abuse programs, a prescription drug program reimbursing out-of-pocket costs, a dental plan, life and accident insurance, a wellness plan, and discounted life insurance rates. Depending on your eligibility, AFTRA's retirement fund may pay you an income when you reach retirement age as well.

A major distinction between the AFM and AFTRA is that the AFM handles instrumentalists, and AFTRA represents vocalists. This means that if you both sing and play an instrument on a union-covered recording session, for instance, you could potentially end up being a member of both unions.

Other Union Benefits

As if the advantages of joining AFTRA discussed earlier were not enough, there are more. The following are some of the other benefits you will receive by becoming an AFTRA member.

+ AFTRA will track and monitor the recordings on which its members sing. When these recordings are used in new mediums like motion pictures, television, or commercials, AFTRA will collect and pay you residuals.

+ Under something called AFTRA's Sound Recording Code, AFTRA members who are also signed recording artists will receive additional health and retirement payments from their record company based on the number of royalties earned (this is whether your record company has recouped its expenses or not).

+ Members will be encouraged to register with an organization called Sound Exchange (www.soundexchange.com), for which AFTRA sits on the board. Sound Exchange licenses the public performances of sound recordings on non-interactive digital channels like the Internet, satellite, and cable TV. If you're a "featured performer" (i.e., a musician who is prominently featured in print in connection to a phonograph recording, and/or a group signed to a recording agreement), and/or if you own your master recordings, Sound Exchange will distribute licensing royalties to you. **Note:** Though Sound Exchange is a benefit in alliance with the union, you *do not need to be a member to receive these monies—* although you must be a member of Sound Exchange.

+ If you are a "nonfeatured" performer on recordings that are broadcast on noninteractive digital channels like the Internet, satellite, and cable TV, you will receive monies first collected by Sound Exchange and then distributed through the AFTRA under something called the AFTRA/AFM Property Rights Trust Fund (www.raroyalties.org), for which AFTRA sits on the board. **Note:** You *do not* need to be a member of AFTRA to collect these monies, but you must be registered to the Property Rights Trust Fund.

+ Members of AFTRA will have access to a professional staff who can answer your questions about contracts and salary minimums. Additionally, there will always be a helpful staff available to assist you in payment disputes and other important issues.

+ Joining AFTRA also entitles you to new employment opportunities. For instance, AFTRA's local branch offices cater to vocalists in their area by offering job listings, programs to increase your résumé-writing skills and audition techniques, and seminars where you can meet potential employers.

+ By becoming a member of AFTRA, you may be able to qualify for special scholarship programs through the George Heller Memorial Foundation.

+ AFTRA provides its members with low-fee credit card options, high-yield savings accounts, low-interest loans, and other services offered through the AFTRA/ Screen Actors Guild Federal Credit Union.

+ When joining AFTRA, you will receive a subscription to *AFTRA* magazine, which will help keep you up-to-date on various developments in the music industry.

Requirements for Membership

To receive the many benefits offered by AFTRA, you'll have to meet a number of qualifications discussed below. Note that some of the rates discussed are subject to change. Be sure to contact a local AFTRA branch office for updated information.

✦ To join AFTRA, you are required to complete an application for membership, fill out an enrollment card, and attach a check for the initiation fees, which are $1,300 at the time of this writing. Minimum dues for the first period are $64. Dues are payable every six months (May and November) and are usually based on gross earnings combined from all AFTRA work done in the previous year.

✦ As an AFTRA member, you must be sure before accepting work that the employer (i.e., the record company, producer, etc.) for whom you are working is a signatory to AFTRA. Members who accept nonunion gigs are subject to disciplinary action and expulsion. Employers are required to pay minimum scale wages and make contributions to the AFTRA Health & Retirement Funds on the member's behalf.

✦ To be covered by AFTRA's major medical and hospitalization, your gross earnings must be at least $15,000 within twelve months of beginning work under AFTRA's jurisdiction. For gross earnings over $25,000, you are entitled to dependant medical coverage for family members.

> Contact AFTRA's Health & Retirement Funds office at (800) 562-4690 or at www.aftra.com.

✦ To qualify for retirement benefits, you must have five years of AFTRA-covered earnings. You must earn $7,500 each year, for five years.

Is Joining the AFTRA Right for You?

The major benefits of joining AFTRA are the eligibility for minimum scale wages and the fair treatment from employers. Unfortunately, however, not all employers are union signatories who comply with union requirements. When you accept work from nonunion employers, you not only undermine the strength of the union but also forfeit the benefits of the health care and retirement funds. Even if you only work AFTRA-covered gigs, you must still work a minimum number of gigs to meet the health and retirement requirements listed above.

By speaking with your local AFTRA office, you'll have a better sense of whether joining the union at this time in your career is right for you. One thing is certain: Whether you join or not, there are thousands of singers who swear by AFTRA's membership. Jon Joyce, a well-known session singer on recordings, television, jingles, and motion pictures, says, "If there were no such thing as AFTRA today, we would be meeting together to form such a union. It is run for members by members, and AFTRA membership is the best bargain in the business."

Kevin Dorsey, backup singer for top recording artists, adds, "I have been a member of AFTRA for thirteen years and currently serve on both the Los Angeles Local and National Board. Whether representing me in the workplace or making me feel at ease knowing that my health and retirement benefits are there, AFTRA has always been with me throughout my career."

Finally, Jevetta Steel, Columbia recording artist, sums things up with, "AFTRA is a union united for the good of all artists. AFTRA is the prototype of the future."

NEGOTIATING YOUR EMPLOYMENT AGREEMENT

Regardless of what the AFM and AFTRA have to say about fair treatment and minimum scale wages for musicians, the truth is that there's nothing "fair" in the music business . . . unless you're referring to the county "fairs" at which aging rock stars end up playing during the course of nostalgia tours to pay their rent. All jokes aside, it's no secret that gigs in the music business don't simply grow on trees, and musicians often have to accept whatever gig is presented them—bad or good—just to survive. In either case, you should look out for the following things. Note that some rates are subject to change.

Working for Employers with Limited Budgets

As either a contract employee or a self-employed musician, especially early in your career, frequently you'll be offered work that pays substandard wages far below minimum scale. This may be due to your inexperience, or to an employer's greed, or to a group's financial restrictions (i.e., a limited budget). When you accept employment from an employer who has a limited budget, there are really no fairness guidelines, but you should at least establish that your pay will increase when the group starts to make more money. This is especially important if you're a contract employee working with one employer on a regular basis. Otherwise, you may continue to be paid the same low fee in spite of the group's newfound success and subsequent profits. It's common sense to establish that safeguard.

Working for Employers with Larger Budgets

The day will eventually come when you're asked to work with successful and reputable employers who are willing to pay fairly and offer special perks—even greater than the minimum scales and treatment suggested by the union. But after adapting an "anything goes" approach to business for so long in your formative years, you may end up undercutting yourself in these new and potentially advantageous situations. To avoid that, you need to understand what you may be entitled to. The

SINGING THE BLUES! A group of musicians agreed to work with an up-and-coming blues guitarist for a minimal fee of $275 per week, due to the guitarist's limited budget. As the tour progressed, the guitarist's new record began to do extremely well. In no time, the group was performing in larger venues with the Rolling Stones and Aerosmith and appearing on national television shows such as *The Tonight Show*. The guitarist was now earning substantially more and could afford to pay his musicians comparable union scale. When the group requested a raise (which was only fair), they were replaced on the following tour with musicians who were "hungry" and looking for a break. This "burn and churn" philosophy is unfortunately used by a lot of employers in the music business to avoid paying their musicians higher fees. Taking this type of shrewd thinking one step further, Chuck Berry has never hired permanent musicians to go out on the road with him. Instead, he uses pick-up musicians (willing to work for cheap) in every city of his scheduled tour, who rehearse his material prior to his arrival. The following discussion sheds light on your wages, per diems, retainers, equipment, equipment techs, buyouts, and much more. Keep in mind that the agreement you're able to negotiate here as either a contract employee or as an independent contractor is substantially influenced by your reputation and experience and/or how badly a potential employer may want to work with you.

Wages

The wages you can expect from employers that have larger budgets will naturally be much greater than the compensation offered from employers with limited budgets. For instance, in 2007, Justin Timberlake paid a relatively unknown horn player a weekly salary of $4,000 to tour (which is a far cry from the $275 salary our blues artist friends in the previous text box was paid). *Session musicians sometimes get paid double or even triple the union minimum scale (a basic sideman union minimum session scale for three hours or less is about $375)* to record an album or to overdub a solo. When negotiating your fee, take notice of the strength of the record company for whom you're recording, the capacity of the venue in which you are playing, the time of year in which you're working (such as on a national holiday), and the length of the tour on which you may be embarking. Consider other factors as well: How much work will you be giving up to take on a new job? What are your personal monthly bills? How much will you net after your basic expenses? How long will you be able to survive financially after the completion of a tour? Drummer Kenwood Dennard, who has worked with Sting, Vanessa Williams, and Miles Davis, adds, "I negotiate my fee based on the obligations a specific employer is requesting and on what I feel I'm worth. As long as the resulting figure is not below my personal minimum standard, I take the gig. As for your readers, I suggest they contact the appropriate union, refer to the minimum scale wages, and use these as a starting point to negotiate their fee."

Should you one day take on a more permanent position in a group (working extensively with one artist for several years), note that some musicians are often offered a guaranteed annual salary covering all of their services (rehearsals, recording, touring, and special appearances). A number of highly successful bands, while they may appear to the general public to operate as a band or "equal partnership," function this way. One high-profile drummer I know was paid an annual salary of $100,000 over the course of several years while working with one of the greatest rock groups in the world—KISS.

Rehearsals

You've probably been participating in rehearsals with little or no pay for years, but employers with larger budgets will typically compensate you for rehearsals in preparation for "phonograph" recording sessions, single live performances, and extended tours. The amount will vary between employers, but minimum compensation of around $100 for a two-and-a-half hour rehearsal is not uncommon.

Per Diems

Per diems are standard in the industry, and negotiating a reasonable one is usually not too difficult. A per diem is a daily allowance for food. The amount varies greatly but can range anywhere from around $50 to $250 per day. Keep in mind that if you're performing a gig out of the country, your per diem should be adjusted to reasonably accommodate the exchange rate.

Buyouts

In addition to receiving a per diem, employers with larger budgets may offer you money in something called a buyout. A buyout occurs when the concert promoter does not fulfill his or her contractual obligation to provide food and drink backstage. This obligation is stipulated in a band "rider," a contractual addendum in live performance contracts that also includes lighting and sound requirements for the group, dressing room accommodations, and security needs. For one reason or another, a promoter may not be able to provide the requested food, so he "buys" the band "out." A buyout is based on the number of people traveling with the band; a group may provide you with additional funds ranging from around $20 to $60 per buyout (and more). There are cases where musicians receive hundreds of dollars in buyouts over the course of a tour. The amount is subject to the individual situation.

Equipment

Musical equipment is another important factor to consider when arranging your deal with an employer. Instruments and protective travel cases may be provided via your employer's recording and/or tour budgets. For instance, a musician hired to play drums on a band's record negotiated to have the group pay for the rental of high-quality drums for the session. In another situation, a drummer needed heavy-duty travel cases for an upcoming European tour, so the group paid over $4,000 to have the cases custom built. When he parted ways with the band, they offered him the option of purchasing the gear at a bargain price.

Equipment Endorsements

Your employer may cover minor equipment expenses for maintenance or usage of items, such as guitar picks, guitar strings, amplifier tubes, drumsticks, and drum skins. If your employer doesn't cover the cost of these expenses, you may try to obtain sponsorship from a variety of equipment manufacturers if your group is already successful or gaining additional exposure from radio play and record sales. Most companies will begin your relationship by offering you a reduced price on equipment (usually 60 to 70 percent off the retail price). If you're currently working regularly for a very large and successful organization, some companies may offer you free equipment and advertise your name and likeness with their product.

Develop as many relationships with manufacturers as possible, but focus on companies whose products you truly desire; a company will want to know that you're not just looking for free equipment. Introduce yourself in a telephone call or at trade shows such as the annual National Association of Music Merchants (NAMM) conventions (www.namm.com). Send manufacturers your recent record releases, updated tour "itineraries" (i.e., performance dates and locations), performance reviews, and magazine articles.

Bill Zildjian, vice president of the Sabian cymbal company, offers this advice: "Show manufacturers that you are attracting attention from the community, especially from the demographic of fans between the ages of eighteen to twenty-four. This age-group is more likely to buy manufacturer's products, and that makes manufacturers happy!"

Equipment Techs

The care and maintenance of your musical equipment is critical, both in the recording studio and out on the road. When you're working for employers with larger budgets, they may hire studio techs

HOW TO GET, AND KEEP, AN EQUIPMENT ENDORSEMENT

✦ Get your priorities straight and hone your craft first.

✦ Pay your dues and build your list of professional accomplishments (i.e., artists you've played with, number of students you have, record labels for which you are signed, producers you've recorded for).

✦ Put together a press kit, including pictures of your current setup, upcoming/past tour dates, CD samples of your playing, and proof you're generating "attention" in your community. Remember, it's not just about how well you play but rather how well you can help expose and sell an equipment manufacture's products.

✦ Don't send your press package to every equipment manufacturer on the planet. Only solicit to those manufacturers whose equipment you love and know well.

✦ Be very polite, courteous, and humble when making follow-up calls.

✦ Get out and network in the industry—attend the NAMM convention and introduce yourself directly to product reps.

✦ Keep an eye open for new and developing companies—their craftsmanship is often comparable to the larger companies and they are often more interested in working with less established artists.

✦ Conceive new product ideas of your own and then pitch them to various companies. Manufacturers are usually very receptive to useful ideas.

✦ If you get an endorsement, be sure to honor your contract terms: Expose the brand name whenever possible, don't attempt to hook up friends with free gear, and always give your product rep VIP treatment at the shows he attends.

to tune and maintain your equipment when recording. On a tour, road techs are usually hired to handle the setup of your musical equipment and to ensure its proper functioning before a concert performance. Techs also help during a performance when a guitar string or drum head breaks, a vocal mike needs to be replaced, or a cord is accidentally pulled out of an amplifier. At the end of the night, techs are responsible for breaking down musical equipment and making sure that it's loaded in the vans, trucks, or buses. A tech adds to the professionalism of a tour by allowing musicians to concentrate on their principal job at hand—performing. Should an employer fail to provide you with a tech, negotiate your fee accordingly so that you can afford to hire one yourself. **Note:** Whoever ends up providing an equipment tech, know that if your musical equipment is lost or damaged on the road (e.g., if an amplifier is dropped from a truck or a guitar is left at the last gig), the group's organization or, in some cases, the venue in which you are performing should cover the repair or replacement costs under their own insurance coverage.

Travel and Lodging.

Although your employer will generally cover or reimburse you for air travel costs and lodging, the quality of service is usually uncertain. Employers with larger budgets may take more care in providing the best possible travel and hotel accommodations; you may be provided with first-class airline tickets and/or single hotel room accommodations. Although this may seem unimportant, after being out on the road for several months, your comfort can mean the world to you. Whether you receive this type of special treatment depends on your employer, but keep in mind that it does exist. **Note:** Hotel "incidentals," such as phone calls, room service fees, and movie rentals, are your responsibility. So be careful! Incidentals can add up quickly—especially telephone and online costs. Employers with larger budgets also pay for the costs for traveling to gigs in or around your hometown. Reimbursable expenses include mileage on your car, cartage (the costs of transporting heavy or multiple pieces of musical equipment), and parking expenses. Check with your local union to see what else you can have covered in your agreement with an employer.

Employers typically purchase airline tickets for you, but be sure to personally register with the frequent-flyer programs offered by most major airlines. You'll be surprised at the mileage you can rack up and the number of free flights you can earn over the years. These tickets can come in handy for personal use, but more important, they can come in handy when you have an opportunity to audition for an act that may be three thousand miles away. Make sure to register your name with every available airline and keep updated records of the mileage you earn.

Special Clothing

If specific clothing that is not "standard" or "ordinary" is required for a promotional video shoot, stage show, or tour, the group will usually reimburse you for the cost of that clothing. For instance, one musician was allotted $750 to buy clothes for a video shoot that only lasted a day. The artist and video director specifically wanted the band and dancers to dress in black and studded leather pants (in case you're wondering, the shoot was for a hardcore rap artist). Keep in mind that the amount of money you're offered depends on the specifics of each individual situation.

Retainers

In times of temporary unemployment, such as during a break in a tour schedule, employers with larger budgets may provide you with additional benefits such as a "retainer." A retainer enables you to maintain an income while your services are on hold. You are expected to be, more or less, on call and are thus limited or excluded from taking on other work. A retainer is usually 50 percent of your weekly salary. Retainers are most common when you're working regularly for one artist.

Working for Employees under a Salary/Percentage Involvement

In some situations, established artists employ musicians and offer more than the typical salary for such relationships. These are called "salary/percentage involvements," and they often occur when an established artist desires your contributions to the writing and recording of an album as well as your participation on a tour in support of that album. An employer may offer you percentages of profits from record royalties, music publishing royalties, and merchandising monies. The process by which percentages are determined depends on each individual situation, although the percentages you get should be equal to the level of your contribution to the project.

Salary/percentage involvements may be one of the most difficult business relationships to understand. You may feel as if you're occupying the gray area between being an employee and a band member. Yes, the opportunity to offer your creativity to a band and the inclusion of percentages in your agreement are two attractive aspects of the relationship, but don't be misled—you're still an employee! (Or as a high-profile New York attorney once put it, you are a glorified sideman.)

Below are a few issues you should look out for when arranging your deal with an employer under a salary/percentage involvement. There are other areas which also need to be considered. However, this should at least show you how being on guard can work in your favor.

Salary

As an employee, you should always be compensated fairly for your services. If, however, you are offered percentages, you may be expected to make some of the same sacrifices that the members of the band have to make, such as attending "promotional events." Promotional events include, for instance, group photo shoots, video shoots, press interviews, radio interviews, record store promotions (i.e., in-stores). These events usually do not generate a direct source of income to the band, and therefore the group may feel that it should not have to personally compensate you for your time. Keep in mind, though, that if you're asked to work for free, it shouldn't cost you a dime to do so; you should always receive a per diem and have all your expenses paid.

Record Royalties

Record royalties are percentages the record company pays the artist for the sale of his record. While owning a percentage sounds tempting, as you'll see in Chapter 10, it could very easily mean zilch. Your objective is to negotiate record royalties in your agreement with the band. But don't be deceived by the apparent significance of these royalties when negotiating other aspects of your deal.

Music Publishing Royalties

If you're asked to participate in the songwriting process and it appears that you'll be contributing a great deal of time, establish an agreement with the group that stipulates some form of guaranteed compensation. Since no one can foresee whether the songs to which you contribute will make the final cut on the album (everyone but you will have the final say), you could end up investing weeks or months of your time arranging and making demos for the group's song ideas without gaining much, if any, in music publishing royalties on the record. Therefore, ask the group for a guaranteed minimum share in the compositions. If the group reacts unfavorably to this request, ask for an

READ THE (SONG) WRITING ON THE WALL Preliminary agreements are a must. According to a former employee of a well-known guitarist, after completing a successful tour of Japan, the guitarist suggested that he and his band begin "throwing around ideas" for songs on his next album. Together, they met for two and a half months, five days a week, working exclusively on the guitar player's ideas. When it came time to record the album, the guitarist chose to replace his band with a new group of musicians; the old band had donated approximately 250 hours of its time arranging the guitarist's material, received zero compensation, and were all out of work!

hourly fee. Either way, a preliminary agreement insures that you're going to be compensated for your time and hard work. (Music publishing is covered in detail in Chapter 11.)

Merchandising Monies

If your beautiful face (i.e., your image) is used on T-shirts and hats or if merchandise generally reflects work in which you were involved (e.g., a T-shirt including a lyric from a song you helped to write), you may receive some percentage of the merchandising revenue. If the group handles its own merchandising, your agreement may consist of a percentage of the net profit during the time that you're with the group. If the group is signed with a merchandising company, you might get a portion of your royalties up front from the advance monies offered in merchandising deals. In any case, when negotiating your agreement, ask for statements of merchandising sales, promotional giveaways, and expenses. This will help you to keep track of your share of merchandising revenue. (Merchandising is covered in more detail in Chapter 13.)

UNDERSTANDING YOUR TAXES: UNCLE SAM'S CUT

Taxes may not be the most exciting topic, but they are something all of us have to deal with eventually. As I mentioned earlier, here's where the distinction between contract employees and those who are self-employed (i.e., working on a freelance basis) is especially important. Why? Because the Internal Revenue Service treats contract employees and self-employed individuals differently, and the difference in taxes can be substantial. **Note:** Keep in mind that rates and regulations are subject to change.

Contract Employment

If you're a contract employee in an ongoing working relationship, then your employer is responsible for deducting taxes from your paycheck. But if you're wondering why your pay (after taxes) ends up being significantly less by the time you receive your check, then here's some information you'd better know. Remember, this is your money we're talking about here, so listen up!

Income Taxes

Income taxes make up the largest portion of your total annual tax bill, which can consist of federal, state, and/or local income taxes. You are required to pay these taxes on business income and on other compensation—wages, a portion of per diems, etc.—for services rendered. Your employer is responsible for withholding these taxes—indicated on your paycheck as FITW, SITW, and/or local tax withholdings—from your pay. The amount withheld only represents an estimate of the taxes you owe and is based in part on the information that you provide on federal tax form W-4 (and the state equivalent) as to whether you are single or married, have children, own a home, etc. You should complete and turn in a W-4 form to your employer at the time your employment begins. If you have any questions about completing this form, your employer should provide you with assistance, or you can contact the Internal Revenue Service.

> Contact the Internal Revenue Service at (800) 829-1040, (800) Tax Form, or at www.irs.gov.

Social Security and Medicare

Employers are also required to withhold Social Security and Medicare taxes—indicated on your paycheck as FICA-OASDI and FICA-HI withholding, respectively—from your pay. In general, these taxes provide retirement and health insurance for people over

Contact the Social Security Administration at (800) 772-1213 or at www.ssa.gov.

sixty-five. The Social Security tax you pay is 6.2 percent of your income, up to a maximum of \$97,500 (for the 2007 tax year). The Medicare tax you pay is 1.45 percent, with no limit on your income.

State Unemployment Taxes/Insurance

In addition, state unemployment taxes/insurance, normally indicated on your paycheck as SUI, must be withheld from your pay by your employer, except for those employers who reside in Alaska, Florida, Nevada, Texas, South Dakota, Washington, and Wyoming. These taxes provide benefits to employees who are laid off or are between cycles of seasonal work (e.g., touring). Eligibility for state unemployment benefits is based on a specific minimum amount of dollars withheld by your employer for taxes during a specified period of time. Because laws vary from state to state, it's important to contact your state unemployment agency to make sure you qualify for assistance. If you're unemployed, be sure to contact them immediately. A little extra cash can come in handy until you resume work.

State Disability Insurance

Employers who reside in California, Hawaii, New Jersey, New York, and Rhode Island must withhold state disability insurance—normally indicated as SDI—from your paycheck as well. State disability insurance provides benefits if you are injured off the job or if you become sick or pregnant. If you're unable to work for several months due to an injury, disability insurance can be a lifesaver. Your employer is required to provide you with information about state disability insurance at the time of your employment. **Note:** Workers' compensation insurance, which covers you for job-related injuries, is discussed below.

Year-End Reporting

At the end of the year, your employer will issue you tax form W-2, which indicates both your total income and the total amount of taxes withheld from your paycheck during the calendar year. This form must be issued by your employer no later than January 31 (following the tax year). After reporting your total taxable income and the applicable taxes withheld from it on your returns, you must then attach a W-2 to your returns and send both to the Internal Revenue Service and/or state tax authorities. In general, the lastest date to file your tax return is April 15 (after the end of the applicable tax year). Keep in mind that the amount withheld from your paychecks throughout the year only represents an estimate of the taxes you owe. Therefore, it makes sense to seek the advice of an experienced entertainment accountant or tax attorney to help you minimize your ultimate tax liability. This may be accomplished in part by "itemizing" (i.e., listing) and deducting the business expenses related to your employment that you incur throughout the year for which you have not been reimbursed.

Itemized deductions, also called "Schedule A" deductions (reported on tax form Schedule A), include miscellaneous expenses such as home office expenses, magazine subscriptions, union dues, stage clothing costs, dry cleaning costs, educational expenses, travel costs, legal fees, tax preparation charges, etc. You may be surprised at what you can write off, so hang on to all the business-related expense receipts for which you are not repaid, and be sure to hire an experienced entertainment accountant or tax attorney to review the expenses you can and cannot deduct. (See the box that follows for a comprehensive list of deductions to which you may be entitled.)

Self-Employment/Independent Contractor Status

For self-employed musicians working on a freelance basis, the tax laws differ from those governing contract employees. As you'll see below, you'll also have a lot more responsibilities.

Income Taxes

Similar to contract employees, self-employed musicians are also subject to income taxes, including federal, state, and/or local taxes. However, if you're self-employed and working as an independent contractor, taxes are not taken out of the payments made to you by the various organizations for whom you work.

You're responsible for estimating and paying your own taxes throughout the tax year. As a self-employed musician, you're required to make estimated payments on a quarterly basis: on April 15, June 15, September 15, and January 15. In addition, you may have to pay a "self-employment tax"—approximately 15.3 percent on net earnings—consisting of 12.4 percent for Social Security and 2.9 percent for Medicare *on net income*. This tax is approximately double that of the Social Security and Medicare taxes that you pay as a contract employee.

Year-End Reporting

At the end of the year, the bands or organizations you have worked for should provide you with tax form 1099 Misc, which indicates the total income that you received from them for the calendar year. You must then report the total income received as reflected on all 1099 forms (and related expenses) on your federal and state returns. You may be able to reduce the amount of money you owe in taxes throughout the year by deducting what the IRS considers "ordinary" and "necessary" expenses related to your trade/business. These expenses, called "Schedule C" deductions (filed on IRS tax form Schedule C), are for office supplies, business travel expenses, car expenses, legal expenses, union dues, etc. Just be sure to hang on to all of your business expense receipts throughout the year. The rules regarding tax deductions for independent contractors, as well as for contract employees, are tricky and subject to interpretation. Therefore, it's always a good idea to contact an experienced entertainment accountant or tax attorney for assistance.

WORKERS' COMPENSATION INSURANCE

Like taxes, insurance is not the most exciting subject, but your risk of injury is increased when traveling from city to city, night after night, and it should not be underestimated. Contract employees and independent contractors are treated differently when it comes to insurance, and it's important that you understand exactly what your employment status entitles you to. **Note:** Rules and regulations are subject to change.

Below are some examples of deductions that you may be able to claim on your tax returns— either miscellaneous itemized deductions if you're a contract employee (Schedule A deductions), or trade/business deductions if you're an independent contractor (Schedule C deductions).

♦ Union dues

♦ Mail and fax expenses: résumés, promotional kits, etc.

♦ Dry cleaning costs for stage clothes, etc.

♦ Conventions: music conferences such as the NAMM show

♦ Business gifts: greeting cards, etc.

♦ Attorney fees

♦ Tax preparation costs

♦ Educational expenses: music lessons, seminars

♦ Telephone calls for business: If originating from your residence, it's a good idea to have a second line; otherwise, you must be able to determine what percentage of calls made from a single residence phone were business related, and what calls were personal.

♦ Entertainment and meal expenses for business: Deductions may include show tickets, etc.

♦ Related work tools: Recording gear, drumsticks, guitar strings, instrument fees, repairs, maintenance, and insurance may be deductible. The cost of CDs and cassettes may also be considered a deductible expense as long as the music was purchased in connection to your work, rather than for your leisure enjoyment.

♦ Depreciation of work tools: You can deduct a portion of your equipment's cost over several years as it depreciates in value.

♦ Subscriptions: magazines such as *Billboard, Guitar Player, Rolling Stone*

♦ Home office expenses (office space in your home or apartment used exclusively for business, such as home studios and rehearsal rooms): Deductions may include a portion of your rent, utilities, cable (for MTV, VH1), and the like.

♦ Travel expenses: airline tickets, lodging, taxis, limousines, food, personal grooming related to work (shampoos and conditioners, etc.), uniform clothing (stage clothes that are not used in everyday circumstances), tips (for meals, baggage handlers, etc.), travel costs for an associate (if for a bona fide business reason), passport photo, and application fees.

♦ Car expenses or standard mileage on vehicle: There are two ways to deduct auto expenses. You can deduct car expenses such as leasing fees, insurance, gas, tolls, parking, depreciation of vehicle, and fees for hauling a trailer, or you can deduct mileage. If you deduct mileage, you can do so only when your vehicle is used for commuting to a temporary but not a regular place of business.

Contract Employees

State laws provide that all employers must purchase insurance to cover their employees in case of an injury that occurs on the job. As a contract employee on your employers' payroll, you should be covered by this insurance. "Workers' compensation insurance" covers medical expenses and pays you an income while disabled. If you're permanently unable to return to work, "vocational rehabilitation" may also be provided. Don't confuse workers' compensation with state disability insurance, which is deducted from your paycheck. Workers' compensation insurance must be purchased by your employer from a licensed workers' compensation carrier or state disability insurance office. **Note:** The laws regarding workers' compensation vary from state to state. For instance, in some states an employer with two or fewer employees may not have to purchase workers' compensation insurance. Ask your employer about your rights to workers' compensation insurance at the time of your employment. This is important!

Self-Employment/Independent Contractor Status

Unlike contract employees, when you're working on a freelance basis as an independent contractor, the people for whom you work are *not* responsible for providing you with workers' compensation insurance. This means that you're responsible for providing your own insurance (i.e., disability insurance) for injuries that might occur, or if you become sick or pregnant, and are unable to work and maintain an income. Disability insurance is rather expensive, but know that you can become eligible for health insurance coverage by joining the music unions. If you have a spouse who works a steady job, you may even be able to receive coverage on his or her policy. Drummer Kenwood Dennard adds, "The real bonanza for me in terms of health insurance comes from taking on a more full-time-employee work, in addition to my sideman work—teaching at Berklee College of Music." And while on the general topic of insurance, you may also want to know that you're personally responsible for investing in insurance for theft and damage to your musical instruments. This is important and should not be underestimated. Instrument insurance can also be obtained through the music unions. Unions were covered earlier in this chapter.

> Further health care advice/assistance may be provided by contacting the MusiCares Foundation (www.grammy.com) and the Actors Fund's Musicians' Assistance Program (www.actorsfund.org).

SHIT HAPPENS! In 2005, Eminem's tour bus crashed while swerving to avoid an eighteen-wheeler truck. Eminem's rapper "The Alchemist" and several crew members were hospitalized. In 1992, Metallica's guitarist/vocalist James Hetfield suffered first- and third-degree burns after a stage prop exploded during a show in Montreal, Canada. And in 1996, in a near-fatal incident, one anonymous musician was struck by a car while on the way back to his hotel after a performance in New York City. He suffered a pulmonary embolism and was very grateful to be covered by his employer's insurance, even though it took two frustrating years before the insurance company paid a total of $43,000 in hospital bills and compensated him for the many months he was not able to work. Without the aid of insurance, he would have been wiped out.

CONTRACT EMPLOYEE OR INDEPENDENT CONTRACTOR?

By now it should be apparent that there are major differences between contract employees and independent contractors when it comes to tax issues and workers' compensation insurance. But do you have a choice between one kind of employment status and the other?

An employee may prefer to be treated as an independent contractor so he or she will not have any taxes taken out of his or her paycheck and therefore, in theory, have a bigger paycheck. As you know, an employer is required by law to withhold taxes from an employee's paycheck, reducing his or her before-tax salary or gross income significantly. If those taxes aren't withheld, the amount of money you make will appear significantly larger. Remember, however, that you can run from Uncle Sam, but you can't hide; and eventually you'll need to report your income to the IRS, and you will owe taxes on what you earned. Also keep in mind that if you're treated as an independent contractor, you won't be eligible for state unemployment benefits.

An employer may prefer to treat you as an independent contractor rather than as a contract employee because it limits his or her responsibility to you. Employers are required to withhold 6.2 percent of your income for Social Security (up to a set limit) and 1.45 percent for Medicare (unlimited), for a combined total of 7.65 percent. Employers are also required to make a matching contribution for Social Security taxes on the income paid to you. By treating you as an independent contractor, however, employers can avoid making this payment, as well as payments toward workers' compensation insurance. This means that you either have to purchase your own disability insurance or risk not being covered.

The IRS has very specific guidelines as to whether a musician should be considered a contract employee or an independent contractor. Employers may tend to bend these rules from time to time, however. To be sure you conduct your business lawfully, below are listed a few factors used by the IRS to help you determine your work status. (A more comprehensive list offered by the IRS can be found at the end of Chapter 4.)

The IRS considers you a contract employee if you meet the following criteria:

✦ You're given specific directions as to how your job should be performed.
✦ You're given set hours as to when work must be performed.
✦ You're paid in regular intervals, such as by the week or bimonthly.
✦ The work you perform with an employer is on an ongoing and continuing basis.
✦ The person for whom you work pays for your travel expenses.
✦ The work you do is on a full-time basis or prevents you from taking on other work.
✦ You can be terminated, or you have the right to quit at any time.

Note: Anyone who does not meet the above criteria may be classified as an independent contractor.

EMPLOYEE OR NOT—THAT IS THE QUESTION Suppose you were hired by a band to go out on the road for three months and were promised a weekly salary as compensation for your services. Before the tour starts, you're required to show up for rehearsals Monday through Friday from 8 P.M. to 12 midnight to learn the band's material at the direction of the group's musical director. The day before the first performance, you're flown out on a commercial airliner (at the band's expense) to the city where the first date of the tour is to begin. From that point forward, you travel on a tour bus under the direction of a tour manager, who makes sure that you get on stage on time and that you're on the bus every morning when traveling to the next city. Additionally, all of your hotel accommodations are paid for. In this scenario, you would be considered an employee by the IRS.

CHAPTER 4

Solo Artist
and Employer

> "And what is the greatest number? Number one."
> —DAVID HUME

The solo artist is a rare and special breed of musician—an exceptional writer or instrumentalist who plays a melodic instrument, a skilled vocalist who's blessed with undeniable looks and image, or a highly motivated individual who possesses the desire to lead (or any combination of the above). Although your name and likeness may be individually displayed on album cover artwork and venue marquees, you'll rarely be working alone. You'll lead a group of studio and gigging musicians, and you may even collaborate with skilled songwriters and producers. As your career develops, it's also likely that you'll have a team of advisors consisting of an attorney, a personal manager, a business manager, and a talent agent. The solo artist sits at the helm, steering this musical battleship into the turbulent waters of the music business.

THE ADVANTAGES OF GOING SOLO

While being a solo artist, or the "captain of your own ship," may not be for everyone, it has its advantages. These include fewer hassles over making decisions, increased earning potential, greater job security, and more freedom to "sail" alone.

Fewer Hassles over Making Decisions

Perhaps the greatest advantage of being a solo artist is that the decision-making process is far simpler than for that of a band. Bottom line: You don't need approval from three other band members on every creative, personal, and business matter that comes up (which also means—in case it hasn't sunk in—you can avoid those infamous "band meetings," arguing about issues like your set list or the number of bars in one of your songs before the second verse). It's no surprise that many bands break up due to difference of opinion (the Who, the Beatles, and the Police were no exceptions).

While it is often the creative polarity between members that helps shape the best music of our time, many solo artists prefer the autonomy of going solo.

"You have to listen to each other as a band, not only musically, but also verbally," said former Alice in Chains guitarist Jerry Cantrell in *Guitar Player* magazine. "It's a human thing, full of errors and surprises, and all kinds of bullshit."

Commenting on the Police and his career as a solo artist in *Rolling Stone* magazine, Sting said, "I'll argue till the cows come home about something I believe in, and so will Andy [Summers] and Stewart [Copeland]. A band is not an easy relationship by any means. Though I can't think of two musicians I'd rather play with, I don't think history is made of mass movements or teams. History is made of individuals."

And in *Rolling Stone*, John Lennon replied to a question about what had happened to the four parts that were the Beatles: "They remembered they were four individuals. After Brian Epstein died, we collapsed. Paul [McCartney] took over and supposedly led us. But what is leading when we went around in circles? We broke up then. That was the disintegration."

Increased Earning Potential

The "love of your music" should be your number one motivator, but money is an important part of life. That said, another advantage of going solo over being in a band is that you will earn a greater share of the profits as your career develops into a fruitful endeavor (or shall I say, "when it does"). After all, you're the boss and essentially call the shots in regard to how you'll split profits and pay your musicians. Revenue streams may include record royalties, music publishing, merchandising, concert monies, and sponsorships funds. (These topics are all discussed in more detail in chapters 10 to 13.)

Greater Job Security

Job security may be another advantage to going solo as opposed to being in a band. One things for certain: You'll never have to worry about getting kicked out of your own solo project due to something like creative differences—unless, of course, your dual personality begins to hate you. And if this happens, job security is the least of your problems. [Grin].

More Freedom to "Sail" Alone

Going solo can also mean that there's more freedom to come and go as you please—there's simply no "dead weight" (aka other band members) holding you back. It's the indie artist at the beginning of her career who can hit the road armed with no more than her voice and guitar if she should so choose (no vans and trailers hauling drum kits and amps needed here). In fact, I've even seen some do-it-yourself artists brave enough to hitchhike from state to state on their "bare bones" tours—something four band members certainly would have trouble pulling off. As a solo artist you make your own schedules and timelines and essentially do as you please. As indie artist Gilli Moon eloquently states, "There's more freedom to sailing solo."

THE DISADVANTAGES OF GOING SOLO

Although being a solo artist may liberate you from the democracies of being in a band, offer more job security, and increase your earning potential, there are several disadvantages to going solo.

These include greater financial burdens, increased workload, greater leadership and business demands, fewer people to blame or hide behind, and more pressure to succeed.

Greater Financial Burdens

Being a solo artist means that all financial burdens rest entirely on you, including all expenses, investments, debts, and loans. For the indie artist just starting out on a limited to zero-dollar budget, this usually presents a serious challenge. There are costs for rehearsing, copying flyers, recording your music, manufacturing CDs, putting together press kits, building websites, and shooting professional photos—expenses that are all far easier to split between four band members. Going solo can be a costly proposition. On this note, have you ever noticed the number of artists that were first part of self-contained bands and established a name before they went solo? One must wonder if there's a correlation. Nonetheless, just never opt for being what I call a solo "artist in disguise": someone who forms a "band" only with the intention of going solo once his/her finances are right. That's just bad karma and unfair to the other members. Enough said!

Increased Workload

Being a solo artist also means that the brunt of the work falls on you. Unlike being in a band, where each member shares sacrifices on the road to success, you're essentially working 24/7. Whether it be a phone interview with a radio station, making appearances at retail stores, conducting interviews with the press, responding to e-mail, updating your personal website, or composing all of the songs, you're essentially on your own! Even when your career progresses into the big leagues when you're signed and you can afford to hire a professional team to help, your job is really never done. Make no mistake, bands may break up, but solo artists break down.

As veteran rocker Vince Neil of Mötley Crüe reveals in the band's book, *The Dirt*, "Now that I was solo, I had to do all the interviews, write all the songs, make up the set lists, figure out the marketing, approve all the artwork, and deal with everything."

Greater Leadership and Business Demands

Solo artists must also endure the pressures of leading their musicians and keeping them happy. First, if you want to surround yourself with talented and experienced players, you must offer them something substantial, such as good pay, good gigs, and career growth—it's only so long that your musicians are going to play at the corner bar in front of three people while being compensated with Subway sandwiches or free drink tickets. Second, you need to always make your musicians feel appreciated, while at the same reminding them who's in control. This can be one of the more difficult aspects of your job. It's important to recognize the fine line between being your employees' friend and their leader.

Solo artist Henry Rollins notes, "You have many factors to take into account as a solo artist: the needs of others, what's best for all in the long run, and what the objectives are. I am very

GOT MUSICIANS?

The best method to find musicians for your solo project is through recommendations from people you trust: musicians, producers, managers, local music schools (like Berklee in Boston and the Musicians Institute in Hollywood), stores, club promoters, music seminars, etc. You can also try calling your local musician's union, attending local jam sessions and open mikes, checking out the hottest bands in your area, placing ads in your local music paper, and by posting announcements in message boards and blogs on the Web.

BE A LEADER, BUT NEVER A DICTATOR! Although most solo artists understand the importance of treating their musicians with respect and fair compensation and they strive to abide by this rule (as, one day, you will), many superstar performers are known to dangle the proverbial carrot of fame before their musicians' eyes. However, this attitude usually prevents bandleaders from keeping great players over the long term. One very popular vocalist (who will remain anonymous) prohibited all of his musicians while out on tour from talking to all females within fifty feet of his presence. In fact, one keyboard player was fired on the spot when he was talking to a female fan in the hotel lobby just as the singer had passed through to go to the restaurant. Even worse, the keyboardist wasn't allowed to go back up to his room to pack his bags. True story!

protective of the people I work with, from the band to the crew. I strive to earn their respect and I hope to get the same back."

Fewer Members to Blame or Hide Behind

Being a solo artist also means that you accept all the heat, the criticism, and the stress. From CD critiques to press reviews to concert performances, you sink or swim on your own. Simply put, there's no band members to blame or hide behind for the creative and business choices you make. It's all on you!

"It's my shit," Jerry Cantrell has commented. "My name is on the marquee, as well as on the paychecks, so it all comes down to me."

More Pressure to Succeed

Last but not least, many solo artists feel the added pressure of living up to the title "solo artist." Lets face it, the very nature of the term practically screams out, "I don't need no one but my superstar self." Even worse, some solo artists may feel the squeeze of living up to the successes of their former bands. Critics in the press will never judge them purely on the strength of their music alone. Although many artists have gone on to succeed in their own right (Beyoncé Knowles of Destiny's Child, and Justin Timberlake of *NSYNC), there are just as many solo artists who have fallen short (U-God of Wu-Tang Clan and MC Ren of N.W.A.).

THE RECORD COMPANY'S RIGHTS TO SOLO ARTISTS

Since many artists are first part of self-contained bands that progress forward to signing recording agreements and releasing albums *before* they go solo, it's important to take a look at something called a "leaving-member clause." When a band signs a recording agreement with a record company, understand that the label usually wants the rights to all members as a band, as well as the rights of any leaving member who becomes a solo artist or member of another band. In case you're not paying attention, this means that if you're an artist who was once a member of a signed group (successful or not), *their record company may own the rights to your new solo career!* This is called a leaving-member clause and it may be found in your former band's recording agreement.

Leaving-member clauses are especially useful to record companies when a band is unsuccessful. It basically gives the record label another shot at recouping its initial investment (in a minute you'll see how that works). At the same time, if your band ends up being a success, a leaving-member clause benefits the record company by securing its right to continue making money from you if you have a successful solo career of your own. Their rationale is that if the company is going to invest a lot of money into developing your career and making you a star, then it has the right to reap the long-term benefits as well.

Leaving-member clauses can be good or bad for you. They can be good because you have a record company that's potentially interested in releasing your solo material. They can be bad because your royalty rate and advances are typically less favorable than your initial recording agreement with your band. Additionally, all debts incurred by your former band automatically carry over to you! That's right, just when you thought you were breaking away from the group of guys/girls that you grew to hate, you find you have continued financial responsibility to them. Here's how it works.

Let's say you decided to leave your group because their last record was a flop and they had an outstanding balance to the record company of $400,000. Before you even see a dime in record royalties from sales of your new record, all monies will go toward paying your former band's unrecouped balance as well as your new debt to the record company. If you spend another $250,000 recording your new record, you'll now be $650,000 in debt to the record company. But before you decide to throw the idea of your solo career away, consider the following.

In most instances, you can negotiate an agreement with the record company that stipulates that only your share of your band's unrecouped balance carries over to your new account as a solo artist. This means that if there were four members in your former band, only a quarter of the unrecouped balance can be charged against your royalty account. Therefore, staying with the previous example, only $100,000 can be carried over to your new account. Hey, it's better than $400,000! Conversely, keep in mind that if your former band stays together and goes on to record new records that are also flops, typically, no new debts to the record company will affect you. You had nothing to do with these records and are not responsible for any debt associated with them.

THE BUSINESS AND LEGAL RESPONSIBILITIES OF SOLO ARTISTS AS EMPLOYERS

When solo artists are making little or no money in the early stages of their careers, their business responsibilities to their musicians might simply consist of supplying lunch after rehearsals or buying a round of drinks after gigs. As long as these musicians aren't misled into believing the relationship

PEARL JAMMED Because of the leaving-member clause, Pearl Jam already owed $500,000 to their label before ever recording an album. This debt carried over from Stone Gossard and Jeff Ament's first band, Mother Love Bone. Mother Love Bone's singer died of an overdose before their debut record *Apple* was ever released. Mother Love Bone broke up, but their label had the rights to Stone and Jeff as individual artists. When Stone and Jeff went on to form Pearl Jam, their debt followed, as per their contract.

is something more substantial, like that of a partnership (i.e., a band), this may be an acceptable course of action for right now. However, as your career starts evolving as a solo artist and employer, you will need to start treating your business affairs more professionally. You may be responsible for paying your musicians minimum scale wages, deducting payroll taxes, and providing workers' compensation insurance. Although I highly recommend you seek the advice of an experienced entertainment accountant, business manager, or attorney on these often complex and tedious issues, the following information will provide a brief overview.

Wages and Commissions

Employers must abide with minimum wage obligations imposed by state and federal laws. Information regarding wages, hours, and working conditions can be obtained by contacting a local state department of labor. The American Federation of Musicians (AFM) and the American Federation of Television and Radio Artists (AFTRA), discussed in detail in Chapter 2, also provide information regarding "fairness" guidelines and recommended compensation.

The method by which most employers choose to pay their employees is determined by the value they place on keeping them. Employers may choose to compensate their musicians by either paying them a flat salary or hourly wage or a salary plus a percentage of the future profits (record royalties, publishing royalties, merchandising, etc.).

Keep in mind that an employer-employee relationship must be a win-win situation to be successful. If an employer resorts to a take-it-or-leave-it approach regarding compensation, it will eventually lead to the "revolving door of musicians" syndrome. For instance, you'll find yourself replacing bass players on every tour you do. Note that this typically diminishes your credibility in the eyes of your fans. Although you may feel like the "star" of the show, it's important to realize that your audience is there to see the other musicians in your band as well. It's not only about you and the extra dollar you can squeeze into your pocket. The happier your musicians are, the better they're going to make you look and sound. Henry Rollins adds, "I pay my musicians the same salary I pay myself." This is sound advice! As the old adage implies, "If all you pay is peanuts, then all you get are monkeys."

TAX ISSUES FOR INDEPENDENT CONTRACT STATUS Employers are not responsible for deducting income, Social Security, and payroll taxes from the earnings of individuals working on a freelance basis (also called "independent contractors status").

INDEMNITY PROVISION SUGGESTED Attorney Burgundy Morgan cautions that you, the solo artist, may be held responsible for the acts of your employees occurring within "the course and scope" of their employment. For example, if your drummer gets into a brawl at a gig, you could be held responsible. Also, if an overzealous fan gets on stage and knocks the entire drum kit off the riser (true story), your drummer may look to you for reimbursement. In 2005, the bus driver for the Dave Matthews Band dumped approximately 800 pounds of human waste from the bus's septic tank while driving over a bridge. The waste went through the metal grates of the bridge and onto a sightseeing boat filled with tourists, which was under the bridge at the time. A civil lawsuit was filed against both the band and the driver, even though the driver was the only one on the bus at the time. With these stories in mind, it is always a good idea to have employees (session players, roadies, etc.) sign a release stating that the employee is responsible for their own actions, including any injuries to people or damage to property, with an indemnity provision requiring them to reimburse you for any money or loss you incur as a result of those same actions. When you can afford it, a solid insurance policy is also a wise move. For additional information on this issue, you can contact Burgundy Morgan, Esq., at BurgundyMorgan@aol.com.

Income, Social Security, and Payroll Taxes

As an employer, you are also responsible for deducting taxes from your employees' paychecks, including federal, state, and/or local income taxes, as well as Social Security taxes. The IRS has severe penalties for employers who don't comply with federal and state withholding and other payroll tax requirements. Although it's likely you'll have an experienced accountant or business manager assisting you in these matters, it's important to have a basic understanding of the mechanics of taxation—no matter how dry and boring tax laws may seem. Please refer to Chapter 3 for a brief overview.

Workers' Compensation Insurance

As an employer, you may also be required by state law to purchase workers' compensation insurance, which covers injuries that occur on the job, pays your employees' medical expenses and income while they are disabled, and provides vocational rehabilitation should an employee be permanently unable to return to work. Once again, please refer to Chapter 3 for an overview of this subject.

WORKERS' COMPENSATION ISSUES FOR INDEPENDENT CONTRACT STATUS You're not responsible for providing workers' compensation insurance for musicians working on a freelance basis or with independent contractor status.

CONTRACT EMPLOYEE VERSUS INDEPENDENT CONTRACTOR STATUS: WHO IS AN EMPLOYEE?

Making the distinction between an employee and independent contractor can get tricky, but it's necessary for both tax and workers compensation purposes. Be sure to contact an experienced entertainment accountant or tax attorney and the IRS to make sure that you're complying with the law. If you, or an employer, are examined by the IRS and found accountable for mishandling business, the IRS can charge extremely steep fines. For this reason, it's extremely important that you have a clear understanding of the factors that the IRS uses to determine who is an employee.

The IRS outlines several factors that help you to determine whether a musician working for you is considered an employee or independent contractor (from the IRS guidelines for employee or independent contractor status, available in Publication 1779, Form SS8). Here are a few of these factors:

Instructions: A worker who is required to comply with another person's instructions about when, where, and how he or she is to work is ordinarily an employee. This control factor is present if the person or persons for whom the services are performed have the right to require compliance with instructions.

Continuing relationship: A continuing relationship between the worker and the person or persons for whom the services are performed indicates that, where work is performed at frequently recurring although irregular intervals, an employer-employee relationship may exist.

Set hours of the week: The establishment of set hours of work by the person or persons for whom the services are performed is a factor indicating control and an employee-employer relationship.

Payment by hour, week, month: Payment by the hour, week, or month of regular amounts at stated intervals to a worker strongly indicates an employer-employee relationship.

Full-time required: If the worker must devote substantially full time to the business of the person or persons for whom the services are performed, such person or persons have control over the amount of time the worker spends working and implicitly restricts the worker from doing other gainful work. This suggests an employee-employer relationship.

Training: Training a worker by requiring an experienced employee to oversee the worker, by corresponding with the worker, by requiring attendance at meetings, or by using other methods, indicates that one person or persons for whom the services are performed want(s) the services performed in a particular manner and suggests an employee-employer relationship.

Payment of business and/or traveling expenses: If the person or persons for whom the services are performed ordinarily pay the workers business and/or traveling expenses, the worker is ordinarily an employee. An employer, to be able to control expenses, generally retains the right to regulate and direct the worker's business activities.

Right to discharge: The right to discharge a worker is a factor indicating that the worker is an employee and the person possessing the right is an employer. An employer exercises control through the threat of dismissal, which causes the worker to obey the employer's instructions.

CHAPTER 5

Your Attorney

> "A man who is his own lawyer has a fool for a client."
> —PROVERB

Just mentioning the word *attorney* is enough to send most new and developing artists into a state of panic. After all, how can you pay an attorney's fees when you can barely afford to pay for your band's rehearsal space? Even if money isn't an issue, the fact is that most people don't trust attorneys. Part of this mistrust comes from the media's frequent portrayal of lawyers as self-serving mercenaries, and part of it is simply based on myth. We often don't trust what we don't understand—and nothing is more confusing to most of us than the language of lawyers. I once heard a musician joke that he needed an attorney just to explain to him what his other attorney was talking about and a secretary willing to try all day to get either of them on the phone. Nonetheless, attorneys are necessary to the business of music—and to your career. If you're going to survive in the business of music, you're going to need a lawyer you can trust.

THE ROLE OF AN ATTORNEY IN YOUR CAREER

Despite the number of bad attorney jokes that plague the music industry today (and I'm sure you've heard at least a few of them), an attorney plays a key role in your career and may very well be one of the most important members of your team. Not everyone understands what an attorney does, so let's begin with a brief rundown. A great attorney does the following:

✦ Helps with limited legal services early on in your career, like drafting a band membership agreement or helping out with getting your band name (i.e., trademark) registered

✦ Provides, in some cases, "shopping services" to record labels (i.e., tries to get you signed). Record companies know that a reputable attorney doesn't have time to represent a band he or she doesn't believe in, so when a lawyer they respect comes calling, they're likely to respond quickly

+ Maintains relationships with industry professionals, including record label personnel, publishers, TV people, merchandisers, and personal managers, all of whom can potentially help shape your career

+ Reviews contracts you receive with your best interests in mind

+ Translates contract clauses and complicated writing (called "legalese") into terms you can understand

+ Knows what issues are most important to negotiate for in recording agreements — for instance, recording and video funds, cross-collateralization, tour support, guaranteed release clauses, pay-or-play clauses, and controlled composition clauses

+ Strives to ascertain what issues are important to you, such as creative controls or advances, and then negotiates within reason for these issues

+ Provides all information you need to make the right business decisions, which could be taking or declining a deal, but never tells you what to do

+ Stays current with changing business models in the music industry, especially with what's happening in the digital arena and with what might happen beyond

+ Represents you in lawsuits with other musicians and music companies, or in the case he or she doesn't litigate, refers you to colleagues who do

+ Helps you get out of a bad deal you signed long before you were inclined to read this book and be advised to hire an attorney

In short, attorneys see the "big picture"; they handle all the business and legal matters involved in your career.

HIRING YOUR ATTORNEY

There's a general misconception that attorneys know "everything" about "anything," but keep in mind that attorneys, like doctors, have their own areas of expertise. An attorney may specialize in family law, patent and trademark law, taxation, workers' compensation, real estate, or criminal law. Be sure to hire an attorney who has experience in the music business and who understands the ins and outs of recording contracts. In case this hasn't sunk in, don't hire your dad's real-estate attorney! Got it? Good, let's move on.

So how do you go about finding an attorney who specializes in your area of concern? What qualities should you be looking for once you've got a few referrals?

Finding an Attorney

Attorneys can work in firms consisting of hundreds of attorneys, boutique firms consisting of two or more lawyers, or in individual firms. Finding an experienced music attorney is far simpler in entertainment centers like New York, Nashville, and Los Angeles, but this doesn't mean that finding a great attorney elsewhere is unlikely.

To find an attorney appropriate to your needs, begin by utilizing all available resources. These include personal referrals, lawyer referral services, music publications, music conferences, and college and adult education courses.

SOME CRAZY CONTRACT LANGUAGE DEFINED
These definitions will get you up to speed on some common contract language, but don't get too excited and try to negotiate your own agreements. An entertainment attorney is always advised.

Licensor: The person who grants a license

Licensee: The person who is given a license

Agent: A person authorized to represent another

Fiduciary: A professional responsibility or duty to another (e.g., an attorney's *fiduciary* duty to his client)

In perpetuity: Forever

The universe: The world and the entire celestial cosmos. Commonly used with "perpetuity" in regard to a grant of rights (e.g., in perpetuity throughout the universe)

Intellectual property: A process, creation, or idea derived from the mind or intellect, and a right or application relating to this (e.g., artwork, compositions, books)

Pecuniary: Money, or relating to money

Herewith: Contained within; in this writing or contract

Hereinabove: In some earlier part of a writing or contract

Hereinafter: In the following part of a writing or contract

Heretofore: Up to this point in time; until now

Henceforth: From this point in time onward

Notwithstanding: Despite; however; regardless (e.g., "*Notwithstanding* anything contained herein to the contrary") (i.e., whatever was just stated, the following now prevails)

Indemnify: To secure against hurt, loss, or damage

Warranties and representations: A promise that a statement or fact (e.g., you own your compositions, or masters) is true

Exclusive: To the exclusion of anyone else

Nonexclusive: That which does not limit the rights of another

Boilerplate: Common; standard; the same (e.g., *Boilerplate* clauses like warranties and representations found in contracts)

Note: For a similar but complete and expanded list of terms, be sure to check out *The Music Business Affairs Glossary* by Robert J. Nathan.

Personal Referrals

The best way to find a good attorney is by asking for referrals from other musicians and industry professionals. Just be sure to consider the source of the referral; just because a musician is successful doesn't mean his attorney is right for you. If you're still in the minors, a big-league lawyer may not be able to give you the personal attention you need. Consider the motive of the person making the referral as well. For instance, an individual who's an accountant may simply be returning a favor to an attorney who referred someone to him. If a record company or personal manager with whom you're doing business recommends a lawyer, you may need to consider a situation called a *conflict of interest* (discussed later in this chapter). In short, you not only need to use discretion when choosing your attorney but also when asking for referrals.

Lawyer Referral Services

Another way to find an attorney is through a referral service. Ask your state or local bar association whether there is a referral service available in your area. The California Lawyers for the Arts, located in San Francisco, refers callers to lawyers throughout California who deal exclusively with the arts. In Los Angeles, you can call the Lawyer Referral Service of the Los Angeles County Bar Association, and in Beverly Hills, there's the Beverly Hills Bar Association Lawyer Referral Service. In New York City, you can call the Association of the Bar of the City of New York, and in Nashville, there's the Lawyer Referral Service for the Nashville Bar Association. You get the point. Operators at referral services will listen to your legal concerns and direct you to one of the attorneys on their panel. These operators will not, however, guarantee the quality of an attorney's services or tell you which attorney you should choose. It's up to you to set up a phone consultation and assess the attorney for yourself. There will typically be a small fee for the initial consultation; fees for continued services are discussed between attorneys and clients on an individual basis. Since big-league "heavy hitters" aren't part of referral services (you may not be ready for one of these guys anyway), it's unlikely you'll be referred to the attorney representing Metallica and Dr. Dre. Nevertheless, it's well worth your time to call a service in your area to learn what it has to offer.

Music Publications

Music publications may also be helpful to you when searching for an attorney. Books such as *The Recording Industry Source Book* (published by Artistpro), *Music Attorney, Legal and Business Affairs Guide* (published by Music Business Registry), and *Billboard International Talent and Touring Directory* (published by Billboard Books) list hundreds of attorneys, agents, and personal managers. These resources can all be found either in bookstores or online. Weekly trade magazines such as *Billboard* magazine are also good sources of information; they'll tell you which attorneys are signing the hottest bands. Finally, try checking to see whether your favorite band has listed its attorney's name and contact number on its CD artwork.

Music Conferences

Music conferences such as the National Association of Music Merchants (www.namm.com), South by Southwest Music and Media Conference (wwww.sxsw.com), and the National Association of Recording Merchandisers Convention (www.narm.com) are sure ways to meet people in the music business. Attorneys and other industry professionals usually speak as panelists, which gives you a good opportunity to ask them a few questions, introduce yourself, and at the very least ask for a business card so that you're able to get in touch with them again later. Keep in mind, however, that music conferences usually draw the heavy hitters of the business, so don't despair if a panelist or speaker is unwilling to take the time to help you—they're just in high demand.

College and Adult Education Courses

Another way to find and meet a good attorney is by taking college and adult education courses in the music business, such as the ones offered in Los Angeles at the UCLA Extension program (www.uclaextension.org). Check a college near you for music-related classes. Attorneys active in the business often teach entertainment courses at the Extension program. Taking their class will not only teach you a great deal about the business, but it will also provide you the opportunity to form new business relationships as well. Perhaps this may lead to a working relationship down the road.

Qualities to Look for in an Attorney

Once you've compiled a realistic list of potential attorneys, you can begin the process of contacting them and setting up a first appointment. In most cases, an attorney will be willing to speak with you over the phone to discuss your needs and determine whether you even need legal assistance. Just be prepared to articulate your legal problems and concerns clearly, to ask questions about the services each attorney provides, and to discuss potential fees. If you're seeking an attorney to shop your band, you should also be ready to send him a press kit or a link to a site on the Internet where he can check out your music, pictures, and biographical information. At worst, if an attorney doesn't have the time to get involved with you, he may be willing to refer you to someone who does. Last, and perhaps most important, when speaking with, or visiting, an attorney for the first time, it's important to evaluate two important qualities in him: personality and clout.

Personality

When you meet with an attorney, it's important to assess his personality. You don't have to be the best of friends, but you want to at least feel comfortable when you're sitting in the same room or talking on the phone with him. Does he take time to explain things to you, or does he rush through the conversation or talk down to you? Does he have a genuine interest in your career and music, or do you feel that he's meeting you because you were referred by "so and so." Also of concern is your attorney's personality and his attitude toward other business professionals. You don't want a hothead for an attorney who can blow deals for you, or conversely a wimp who won't make any deals happen. These are all important concerns and ones that should be taken seriously before choosing your attorney.

Clout

An attorney's clout can mean getting you before the biggest and best companies and leveraging the biggest and best deal. When you speak with lawyers, don't be afraid to ask them the names of the clients they represent and then check these references. If they "shop" CDs to record labels, ask them about the groups they've helped to get signed. Don't expect to get detailed information about the actual deals that they've negotiated, however. That is privileged information, and you should be wary of any lawyer who violates the Attorneys' Canon of Ethics.

Keep in mind that powerful and well-connected attorneys are more likely to get their calls returned more quickly than are attorneys who are newer in the business; however, if a star attorney is too busy handling star clients, you may very well get lost in the shuffle. Young, ambitious attorneys with great networking skills may be even more valuable to you because they'll have more time to devote to your career. In any case, you should be aware that the attorney you choose to represent you will not always be the person who does most of the work. Many attorneys are gregarious types who work aggressively to bring in new business while their associates do the actual work of drafting the contracts. Be sure to ask attorneys who else will be involved in some of their day-to-day work and how long they've been working with those people.

ATTORNEY FEE STRUCTURES

Samuel Butler, the renowned nineteenth-century English novelist, once said, "In the law, the only thing certain is the expense." People know attorneys aren't cheap, and that's why they avoid calling them in the first place. As a result, musicians often fly blindly and work without contracts or accept terms to agreements they barely understand. Inevitably, they run into legal problems.

When you set an appointment and meet with an attorney for the first time, be sure to ask about the fee structures he or she uses and for an estimate of what it may take to resolve your matters. If he or she estimates that your bill will total more than $1,000, you have the right to ask for a "fee agreement" in writing. A good attorney will suggest that you have your fee agreement reviewed by another professional to make sure his/her charges are reasonable.

The fee structures typically used by attorneys are as follows: an hourly rate, a flat fee, a percentage of the deals he/she negotiates, a percentage of the deals he/she both *finds* and *negotiates* (the latter of which I will specifically refer to as a label shopping agreement), and something called a retainer.

Hourly Rate

While an hourly rate is not the most common method of attorney billing there are still a few issues worthy of highlighting. These include the range, increments of the hour, caps or maximums, expenses, and billing policies.

Range

The hourly rate an attorney charges can range anywhere from $100 for a young attorney to $600 or more for a high-powered attorney. Once again, before completely freaking out, remember that hourly billing is not the most common form of billing.

Increments of the Hour

Be sure to ask about billing policies for increments of the hour. In other words, a phone call that only takes your attorney three minutes to make might be billed at a quarter of an hour's fee.

Caps or Maximums

A total maximum in hourly costs can sometimes be arranged with your attorney. A cap can help protect you in the event your case unexpectedly drags out for an extended period of time. As I'm sure you are aware, there are always unexpected twists, turns, and delays when dealing with business and legal matters, and the last thing you want to do is tell your attorney you can no longer afford him/her before your legal issues are resolved.

Expenses

Certain costs for postage, messenger services, or even administrative work are often charged to you in addition to your hourly fee. In any case, be sure to discuss these expenses with your attorney when discussing your hourly rate, so that you don't have any surprises when you see your bill.

Billing Policies

Fees for hourly billing are usually sent on a monthly cycle. Your bill should be easy to understand and should clearly outline what you're paying for. Find out whether you can use a credit card to make payments, and ask if you'll be charged interest for any late payments you make.

Flat Fees

Most attorneys are willing to provide a flat estimate of what their services will cost; in actuality, this is their hourly rate multiplied by the number of hours they expect it will take to complete a job. To draft a short agreement, for instance, your fee may be $500 plus out-of-pocket expenses such as faxes and phone calls. Negotiating a recording agreement can cost a flat fee of anywhere from $2,000 to $20,000, sometimes more. Of course, if you have a friend who's an attorney, you may be able to talk him into charging you much less.

Percentage of the Deals

Most attorneys are also willing to work for a percentage of the deals they negotiate. For example, an attorney may agree to work for 5 percent of the fund you receive (which, by the way, is the industry standard), for negotiating a recording deal. Out-of-pocket expenses for postage, messenger services, or even administrative work are separate.

Label Shopping Percentages

The fee most attorneys charge for a "label shopping agreement" is structured on a percentage basis, typically 10 percent (sometimes, as much as 20), based on the deals your attorney both *finds* and *negotiates*. Since shopping your band and finding deals takes more time and work than simply negotiating a deal you or your manager initiated, the percentage is obviously higher. And note that this percentage usually applies *for the full length of the deal*. For instance, for every album your band records — long after your attorney's job is done — he may earn a 10 to 20 percent fee for initially shopping your band.

A cap or maximum can be negotiated that determines the total amount the attorney's percentage will yield (e.g., $100,000 over the life of the recording deal). Sometimes a de-escalating percentage can be established over the course of the deal (i.e., 10 percent on the first recording, 7.5 percent on the second, 5 percent on the third, etc.).

Attorney Stan Findelle adds, "From my point of view, 'shopping' a deal is worth as much as 20 percent. Why? Because this lawyer has turned water into wine: He or she got the artist plucked out of the unwashed mob and into the ballpark."

A Flat Retainer

Some attorneys may ask for something called a retainer, which is basically a flat sum of money paid up front to cover the legal services you haven't even received yet. It's like paying a bill up front. For example, if you pay a retainer of $500, and your attorney provides you with his or her equivalent of $1,000 in legal services, the $500 retainer will be deducted from your bill. At this time, you may be asked to pay the $500 balance as well as another retainer to be held in trust for further services rendered. In the event that your attorney never earns the amount of the initial retainer and you decide to discontinue your business relationship with him/her, the remaining retainer should be paid back;

YOU GET WHAT YOU PAY FOR To save money, or perhaps because they just don't have any, many musicians hire attorneys who are willing to represent them for a discounted fee. If you're lucky, you'll get all the attention you need and your issues will be resolved to your satisfaction. *This isn't always the way things work out, however!* For instance, one musician hired an attorney who was a friend of a friend to review a short, eight-page contract. As a favor, the attorney quoted the musician a flat fee of $250, but the job ultimately required much more time than the attorney had initially estimated. The attorney was obviously frustrated with the matter and began rushing the musician through phone conversations and taking a long time to review second drafts of the contract. It was clear the job wasn't a priority to him. The attorney considered certain contractual terms important to the artist, like creative control, unimportant for negotiation. The attorney essentially reviewed the boilerplate terms of the contract to make sure the musician was protected but didn't put much effort into reviewing the finer points. In the end, the musician was dissatisfied with the final contract, and this had a negative effect on his enthusiasm for the project. You always get what you pay for.

if you pay a retainer of $500 and your attorney's charges for the month are only $300, the attorney should return the extra $200.

GETTING THE MOST OUT OF YOUR ATTORNEY

Once you've hired an attorney, you want to make sure that the relationship runs as smoothly as possible. Attorneys are not inexpensive; nor do they have a lot of free time. Keeping this in mind, when you contact your attorney, make sure to get the most out of him/her. Consider the following tips.

Be Prepared

Before contacting your attorney on any matter, be clear about what you want to accomplish. Make a list of all the points you'd like to discuss and write a list of questions for each. Although your attorney might object (for fear of providing evidence to a misstatement they may make that could fuel a frivolous lawsuit), you might ask if you can tape-record your meetings (I just recorded a meeting the other day). This way, if something isn't immediately clear, you can replay the conversation later to figure it out. This is also helpful if you're in a band and one of the members can't be present.

Is it necessary to hire an attorney when all you need is for a few short business or legal questions to be answered? It depends on each case, but many attorneys are fine with speaking with you for a few minutes on the phone for free—with the hopes that you may become a client down the road. Websites like Nolo's Self-Help Legal Center (www. nolo.com), in addition to the many books about the music business available today, are also helpful.

Be on Time

It may be easy for one band member to arrive at a meeting on time, but when all members of a group will be attending, you might consider driving together in one car to ensure that everyone is on time. Your attorney won't be thrilled to have to repeat what has already been said for a member who walks in the door fifteen minutes late.

Appoint a Band Representative

It's also best to appoint one band member to serve as your liaison between the attorney and the rest of the band to avoid having every member of the group call whenever they have a question or want an update on a particular matter. Attorney Stan Findelle says, "This is a must, especially if the artist is being charged by the hour. I've had four different guys call from a group constantly, where I should've billed four times the amount." Appointing one member to make calls will also make life easier for your attorney, who won't have to re-explain issues to each band member, and will also prevent the awkward possibility of each member getting his/her own take on a matter. By having a liaison, your group can put together a list of questions, and then one individual can make the call or attend the meeting. As long as your liaison is effective in relaying information to the other members of the band, this system usually works adequately. Nevertheless, at times the other members may feel they're relinquishing control and are at the mercy of the appointed liaison. In these cases, your band can always make group phone calls via speakerphone so that everyone can participate in the conversation. A second solution is to have everyone attend meetings but to appoint one representative to do all the talking.

Keep Your Attorney Informed

It's important to keep your attorney up-to-date regarding business matters. For instance, if your attorney is shopping your band, and you're unexpectedly approached by an A&R representative from another label after one of your shows, your attorney should be the first person to hear about it.

Attorney Stan Findelle adds, "It's surprising how many acts may actually NOT inform their attorney that they've been approached directly by an A&R person—suddenly, they feel the worm has turned, and they can cut the deal themselves or look for a name lawyer. Thus, if a lawyer does take on an act for 'on the come' shopping, there should be a document involved that says the lawyer is in for a percentage of the record deal, regardless of the source of the offer."

Keep Good Records

Keep clear records of all business correspondence and be prepared to bring copies to business meetings or to fax copies to your attorney before a phone conversation. It can be difficult to explain to your attorney from memory what a producer is offering your band. You can ask the producer to put a proposal in writing so that your attorney has something tangible to review. Another effective way of keeping good records is to ask anyone you have an important phone conversation with to put a summary of your discussion into a letter. It's also helpful to save all e-mail correspondence in a file in chronological order.

Tell the Truth

It's extremely important to be forthright with your attorney from day one. Your lawyer is there to help you, and if you're working at cross-purposes, the only one you're hurting is yourself. An attorney needs to clearly understand the details of a situation to do his/her best to solve the problem. If someone is suing you, for instance, because you threw a bottle into the audience and cut a fan's face (this has actually happened), don't tell your attorney that you have no knowledge of the incident; later someone may turn up with the whole incident on videotape, and by that time, your attorney may be able to do little to defend you.

Pay Your Bills on Time

A surefire way to avoid putting a damper on your relationship with your lawyer is to pay your bills on time. Your attorney is running a business, just like you are.

Never Sign Anything Without Your Attorney's Involvement

To avoid a lot of potential problems, never sign anything without having your attorney review it first. After all, that's why you retained legal counsel in the first place.

Keep Your Attorney in Constant Check

Some lawyers drive fancy cars, have impressive offices, wear expensive clothes, graduate from well-known schools, appear super smart, and have famous clients, but this doesn't mean they're always going to handle your business affairs timely or even ethically. Be sure to create a checklist of important questions in which to evaluate your attorney's progress. Here are a few examples.

Is Resolution to Your Legal Problems Taking Forever?

If it's been several months and your business matters aren't moving along, it might be because your attorney lacks the clout or experience needed to get the job done, he/she's lost confidence in your project, or is unmotivated by the fee agreement you arranged. Get used to the expression "Hurry up and wait." Things usually take longer than you'd like in the music business: A record contract contains several pages that must be carefully scrutinized, and a deal can take a long time to negotiate. Aside from this, you at least deserve a logical explanation from your attorney if you're dissatisfied with the speed at which things are moving along.

Do You Feel You're Being Fully Informed on all Matters Dealing with Your Case?

If you're being told things like, "Don't worry about the details," and that "Everything is under control," you're attorney may obviously lack the personality, patience, and understanding you need. There's an old joke: "How many lawyers does it take to screw in a light bulb? None, it's easier to keep you in the dark." It's your responsibility to educate yourself about the very basics of the music business and to at least know something about a few key terms, but your attorney should never make you feel left in the dark, stupid, or afraid to ask specific questions. Remember, there's a fine line between working with a smart lawyer who's a tough, go-getter attorney *for* you, and one who's a smart, tough, insensitive person *with* you.

Are You Considered a Priority by Your Attorney?

If the receptionists always tell you that your attorney is "out of town" or "unavailable," or you feel you're being rushed through your meetings or phone conversations, these may be clues you're a low man on a roster of more successful clients. Just remember, a high-powered attorney will not always be high-powered for you.

Are You Being Billed for Services That Are Compatible with the Actual Time Your Business Relationship Endured?

If you feel your bill is much higher than you anticipated, or if there are charges you don't understand, there is obviously a miscommunication that must be immediately looked into.

Are Your Best Interests Being Looked After at All Times?

If your attorney is representing an opposing party in a deal, and you feel your best interests are at risk, ask him/her to disclose any potential "conflicts." This is important. So read on.

A CONFLICT OF INTEREST

An important matter worthy of isolating and expanding on in regard to working together with an attorney is something called a conflict of interest. In situations in which your attorney represents another party with whom you are conducting business, a conflict of interest may occur, since the attorney cannot represent the best interests of each party fairly.

An ethical attorney should disclose when a conflict of interest exists, or could exist, and advise you to seek representation elsewhere. The exception to this rule is a situation in which both parties consent to the representation of the same attorney. The attorney must show that both parties can be represented fairly and then ask both parties to sign something called a "conflict waiver." A conflict waiver protects the attorney in case either party later claims it was represented unfairly. Let's take a look at a few examples where a conflict of interest may exist.

Suppose you're on the verge of signing a record agreement and have hired the same attorney who is representing the record company. This is unlikely, but bear with me. You want the biggest advance and royalty rate you can get, while the record company wants to get away with giving you the smallest advance and royalty possible. How can an attorney look after the best interests of opposing sides in a business negotiation? This situation is called a "conflict of interest," because again, each party's best interests are at stake, and the same lawyer cannot possibly represent both fairly.

A conflict of interest may also exist when an attorney is representing the members of a band who are putting together an internal band membership agreement if the members decide not to divide the profits equally at the direct advice of their attorney.

Another instance where a conflict of interest may exist is when a band hires its personal manager's lawyer to review its management agreement. How can the attorney possibly represent both sides fairly? Who will he/she favor? You get the idea!

In a final example, a conflict of interest might exist when your attorney is shopping your CD and he/she is working for a percentage of the deals he negotiates. If your attorney appears exceptionally aggressive in negotiating for large, and perhaps unreasonable advances (remember, the larger the advance the larger the commission), and he is letting business deals and opportunities slip by as a result, this is a situation that may be perceived as a conflict. Hey, I'm not making these scenarios up; they're known to happen occasionally.

Remember, when hiring an attorney, or even after hiring one, it's always advisable to keep your eyes open for potential conflicts of interest. If you think a conflict exists, it's probably fair to assume that neither side can be represented fairly and that you should therefore immediately seek representation elsewhere.

CHANGING YOUR LEGAL REPRESENTATION

In his play *Henry VI,* Part II, William Shakespeare wrote, "The first thing we do, let's kill all the lawyers." If you're having problems with your attorney or if you don't feel you're receiving adequate legal representation, what can you do? The best way to resolve any problem is to bring it out in the open. Even when dealing with an attorney who's become your friend, it's important to remember that you're talking about business, and immediate steps must be taken to amend any situation gone awry. If a situation can't be resolved, you should know that it's your legal right to change attorneys at any time.

Before you hire a new attorney, however, you must sever your relationship with your first attorney. At your request, your former attorney must allow your new attorney to review and photocopy all confidential records regarding your case, even if you have an outstanding bill. If there's unused money in your retainer, your former attorney must return it to you at the time you terminate your relationship.

Firing anyone is never an easy thing to do. But your career should be foremost in your mind. If you're not getting the kind of legal representation you need, don't be afraid to make a change.

CHAPTER 6

Your Personal Manager

"Leadership is defined by results."
–PETER F. DRUCKER

The close-knit relationship that exists between an artist and a personal manager is not much different from that between a professional athlete and coach. As an artist, you fully entrust the manager to envision your goals and help put a strategic plan of attack into effect that will allow you to attain those goals. The artist relies on a manager to be a motivator, counselor, confidant, diplomat, and day-to-day business person. Having the right personal manager at your side can assist in bringing you success beyond your wildest imagination. Having the wrong personal manager, however, can be devastating to your career. Needless to say, knowing what to look for in a personal manager, where to find one, and most important, *when you're ready for one* (the best personal manager just might be you right now), are crucial to your success.

THE ROLE OF A PERSONAL MANAGER IN YOUR CAREER

If you ask musicians to define what a personal manager does, their answers will vary (depending on their level of experience) from "They take care of business stuff like making flyers and collecting e-mail addresses" to "They shop your music to record and publishing companies" to "They book you on successful tours." Well, making flyers and collecting e-mail addresses is something every band (or its fans) must do for itself early on, shopping your music to record labels is probably better suited for a well-connected music attorney (as you'll see later in this chapter and also in Chapter 5), and booking you on successful tours is legally the job of a talent agent (see Chapter 8). Puzzled, you might ask, "So what does a personal manager do, and why do we need one?"

Managers have been described as the chief operating officers of an artist's company. I like to think of managers as air-traffic controllers and of the artists, producers, publicists, fashion consultants, A&R reps, attorneys, and business managers (and just about anyone else you can think of in the industry) as pilots. The air-traffic controller has complete control of the runway and guides the pilots flying in and out of the airport to safety. If the air traffic controller gives one wrong signal to any one pilot, complete disaster could ensue.

By strict definition, a manager's role is to advise and counsel you in all aspects of the music business. The manager provides guidance and ensures that everyone involved in your career pulls together in the same direction to achieve success. Interestingly, in management, there are no sure-fire methods to achieve success. Every manager may take a different approach—whether conventional or unconventional. Therefore, the best way to understand what managers do is to take a look at the various ways they're involved in the different stages of your career—from before securing a record deal onward, including artist development, securing contracts, dealing with record companies, and assisting with live engagements and touring.

Artist Development

Your manager helps you define your "target demographic audience," making sure that everything from your publicity photos to your public image to your stage presence to what you say to the press is consistent with your vibe and style of music. Your manager's role is to fully develop and package you as an artist so that, should you progress to signing with a record company, the label will be less inclined to remake you as something you're not. A good manager will help you find what feels most comfortable and natural to you. In a lecture he delivered at UCLA, manager Andy Gould, whose clients include Rob Zombie, Linkin Park, and Static-X, said, "The job of a manager is to let [his or her] artists breathe and develop into who they are."

Your manager may even find unique ways to associate you with certain "lifestyles" to create a specific image for you. This is called "lifestyle marketing." For instance, since heavy metal appeals to kids who skateboard and snowboard, if you were a member of a heavy metal band, your manager might try to find sponsorships for the group through skateboarding or snowboarding companies. Your manager might even look to certain clothing manufactures for endorsements. The options are limitless. Associating you with a particular lifestyle helps to define and make your image that much more believable and real.

Securing Contracts

Your manager helps get you exposure by setting up industry showcases with potential record and publishing companies. Your manager must research what labels and A&R reps are best suited to your talents and musical style, based not only on a company's past signings or successes but also on a company's financial stability—whether they're in trouble and about to consolidate or go under. Your manager must also be able to distinguish between an A&R representative who understands your music and your vision and an A&R rep who's just blowing smoke up your rear end, so to speak.

Your manager may also help you to find an attorney who can shop your music to various record companies. Attorneys deal with hundreds of clients in the course of their careers, while managers may deal with just a few; therefore, many attorneys are very well connected in the industry and may provide the extra push you need to get a deal. In such an instance, your manager will work with the attorney on key contract points in your recording and publishing deals. For instance, your manager must understand essential points of negotiation in recording agreements, such as recording and video funds, cross-collateralization, tour support, guaranteed release clauses, pay-or-play clauses, and controlled composition clauses. He must also stay current with how record companies are changing their business models, for example, in acquiring additional income streams from artists like publishing, merchandising, and touring; and with the indies "upstreaming" artists to majors after certain sales criteria are met. But in the words of Gary Borman, manager for artists such as Garbage, Faith Hill, and James Taylor, "The manager will also know when to shut up and let the attorney do his job."

Dealing with Record Companies

Another of your manager's responsibilities is to meet with the various departments at the record label, from radio promotion, new media, licensing, press, sales, and marketing, to make sure that everyone is acting in concert in preparation for an album release. Manager Andy Gould adds, "The manager must keep the entire record label talking. Believe it or not, the people at a label don't always talk to each other."

Under newly structured recording deals, some record companies are partnering with management companies to act more like venture capital firms, sharing in additional income streams like publishing, merchandising, and touring. In essence, the label and management companies are acting as one. Is this a good thing? Time will tell.

Your manager puts together a marketing plan and tries to sell the label and the A&R rep on making you a top priority. A marketing plan may include ideas for when your CD should be made available for sale in stores and on the Internet, how retail buyers can get excited about ordering the album, what quantity of records should be shipped to retailers, how the record is going to be priced (either at a full price or a developing artist price), and what advertising will be in place to generate sales.

A marketing plan may also tactfully suggest what the first radio single and format could be, how far in advance of the record release date the single should be "serviced" to radio, what avenues might be explored to promote the single (independent radio promoters, advertisements in trade magazines like *Hits* and *Radio and Records*), and when a promotional video for the single should be filmed.

A manager might also indicate in a marketing plan how the new media department might create hype online through contests and product alliances, how the licensing department might opt to exploit TV shows and video games, what magazine and newspapers the press departments should send advanced copies of your music to for reviews and stories, and whether the international departments at the label might consider the release of your record in foreign territories and when.

Last, your manager might outline in a marketing plan strategies regarding what he or she thinks is the best time for you to begin touring in support of your album. Attorney Jeffrey Light suggests, "Get the band touring three or four months before [its] record comes out. The buzz will start building, and by the time the single starts getting some love on the radio, there'll be something for people to connect to. If they buy the record—boom, there's a fire." It's also advisable that once it has been decided when a band is going to tour, the manager inform the record label of all the band's touring dates so that the proper departments can push the band's single in those key cities.

Assisting with Live Engagements and Touring

Your manager will also help you to find a licensed talent agent who specifically works on procuring live performances. Your manager will work together with this agent to determine what tours are best for you, to make sure that you're getting the best offers from concert promoters, and even to help direct your performances from city to city. Notes Rob "Blasko" Nicholson of Mercenary Management: "From my perspective as a manager of indie bands, the roll of the agent is priceless. Because the indies don't have the same resources as the majors have, touring is the band's main source of visibility. A great agent is crucial to getting the band in front of the most people possible. Of course it is the band's job to deliver the goods, but a bad agent could be the sole demise of your career as an artist."

Your manager will work with your business manager to put together a tour budget and then arrange hotel accommodations and transportation, hire stage and lighting crews, and even help get equipment endorsements. Your manager may even travel with you or will hire a "tour manager" who is responsible for keeping a watchful eye on all activities on the road. Your manager makes sure that you are meeting and mingling with radio station personnel, retail sales people, magazine and newspaper journalists, and, of course, that you're shaking hands with fans all over the country. John Leshay, manager of pop sensation Mandy Moore, adds, "The idea is to get the fans to feel they own a piece of the band from the start. That can be potentially worth millions in the long run." As you can see, a manager's touring responsibilities and concerns are endless, and he or she must be on top of them all. Touring is when you can build a grassroots following with your fans and an identity, or "brand," that can keep you earning money for years.

Manager Richard Bishop, who handles clients such as Henry Rollins, emphasizes that "Just as important to touring, a manager must know when to take their artist off . . . the road. The last thing you want to do is oversaturate the artist. Too much time between an artist's first and second record is not always good." (Chapter 12 covers touring in detail.)

To sum things up, personal managers are responsible for a great deal—and we've only touched the tip of the iceberg. Now let's take a quick look at your management options.

TURNING BAD INTO GOOD To illustrate yet another of a personal manager's roles, Bud Prager shares a classic road story concerning one of his bands, Foreigner. Tickets were not selling well for one of the band's performances, so Prager and the concert promoter put their heads together and decided to charge a "one car, one price" admission to the show. This meant that regardless of how many people could squeeze into a car, the car would only be charged for the price of one. To everyone's disbelief, the plan backfired when a tractor-trailer truck showed up with over 130 people crammed into the cargo space. Rather than turning the truck away, Prager quickly phoned up the local news media, and in minutes helicopters were buzzing above with cameras rolling. The exposure the band received on television that night was priceless. Prager took a potentially bad situation and made it good. In Prager's words, "That's the true essence of management."

MANAGEMENT OPTIONS

Before seeking out and hiring a personal manager, it's important to understand the various types of management options that are available to you. The most common choices, depending on how far along you are in your career, are self-management, start-up management (by an individual attempting to break into the music business), and established professional management.

Self-Management

In the early stages of your career, unless one of your relatives happens to be the president of Warner Bros. Records, *no one is going to help you until you first help yourself!* Remember that good management *must always* begin with the artist. Too often, musicians believe that the solution to their problems is finding some third party to magically whisk them up from rehearsal room to superstardom. It's true that an experienced manager can make good things happen fast, but having a motivated manager does not make it okay for you to be lazy. First, you must seriously ask yourself if there's anything you can be doing yourself:

- ✦ Are you writing a large repertoire of songs or even co-writing with professionals?
- ✦ Are you professionally recording your music, manufacturing CDs, and selling a respectful number of units at your live performances and over the Internet?
- ✦ Are you booking your own shows and drawing large numbers of fans?
- ✦ Are you getting your fans involved in promoting your music and creating strong legions of "street teams" in your state and around the country?
- ✦ Are you utilizing print media and the Internet to stimulate excitement?
- ✦ Are you getting played on college, Internet, and satellite radio?
- ✦ Are you placing your songs in films, TV shows, and video games?
- ✦ Have you aligned your band with local and corporate sponsorships?
- ✦ Have you recorded a video and posted it on Internet sites?
- ✦ Have you given serious thought to your career vision or goals, and do you know exactly what you want to accomplish?
- ✦ Are all members of your band united by a common goal?

You must acquire a basic knowledge of the music business and promote your ass off before ever thinking about getting a personal manager. This is the digital age, where doing it yourself is far easier than ever before. Even classic bands like Mötley Crüe, whose chaotic demeanor made them appear completely incapable of functioning at a professional business level—and whose generation didn't have the advantages of the Internet—worked their butts off the old-fashioned way and generated career momentum, *long before ever getting involved with their first manager.* Some artists have it so together that the first time a personal manager comes into play it's after they've signed an agreement with a record company. A band may then be better positioned to pick a more powerful manager. But even then, the band must continue to monitor the progress of their business and work with their personal manager to build a successful career. After all, the personal manager ultimately works for the band!

Start-up Management

So, when is the right time to get a personal manager? Perhaps you've reached a point in your career when the time you spend running your business is inhibiting your creative development—or maybe you've done everything in your power to advance your career and can't go any further without a helping hand. If either of those things is true, perhaps finding a personal manager is the right solution. But the reality is that until you're a signed act or are close to being signed, most managers with any clout or power will not be interested in working with you. These managers are simply too busy handling artists that bring them an immediate return on their investment of time. Surely there are always exceptions to this rule, but it's likely that your first manager will be one of the following:

✦ A close friend who's willing to make phone calls and help promote shows without getting paid for the first few months or years. In fact, he may not even be called a "manager" at all, working with the understanding that as soon as your career progresses, he will be replaced by an established professional manager and offered some other position in the band.

✦ An experienced musician who wants to "right all the wrongs" he/she's encountered in his/her professional career and has got all the passion and drive needed to set you on course. Or a businessperson who's always dreamed of being in a band and has the desire to live those dreams through you.

✦ A club owner in your hometown who sees hundreds of bands perform each year. This individual has a good idea of what works and what doesn't and is willing to offer you an objective point of view and career guidance.

✦ An intern or junior assistant of a professional manager by day who's looking to cut his teeth on managing his own band on his downtime at night. He's got the advantage of having his boss's ear for guidance and observing how a professional office is run all day.

Regardless of the possibilities here, these people all have one thing in common: They are relative newcomers to the management business—or, as I once heard someone devotedly call them, "start-up managers." Start-up managers are usually young, aggressive, and ambitious individuals who are willing to work their tails off for you. They'll devote every minute of their day to helping you reach your goals. They're business savvy, good talkers, and eager to learn. These traits are exactly what you will need from a manager in the early developmental stages of your career.

But take note: The early stages of your career are when you have to be the most careful about picking your manager! A lot of wannabees will feel that they can adequately manage your career. Despite their good intentions, their inexperience and lack of connections may end up costing you time and money. They may promise you everything but deliver absolutely nothing. Keep in mind, becoming a personal manager does not require getting a license or

Many start-up managers handling a band whose career is taking off often become overwhelmed because of their inexperience. In these circumstances, it is not uncommon for a less experienced manager to partner with a large, more experienced management firm. And as an afterthought, under newer structures of record contracts, these management firms may even be partnered with record labels.

state certification—anyone from a used car dealer to a snake oil salesman can be one—so proceed with caution when making your choice! There are managers in the business, and there are damagers. Watch out for the damagers.

Established Professional Management

If you're ambitious and able to develop your career on your own to the point at which you're creating a buzz in your hometown clubs, in the press, and on college radio, and perhaps record companies are even beginning to ask about you, or if you've gone as far as signing a record deal, then your management options are going to open up considerably. (In fact, under newer structures of record deals, the label may even have its own management division. Will this mean you'll have no choice in your manager? Stay tuned.) At this point in your career, things are going to begin moving fast for you, and you'll need an experienced pro to take the reins. Keep in mind that managers are in business to make money just like anyone else, and now that you're in a position to potentially make them money, they have a bigger incentive to work with you. You've come a long way on your own, and unless your ego starts to expand drastically or you decide to start shooting drugs (hey, it's been known to happen), you've already proved you have what it takes to go the long haul. The term "established professional management" covers a broad spectrum of types, but for the sake of clarity, we'll divide them into two distinct categories: midlevel managers and big-league managers.

Midlevel Managers

Midlevel managers are those who have a great deal of experience in the industry but have not quite broken a band into superstardom. Maybe they have one client on their roster who was able to sell a respectable couple hundred thousand records but still don't have a gold or platinum record hanging on the walls—and that's what they're shooting for! These are the guys who are typically very well liked in the industry for their enthusiasm and well connected enough to open some doors for you. They may be exactly what you need to get the record companies from just being interested in you to actually closing a deal. Midlevel managers usually have a great understanding of the business and perhaps were even A&R representatives or marketing managers at a label before getting involved in the management business. They enjoy the entrepreneurial spirit and freedom provided by managing bands. The problem is that they are not as powerful as someone like a big-league manager, and therefore it may take them longer to get things done.

Big-League Managers

Big-league managers are, needless to say, very well connected in the industry. The relationships they've formed, the respect they've earned, and the favors they can trade give them the power to make things happen for you with just a few phone calls. These guys have been around for years and have lots of gold and platinum records hanging on their walls. They may even run a large firm and have a number of managers working under them. The clients these managers represent provide a number of touring opportunities for your band. In addition, these managers have established strong

There are dozens of experienced, professional, established managers out there, any one of which are capable of doing the job. The important thing is picking the one that really *wants* to do it, not the one with the biggest star on the roster. Your manager must possess a genuine enthusiasm for your music and a commitment to going the long haul through thick and thin.

relationships with record companies over the years representing other clients, and the labels are happy to have them representing you. If a big-league manager is truly dedicated to making you a huge success, then it's a pretty good bet that things are going to start moving fast for you. Everyone from your peers to people in the press are in awe that you've signed with such a powerful management company and you're already planning your getaway house in the Nevada desert. It's very possible that you're going to become a huge star!

The danger, however, with a major-league manager is that you may not always get the attention you deserve. Maybe you were taken on just so someone else couldn't sign you. Perhaps you were taken on as a favor to someone else in the industry. Maybe you're going to be turned over to a less experienced manager of the firm. Regardless, when push comes to shove, you can bet that your manager is going to prioritize his or her more successful clients before you. After all, this is how the mortgage on that summer home in Hawaii is paid. One group, signed to Atlantic Records and managed by one of the most successful rock management firms in the world, was actually told that it should not even think about going on the road until it had three singles released to radio and three videos in rotation at MTV. (At the time, most bands were lucky to have one single in rotation!) Needless to say, the band bit the dust. Were the managers unhappy with the record the band delivered and wanted to see if the album "had legs" on its own with minimal effort? Or was it just not worth their time to send the band out in a passenger van and slowly build a buzz over the next two years? Who knows really. But one thing is for sure—a manager who's been involved with a band from the very beginning has much more invested emotionally than someone who comes aboard later. These are typically the guys that will go down with the sinking ship before giving up. In the long run, this may be exactly what you need.

> It's become a trend recently for management companies to merge together under one management umbrella. Although it may appear that the bigger a firm is, the better it is, sometimes the priority of many of these larger firms changes from quality to quantity. In other words, the more bands they sign, the better their chances of one of those bands hitting it big. In fact, the firm may never have any intention of getting behind your band and giving you the full-court support you deserve over the long haul.

HIRING YOUR PERSONAL MANAGER

Once you've reached a point in your career where you feel you need the assistance of a personal manager, there are a few things you must understand before beginning your search, and it's vital that you know the most important qualities a manager should possess.

Finding a Manager

The first thing to realize before looking for a personal manager is that the person you hire is going to be working closely with you for a potentially long period of time. Unlike dealings with your attorney, who, once a deal is negotiated, moves on to another client until the next time you need him, your relationship with a personal manager is, well, more personal. Are you going to look in a publication such as *The Musician's Atlas* or *Billboard's International Talent and Touring Directory* and begin randomly calling managers? You can try, but the managers listed in these books probably won't have the time to work with you unless you're fairly advanced in your career. Are you going to call a manager referral service, where an operator refers you to a manager who's suited for your needs? I don't think a service like this exists, and even if it did, remember that *you need to think about your personal needs when looking for a personal manager!* The best way to find a manager is probably by asking people you trust for personal referrals. Just keep in mind that in the early stages of your career, your options are going to be limited, and once you've progressed to the point where you're about to sign, or have signed a recording agreement, your options will open up. If this seems like a paradox, it is. But hey, that's just the way the business works. This brings the old saying to mind: "The only time a bank will loan you money is when you can prove you don't need it."

In the early stages of your career, the best way to find a personal manager, besides looking to a friend or relative to manage you, may be to get out on your local music scene and begin asking other artists or club owners what bands are moving ahead most quickly with their careers. You might even try looking in your local music papers or keeping your ears glued to your local college radio stations to determine which bands are making headway. In either case, it's quite possible that behind the most promising bands on your local scene you'll find a motivated individual who may be interested in giving your band some help. There will be plenty of people around town who can vouch for this manager's credibility, and you'll have the opportunity to meet with the manager yourself to determine whether there's a good working vibe between you. Sometimes you may be able to create enough career momentum around town yourself so that personal managers begin approaching you. In these cases, you must still ask for personal references to ensure that the person to whom you're about to entrust your career is someone reliable and able to help you to accomplish your goals.

If you're close to signing a recording agreement or if you have already inked a deal, you can look to your attorney or record company A&R representative for suggestions as to who they think should manage you. Of course, the decision will ultimately be yours, but as I mentioned before, at this point your options will be considerable. It's also possible you may already have a good idea of whom you want to manage your band based on stories you've read in the press or listings on the liner notes of your favorite band's CDs. You may have even had the opportunity to meet and speak with a manager at one of the many annual music conventions such as South by Southwest (sxsw.com) or you may have met a manager who was lecturing at a program held at a university or in an adult-education class such as UCLA's Entertainment Extension program (www.uclaextension.org). You may even know someone in a successful band who wants to introduce you to his or her manager. The possibilities are endless, making your search for a manager less difficult than ever before. However, now that your options have expanded greatly, how do you really know who the right person to manage your career is? Read on.

Qualities to Look for in a Manager

The classic concert film *The Song Remains the Same* features a scene in which Led Zeppelin's manager, Peter Grant, a 270-pound former wrestler from East London, is backstage screaming at one of the promoters at Madison Square Garden. Many artists may think that an intimidating personal manager is exactly what they need. But Jeffrey Jampol, who has managed artists such as the Doors, says, "The days of the Peter Grants in this business are over." People in the music industry prefer to do business with nice guys. A manager must be able to nurture and maintain relationships while at the same time standing firm, being sensible, and demonstrating a strong knowledge of the business. (It's a balance between ticking people off and not being a pushover.) If a manager walks into the record company and starts pounding desks, insisting that things get done his way, he's bound to get absolutely nowhere!

So what are the most important things to look for in a manager? In addition to being ambitious, well connected, a good negotiator, powerful, and accessible, a good manager should be someone who inspires your *trust and respect*.

Trust

Trustworthiness is an incredibly important attribute in a manager. Think about it: You've worked for many years learning how to play your instrument and write your songs, and your band has been rehearsing and promoting its shows for years—and now you're going to turn over a great deal of responsibility to someone you barely know! Sounds scary, doesn't it? Trust must be earned over time, but if a manager doesn't show a genuine caring, enthusiasm, and understanding for your dreams and passions, you may not have the right person for the job.

I remember one very famous manager firmly saying to a group that he didn't need to like their music to do business with them. Sounds rather insensitive, but because of his power and clout, the band decided to go ahead and work with him. Needless to say, the relationship ended in disaster. The band drove all the way across country in a van to perform a showcase, and the manager didn't even show up—nor did any industry people! True story. In fact, after that, the manager didn't even return the band's phone calls. Nice! In similar situations, many bands are promised that a record contract is waiting right around the corner and that the labels are ready to ink the deal. One or two years later, the band is still unsigned and playing the same shithole clubs.

A manager isn't a magician and can't predict the future, but he can't lie to his or her artists to keep them optimistic (i.e., dumb), to keep them under his control, or even to lure them into romantic relationships (it wouldn't be the first time a sleazy manager type lies to his female artists about making them stars so that he can get a crack at them). Again, an initial feeling of genuine caring, sincerity, and trust is a major quality to look for in a manager. Without it, you may end up with a lot of broken promises down the road.

Respect

A manager must also be someone that you can respect. We're not just talking about the impressive number of successful bands this individual has managed or how many gold and platinum records he or she has on the wall; we're talking about morality and ethics. What does your manager really stand for? Is he well educated? Is he well groomed? Does he show a genuine loyalty to other business partners and associates? Does he show an interest in win-win relationships in other business ventures? Is he a family man? Does he do anything to give back to the community? Or is your manager all about making money and being flashy—big houses, expensive cars, and arm-piece girlfriends at any expense? Is he a spoiled rich kid or a businessman who got into management to fulfill some showbiz fantasy? Is he a former drug dealer or dubious businessperson? Does he hang out and party twice as hard as you?

Hey, I'm not making these examples up! Surely, it's not like you're an angel looking for a saint, but overall a manager must maintain a level of authority and respect and perhaps even be somewhat of a father figure to you. Many bands, not that they'll always admit it, want someone whom they can look up to and feel protected by. They want both someone who's going to take them under their wing and keep everything under control—a superhero who can do no wrong, and someone who knows how to be down to earth and admit that he doesn't have an answer to a particular situation.

Of course you may initially be impressed with someone who makes a lot of noise, blows a lot of smoke, wines and dines you, and flexes a lot of muscle—but are you really going to trust your whole career to a guy like this? A manager must be secure, grounded, firm, confident, educated, and well respected—far above all the bells and whistles and shallow surface stuff. Without these positive and respectful attributes, you're only building a relationship in a personal manager that is doomed eventually to fail!

MANAGEMENT AGREEMENTS

Trust is a crucial factor in the union between an artist and his personal manager, yet it's still extremely important to have a written contract between both parties defining the terms of their business relationship. In the event of a falling out, a written contract leaves no doubt as to what each party initially agreed upon. Manager Gary Borman agrees: "I believe in agreements from the very beginning simply because people tend to forget."

But many managers, even those at larger firms, don't believe in detailed written contracts. They feel that the artist/manager relationship will either work or it won't, regardless of the words written on a piece of paper. If the artist is unhappy, he/she should always be free to go. However, when you consider historic disasters like the one with Bruce Springsteen, who found himself trapped in a legal battle for over a year after firing manager Mike Appel in 1976, then perhaps you'll agree that there's a lot more to formulating a professional relationship than just a verbal or handshake agreement.

Key elements that all management contracts should include are exclusivity, a key person clause, the term of the agreement (period of time for which it's valid), the manager's commission, expenses, power of attorney, a talent agent disclaimer, and post-term provisions.

Exclusivity

When entering into a relationship with a personal manager, you're taking on an "exclusive" manager. This means that during the full term of your agreement, you cannot be managed by anyone else. Consequently, before entering into a relationship with a personal manager, be sure you're absolutely confident in that individual's ability to represent you. Remember, you're going to be working together for a long time.

Key Person Clause

When signing a management agreement, you're often not just signing with an individual but also with a management firm consisting of a few managers. But what happens in situations where your manager decides to leave the firm, he is terminated, or he becomes disabled or diseased? The reality is that you could get stuck with the company and be assigned to another representative you don't like. This is why you want to make sure there's a clause in your agreement called a "key person clause." A key person clause is exactly what it sounds like. The manager with whom you initially signed is your key person. If this individual leaves the firm, for instance, your agreement becomes void and you're free to follow.

A key person clause may also protect you from cases in which the sport who wined and dined you and inspired you to enter into a management agreement in the first place never seems to be doing much of the managing. Instead, he or she turns the bulk of the work over to a partner or office representative. Under the key person provision, you may be able to void your agreement if you insist that your key person clause expressly states this. But keep in mind, it's normal for a manager to delegate some of the less important responsibilities to other people on the team. A representative of the firm is just as capable of getting you equipment endorsements and, as a result, provides your manager with more time to do something really important—like work with an agent to get you a national tour. Manager Gary Borman adds, "Artists begin to understand that it's a waste of time to be directing issues to the wrong person. Managers don't have to show up at every gig. As long as they're available at the more crucial times in your career, you don't have to feel uncomfortable in their absence."

The Term of the Agreement

The term of management agreements can be based on a set number of years (from one to five, with three years being the norm) or on "album cycles" (from the day the recording of an album begins to the last day of promoting it). Two to three album tour cycles is standard in management agreements. Understandably, the manager will want a chance to make a return on his investment of time and hard work and therefore will shoot for the longest term he can get.

The artist, on the other hand, will want to commit to an agreement with the shortest term possible. Their fear is of being trapped in an agreement with a manager who's just not making things happen! As a result, the manager may be willing to stipulate certain "performance guarantees." For instance, the manager may guarantee you a recording deal within the first year. Or, once you're signed, the manager may guarantee that a licensed talent agent will be hired to work toward getting you an opening slot on a national tour. Or you'll be guaranteed a publishing deal. In any case, these performance guarantees must be fairly reasonable for your manager to achieve if you expect your manager to agree to them. It's not likely, for instance, that a young manager will be able to secure a recording agreement for a new band in a period of six months. On the other hand, it may be possible that you're not ready for a deal in the first place. Remember, managers aren't magicians. Even if you have a lot of talent, the best manager may not always be able to make things happen so quickly.

In addition, performance guarantees may apply to income. The artist may want a guaranteed specific income over a certain period of time. For instance, in a deal with three album cycles, a recording artist may expect to earn up to $200,000 over the first cycle, and as his career becomes more established, up to $300,000 in the second cycle, increasing up to $400,000 in the third cycle. Keep in mind that these numbers are arbitrary and not necessarily based on reality. These figures will change according to the state of the economy, and there are many other factors that can affect an artist's earning ability. It's easy to see that a jazz group playing small clubs will produce less income than a young rock group playing larger venues.

The source from which money is earned should also be stipulated in a performance guarantee. For instance, the artist may stipulate that $200,000 in earnings be derived from live performances. Assuming you don't want to play circuses all year, you may need to clarify the types of live performances you have in mind. Thus, your agreement could state "live performances that can reasonably advance your career in the commercial marketplace and that cater to your demographic audience."

Lastly, and in all fairness to the manager, your performance guarantee must be based not only on the monies you make but also on the work you turn down. In other words, if your lead singer decides he'd rather hang out with his girlfriend for five months and turn down work, that should not be held against the personal manager and used as an excuse to break your contract with him.

The Manager's Commission

Personal managers risk a great deal when taking on new clients—they invest their time, reputation, and money with no guarantee of a big payoff. Therefore, managers can commission their artist's earnings (e.g., from records, publishing incomes, and tours) at anywhere from 15 to 30 percent, with the norm being 20 percent (some say the norm is 15 percent). Just keep in mind that there are no regulations dictating the amount a personal manager can charge; it varies with each individual situation.

Gross Earnings and Customary Deductions

A manager's commissions are commonly based on your gross earnings. But note: The word *gross*, which typically means total earnings, must be defined here as *all monies other than those that pass through your hands for customary expenses*. Without a clear definition of what these expenses include, the manager may be taking a bigger commission than he or she deserves. Consider the following example.

Since there are so many expenses incurred on the road before the artist sees a profit, sometimes a manager's commissions are based on the "net" touring profits, while his or her commissions for records and publishing are based on the "gross" after certain customary deductions.

Suppose you're advanced a healthy recording fund of $300,000, and your manager earns a 20 percent commission off the top. The manager's take would be $60,000 ($300,000 × 20% = $60,000). This leaves you with a new balance of $240,000 ($300,000 − $60,000 = $240,000). If the costs for recording your album are $200,000, you're left with $40,000 with which to pay your attorney and business manager a commission and to pay Uncle Sam taxes. If there are four members in the band, each member could receive as little as $3,500.

As you can clearly see, your manager's commission of $60,000 is far greater than each member's earnings of $3,500. How could this be? After all, you're the star! But before freaking out, remember that your manager's commission is based on monies *after* certain expenses are deducted. Recording costs, you'll be happy to know, are considered one of these deductions. Now let's take another look at our numbers.

Three hundred thousand dollars (your recording fund) minus $200,000 (your recording costs) equals a balance of $100,000. One hundred thousand dollars multiplied by your manager's commission of 20 percent equals $20,000—a far cry from the $60,000 in the above example. After subtracting your attorney and business manager's commissions and paying uncle Sam taxes, you might have approximately $42,000 in which to divide between four band members, which is $10,500 each—as opposed to the $3,500 in our first example.

It doesn't take a genius to see that the second situation works out much better for the artist. Although most reputable managers will deduct the recording fund and other customary deductions before taking a commission, *it's vitally important that all monies that are not to be commissioned are detailed in the written agreement with your manager.*

Here are a few more examples of monies that are not to be commissioned by the manager:

✦ Advances to record producers (usually considered part of the recording costs) and any royalty payments due

✦ Tour support, which is money advanced by the record company to help cover expenses on the road

✦ The costs for filming a promotional music video, which are advanced by the record company

✦ Monies that may be allocated as an expense in live performance agreements to cover sound and lights

✦ Monies that may be allocated to pay opening acts (once you're a headliner)

NINE INCH NAILS COME SCRATCHING . . . In 2003, NIN front man Trent Reznor was shocked to discover that though he had earned millions in the past fifteen years, he only had around $400,000. Reznor's claim was that his manager John Malm tricked him into signing a contract that permitted Malm to collect 20 percent of the gross earnings, without factoring in customary deductions or offering a deal based on the net for touring income. Malm defended himself by stating that he never hid any of his dealings from Trent and that Reznor had simply not paid attention to his finances at all throughout the years when he was drugged out and irresponsible. When the jury found Malm guilty for breach of contract and fraudulent action, Reznor was awarded $2.95 million by the court. After adding interest, the damages were as much as $4 million.

Escalating and De-escalating Commissions

Personal managers sometimes work on an escalating or de-escalating commission scale, depending on their artist's success. For instance, when you're first starting out and not making much money, a manager may agree to a 15 percent commission based on the premise that when you begin to earn more money, the commission escalates to 20 percent. Sounds fair enough, right? But what happens when the same concept is applied in reverse and your manager works on a de-escalating commission?

Suppose that in the beginning of your career, when there's not a whole lot of money, your manager asks for a commission of 20 percent. Later, if you're successful and earning more money, your manager's commission drops to 15 percent. At first, this may seem to make little or no sense. Why should a manager promote you if his or her commission continues to drop as you become more and more successful? If you do the math, it becomes clear how this type of arrangement works. A hundred thousand dollars in earnings multiplied by a commission of 20 percent yields a payment of $20,000. However, $500,000 multiplied by a commission of 15 percent equals

In the very early stages of your career when you're barely making enough money to pay your rent, most managers will defer their commissions altogether on what little money from live performances and merchandise you having coming in.

$75,000, and so on. The manager makes more money as the artist does, even though his or her commission is less.

Limitations and Exclusions

Sometimes your personal manager may agree to charge you a lower commission, or even no commission at all, on money earned in areas in which you're already established. For instance, if you're a successful songwriter who writes for television and film or if you're an accomplished musician who plays on a number of recording sessions, your manager may agree to only charge you a 10 percent commission on these incomes, as opposed to the standard 20 percent commission on everything else. It's also possible that if the manager is not going to be involved in furthering your career in these areas (because of lack of time, expertise, or interest), he or she will usually agree not to charge you a commission at all.

In situations in which a band signs a recording agreement before hiring a personal manager, you may wonder whether a personal manager still receives a commission from the artist advance when this individual comes onboard later. Major-league managers may want their usual fee, midlevel managers may accept a reduced percentage of their standard fee, and some managers may take no commission at all. Nevertheless, if signing a recording agreement before hiring a manager, the band's attorney will typically advise them to put aside a portion of the fund for the manager, just in case. The initial advance can be the factor that decides whether a manager chooses to work with a band.

You must also consider what the manager will be able to commission for work that becomes available after you become a successful artist. What if you get the opportunity to act in motion pictures, or write a book, or start your own clothing line? Will your manager be entitled to a commission? If these new opportunities are a direct result of your manager's years of hard work, *then yes!* But for the sake of clarity, it's extremely important to discuss these issues in advance.

Expenses

Besides the commissions I've outlined, your manager will also be entitled to be reimbursed for certain expenses. The expenses necessary to run the business, such as rent, office machines, and personnel, are typically your manager's responsibility, but what happens when he or she has to FedEx your tape to an interested A&R representative? Even better, what happens when your manager has to fly to New York to conduct business on your behalf? These costs are charged to you, and don't be mistaken, expenses can add up quickly.

To monitor the expenses that are reimbursed to your manager, a limit is usually set on what the manager can spend. For instance, a single expense above $200, or total monthly expenses that exceed $1,000, should be approved by you first. In cases in which a manager handles more than one client, expenses may have to be prorated. I once knew a manager who flew out to an industry convention in Cannes, France (MIDEM—www.midem.com) and charged the entire trip as an expense to one of his primary bands. He justified the expense by setting up a meeting or two, but he also spent time shopping his other artists to record labels. The manager should have prorated his expenses and charged each band accordingly. If he was representing three bands, and each band was given equal attention, expenses should have been split three ways. However, a band that is not yet earning money should not have to take money out of its own pockets to pay its manager. Expenses are paid at a later time once the band has an income to do so.

So who actually monitors and pays the manager expenses and commissions? After all, if you wanted to handle your money, you probably would have become an accountant yourself. Although most managers may initially insist monies flow through them, they will accept an outside accountant or business manager (see Chapter 7). The business manager will usually collect and deposit money into an account on your behalf. Expenses and commissions are monitored and paid out as the manager submits them.

Power of Attorney

Power of attorney is a clause found in management agreements that could give your manager the legal right to act for you in making major career decisions, cashing checks, and signing contracts. Needless to say, there are far too many nightmarish stories involving unscrupulous managers for you to agree to any more than a limited power of attorney. In other words, you might stipulate that your manager, in the event that you're out of town, can sign an agreement on your behalf only after you approve the deal verbally. The paperwork can then be faxed to you. Your manager may also be able to approve live performance engagements under a certain number of dates, and only after you've approved the time in which you want to tour. Realistically, offers of engagements by promoters don't stay open long, and your manager may have to make these decisions quickly.

Remember, there's a reason you hired your manager in the first place. When you're on the road or in the studio trying to be creative, you don't want to be bothered with business issues. On the other hand, you don't want to get screwed either. It's not that you should distrust your manager, but putting limitations on how your manager can act on your behalf helps ensure that you'll always know what's going on.

Talent Agency Disclaimer

Some management agreements (depending on the state) will include a talent agency disclaimer clause, which stipulates that your *manager will not act as your agent to procure employment or engagements, and that you will at all times have a licensed agent*. If this sounds confusing, since booking gigs is exactly what most managers do in the very early stages of a band's career, you should know a few basic facts here.

Under California state laws (as well other states, notably New York and Massachusetts), anyone who engages in the occupation of procuring employment for their artists *must be licensed as a talent agent*. The problem here is that most managers don't care to obtain this license, for a number of reasons. For instance, in the state of California (which we all know is where a great deal of the music industry is centered) the personal manager must submit an agency contract form to the state labor commissioner for approval. Although there are some exceptions, the labor commissioner will not approve more than a 10 percent commission for an agent. As you know, managers typically earn 20 percent and simply don't want to work for any less.

Additionally, the agency contract will need to provide a clause stating that the artist is free to leave and the contract void if they have not worked within a ninety-day period. This could cause a lot of problems for the manager, since there must be some discretion in the gigs that their artist performs. It's possible that, in an effort to meet the ninety-day requirement, the manager may find himself or herself in approval to working certain gigs that may not be in the best interests of the artist. It's easy to see why a manager would not want to work under these circumstances. In fact, it's safe to say that very few managers ever become licensed agents.

So, does this mean that your manager is in violation of California state law when gigs are booked without a license? We all know this happens—managers book engagements for their young bands in order to help them develop into seasoned acts. In fact, attorney Richard Schulenberg (author of *Legal Aspects of the Music Industry*) cautiously goes as far as saying, "In California, if a personal manager is not breaking the law, he's not doing his job." Well, it's not like someone is going to come and take your manager away in handcuffs, *but it could provide a way for you to get out of your contract with your manager if you are justly unhappy and your manager won't let you go any other way*. In fact, in California your manager may even have to pay back all commissions he earned while procuring employment for you. Of course, it's not as easy as it sounds—you'd still have to go through legal proceedings and prove your manager booked gigs—but if you're ever in a position where you want to get out of your contract badly enough, it may be an option. This is not meant as advice; it's the law, and you should always speak to your attorney first.

So, getting back to square one and the disclaimer clause, understandably, it's not a personal manager's general intention to book gigs for the artist but rather to work together with a licensed talent agent who will be responsible for initiating engagements. But again, the problem here is that a young band usually can't attract the interest of a talent agent because young bands don't earn enough money to make them worth the talent agent's time. So, we're back to where we started once again. If this sounds like a catch-22 scenario for the manager, it actually is—and managers, especially in California, should understand this. Nevertheless, it's important that managers look at their state laws to help them decide whether a talent agency disclaimer clause is useful. At best, notes Richard Schulenberg, should a claim arise against the manager, the clause might serve as proof that he had no intention to, and did not, book the band. But, of course, if evidence shows he did book the band, the clause is meaningless.

Note: There are some exceptions to talent agency laws. For instance, in California anyone can procure a recording agreement on behalf of an artist without a license. In New York, anyone can book "incidental" performances, such as a showcase, to generate interest from record companies. Again, it's important that managers look at their individual state laws to make sure they understand their legal boundaries.

Post-Term Provisions

When the term of your manager's agreement expires, he or she is still entitled to earn a commission on royalties from contracts entered into or substantially negotiated during that contract term.

ARSENIO HALL DOES THE TALKING! As noted in Richard Schulenberg's book *Legal Aspects of The Music Industry*, the ex-managers of entertainer and former talk show host Arsenio Hall (known as X-Management) were ordered by the labor commissioner to repay $2,148,445.78 in commissions earned over one year (you read right!). The labor commission found that the managers had engaged in the occupation of a "talent agency" without being licensed. Ouch! Be sure to check out Schulenberg's book for further details on this and many other cases. Interesting stuff!

For instance, suppose you sign a whopping five-record deal with a label a few months before the manager's term expires. Technically, your manager is entitled to commission royalties from all five records—even without being involved with your career anymore. Is this fair? To make matters worse, if you hire a new manager, you'll be required to pay that manager a commission on your earnings as well. If both your former manager and your new manager are charging a 20 percent commission, you're now paying out 40 percent in commissions. Let me repeat this: 40 percent!

To limit the amount your manager can commission after the contract term expires, he or she may be willing to agree to something called a "sunset clause." A sunset clause gradually "ends the day" on the commissions to which the manager is entitled. For instance, in our above example, the manager would continue to earn a commission after his or her term on all five records. However, with a sunset clause, your manager may be willing to accept the full commission on royalties for a limited period of five years after his or her term and then no royalty. Or, the manager may agree to the full commission for the first three years after the lapse of the term, a reduced commission for the next two years, and then no royalty. Lastly, you may be able to exclude your manager altogether from earning a commission on the albums recorded after the term. A variety of interpretations can really exist here, depending on your personal manager, your bargaining strength, and on the type of money (records, publishing) on which a sunset clause is being negotiated.

Obviously, not all managers are going to be happy with a sunset clause. In a UCLA lecture, veteran managers Bud Prager (Foreigner, Bad Company, and Megadeth) and Mike Gormerly (Bangles, Oingo Boingo, and Danny Elfman) revealed that they don't believe in sunset clauses. After all, it's the manager who helps take the artist from obscurity to popularity. If the artist continues to make money from recordings, then shouldn't the manager do likewise? Although this argument may be valid, your attorney will be able to advise you as to what is appropriate in your individual situation. An attorney who is skillful at negotiating should be able to reach terms that are acceptable to both sides.

CHAPTER 7

Your Business Manager

"Money is better than poverty, if only for financial reasons."
—WOODY ALLEN

If you can make money in the music business playing the music you love, you're doing well. If you can make money, hang on to it, and make it grow, you're exceptional.

Unfortunately, we've all heard stories of musicians who hit it big and sell millions of records yet end up penniless. Just think about infamous stories like that of rapper MC Hammer, who was once reported in *Forbes* magazine as being worth $40 million, only to end up filing for bankruptcy. If you don't want this to happen to you, remember that the assistance of a good business manager is crucial.

In the early stages of your career, when you're trying to get noticed and you're making no money or just making ends meet, you're probably not ready for a business manager. In fact, all you may need is a certified public accountant experienced in music to help with taxes and to provide general business advice. Some acquired basic business smarts wouldn't hurt either (see "How to Self-Manage Your Personal Finances and Life" at the end of this chapter). Nonetheless, learning about what a good business manager can do now, before you hit it big, can be worth millions to your career and to your future. And besides, who doesn't like to read about money? Those that say, "money isn't everything," are usually those that never had to worry about it. Read on.

THE ROLE OF A BUSINESS MANAGER IN YOUR CAREER

The role of a business manager is not to be confused with that of a personal manager. A personal manager is more like the chief executive officer (CEO) of your company, who helps *generate income* by setting up recording deals, publishing deals, and tours. A business manager, on the other hand, is more like the chief financial officer (CFO) of your company, who helps *manage the income* from these deals once they're in place. A business manager handles all financial issues, such as investments, financial planning, bookkeeping, tour account services, asset administration, tax services, insurance monitoring, royalty examination, and in some cases even publishing administration.

Investment Strategies and Financial Planning

One of the most important roles that a business manager can play in your career is to help you plan for your future. As a musician, there are many sacrifices you'll make while pursuing your dreams. You'll shell out money for rehearsal rooms, recording sessions, CD manufacturing, Web hosting and design, press kits, photographers, and van rentals to haul your gear from one gig to the next; all without ever making much money in return. If your sacrifices and hard work pay off and you can make ends meet as an independent artist, you're a huge success. If your sacrifices and hard work pay off and you have the full-court support of record label and publishing company, a song climbing up the charts, and a substantial amount of money coming in, then the gods are on your side. In the latter case, you'll almost immediately sense the natural urge to reward yourself. You can finally afford to eat in upscale restaurants, drive a nice car, and perhaps buy a comfortable home. As long as your spending is in moderation, then fine, why shouldn't you enjoy the fruits of your labor? After all, your adoring fans would expect nothing less; public image is everything, right?

But what practically all artists fail to recognize is that their days in the limelight are numbered. The average career of an artist lasts anywhere from five to seven years, and you're doing really well if you last longer than that. With time, the public's perception of you slowly but surely diminishes. In other words, you'll inevitably find yourself "yesterday's news" or "a thing of the past" (see "Overcome Age Discrimination in the Music Business" in Chapter 1). If you've spent your money lavishly, you may also find that you've become used to a lifestyle that you can no longer afford. Even worse, with dwindling royalties and diminishing concert sales, you may find yourself faced with a very difficult decision about what to do next with your life.

This is where the assistance of a business manager is essential. As Samuel Butler once said, "The future is purchased by the present." A good business manager helps his or her clients plan ahead by first determining what investment strategy is best suited for their needs. For instance, is a high-risk, short-term strategy (such as stock investments in emerging technologies) a wise plan, or is a long-term, low-risk strategy (such as investing in pension plans, mutual funds, and municipal bonds) a more appropriate scheme? Jeff Hinkle of the Los Angeles–based business management firm Gudvi, Sussman & Oppenhiem (www.gsogroup.com) says, "We like to think in the long term for our clients. One of the first things that we would do, especially for our younger clients, is to set up a pension plan and start saving for their retirement. Depending on how much they can afford to put aside, we'll probably use the assistance of a professional money manager. The money manager opens the investment accounts and recommends appropriate investments such as stocks, mutual funds, treasury bills, and high-quality bonds. Once the investment choices have been made, the money manager then oversees the portfolio on a day-to-day basis; he makes ongoing recommendations as to the mix of investments to maximize the client's return on their money and also minimize their downside risk. The business manager is always involved in these decisions, but the business manager is not a stock picker. That's the money manager's job."

The point of all this is not to get caught up on what all of these financial terms mean; that discussion is beyond the scope of this book. The message to absorb here is that a business manager is a skilled money person who plays a key role in making sure that the money you're making today is invested in such a way that your future is a bright and well-secured one.

Bookkeeping and Accounting

Business managers not only look out for your future by helping with investments and financial planning, but they help manage your money on a daily basis by reviewing invoices, paying monthly bills, collecting royalty earnings, depositing money, and monitoring your bank accounts. All of these issues fall under a service known as bookkeeping and accounting.

Business managers have long-established relationships with local banks that are familiar with the business management firm and its clients. Business managers open accounts with these banks usually consisting of a checking account (to pay all of your bills) and what's called a pocket account (for whatever personal expenses you may have, ATM withdrawals you may make, etc.). Of course, these accounts are open under your name, and you have to provide your signature to the bank. Your business manager then collects all of your income, which can range from touring and merchandising monies to publishing and record royalties, and deposits it into these accounts. He or she monitors your bank accounts to make sure there's enough money to meet your expenses, reviews your bills (car payments, credit card bills, home mortgages, gardener, personal trainer, etc.) to ensure that all charges are justified, requests your approval and signature (unless you authorize him or her to sign on your behalf), and then pays your bills. Jeff Hinkle notes: "We really encourage our clients to be involved in the bill-paying process. Not paying your own bills can be a dangerous thing; it's the old 'out of sight, out of mind' problem. We prefer for clients to sign their own checks, although this isn't always possible due to their generally busy schedules. I've had clients who seemed to have a phobia when it came to bills and discussing their spending. Sometimes as long as they know they can meet all of their expenses, they would rather not deal with any of it at all."

Touring Services

Another important role played by your business manager is the handling of all financial matters pertaining to touring. Business managers are involved with a tour from its inception and planning to the very last show a band performs.

Pre-Touring

Your business manager, along with your personal manager, is responsible for putting together tour budgets when you're planning to hit the road. He or she will review all of the performance deals offered by concert promoters around the country to determine the total gross earnings of the tour. A projection of expenses is then made to determine what the potential net profit or loss of the tour may be. Expenses may include the following:

- ✦ Tour bus
- ✦ Airfare
- ✦ Hotels
- ✦ Insurance (for personal injury, theft, if you miss a show—called "nonappearance")
- ✦ Rehearsal fees
- ✦ Per diems (daily allowances paid to the band and crew for food)

- ✦ Salaries for the band
- ✦ Salaries for the crew
- ✦ Production costs (for the sound and lighting equipment)
- ✦ Trucking cost (to carry the sound and lights)
- ✦ Contingency (an additional percentage [usually 5 percent]) calculated into the budget in case expenses are estimated low or there are unexpected emergencies
- ✦ Your agent's fees
- ✦ Your manager's commission
- ✦ Your business manager's fees

The expenses listed above are an oversimplification of what is usually incurred by a band on the road; the list can easily be a page long. Nevertheless, after determining the total expenses of a tour and then deducting them for the projected gross income, the business manager then works at making adjustments in areas where he or she feels money could be saved. Careful planning is required. Any miscalculation of expenses can lead to serious problems at the end of a tour, and instead of making money, you can find yourself thousands of dollars in the red.

So what happens when your business manager projects a loss in profits for a tour? Do you stay home or go out on the road anyway? In the early stages of a band's career, a tour almost always shows a loss. But since a live performance is a valuable way for you to reach your audience and help sell albums, your record company may provide you monies in the form of something called "tour support" to subsidize a tour. However, this amount is always charged against any record royalties you may have earned. In other words, the money your record company may provide to make a tour economically feasible may feel like it's free, but it all comes out of your pocket in the end.

Once the Tour Starts

Once you're on the road, your business manager's work does not end by any means. He or she collects monies taken after from each performance and makes sure that the concert promoter paid the appropriate sum. Your business manager then pays all bills owed to the tour bus companies and trucking companies and pays salaries to the band and its crew. He or she also makes sure a tax return is filed in every state in which a tour is planned. By submitting a budget to the appropriate authorities in each state, your business manager can limit the band's tax obligations by making sure the band is taxed on the net profits of a performance rather than on the total gross earnings taken. Lastly, your business manager makes sure your band is properly insured while out on the road, especially with something called "non-appearance insurance." This means that if a concert is cancelled because your lead singer gets sick or your tour bus breaks down, the insurance company will pay the band the amount it was expecting to earn from that performance. As you can imagine, non-appearance insurance is extremely important. One or two live performance cancellations can cause a band to lose incredible sums of money.

Asset Administration

What happens once you have a little money rolling in and you decide you want to start making expensive purchases like a home or a car? This brings us to your business manager's next important role, known as asset administration.

Shopping for a Home

When you're shopping for a home, your business manager will advise you as to what price range you can afford. Unless you're exceptionally fortunate and can pay cash for a home, your business manager will rely on relationships with mortgage brokers to arrange loans. A good business manager understands all the various factors involved in buying a home, including loan fees, points, title insurance, and credit reports. Depending on your income and the cost of the house you want to buy, your business manager may even be forced to inform you that buying a particular home may not be a wise choice to make.

Shopping for an Automobile

After your business manager is informed as to what kind of car you want, the options you'd like included, and the color you'd like the car to be, he or she usually contacts an automobile broker. Jeff Hinkle remembers one instance where a client wanted a particular Mercedes model, which was a particularly hard car to find. An automobile broker located the car down to the exact specifications, in Texas, and delivered it to Jeff's client in California in a few short days; how's that for service!

Your business manager will also explain the advantages and disadvantages of either leasing or financing an automobile. When leasing, you can make low monthly payments and turn your car in for a new lease in two or three years with no money owed. When financing, you may have higher monthly payments, but you'll own a car with some equity after a few years. Your business manager will help you to weigh these pros and cons and in some cases may even have to advise you that purchasing that $130,000 car is not at all practical for you. But in the words of Jeff Hinkle, "All we can do is advise our clients as to what's best for them to do. The rest is up to them."

Financial Reporting

Every month, your business manager must send out a detailed statement to his or her clients that includes every deposit made, every transfer of funds made in and out of investment accounts, and every check written. Rather than these reports looking like something a bank would send out, your business manager may categorize items under certain headings, such as recording expenses, housing expenses, and business expenses. This makes it much easier for you to read and understand your statements. Your business managers will also meet periodically with you to review financial statements and to make projections as to where they see your finances in six months to a year. Jeff Hinkle adds that this is one of the most challenging parts of his job: "Communication with the client about their money is the key. Most artists would rather think about mixing their new album or an upcoming tour than their finances. That's why we make it a point to have regular financial meetings with all of our clients. Since most of our clients are touring artists, finding the time and place to meet can be difficult. So several times a year, we will get on an airplane and fly out to meet with a client who is on tour. I've had plenty of business meetings on tour buses and backstage in dressing rooms. Sometimes that's the only way to get in front of the client."

Tax Planning

Another important function undertaken by your business manager involves tax planning. This crucial responsibility can be divided into three categories: determination of an appropriate business entity, handling of payroll and income taxes, and estate planning.

Determining a Business Entity

One of your business manager's major responsibilities is helping you determine what business entity best suits your needs. Should you be a partnership, a corporation, or an LLC (limited liability company)? (See the interview with attorney Jeff Cohen in Chapter 2 for a more detailed analysis.) Your business manager, together with expert lawyers, will help you set up the business entity best suited to your needs.

Payroll and Income Taxes

Your business manager also handles payroll and income taxes. He or she writes checks and pays all personnel, from the crew to the side musicians to the band itself, and deducts all applicable taxes. He or she also prepares all W2 and 1099 forms for the purpose of filing tax returns. Having a working knowledge of the special deductions that entertainers are allowed to take, your business manager also prepares your tax returns (or in some cases, business managers hire an outside firm to do this). Should you ever be audited by the Internal Revenue Service, your business manager will have the authority (granted by you under contract—discussed later in this chapter) to meet with the IRS field agent and show all proper documentation of receipts and deductions taken on your returns. If your business manager is doing his or her job correctly, this is usually not too difficult. But without a business manager working for you, an audit by the IRS can be a nightmare unless you have been extraordinarily organized and careful with your record keeping.

Estate Planning

Lastly, your business manager helps you with estate planning. In plain English, this means that he or she will assist you in preparing for what will happen to your assets when you die. It may not be something you want to think about while you're young and healthy, but if you've worked hard all your life and are finally successful, you want to be sure your assets are left with the people you love. Estate planning includes such important issues as setting up wills, trust funds, life insurance, and gifting (the process of giving equitable gifts such as cash or property in order to reduce estate tax liability on inheritance). Your business manager will work with expert attorneys specializing in estate planning to make certain that you and your family are protected.

Monitoring Insurance

Your business manager also makes sure that you have all of the appropriate insurance coverage in place, including general liability, workers' compensation, auto insurance, home insurance, and non-appearance insurance.

When taking on a new client, a business manager typically contacts that client's current insurance broker to determine what insurance is already in place. If the broker is not experienced in entertainment, the business manager will recommend someone who is. Although business managers typically have established relationships with experienced entertainment brokers, they will not take their advice at face value. The business manager makes sure that his or her client is getting all the best rates, premiums, and deductibles. Jeff Hinkle notes that insurance is a very important responsibility for business managers. If their clients are sued and don't have the adequate coverage, or the right kind of coverage, or have no coverage at all, it can lead to substantial losses and even bankruptcy.

Royalty Examination

Most business management firms have royalty-examination departments that understand the detailed aspects of royalty earnings, such as when your record royalties should be paid, whether your royalties are being computed properly, and how many records you should be credited to date. In cases where your business manager finds discrepancies, he or she will contact your record company with a series of detailed questions concerning the matter. If the problem at hand cannot be reasonably resolved, the business manager will contact a royalty-auditing service and conduct a field audit on your behalf. Jeff Hinkle says that these audits usually result in sizable settlements for the artist. (Disturbing, isn't it?)

Your business manager will also monitor royalties from publishing monies such as mechanical and performance royalties and make sure you're paid appropriately for merchandising sales (T-shirts, hats, posters, etc.), should you have signed a deal with a merchandiser. Needless to say, your business manager must have a complete understanding of all contracts and deals you enter into to provide you with an efficient royalty-examination service. (Royalties are covered in chapters 11, 12, and 13).

Publishing Administration

Last but definitely not least, some of the larger business management firms have publishing administration departments that can function as administrators for the compositions you write. In other words, in addition to collecting royalties and making sure you're paid, the publishing administration department can negotiate licenses for the use of your songs in film and television and also issue licenses for print uses (like the sheet music you see on the racks at your favorite music store). The publishing administration department may also handle the licensing of your songs in foreign territories and can arrange deals with publishers in foreign territories called foreign subpublishers.

ONE-CENT ROYALTY AND A $19 MILLION AUDIT Most of the horror stories you hear in the music business pale in comparison to what took place in the early days of rock 'n' roll. Take the Beatles, for example. If anyone should have been able to get a good deal, it's the "Fab Four" right? Wrong! In 1962, music attorneys didn't even exist. The Beatles' first recording contract with EMI called for a paltry one-cent-per-album royalty. Not 1 percent—*one cent!* And due to several one-year options contained in their contract, it wasn't until 1967 that personal manager Brian Epstein was able to renegotiate the band's record deal. To make this story even juicier, business manager Jeff Hinkle adds that in 1980, ten years after the Beatles broke up, an accounting firm was hired to audit EMI on the Beatles' behalf. The audit resulted in a settlement in the Beatles' favor of around $19 million. (You can double that amount to get an idea of the money's value in today's dollars.) If you made a list of all the rock stars who signed one-sided contracts early on in their careers, your list would read like a "who's who" of the music world. So first and foremost, be extremely careful what you sign and what you agree to when you're nobody. If you later become somebody, I guarantee you that those early deals will come back to haunt you.

However, owing to the complex nature of publishing issues, you may choose to contract with an outside publishing company (independent of the business management firm) to handle these matters instead. (Chapter 11 covers music publishing.)

HIRING YOUR BUSINESS MANAGER

Now that you have a pretty good idea about the role a business manager plays in your career, you'll wonder what the best time to employ their services is. And once you determine that you're ready for a business manager, how do you go about finding him or her? More important, what are some of the qualities to look for in a business manager?

When to Hire a Business Manager

In the early stages of your career, before you've released an album or gone out on a major tour, you can usually rely on the "per hour" services of a certified public accountant (CPA) experienced in the music business to help you file your tax returns and provide general business advice (incorporating, filing a fictitious business name statement, etc.). But once there's a substantial amount of money passing through your hands, the assistance of a business manager is necessary.

> Early in your career, a certified public accountant (CPA) may be all you need. CPAs usually charge by the hour. Rates vary depending on the experience and skill level of the individual and his or her staff. Sometimes a flat fee per tax return can be negotiated based on the complexity of your particular situation. Be sure to get referrals from people you trust, and always choose someone with experience in the music business.

Jeff Hinkle warns: "Many artists wait until the last possible minute before hiring a business manager. Usually this is done to avoid paying the business manager a commission on their first round of advances. However, this can end up costing the artist more than they save in fees. The problem with waiting is that their money is often wasted or mismanaged, and more times than not, they forget to file their tax returns. By the time the artist decides to hire a business manager, they may have already blown through the advance, but no taxes have been paid. Remember, advances are almost always taxable income in the year received. Once the delinquent tax returns are filed, the IRS adds penalties and interest to the tax bill, compounding the problem. As long as the artist hires a reputable CPA to handle tax issues in a timely manner, he or she can probably get away with waiting to hire a business manager until right before the next record is released and the tour starts."

Finding a Business Manager

Finding the right business manager may be one of the most difficult processes you experience when putting together your professional team. Why? Because unlike your personal manager or attorney, the business manager is the one person to whom you're usually giving significant control of your money! And if that doesn't sound scary enough, did you know that a business manager needs no credentials, licensing, or educational qualifications? You do need a license to give investment advice (such as the ones stock brokers have), but you'll find that most business managers don't have it—probably because they refer you to a stock broker anyway when investing in stocks. Taking all things into consideration, the best way to go about finding a business manager is usually through personal referrals from people you already know and trust.

Personal referrals from members of your professional team, such as your personal manager and attorney, are probably the most reliable source for finding a business manager. However, you may have to watch out for a potential conflict of interest here. Suppose your personal manager has three bands on his or her roster that all work with the same business manager? If you also take on the same business manager, and there's a dispute between you and your personal manager regarding money, who is your business manager going to side with? If your business manager sides with you, he or she may lose your personal manager's other artists. On the other hand, if the business manager sides with your personal manager, all he or she stands to lose is you as a client. Jeff Hinkle understands and is empathetic about how this can be a concern for the artist, but he believes that when dealing with a reputable business management firm and personal manager, it's not likely this type of conflict issue will exist. Nevertheless, to give you some peace of mind, if your personal manager or attorney refers you to a specific business manager, ask for more than a single recommendation and then be sure to meet with all of them before making your final decision. A good alternative is to ask for recommendations from other artists who are more successful than you are.

Qualities to Look for in a Business Manager

Once you have some business managers in mind and have scheduled some appointments, there are a few things you need to consider before deciding whom to hire:

Is the business manager a certified public accountant?

Being a CPA doesn't necessarily provide you with the skills to be a business manager (many great business managers aren't CPAs), but it does give you some assurance that your business manager is at least a college graduate, is board-certified, and has some organizational and accounting skills. Remember, there are no qualifications needed to be a business manager, so essentially anyone can be one.

Is the business manager part of a larger firm or a smaller firm?

Some smaller business management firms (ranging from a one- to twenty-person staff) simply don't have the same resources larger firms do. For instance, they may not have the capabilities for undertaking a royalty examination. You don't want to be with a firm that you're going to quickly outgrow. On the other hand, if you start out at a larger firm (ranging from a fifty- to one-hundred-person staff), they may have more resources, but you risk the possibility of being overshadowed by their larger, more successful clients.

Who are some of the business manager's other clients?

If you haven't heard of any of the clients the business manager represents, it may not be a good idea to go with him or her.

How long has the business manager been in business?

An established business management firm is one that has usually been in business for about ten years. That's not to imply that anyone who has been in business for less than ten years is not any good; it just means that they haven't handled as many clients and are not as experienced.

Does the business manager specialize in music?

This is perhaps one of the most important questions to consider. If the business manager handles entertainment clients in only film and television, he or she may not be right for you. Your business manager must understand the complexities of touring and royalty issues.

Does the business manager handle new and developing artists?

This is important! You want to know that this business manager has the patience and know-how to make your pennies grow into nickels and your nickels to grow into dollars.

Is the business manager approachable and pleasant?

If you can't communicate with your business manager, or if you feel uncomfortable or stupid discussing money in his or her presence, then no matter whom he or she represents, you should look for someone else to hire.

Does the business manager welcome your questions?

You want someone who's going to be helpful enough to take your calls on weekends or at home if you have an important question or concern.

Can you trust your business manager?

This is an obvious concern, but extremely important. You want a business manager who projects a genuine feeling of concern for the security of your future.

What investment strategies does the business manager have in mind for you?

As previously discussed, does the business manager have a long-term, low-risk plan, or a high-risk, short-term plan in mind for you? You probably want to look for someone who is thinking about the long term.

Is the business manager independent of the deals and investments they're putting your money into?

If the business manager owns a share in a shopping center and wants you to invest in it as well, you should be wary of his or her advice. Or if your business manager aggressively pushes you in the direction of investing in a particular stock, he or she may be getting a commission from the stock broker for making the referral.

What kind of financial reports will the business manager give you?

Will the financial reports be issued monthly? Will they be categorized in a way that is easy to read and that you can understand?

Will the business manager handle your tax returns?

Some business management firms hire outside CPAs to handle tax returns, and as a result they charge you extra. You want to know this in advance.

Is the business manager an expert in handling royalties?

Royalties from publishing and record sales can be a great source of income for you. A business manager needs to understand this very complex and detailed area to ensure that no money is lost or uncollected.

Has the business manager ever been sued before?

If there was ever a heated question with which to end, this one tops them all. It's sure to narrow down your choices, don't you think? Sharon Chambers of Down to Earth Business Management in Sherman Oaks, California, suggests, "Never be intimidated to ask this question to both the smaller and larger firms. It's often the smaller firms that get the bad rap for unscrupulous activity, but nine times out of ten it's the big firms that rip you off. The reason why you rarely hear about these cases is because they settle out of the courts. You should never prescribe to the 'the larger the firm the safer you are' way of thinking."

As you can see from this list of questions, there is a great deal to consider before hiring a business manager. Keep in mind that it may be impossible to ascertain which individual or firm is right for you in a brief, one-hour meeting. The most important thing is not to be afraid of trusting your good old gut instinct. If things don't feel right from the start, they're probably not!

IMPORTANT TERMS OF YOUR AGREEMENT

For many years, formal contracts between business managers and their clients were not standard, but this is no longer the case—at least for many firms. The basic terms of an agreement might include the payment structure, audit rights, power of attorney, and termination rights.

Payment Structure

There are three methods by which business managers are typically paid: a flat monthly retainer, an hourly fee, and a percentage of the deals negotiated.

Flat Retainer

A retainer is a fixed monthly sum that is based on the success of the client. Obviously, the more successful a client is, the more attention he or she will need. A retainer gives the client a sense of predictability regarding what they can expect to pay each month. On average, a monthly retainer can range from $500 to $3,000 for new artists, and far more for successful clients.

Hourly Fees

A straight hourly fee is just that: You're charged by the hour for your business manager's services. The hourly fee is based on the professional level of the person working with you. For instance, a file clerk can get around $30 per hour, while a partner of the firm can get up to $300 per hour or more. It's usually not possible to pay one hourly rate for everyone involved with your career, so your bill will reflect various rates and charges. For instance, during the tax season (January–April 15), you may see higher charges on your bill since the higher-level CPAs may be preparing your returns. The "by the hour" system of paying a business manager usually works best for artists making substantial sums of money. As you'll see in a minute, when you choose to pay your business manager a percentage of the deals you enter into, he or she can end up with substantially more money—especially if you're earning large sums from concert performances or publishing deals.

Percentage of the Deal

The last method of payment is for your business manager to take a percentage, typically 5 percent, of your gross income *excluding investment income, tour support, and recording "costs."* Jeff Hinkle notes: "When budgeting a tour, business management commissions can either be a percentage of the tour's gross (artist guarantees plus overages, but not production reimbursements) or a percentage of the net (total gross minus all tour expenses)." Your business manager may sometimes agree to set a cap on the amount of income he or she can earn per year. For instance, a business manager may agree to take in no more than $100,000 in commissions, and no less than $30,000. "And make sure to ask your business manager if there is a minimum requirement they must earn in order for you to stay a client," says business manager Sharon Chambers. "Some firms dump you in a year after they've commissioned your initial advances and monies from touring have slowed down."

Audit Rights

Another point that you may want to stipulate is your right to audit your business manager's books. Business managers will always allow their clients to review all financial records. That said, Jeff Hinkle adds, "It's rare that an artist will feel the need to audit their business manager. Nevertheless, an audit can actually be a healthy exercise for the artist. If anything, they'll get a greater appreciation for what the business manager does by seeing that everything is in order. And in the worst-case scenario, if the business manager is up to no good, an audit may help reveal whose pockets the artist's money has been going into. The stories you often hear of unscrupulous business managers, personal managers, attorneys, or whoever else ripping off unsuspecting artists occur when the artist allows one person to have too much control over their career and finances without having any checks and balances. *The artist must always pay attention to what's going on around him or her, and not get caught up in the whole fantasy of being a star"* [my emphasis].

Power of Attorney

Power of attorney simply grants another person "the right to act for you." Jeff Hinkle says, "Generally, all we ask for is what is called a limited power of attorney for handling certain IRS matters (like representing you in tax audits) and signing bills on your behalf (when you're out on the road and too busy to deal with this matter). Always think twice about what rights you grant under a power of attorney, and think three times—no four—about granting someone full power of attorney—or you might find someone buying a home or financing new automobiles using your money without you knowing about it. Remember, your business manager should only have a limited power of attorney, with what rights you're giving him or her clearly stipulated in writing."

The Right to Terminate

Last, but not least, in all relationships between a business manager and client, the client must have the right to terminate at will. It's your responsibility to be aware of your finances at all times! Stay involved with what your business manager is doing. Examine the monthly reports he or she sends you, ask questions, and listen to your business manager's advice. If you suddenly snap out of rock stardom and realize that you're running out of money due to excess spending or neglect of your finances, the only person to blame is yourself. No one should care more about your future than you!

HOW TO SELF-MANAGE YOUR PERSONAL FINANCES AND LIFE

✦ Determine your exact monthly expenses (rent, car insurance, phone, food, health insurance, Internet) and decide on what expenditures you can really do without.

✦ Set your sights on earning twice as much as your expenses. You might not be able to accomplish this, but you can at least push for this!

✦ Don't "fake it till you make it." In other words, don't live above your means. You can find ways to make a good impression by shopping around for great deals, buying secondhand, etc., without putting yourself in debt.

✦ Keep track of your bills. Pay your bills on time to avoid paying late fees, and always check your bills for accuracy—even major corporations make mistakes!

✦ Watch your money daily. Keep track of what you're spending your money on and what's in your checking account. You can balance your checkbook the old-fashioned way (using the register your bank gives you) or by learning to use financial software programs like Quicken.

✦ Find ways to limit "necessary" expenses: Reduce monthly banking fees by limiting ATM use, finding a bank that offers free checking, raising your car insurance deductible, shopping around for long distance and cell phone rates, moving into a smaller apartment or getting a roommate, packing a lunch, and drinking at home instead of drinking in a bar (that is, if drinking is really necessary).

✦ Pay off your credit cards in full each month to avoid paying interest charges, and consider using convenient secure cards (i.e., cards in which your limits are pre-deposited into an account so that you'll never find yourself in debt).

✦ If you're in debt, make it a priority to start getting out now. There is nothing that weighs on your mental well-being more than worrying about money. Check out the Internet for advice, or speak with your local bank or personal accountant.

✦ Don't borrow money unless you absolutely have to. If you're trying to fund your next recording project, get creative. Set up a barter deal with a local producer in which he/she records you for free in return for playing on his/her other sessions for free.

✦ Save some amount of money each month. No matter how little it is, save something!

✦ Speak to your bank about opening a low-risk, high-interest certificate of deposit (CD) account. CDs usually start as low as $1,000 with a minimum of one- to three-month terms and allow you the flexibility of withdrawing money if you absolutely have to.

✦ Save all of your business-related receipts, and file them in separate envelopes by the month. If you're really good, also separate them in various categories like gas, auto repairs, entertainment and meal receipts, business phone charges, subscriptions, and union dues. These may help you save money when doing your taxes.

✦ Read motivational and business books like *Think and Grow Rich* by Napoleon Hill, *The Money Book for the Young, Fabulous, and Not Broke* by Suze Orman, and *Get a Financial Life* by Beth Kobliner, or take a class on bookkeeping or money management at a local college.

✦ Find a good CPA experienced in the music business by using referrals from people you trust.

CHAPTER 8

Your Talent Agent

"Ten percent of zero is zero"

—THE LATE IAN COPELAND (founder, Frontier Booking International)

Talent agents are on the minds of almost every developing band and solo artist. After all, talent agents are those industry professionals ready to help you (and anyone else) get really cool gigs and tours all over the country. Right? Well, not exactly. . . .

Most talent agents with clout focus only on clients who are already generating substantial live performance fees, drawing large local crowds, or getting attention from labels and publishers. Surely, you can always find persons known as "local and regional bookers" willing to work with you on a monthly fee basis or "pay to play" system (where you have to buy and pre-sell tickets), but these folks are not to be confused with professional talent agents working with well-established agencies.

While the best game plan for you right now may be to continue booking and promoting your own live performances (see the box "How to Be Your Own Booking Agent" at the end of the chapter), the day will eventually come when a talent agent's services are in order. Therefore, you need to understand what a talent agent does, when to hire one, what qualities to look for, and what agreement terms are standard before your career takes off. So, pull out a yellow highlighter pen and get ready to mark this section up.

Note: A significant portion of this chapter includes excerpts from a candid one-on-one interview I conducted with the late Ian Copeland (founder of Frontier Booking International). His contribution to the world of touring and the music business will always be valued.

THE ROLE OF AN AGENT IN YOUR CAREER

Agents are not to be confused with personal managers. By definition, the role of an agent is to *procure employment*, whereas the personal manager's role is to *advise and counsel* the artist. Personal managers assist you in everything from defining your public image to targeting your demographic audience. Agents secure bookings for you in concert settings, as well as in television, motion pictures, commercial work (for those of you who wish to be actors), and in literary work (for those of you who wish to write books and screenplays). Live performances and touring are the talent agent's primary realms in the music business.

Formulating Your Tour Strategy

After your career has advanced to the point of signing with a talent agency, the first thing that happens is your personal manager (who is almost definitely on your team at this point) and your talent agent come together to formulate your tour strategy. The issues they discuss may include (1) whether you should tour by yourself or open for another artist, (2) what band you should open for, (3) how much you should charge for tickets, and (4) when and where you should tour.

However, Ian Copeland (whose Frontier Booking represented Sting, the Police, R.E.M., No Doubt, and the Red Hot Chili Peppers) noted in an interview that a personal manager and agent can sit down and talk until they're blue in their faces, but a lot of what's discussed may never pan out. The reality is that your agent has to get on the phone with concert promoters around the country and test the waters. Your agent must first determine whether there's a real interest in your band.

As Copeland put it: "It's like an army discussing its plans for going into battle with an enemy they can't see yet. You have to survey the terrain and figure out from where they're going to be shooting at you. Once this is determined, you can begin matching your plans with actual reality. This is an important point for your readers to keep in mind while reading this chapter."

Packaging the Artist

Another important responsibility handled by your agent involves packaging. Packaging is the process of matching different bands with similar styles and demographic appeals for a concert tour. In other words, if you're in a metal band, it's probably not in your best interest to be touring with a country artist, and vice versa for the country artist. Careful consideration is required here, especially for a new group still trying to establish its "brand name" or identity in the marketplace.

While there may seem to be a basic logic that goes along with packaging, individual bands and agents are going to have significantly different ideas. Some agents have a very strict conservative approach, while others have a looser game plan. The truth is that no one really knows what will and won't work. For instance, it was the incredibly varied lineup that made Lollapalooza (a concert festival conceptualized by Perry Farrell of Jane's Addiction) so popular. The 1997 lineup consisted of Snoop Doggy Dog, Tool, Korn, Prodigy, and Devo—everything from rap to alternative to metal to techno to new wave. It brought different audiences together and exposed fans to music that they might not otherwise have listened to.

Ian Copeland had this to add: "The Police, whose music was basically rock 'n' roll, desired to tour with punk bands because they wanted to be a part of that movement. At the time, which was around 1978, most people in America really didn't even know what punk was. But it didn't matter! The tour went over great! Although there's a common sense rationale that goes along with packaging, sometimes you just have to push that envelope and try new things."

Determining Whether to Open or Headline

Sometimes your agent may determine that it's better for you not to open for anyone at all but to go out as the headlining act. Opening slots aren't easy to get, but when the opportunity comes along, you definitely don't want to settle for opening for a group whose audience isn't right for your music. Most record companies are usually horrified, however, by the idea of a new band headlining their own club tour. They'd rather have you go out as the support act for a major group in larger venues no matter what band you're opening for. The theory is that if your band plays in front of a larger audience, you'll sell more records.

But Ian Copeland noted that there are five major disadvantages to going out as a support act:

1. You're going to end up with a limited use of the stage because the headlining act won't strike their drum set.
2. Because you're crammed at the front of the stage, you're going to end up with a limited use of the lights.
3. Your volume is not going to be as strong as you'd like because the headlining act is going to limit the amount of power you'll have over the PA system.
4. Because you'll only have a limited time to play, your set list will consist of about six or seven songs you'll have to perform early in the evening while everyone is still on their way to the venue. And if this weren't bad enough . . .
5. The audience members who are already seated have probably never heard of your band anyway and are somewhat annoyed by you because you're making them wait for the group they really came out to see.

In Ian Copeland's experience, a band gets much better exposure and can make a better impression by headlining smaller clubs. Although you're playing in front of smaller audiences, the people who come out—from the fans to the publicists to the radio station personnel—are specifically coming out to see you. You own the show! This provides you with the opportunity to really connect with your audience and slowly but surely win over a grassroots following of loyal fans. From there, you can work your way up to playing two nights in the same club, to playing larger rooms, performing in theaters, and, eventually, to playing stadiums. "But it's always a fight with the record companies to take this approach," says Copeland. "It's the same way they run their companies—they're worried about quarterly reports and quick results. If the artist fails to measure up, the label is on to the next act. They'd rather see a new group support a totally inappropriate band in stadiums than to see them headlining clubs in front of a few die-hard fans that really want to be at your show."

Routing the Tour

Routing a tour is exactly what it sounds like. Your agent helps route or map out the direction your tour will take, what venues you'll be playing, and when you'll be expected to perform. This information is then forwarded to you in an itinerary.

When you're the support act for a major artist, you won't have much say in the routing of your tour—you're told when to show up, and you'd better be there. However, when you're going out as the headlining act, your personal manager needs to supply your talent agent with as much information as possible before your agent can begin molding the tour. This information might include the following:

+ When your record is coming out
+ Where your single is getting airplay
+ Where your records are selling the most units
+ When you want to tour
+ Where you want to tour
+ How many months you want to tour
+ How many consecutive nights the singer can handle performing

Agents must take many factors into consideration when routing a tour. For instance, your agent understands that the most strategic time to tour is in the spring and the summer months (when kids are on spring break or out of school) and that the worst time to tour is during the winter months (when snow is on the ground and traveling is more treacherous). But more important, your agent must make sure to route a tour with the least amount of distance between each performance. If possible, a tour should never be routed to backtrack and recross old ground. Even when you're successful and can afford to fly between performances, your agent must consider the road crew that hauls the equipment from one show to the next. If there's too much distance between venues, the road crew may be late setting up the production—and shows may be canceled. And canceled shows make for unhappy fans.

Ian Copeland felt that there really is no set method for the way a tour is routed: "I may get a call from a band in England that gives me no other information than that they want to tour the United States. I then make a few calls, put together thirty or forty dates, arrange them in some sensible order, and then fax an itinerary back to the band. Either they'll think it's great, or they'll get back to me with a number of concerns. They may want fewer consecutive shows in the beginning of the tour, when the singer is still trying to get his voice in shape, or they may want fewer shows at the end of the tour, when the singer's voice is beginning to burn out. I then go back and begin to reformulate the tour from there. So as you can see, the process in which tours are routed and itineraries are established can vary considerably."

Pricing the Artist

When you're the headlining act of a tour, your agent is responsible for determining the ticket price for your show as well. Determining the ticket price for a live performance begins with your agent contacting concert promoters and getting a sense of the marketplace. Although it may seem that the main goal is to get the highest price possible, you don't want to set it so high that you turn people away. Your agent must therefore take on the role of investigator and learn what similarly popular bands are charging for a performance and how well their tickets are selling. And if a similarly popular band had charged a different price for its performance, would its sales have been even better?

Ian Copeland said that pricing the artist has a great deal to do with the style of music they perform and the demographic audience they attract. If you're a classy band whose music caters primarily to an adult audience, you can get away with charging a higher ticket price. If you're a metal act that attracts a younger audience, you have to charge a much lower ticket price, or no one will be able afford to attend. As Ian Copeland put it, "It's all about determining what the consumer is willing to pay and can afford to pay for a product. If you're selling beer, you might only charge four dollars because that's what people expect to pay. But if you're selling cognac, you can get away with charging much more as long as it's high quality, because people won't care what it costs."

Determining When to Put Tickets on Sale

Agents are also responsible for determining the best time to put your concert tickets on sale. Although your agent's plan will vary from city to city, the key is not to put them on sale either too far in advance or too close to the day of the show. If you put the tickets on sale early, you have more time to monitor sales and add another show if you're selling out a specific market. The downside is that you have to commit to a consistent level of advertising over the long haul or the audience may simply forget about your show. On the other hand, if you put your tickets on sale too close to the day of performance, you obviously won't have as much time to devote to promotion. It's a fine balance and requires thoughtful planning and research on the part of your agent.

To avoid direct competition for the consumer's dollar, your agent must also be careful not to put your tickets on sale on or around the same day as another major act. The strategically minded agent may even try to beat another group to the punch by purposely scheduling an earlier sales date. "Sometimes, it's a lot of butting heads with other agents," says Ian Copeland. "If two different agents representing different artists want [tickets for their shows] to go on sale on a particular date, and neither of them wants to let the other go first, the tickets will end up coming out on the same day. But this is rare. Usually things get worked out."

Negotiating Live Performance Deals

In the early stages of your career, when you're the support act for other artists, your compensation may consist of whatever the headlining act wants to offer, which may not amount to very much. Even when going out on your own and headlining small clubs, there may still be little room for negotiation at first. In any case, what generally happens when you're determining your fee for a live performance is that your agent must first determine what's called the "gross potential" of the venue. To simplify, once your agent and the promoter determine the ticket price they can charge for the artist, the agent multiplies this price by the capacity of the venue.

For instance, if the average price of a ticket is $20 and the venue holds 500 people, the gross potential for the show would be $10,000 ($20 x 500 = $10,000). The agent and the promoter then negotiate backward from this price until it makes sense for all parties involved to put on the show. (**Note:** The various methods by which you're paid for a live performance, as well as how these deals are negotiated, are covered in Chapter 12.)

Ian Copeland felt that the negotiation process is really where your agent's skill comes into play. He or she must try to get the promoter to pay more money than your band is actually worth, but not so much that the promoter never wants you back again. It's important to understand that although your agent ultimately works for you, in a sense he or she also works for the promoter. In other words, once your band plays a venue and moves on to the next city, your agent must continue to book other acts in that very same room and needs to deal with the very same promoter. This also works in reverse. The promoter knows that the reputable agent books a number of viable touring acts and will therefore work hard at preserving his or her relationship with the agent.

Collecting Deposits

Besides negotiating live performance deals with promoters, your agent is responsible for collecting a deposit to ensure that you're not screwed out of what the promoter promises you. Most typically, the agent collects 50 percent of the negotiated fee for a performance, usually thirty days in advance of the show.

But Ian Copeland pointed out that, while this is the standard protocol in the business, the amount of money the talent agent can collect depends on his or her negotiating power. When dealing with Sting, Ian collected 100 percent of the money in advance—no questions asked! In fact, this held true for Copeland when booking any band in foreign territories.

Whatever the amount of the deposit, *it is held by your agent on your behalf until after you perform the gig*. Before this, you must be clear that your deposit remains the property of the promoter until the contract for a performance is consummated. After the show, the agent then subtracts his commission and forwards the rest to your business manager.

Hall Fees

Hall fees are discussed in more detail in Chapter 13, but generally they deal with a commission (or fee) the venue (or hall) charges merchandisers for selling your T-shirts, hats, posters, and other goods. Percentages range from 30 to 40 percent of the gross sales. Note that the talent agent does not share in a percentage of your merchandising incomes, so it does no good for him or her to negotiate one way or another. Nevertheless, agents are usually pretty good at reducing merchandising charges. More on this later.

HIRING YOUR AGENT

So at what point should you think about hiring an agent? And if you are going to hire one, where should you look, and what qualities should you look for?

When to Hire an Agent

As already suggested, if you're in a new band that's playing around town, trying to build a local following and looking for a record deal, you're a long way from needing an agent. At this stage of your career you'll be better served by picking up the phone and doing exactly what you're already doing— *booking gigs yourself!* No matter what anyone tries to tell you, the simple truth is that until you've built up a decent following and can generate reasonable fees for your live performance, you're simply not worth an agent's time.

In any case, *talent agents of any caliber usually deal only with promoters on a national level anyway*. Of course talent agents can deal with the very same clubs that you're playing in your own hometown, but this usually only happens when he or she has an artist passing through on a national tour. Keeping you busy for months on end in a local setting is simply not what a professional agent does.

The best time to begin looking for a talent agent is when you're getting signed to a record deal and a tour seems imminent. "But on the other hand," noted Ian Copeland, "some bands will specifically go out on the road for the very purpose of getting a record deal! Take the Police, for example. Although the band already had a deal with A&M Records in England, there were no plans for the label to license the band's album in the United States. I purposely brought the Police over from England to get A&M's offices in the U.S. excited. Although my brother Miles [the band's manager] had to borrow money for airfare and start-up expenses, and the band had to travel with one crew member and sleep in a passenger van that hauled all of the equipment, it was all worth it in the end! A&M was blown away by the band's live performances and decided to release and promote the Police in the States. So as you can see, in some circumstances the talent agent can also get involved with a band before they have a record deal. But in the most typical scenario, I'll have to agree that the agent comes aboard right at the time, or around the time, a band gets a deal."

> In major cities such as L.A., you will find some local agents for unsigned, original bands who can help you get gigs, but if you don't heavily promote your shows and get people to pay an admission at the door, these agents won't be interested in working with you. Check out Sean Healey Presents, at www. webookbands.com.

Hooking Up With a Talent Agency

There are typically three methods by which an artist and a professional talent agency come together: (1) The record company, for which an artist or band is signed, makes suggestions and referrals, (2) an agency initiates a meeting with an artist once he or she is signed, and (3) the band or personal manager utilizes a number of available resources.

> Under newer structures of record deals, the label may even have its own booking division. Will this mean you'll have no choice in your agent? Things are likely already worked out by the time you're reading this, but stay tuned.

The Record Company Makes Referrals

More often than not, once your band is signed to a record company, the label already has a pretty good idea of what agency they'd like to see representing you. They may even go so far as initiating the first meeting between the agency and your personal manager. Ultimately, the final decision is up to you, but the record company has a lot of influence over who will end up representing your career. Keep in mind that the record company usually pays for your first tour by advancing you start-up money in the form of something called tour support. Although you're responsible for paying this money back from royalties you earn from future record sales (I'll discuss this in more detail in Chapter 10), the label still wants to make sure that it's going to get the most out of its initial investment.

Talent Agencies Initiate Meetings

In some cases, the talent agency itself will be the first party to seek you out. As soon as a band with any amount of buzz gets signed, you can be sure that the agencies will start calling—especially the larger ones. This is what's called a lazy campaign. A more aggressive campaign consists of agents actually hanging out in clubs every night and keeping their eyes and ears peeled for new and promising bands. Some agents may even go as far as keeping in touch with what's going on in foreign territories.

Ian Copeland often received phone calls from his connections in England to alert him of any band that appeared to be unstoppable. Copeland was into cutting-edge music and was particularly fond of the punk revolution in London, which had not yet caught on in the United States. When he'd get a call about a band, Copeland would get on a plane, check the group out, and sign them before any other agency could. Squeeze is a classic example of one such band Copeland signed.

The Band or Personal Manager Utilizes Available Resources

Often, a band or its personal manager has to be the aggressor in finding an agent. First, he may make the rounds at all the major agencies like ICM, CAA, and the William Morris Agency. Second, he might conduct a more thorough search by contacting other personal managers in the business and asking for recommendations. And finally, the manager may refer to one of the many resources available on the market today, such as the *Booking Agency Directory* (www.pollstar.com)—a biennial magazine listing practically every agency, its roster of artists, and the names of the agents who work for the agency, or *The Musician's Atlas* (www.musiciansatlas.com)—another valuable resource loaded with agent information. Whatever you use, it's highly advisable for both you and your manager to spend some time looking over the information. From here, you can start contacting various agencies and setting up appointments. But with so many agencies to choose from, how do you really know who's going to be the best one to represent you? Read on.

Qualities to Look for in an Agent and Agency

While it's typically the personal manager who spends the most time working together with the agent (your relationship is usually limited to hanging out after your shows), it's important to understand what qualities to look for in a potential agent and agency. After all, it is your career we're talking about here. Here are a few questions to consider.

Is the Agent Part of a Specialized Agency or a Full-Service Agency?

Some agents specialize in only booking musical acts, or even more specifically, booking musical acts of one genre. A full-service agency, on the other hand, has a broader range of services, representing actors in television, motion pictures, and commercial work, as well as representing producers, directors, writers, and editors. This can be useful to artists who have multiple interests and talents. However, you should never choose one agency over another because they promise to make you a movie star. More often than not, this prospect is only used as a sales pitch to get you to sign with their company.

Does Your Agent Represent a Small Agency?

A smaller agency might be exactly what you need in the early stages of your career. There won't be many bands to compete with on the agency's roster, and you'll probably get individualized treatment. A smaller agency, however, may be limited in the scope of services it provides and in some cases will not have the level of clout and power you need to get into certain venues or on certain tours. You always want to make sure the agency is experienced in negotiating venue expenses like rent, ticket commissions, and merchandising deals. If you're a headlining act, your agent must be experienced at handling these business issues to ensure that you get the best revenue per show. Smaller agencies may not have this experience.

Does Your Agent Represent One of the Larger Agencies?

Larger agencies usually have a broad range of services, as well as the clout needed to get you the best gigs and tours. Concert promoters around the country know that larger agencies represent a number of money-making clients and therefore work harder at preserving their relationships with them. Promoters may even be more willing to "play" young and developing artists like you, knowing that once you're in demand and successful, it's likely they'll have an ongoing relationship with you. The downside of being with a larger agency, though, is that you run the risk of being overshadowed by other artists the agency represents who are more successful and established than you.

Does Your Agent Represent Other Artists Whose Music Is Similar to Yours?

If you're a rock band, it may not be in your best interest to be represented by an agency that only handles new-age artists. But what happens when a new-age agency, for instance, is planning to open up a rock department, and you're the first rock band it wants to sign? Although it may be easy to conclude that you're going to get specialized attention, Ian Copeland warned that you never want to be the guinea pig at any agency, no matter how hard it may try to sell you on the idea.

Is Your Agent Excited About the Style of Music You Perform?

Your agent's enthusiasm for your music will greatly affect how hard he or she will fight for you—both for better gigs and better money. No matter how reputable the agent is, or the agency he or she represents, you want someone who seems genuinely concerned about furthering your career. Ian Copeland felt that this is one of the most important points to consider when choosing an agent. "An agent who has real passion for an artist can make a huge difference," said Copeland. "It can sometimes mean the difference between an artist succeeding and failing. In an ideal situation, the agent should be just as enthusiastic, if not more enthusiastic, about your music than you are. Make sure your agent is someone that's willing to kill for you and not just some person blowing smoke up your ass so you'll sign with their agency."

Will the Agent with Whom You're Meeting Be Your "Responsible" Agent?

It's extremely important that the person with whom you initially meet is the person who will be your responsible agent and not just the person who wines and dines you and gets you interested in signing with his or her firm. Your responsible agent is the key person who will serve as the liaison between you and the rest of the agency and who will do the bulk of the work. Your responsible agent must have the ability to keep everyone within the agency motivated and interested in developing your career.

Where Does Your Agent Stand in the Hierarchy of the Agency?

Is your agent at the bottom rung of the agency ladder or does he or she actually have a position of power and strength? Agencies usually assign specific geographical regions, styles of music, and size of venues in which each of its agents must be responsible. "It's great if the agent who's meeting with you has come out to eighteen of your shows and thinks the world of you," noted Ian Copeland, "but if the territories he or she handles [are] North and South Dakota, you'd better hope the agents handling the East and West Coast also think you're the shit! That said, keep in mind that when signing with a talent agent, you're also signing with an agency consisting of several other agents who will be working on your career. It's important that you're confident [about] everyone's enthusiasm and ability to represent you."

How Long Has Your Agent Been a Part of the Agency He or She Represents?

Is your agent known for jumping from one agency to the next? Does the agency itself have a high turnover rate? If so, you should perhaps be concerned with whether your agent's days are numbered with a particular agency. Once you establish a good working relationship with a certain person, the last thing you want is to lose continuity by having to reestablish what you've already worked hard to build, or in the worst case, get stuck with someone at the agency who's not as enthusiastic about working with you. This is one reason why it's important to get something called a "key person" provision in your agreement with an agency. A key person clause stipulates that if your agent leaves or is fired, you have the right to terminate your agreement with the agency and follow along with him or her.

What Ideas Does Your Agent Have About How You Should Be Packaged with Other Artists?

As I've pointed out, this is an extremely important consideration. The band that you're opening for is a much more important factor in terms of getting your music to the right audience than, for instance, the size of the crowd for which you're playing. If you're a new rock band, and your agent wants to package you with a pop band from the '80s, you may have a problem.

Does Your Agent Display an Open-mindedness About How He or She Will Try to Break Your Career?

In other words, does the agency's plan for you seem to be centered on getting you on tour with its major acts? If this is the case, you should be put off. It only displays your agent's lack of creativity and enthusiasm in finding new ways to break your career. "And more times than not," added Ian Copeland, "you're not going to get on the major support slots anyway. There's probably twenty other new bands signed to the agency who have all been promised the same thing. Some may even be selling more records than you. What's more, the agent isn't the only person responsible for making the decision regarding who will end up on an opening slot of a tour. The headlining act itself is very influential, and so are the record companies. Your agent must have the patience to help you work your way up through the marketplace and rally everyone involved—from the other agents to your record company—to stick with you over the long haul."

Do You Like the Demeanor Your Agent Projects?

Your agent is the person who sells you to potential buyers. You want to know that he or she is going to be aggressive enough to get you the best deals and tours. But while this is an important attribute to look for, Ian Copeland advised, "You want to know that your agent is going to have enough tact and salesmanship to handle business in a way that won't be damaging to your career. You don't want a bully handling your business. As the saying goes, you can get more bees with honey than you can with vinegar. Another important consideration to look for is, while you don't need an agent who's going to be your best buddy, you want someone who is going to be cool enough to hang out with you backstage after your shows. Bottom line: You don't want an asshole representing your career."

Can You Trust Your Agent?

Not only is it important to feel that your agent believes in you and will work hard for your career, but it's also important that you trust that your agent will not participate in unethical behavior. For instance, an unscrupulous agent may promise you one rate for a live performance and then sell you for a much higher rate and pocket the difference. This kind of thing can easily happen if you only see the contracts between you and the agent and not the contracts between the promoter and the agent. The bottom line is that it's in your best interest to keep both eyes open at all times.

TERMS OF THE AGREEMENT

As with any business relationship, there are specific terms in your talent agency agreement about which you need to be extremely clear. These are the agent's fee, exclusivity, the scope of the agreement, the territory, and duration and termination.

The Agent's Fee

Before discussing your agent's fee, it's important to note that many states regulate the licensing of anyone who engages in the occupation of procuring, offering, promising, or attempting to procure employment for an artist. In California (arguably, the entertainment capital), an agent must file detailed applications, submit affidavits from two reputable persons asserting the agent's good moral character, post a bond, and have all contract forms between the agent and client approved by the California state labor commissioner.

In approving forms for representation between agents and artists, as noted by attorney Richard Schulenberg in his book *Legal Aspects of the Music Industry*, the state labor commissioner limits agents' fees, in most cases, to no more than a 10 percent commission—except under certain personal appearance situations by jurisdiction of the American Federation of Musicians (AFM). The AFM and American Federation of Television and Radio Artists (AFTRA) unions only seek the representation of "franchised agents" (i.e., those agents who abide by certain union regulations.) One such regulation by the unions is that the talent agencies only use union approved contracts. These contracts usually limit the agent's commission to 10 percent (see Chapter 3 for information about unions).

Agents earn a commission on incomes from live performances, tour sponsorships, and the work they may generate for you in television and motion pictures. *Watch out for the agent who will try to earn a commission from your record royalties and publishing—this is not an industry standard*. It's also important to make sure that your agent is not charging you any hidden fees. For instance, some agents may try to charge you for making telephone calls and mailing out contracts. Make sure that your agent's 10 percent commission covers everything.

Exclusivity

When you take on a talent agent, he or she will typically want to have an exclusive agreement with you. This means another agent cannot book you during the term of your agreement. You will also be required to inform your agent of all offers made to you personally. Note that the exclusivity clause is a standard in most agency agreements. It would be unfair to assume that your agent should put his or her time into booking you if another agent is doing the same thing. Note that there is an exception in cases where you're able to restrict your agent from booking certain territories, as you will see in a moment.

The Scope of the Agreement

As discussed at the beginning of this chapter, the bulk of your agent's job is to book you for live performances and tours. Nevertheless, most talent agencies will also want the rights to book you in a variety of other areas, including the following:

- ✦ Film (for those inclined to make it to the silver screen)
- ✦ Television (for the "prime time" star in you)
- ✦ Commercials (for the perfect spokesperson)
- ✦ Literary (for those inclined to write a book)

If you're just a rock star and not an actor or writer, you may be happy to have someone who at least promises you the possibility of work in other areas. However, your decision to work with an agency should not be based on this promise. What's more, if you truly believe that you have a chance at a career separate from the music business, or if you have talent in acting or writing, then you'll want another agency that specifically deals with those careers.

When you're an artist being wooed by several agencies because you've got a record coming out and you're the new hot buzz on the streets, all of the larger agencies are going to tell you that they can get you into the movies as a way of getting you to sign with them. They're going to tell you that they represent the biggest directors and producers and that you've got a really good chance at expanding your career horizons. Ian Copeland said that all the different departments at an agency are so separate from each other that they may never come together under one plan of attack for your career; there's no coordination between one agent and the next. Unless you're talking about a major star, it's rarely the case that a musical artist gets the big acting role, commercial, or spokesmodel endorsement for a cosmetic line. And if it happens, it's usually self-generated. In other words, someone will call the agency specifically requesting you. "And I bet you can guess who will then turn around and take the credit for finding you the work: the agency," said Copeland.

"An agency should be run the way doctors' offices are run," Copeland continued. "A general doctor meets with his or her patients and then refers them to a specialist when needed. It would be ridiculous, to say the least, to have one doctor asking for the rights to take care of all aspects of your health. The best advice an honest agent can give a client is to separate [the client's] music career from other endeavors. It's my belief that an agent who's not honest enough to tell you this is simply greedy and only wants more control of your career."

The Territory

Your agent will want the worldwide rights to represent you as well. However, in some cases, you may be able to limit you agent's control over certain territories. For instance, you might be able to limit your agent's control to the United States only and thus be able to contract with agents overseas who are more experienced with handling these areas. Ian Copeland advised that you should always try to hold on to your rights when it comes to booking outside of the states. Although your agency may have affiliations in foreign markets, they may not be the best people to represent you. If you can hold on to your rights, it's likely you'll begin touring the states anyway, and by the time you get to playing overseas, you'll have had the chance to see how your agent performs. Either you'll be confident in their connections abroad, or you can make the rounds of the various agencies yourself and find someone you want to represent you there.

HOW TO BE YOUR OWN BOOKING AGENT

Until you can successfully build a buzz and command "healthy" fees for your live performances, getting a talent agent is unlikely. Therefore, here are a few tips on how to do it yourself:

✦ Put together a list of venues you intend to target in your town and surrounding territories and include the bookers' names, addresses, e-mails, and phone numbers. Start with resources like *The Musician's Atlas* (www.musiciansatlas.com).

✦ Call or e-mail the booker with a clear idea of your style and the dates you'd like to perform. Bookers are busy people, so be patient, but pleasantly persistent.

✦ Keep good records of all correspondences. You don't want to call back a booker in a week when he or she advised you to call back in a month.

✦ Be prepared to mail the booker a press kit or to e-mail him or her a link to a website where music, bios, and biographical information can be reviewed. Sites like MySpace (www.myspace.com) or Sonicbids (www.sonicbids.com) come in handy.

✦ Let the booker know you're available to fill in for cancellations. It might also help to have two sets' worth of material prepared in case you're asked to perform longer.

✦ Understand the deal structures of clubs in your area: You'll either be asked to play for free, receive a percentage of the door, or to buy and then "pre-sell" tickets. Whatever your deal structure, get all terms in writing and understand everything you sign.

✦ Limit the frequency of your performances to no more than two gigs per month within a thirty-mile area. You don't want to oversaturate the marketplace.

✦ Consider alternate venues like colleges: Organizations like the National Association for Campus Activities (NACA) (www.naca.org) can really help. Also, consider playing youth centers, house concerts, bookstores, and art galleries.

✦ Promote your gigs well, making every show a huge event. Remember that moving up in the club circuit is not just about how good you are but about how many people you can draw.

Duration and Termination

The typical term of an agreement between an agent and client is usually three to five years. However, it's not uncommon to negotiate for a shorter term, such as one year. Note that in the contract forms approved by the state labor commissioner, as well as the contract forms used by the unions, there is a clause that states that if your agent does not get you work (or an offer of work) within a specified period of time (ninety days in the state of California), you may have the right to terminate your agreement.

It's also wise to have a key person clause in your agreement with an agency. As previously mentioned, a key person clause gives you the right to terminate your agreement with an agency should your responsible agent be fired or leave the agency. This prevents the possibility of your being passed around the agency from one agent to the next or being stuck with an agent who is not enthusiastic about working with you.

Ian Copeland summed up his overall view on agency agreements this way: "Most agencies will tell you that you must sign a written agreement with them at the beginning of your relationship. But if you have any bargaining power at all, you may want to consider not signing anything at all. Think about it. There's no reason why an agency should ask you to sign a contract with them, because the truth is, the agency works for you. Tell them that you'll be loyal to them till the end of the earth as long as they're delivering 'the goods,' but if they're not delivering, you don't want some loophole in a contract that [prevents] you from moving on."

Furthermore, Copeland stated, "From the artist's perspective, I can't see one benefit of why they should sign an agreement with an agency. You already know that by law an agent can't take any more than a 10 percent commission. You also know that a key person clause is just a means to get out of your contract if your responsible agent leaves or is fired—but if you have no contract, you don't need a key person clause. If an agent adamantly insists you sign an agreement with them, could it suggest they're not confident you're going to stay with them? Assuming it does, then you better consider looking for an agent elsewhere."

CHAPTER 9

Your **Record** **Producer**

"Where business, commerce, and art all meet
at the same intersection."
—ED CHERNEY

The most important thing to you as a solo artist or band is the music you create. You spend months, if not years, formulating a distinctive sound and style before recording your first album. All the hard work you've put into creating a unique, original sound, however, may not be enough to create a successful record. Producing a great album is an art form in itself and it requires the assistance of an experienced professional producer. The right collaboration can take you to creative places you never imagined, but the wrong one can be a nightmare whose implications are far-reaching. Understanding what producers do, when their involvement may begin, how they are selected and hired, and the method by which they are typically paid is vital information you can't afford to miss.

THE ROLE OF A RECORD PRODUCER IN YOUR CAREER

If there were but one phrase to sum up the role of the record producer in your career, perhaps it would be this: "guardian of the recording process," which, depending on your career level, could mean any or all of the following:

+ Helping the artist select the best songs to record, arranging these compositions, and even co-writing and composing complete works.
+ Gathering specific considerations about the artist and musicians (like whether they're comfortable recording with a click reference or comfortable recording in isolated and more restrictive conditions) to determine the best recording approach.

- Helping the artist get the most out of each studio performance . . . "Even to the point of frustration if necessary," adds Geoff Emerick, producer/engineer for the Beatles, Paul McCartney, and Elvis Costello in Howard Massey's book *Behind the Glass*.
- Dealing strategically with the various personalities within a band to keep the environment in the studio productive and creative. Geza X, producer for Black Flag, says, "Playing the role [of a record producer] means being part psychologist, part babysitter, and part social engineer."

> The key to a successful record is to first and foremost have quality songs and the best recorded vocal performance of those songs. The producer must do everything to ensure that both of these elements are in place.

- Making sure that artist's work sounds current in the marketplace—and even several years after its release. Stevie Wonder's record *Songs in the Key of Life*, for instance, still sounds fresh and original thirty years later, as does Nirvana's *Nevermind*.
- Helping the artist bring his or her vision to life and knowing when to stay out of the way. Steve Churchyard, producer for the Pretenders and INXS, says, "As a producer, it's my job to make the artist's dream a reality and actually make it better than the dream."
- Delivering a product that can be commercially successful in the marketplace. Ed Cherney, producer for the Rolling Stones and Bob Dylan, says, "You're going in to represent what the artist is doing, to be as honest as you can, and to hope for the best—hopefully making something where business and commerce and art meet at the same intersection."
- Putting together a recording budget and making sure the recording project stays within its budget and schedule.
- Handling administrative duties associated with recording a record, such as making sure samples are cleared and filing union contracts.

PULLING RABBITS OUT OF HATS

To illustrate one of the many roles a producer must play, in his book *Free at Last* (SAF Publishing), Steven Rosen spoke with legendary producer Eddie Kramer about his magical work with the classic rock band Bad Company. Kramer said: "We didn't have many recording effects in the studio at our disposal, so when the band wanted a swirling or tremolo effect for one of their recordings, I tied a couple of microphones together and spun them around in the air. It actually worked great! Sometimes you just have to try anything to get the right sound on tape." Another Kramer experience involved the late, great Jimi Hendrix. For the intro to the song "Cross Town Traffic," the artist imagined a sound he couldn't quite explain. Musician and producer put their heads together and finally came up with something simple—Hendrix blowing through a comb covered in tissue paper (creating a kazoo sound). Hey, whatever works! To hear this effect, check out Hendrix's classic record *Electric Ladyland*.

When a Producer's Involvement Begins

A record producer's involvement in your career may begin at a number of junctures. Some of the more common ones start out as the barter system deal, the do-it-yourself deal, the demo deal, the production deal, and the record deal. Types of recording deals are covered in more detail in Chapter 10.

The Barter System Deal

In the beginning of a band's career it usually does not have enough money to rent a recording studio and record samples of its sound and music that it will need in order to get booked at local venues. A possible solution is a barter system deal with a novice record producer. Bartering is a type of trade in which goods or services are exchanged for other goods or services. For instance, a student record producer at a local trade school might have access to recording equipment but may not have developed a Rolodex of competent musicians to help record his or her school projects. With the proper permissions from the school, a band can make a decent recording of its work to promote itself—or maybe even sell. The student, in the meantime, can hone his or her skills, develop a Rolodex of musicians, and complete school projects. It's a situation in which everyone wins.

The On-Spec Deal

Another scenario that is very common to young artists and bands is the on-spec deal. The on-spec deal is a situation in which a local producer, perhaps one who owns his or her own recording studio and who may be a friend or close relation of the band, records a CD for *free* under the terms of an informal agreement. Such an agreement may state that if the band goes on to getting a recording agreement, the producer will receive a predetermined fee for services rendered and be considered as a candidate to record the final product for the label. If the band never gets signed to a recording agreement, it never owes the producer any money. I've actually been involved in a deal similar to this, and it ended in a relatively pleasant way. Although the band, unfortunately, never got signed, we didn't have to a pay the producer a dime for his time. In fact, after about a year, I was even given copies of the master recordings along with his permission to do whatever I wanted with them.

The Do-It-Yourself Deal

A proactive approach among musicians in the digital age is to gather enough funds to both record and release a studio CD themselves. From what I've seen with this deal, the producer serves as both the engineer and the studio owner. The artist makes contact with the producer through referrals from other local indie artists or through ads in local music and trade magazines. After discussing recording philosophies, listening to recorded tracks, and getting a sense for how well the producer vibes, the technical elements of the studio are also considered, such as the size of the room, the recording equipment (analog versus digital), and the collection of microphones. Just remember that in a DIY deal, the producer works for you, and he or she does not retain the master rights in the sound recording. You are essentially your own record company and retain full control of your career.

The Production Company Deal

Another scenario in which an artist may first come in contact with a producer is the production company deal. In a typical production company deal scenario, the production company (one that is usually made up of producers) finds and signs talent ranging from the obscure artist who needs grooming (much like those the independent record companies sign) to the commercially viable rock, pop, or urban artists. In any case, the production company develops and records the artist first and in turn attempts to enter into a recording agreement with a record company *on behalf of the artist*. If successful, the production company receives a royalty rate for sales from the label, which it typically splits with you a whopping 50/50. The production company also typically receives a recording advance, and if anything is left over after it covers its recording expenses, it will typically be split 50/50 as well.

The Record Deal

The last and most obvious scenario—and the one I'll expand upon in this chapter—is when you enter into a recording agreement directly with a record company. In this case, the project is artist-driven. You are obligated by contract to hire an experienced record producer to help guide you through the recording process and to deliver a product that has the commercial sales potential to meet the company's expectations. The record company pays you an advance, typically known as the *recording fund*, from which all recording costs must be paid. And as you'll learn in detail in Chapter 10, the recording fund is considered a recoupable advance, meaning that you'll be required to pay the recording fund back from future record sales before you ever see a penny. The recording fund is really your money up front, and you'll have to use it wisely.

Additional Responsibilities of the Record Producer

Besides his or her creative contribution to the recording of your material, the producer typically handles important business responsibilities. These include creating and maintaining your recording budget and handling administrative responsibilities such as paying bills and handling union contracts. Remember, we're looking at this topic from the perspective of being signed to a recording agreement, since that is where there are a variety of complicated issues that you need to understand.

Creating a Recording Budget

As mentioned above, a record company allocates a recording fund from which a recording budget must be established. By contract, creating this budget is typically your responsibility; however, it is usually the record producer and A&R representative that first put it together and who actually work the numbers. The producer gets you to agree on the budget and then submits it to the record company for final approval. If there are a number of producers on a given project, then your A&R representative is responsible for making sure that all of the producers submit individual budgets that, collectively, stay within the fund.

Below are some examples of what's typically covered in the recording budget and deducted from the recording fund, all of which are charged against future record sales:

- ✦ The producer's fee
- ✦ The engineer's fee
- ✦ Studio rental costs (which may fluctuate greatly, depending on the rate you are charged, the advertised rate, or the discounted rate)
- ✦ Editing costs

- ◆ Mastering costs
- ◆ Equipment rentals
- ◆ Sticks, skins, strings, picks, and amplifier tubes
- ◆ Union minimum-scale wages for musicians (or double or triple scale depending on what the band decides to pay themselves)
- ◆ Union-scale wages for hired musicians (for overdubs, guest appearances, etc.)
- ◆ Cartage (to transport your equipment to and from the studio)
- ◆ Lodging (depending on your needs and budget, this could consist of either extravagant or conservative accommodations)
- ◆ Transportation costs

Maintaining a Recording Budget

Equally important to creating a recording budget is making sure that the recording process runs smoothly and that the project stays within the intended limits—but this isn't always the way things turn out. Events in the recording studio aren't always predictable, mistakes are made, and projects go over budget. Whatever the reasons for this, know that it's not uncommon for the record company to spring for the extra cash to complete a recording project. However, keep in mind that the more the record company spends over the amount it initially intended, the quicker the label may pull the plug on providing support should the record not have immediate legs. Furthermore, that overage may come out of your next recording fund or may even be deducted out of mechanical royalty payments (discussed in Chapter 11) that may be due to you. The bottom line is that in almost all cases, when your record goes over budget, it comes out of your pocket!

Administrative Responsibilities

Besides putting together your recording budget, the producer assumes a number of administrative responsibilities when agreeing to work on a project. These include submitting bills to the record company, filing union contracts, alerting the label of samples, alerting the label of guest permissions, and alerting the label of cover songs (all of which will be discussed below).

WHEN THE BUDGET GOES HAYWIRE According to a former member of Billy Idol's band, the singer's days in the recording studio consisted of showing up three hours late, deciding what strip club they were going to visit, going there and getting loaded, and then showing up back in the studio past midnight—with Idol being billed for the studio time all the while. The band Korn reportedly spent $20,000 on Coors Light and Jack Daniels in the studio while working on their album *Follow the Leader*. Even in situations in which everyone is "behaving themselves" in the studio, a band and its producer can eat up thousands of dollars just trying to get the right sounds. Obviously, once a band is successful, record labels are more tolerant of this type of behavior. The truth is that if you're a hit and the money is rolling in, no one really cares. This brings to mind Axl Rose's fifteen-year project recording *Chinese Democracy*. The album was said to cost over $13 million.

Since the producer's time is obviously better spent making records, he or she will typically pass these responsibilities over to someone called a "production coordinator" who specializes in administrative matters. The production coordinator is typically paid a flat fee or a percentage of the recording budget that ranges from 3 to 5 percent.

Here's a brief description of some of the more important responsibilities commonly handled by the production coordinator.

Submitting Bills The production coordinator is responsible for submitting all invoices to the record label (usually the A&R administration department) to be processed and paid. Producer Jeff Weber says he usually pays a visit to the administration department at a label to ask how he can help them help him get bills processed efficiently. Webber also says, "Different departments want different things. Some may want a copy of the original invoice and even want prior approval before most expenses are incurred." In a typical scenario, bills are submitted to the label as they come up, which might include cartage of instruments, copying charges, food bills, the engineer's fee (but usually the engineer is paid 50 percent up front and the other 50 percent after final mixes have been approved), and even studio costs (many studios, however, require payment in advance).

Filing Union Contracts Major record labels and many smaller independent labels are signatories to agreements with the musician's unions, the American Federation of Musicians and the American Federation of Television and Radio Artists. Under these agreements, labels are required to pay their artists, and all other musicians that are hired to perform on a recording, a union minimum-scale wage. The label must also make contributions into pension and health and welfare funds on behalf of their artists. The production coordinator may ensure that all union forms are filed with the musicians' unions and that bills are submitted to the label so that musicians can get paid. If these forms are not filed properly, the unions may enforce penalties. Unions are covered in more detail in Chapter 3.

Alerting the Label of Samples The production coordinator may ensure that all "samples" used on the final recording get cleared in a timely manner by the record label's legal department (or sample clearance specialists) by pointing out where the sample is used, on what song it is used, and from what artist the sample is taken. Samples are bits and pieces of other artists' songs (for example, a bass line from a David Bowie song, or a scream from a James Brown record) overdubbed or mixed into the recording of a new song to enhance its overall feel. If your album is released before you've cleared the sample rights, the owner could insist you pay substantial sums for its use or otherwise he won't grant you permission. Even worse, if you fail to clear samples altogether, the owner could sue you for copyright infringement (see Chapter 11). The owner is typically paid a negotiated fee (or "buyout") for the use of a sample, and when a sample makes up for a significant portion of a composition, the original owner may even want to share in the ownership of your song.

Alerting the Label of Guest Permissions When you wish for another artist to make a guest appearance on your record, the production coordinator may inform your label's legal department so that they may obtain permission from the guest artist's record label. For instance, on Carlos Santana's Grammy Award–winning record *Supernatural*, Dave Matthews appears courtesy of RCA Records. Since there's no guarantee a record company will give the proper authorization, the earlier your requests gets into your label's legal department, the better chance you'll have to make the collaboration you desire a reality.

Alerting the Label of Cover Songs and Mechanical Licenses If you are suddenly inspired to record a cover of another artist's song (of course it will have to get approved by the label first), the production coordinator may ensure that the label's legal department is aware of it so that a compulsory mechanical license (or a license most typically used called a mechanical license) gets filed. For example, when Gnarls Barkley covered "Gone Daddy Gone" by the Violent Femmes, the group had to file a mechanical license. But again, keep in mind that a license must be filed in a timely manner (before the record is released) to avoid copyright infringement charges from the owner. (The compulsory licensing provision is covered in more detail in Chapter 11.)

HIRING A RECORD PRODUCER

You already know how important a record producer is to your career, but how should you go about selecting the record producer? And once you select a producer, who actually negotiates the deal?

Selecting a Record Producer

When a record company signs a new artist to a recording agreement, it will initially insist on having the final say in choosing an experienced record producer. After all, the record company wants to

HIDDEN AGENDAS

Although it's the record producer's role to create and oversee the recording budget, sometimes it is the producer that has other hidden agendas. As illustrated in Moses Avalon's book *Confessions of a Record Producer*, the producer may be able to arrange deals with side musicians, tape vendors, and recording studios, bill the expense at a higher cost, and then receive a payment in the form of a kickback. In other words, besides earning an advanced fee for his or her services, your record producer may be able to scam additional money from your recording budget under the table. If you don't think this type of activity takes place, here's another example. A colleague who wishes to remain unnamed recorded an album for a major label under the direction of two world-class producers. Unbeknownst to this young musician, he was entitled to earn a minimum-scale wage for his work as enforced in the union's collective bargaining agreements with the record labels (see Chapter 3 for more on unions). Instead, the producers kept the musician's payment off the books and kept the money for themselves.

ensure that it is getting the best possible product for its investment, which can run into the hundreds of thousands of dollars.

However, since it makes no sense to have you locked up in the studio with a producer with whom you're unhappy, your attorney can usually negotiate so that the selection of the record producer is mutual. But how does the process of actually selecting the record producer work? First you must interpret your needs and then make a wish list, get in contact, spend time, go into preproduction, choose right before might, know expectations, and maybe use more than one producer.

Are you an unsigned DIY artist looking for a producer? If so, your choices may be limited to local producers and word-of-mouth recommendations. Ask some of the best independent artists in your area where their albums were recorded, and then listen to the production to see what you think for yourself. You might also check out The Record Producer & Recording Engineer Directory.

Interpret Your Needs

Before even thinking about looking for a record producer, you and your A&R representative should give some consideration to the type of record you're going to make. Will it be a slick, well-produced album with a lot of sequencers and samplings, or will it be raw and in-your-face? "These factors," comments producer David Brownstein of Fish Hook Productions, "are going to help you narrow down your choices for finding the best producer for your needs. Every producer has their unique gifts and specialties to bring to the table, but you have to have some idea of the results you want."

Make a Wish List

Most artists will spend hours listening to their favorite CDs, reading the liner notes of top 100 *Billboard* albums, and compiling a wish list of potential producers. "Of course, you'll also have the benefit of speaking with your A&R person, who will have some very definite ideas about who should produce your album," says producer/musician Jay Gordon of Orgy. "Your A&R rep is also likely to have a lot of connections with people he or she has already worked with and is comfortable with and will have a good sense of who is actually affordable considering your recording budget."

Get in Contact

Once your list of prospective record producers has been compiled and then approved by the record company, it's usually the artist (or artist's A&R person) who first makes contact with the producers, sends out recordings, and provides a sense of the overall buzz about the band in the industry.

Spend Time

Once a producer has expressed an interest in working with you, it is extremely important to meet with him or her to review songs and to get a vibe for whether you can successfully work together. Mikal Reid, producer for Ben Harper, says, "It's important that the artist gets a feeling of trust with a producer before ever choosing to work with him or her. Take the time to get to know your producer first so that there won't be any surprises or conflicting situations in the studio later."

Go Into Preproduction

Part of spending time with your producer before entering the studio to record the album should include a couple weeks of preproduction. Producer Robert Shahnazarian Jr. (Killers, Incubus, and

TOP PRODUCERS BEHIND THE ARTISTS

Rick Rubin: Chili Peppers, Johnny Cash, Beastie Boys, Slip Knot

Bob Rock: Metallica, Aerosmith

Pharrell Williams & Chad Hugo: Snoop Dogg, Justin Timberlake, Kelis

Timbaland: Missy Elliott, Justin Timberlake, Jay-Z

The Matrix: Hillary Duff, Britney Spears, Avril Lavigne

The Neptunes: Snoop Dog, Clipse, Busta Rhymes

RZA: Wu-Tang Clan, The Notorious B.I.G.

Swizz Beat: Britney Spears, Gwen Stefani, The Game, Jennifer Lopez

Just Blaze: Kayne West, Jay Z, The Game

DJ Premier: Nas, Gang Starr, Termanology

John Legend) says, "Preproduction includes having the producer attend the band's rehearsal sessions, going over song arrangements, maybe seeing them perform live in front of their fans, getting the band's perspective and vision for each song, and generally solidifying the trust between the producer and band. Preproduction will save the band money on time spent trying to figure these things out while under the clock at a studio and give everyone a sense of direction."

Choose Right Before Might

Choosing a producer should not be based entirely on what he has done but rather on what he can do for you. Arif Mardin, who's produced numerous artists including Aretha Franklin, the Bee Gees, Ani Chaka Chan, and Norah Jones, explains, "Surely, a producer with platinum records on his walls proves he has talent, but you don't want to sound like his other hit artists; you want your record to be unique to you. That said, no matter how well known a producer may be, never be intimidated to ask questions and voice your opinion when first meeting with him. Always remember that it's your record you're talking about, not the producer's record."

Know Expectations

It's not only important to discuss the things you expect to get out of your producer but also what your producer expects to get out of you. Producer Dave Darling says that one of the major expectations he has for his artists once they make a commitment to working with him is that they maintain the highest level of trust. "I like to push my artists to reach new creative heights and to get recorded performances they never thought possible. It's hard work, but it has to stay fun at all times. A positive working attitude is a must."

Arif Mardin adds, "Artists must always be on time, make sure that their musical gear is well maintained, and, if they choose to partake in certain substances, to make sure that it's not going to diminish their musical capabilities—or otherwise I'm out of there!"

Use Multiple Producers

Keep in mind that if a record producer is in big demand, he or she may only be available to produce one or two tracks on the record, in which case multiple producers may be considered. In fact, multiple producers may have been the initial plan. Multiple producers are becoming increasingly common in many genres of music.

Self Produce or Coproduce?

What happens when you feel capable of producing your own record? Prince did and was successful at it, as was Paula Cole. Unless you have had some prior success and the record company believes you're capable of delivering a worthy product, the label will most likely not approve the request. If you feel capable of coproducing your record, the record company will want to be sure that the producer is experienced in making creative decisions and not just someone who will be functioning as an engineer (i.e., the people who are responsible for getting the right sounds on tape).

Producer Humberto Gatica, who has worked with Michael Jackson and many other artists, clarifies the difference in Howard Massey's book *Behind the Glass*: "The whole idea of a great producer is to create a performance that's believable, and the engineer's job is to capitalize on that and put down on tape the best quality possible." Nevertheless, if the artist and A&R person feel strongly that the right record can be made with a particular person, it's possible the record company will approve co-production.

Strive to Keep Everyone Happy

Whoever the record producer is, it's important that everyone involved, especially your record label, be confident that the resulting product will be what they envisioned it would be. If a record company is unhappy with an artist's record, they'll approve additional funds in an effort to remedy certain issues and come up with a marketable product. But note that the more money the record company spends beyond its initial budget, the less committed they'll be to promoting the record if it is not immediately successful. And should the album not meet the expectations of the record label altogether, it can mean the end of an artist's career with that label. Choosing the right producer is not just an important creative decision, it's also an important career decision.

Negotiating the Producer's Deal

Once the producer has agreed to work on a project, and his schedule is free and clear, your contract with the record company will typically hold you responsible for hiring the producer and negotiating the deal. What fee will the producer want? What record royalty is the producer going to receive? How will the credits be listed on the album cover? Of course, this means that your attorney has to draw up contracts and negotiate the deal on your behalf, which means even more money out of your pocket at the end of the day.

Attorney Dina LaPolt says, "I usually build the costs of negotiating the producer's fee right into the record deal. If I have a rock band that I'm signing to Warners and the deal is for $150,000, I know I have to negotiate the band deal, the producer's contract, and maybe a couple of re-mixer agreements. Therefore, I might try to build another $20,000 above and beyond the $150,000, of which a portion goes to me. If it's a rap band I'm working with, I might shoot for an extra $100,000 above the offer because I'll have twenty producer agreements to negotiate, fifteen remix agreements to do, and I'll have to hire a production coordinator or sample clearance person."

Note: In some cases, it is the record label's business affairs department that actually negotiates the producer's agreement on behalf of the artist, while the artist still bears the cost. But since having multiple producers on recording projects is becoming more common and business affairs departments soon become tied up negotiating these deals, the trend lately is to have the artist's attorney negotiate the producer's deal.

THE RECORD PRODUCER'S COMPENSATION STRUCTURE

Now that you have a good sense of the role a record producer plays in your career, as well as who's responsible for selecting the producer and negotiating his or her deal, let's discuss your last contractual obligations to your record company: the producer's advance (or fee), the producer's royalty payment, and master use fees. And just for good measure, let's take a stab at a frequently asked question by artists and writers: When does the producer get a share in the *music publishing royalties?*

> Unsigned artist? Remember, the fees for working with a local producer at this level may consist of an hourly studio charge plus an additional charge for production. Producer Tom Weir of Studio City Sound says studio and production costs are an open market. "You simply have to do your research and make calls to get the best possible product to fit your economic means."

Advances

As mentioned briefly at the beginning of this chapter, most recording contracts today are structured as something called the recording fund. This means that out of the advances that you negotiate in your recording agreement, the producer's compensation must also be considered. For example, if you're a rock band that receives a very healthy recording fund of $250,000 under a traditional deal structure, $200,000 may be budgeted toward the recording cost budget, and the other $50,000 may be used as your advance. The fees typically advanced to a midlevel rock record producer can be in the neighborhood of $50,000 for recording a full-length album and up to $15,000 for a single master. So if the budget for recording an album is $200,000, and the producer earns a fee of $50,000, you'll be left with a recording budget of $150,000.

> Attorney Dina LaPolt says that hip-hop and pop artists may receive recording funds as much as $500,000 to $1 million to record their records, even for newer artists. This is because there is usually more than one producer on these types of recordings (sometimes as many as ten to fifteen and more) and they all want to get paid. Midlevel hip-hop or pop producers, who are often considered as important as the artist, can get as much as $50,000 per track.

Record Royalties

In addition to paying the producer a fee, you're also responsible for assigning the producer a record royalty for future sales. To understand how this really works, let's take a look at the artist/producer all-in royalty rate under a traditional deal structure, when the producer gets paid, the producer's record-one royalties, and who pays the producer.

The Artist/Producer All-in Royalty

Most record royalty provisions in recording contracts are structured as an "all-in royalty." This means that out of the royalty rate you negotiate with your record company, the producer's royalty must also be considered. For example, if the record company offers you a royalty rate of 14 percent of the wholesale price of the record, and the desired producer for a project requires a royalty of 4 percent, you're now left with a what's called a net royalty rate of 10 percent (14 − 4 = 10). For simplicity, let's say that the net rate is equivalent to about one dollar for CDs sold in normal retail outlets in the United States.

When the Record Producer Gets Paid

After enough records are sold (i.e., after enough one-dollar bills are thrown into a big pot to "recoup," or pay back, the costs of recording your album), the record producer will typically start getting paid a royalty. So, for the sake of simplicity, if the recording budget for an album is a high $200,000, and 200,000 one-dollar bills get thrown into a pot, the producer will start getting paid. In more technical terms, this is called *recouping the recording fund at the artist's net rate*. Sometimes, the record producer will get paid after the recoupment of his or her advanced fee only. So if the producer's advanced fee is $50,000, the producer will start getting paid a royalty after $50,000 is made. This is a far better scenario for the producer.

Regardless of how the producer gets paid, note that it is always far better than how things work out for you the artist: All advances given by the record company (i.e., the recording fund, monies for touring, monies for videos, and radio promotion funds) must be recouped before you get paid a penny in royalties. You may have to recoup as much as $500,000 or more before you start getting paid. If it's not clear yet, this means the record producer starts getting paid long before you. And no, you can't produce your own record and get paid in the same way producers do. But nice try.

How the Producer Gets Paid: Record-One Royalties

Also significant to our discussion is how the record producer gets paid. Using our above example, after the record company sells 200,000 units and $200,000 is used to recoup the recording budget, the producer starts getting paid a royalty back to the very first record sold, a system called *record-one royalties*. This means that the producer gets paid a royalty for all 200,000 units and for every unit that is sold after that.

Regardless of how the producer gets paid, once again, it is always far better for him than for you the artist: *You only get paid for sales from the point after the recoupment*. In other words, if it took up to 500,000 units sold before you recouped all the advances to the record company, you would get paid a royalty only after the 500,000th record sold: 500,001, 500,002, 500,003, etc.

Who Pays the Producer?

As you already learned, once the recording fund (or just the producer's advance) is recouped, the producer is entitled to getting paid a royalty back to the very first record sold. And now comes the good part. Guess who is responsible for paying the producer? That's right, YOU ARE! But don't panic just yet.

It's not like the money actually comes directly out of your pocket or that a collection agencies comes after you in the middle of the night. What typically happens, with the help of your lovely attorney, is that the record company will agree to pay the producer's royalties on your behalf. How nice of them! But note that every penny paid to the producer by the record company is charged back to the amount of money you must recoup before you ever get paid a royalty. If you haven't figured it out yet, this means that the more records you sell and the more the producer collects, the deeper in debt you can become. The good news, though, is that if the gods of rock (or pop, rap, or whatever) are on your side and you go on to sell shitloads of records, eventually everything will mathematically balance out and you'll start getting paid.

I'd show you how this works in a diagram below, but I figured I'd spare you the headache. (You'll learn more about record royalties and advances in Chapter 10.)

Should the Producer Get a Share of Music Publishing Royalties?

A common concern of artists and songwriters is if, and when, the producer should get a share of music publishing royalties. The issue really comes down to how involved you want the producer to be in the songwriting process. Is he or she going to sit down with you for several weeks and pen a batch of songs with you one-on-one?

Alanis Morrisette joined forces with producer Glen Ballard to co-write songs. The collaboration not only helped Morrisette to land a major recording deal but also allowed her album *Jagged Little Pill* to sell over 30 million copies worldwide. In this instance, the record producer is clearly involved in the songwriting process and entitled to a share.

But other instances may not be so clear, says Arif Mardin. "All producers will make modifications to the arrangements of your songs by adding or dropping four bars here and there, rewriting a pre-chorus, etc., but they're hired and paid a handsome fee to do so and should not ask for publishing. I suggest all artists/writers should be leery of producers that are overly insistent on taking a piece of the [music] publishing or getting involved in the songwriting process. Your [music] publishing income can be the very money you live on long after your career is over."

Understand that under copyright law, a music or lyric "contribution" to a song, no matter how big or small that contribution may be, could entitle the contributor to a "pro rata" (equal) share of ownership, unless there is a written agreement between the parties that stipulates otherwise. Bottom line: Before any artist/band goes into the studio with a producer, they should have a sit-down with the producer and discuss matters of music publishing, to the point of putting something in writing.

Robert Shahnazarian Jr. says, "I'll always make sure to discuss publishing matters with any band for which I work before going into the recording studio. I want the artist to feel free to create music around me, without being afraid that this will somehow involve me in the songwriting and entitle me to a share. This is for the best of all parties involved." (Music publishing is covered in more detail in Chapter 11.)

CHAPTER 10

Record Royalties, Advances, and Deals

J"He that has a penny in his purse, is worth a penny."
—TITUS PETRONIUS NIGER

ust mention the words *royalties* and *advances* and most artists immediately conjure up images of getting signed to a record deal, quitting their day jobs, and perhaps even buying one of the sports cars or mansions they see on MTV. It's probably the very nature of the words *advance* (which implies getting something before working for it) and *royalty* (which is very regal sounding—you know, something that relates to kings and queens). Put this all together with the word *major* (as in major record company), and it's easy to see why some musicians get delusional.

But before getting too excited about your pot of gold at the end of the rainbow, there are two basic concepts that you need to know about how record royalties and advances are structured:

1. Advances are money that is really given to you by a record label that typically goes toward the expenses of making your record, going on tours, and other fun stuff.

2. Royalties are the monies that go toward paying back *all* of your advances from the record label before you ever see a penny—that is, if you *ever see* a penny. According to the Recording Industry Association of America (www.riaa.com), 90 percent of all bands fail to pay back expenses to their label. Yup, you read right!

In this chapter, we'll expand upon these two simple concepts and show how recording funds and advances can add up to hundreds of thousands of dollars in expenses. Furthermore, we'll take a closer look at record royalties, royalty rates, the five factors that can affect your royalty, royalty computations, and electronic transmissions such as digital downloads, mobile tones, interactive and noninteractive subscription services, and other new revenues sources—including the latest development: planet Uranus royalties (I'm kidding of course). We'll also offer a basic overview of the various types of recording deals that exist, from the do-it-yourselfer to the major label deal. We'll even take a quick look at some do-it-yourself marketing tips on selling your own music and creating a buzz.

TOP-SELLING RECORDS OF ALL TIME If I'm making it sound completely impossible to make mountains of money in royalties and advances after getting signed to a label, one cannot forget about the legions of top-selling artists that have hit the jackpot and sold millions of units. Just for fun, here are some of the top-selling records (in units) of all time:

29 million: Eagles' *Eagles—Their Greatest Hits 1971–1975*

27 million: Michael Jackson's *Thriller*

23 million: Led Zepplin's *Led Zeppelin IV*

21 million: Pink Floyd's *The Wall*

21 million: AC/DC's *Back in Black*

20 million: Billy Joel's *Billy Joel Greatest Hits Volume I & Volume II*

20 million: Garth Brooks's *Double Live*

19 million: Shania Twain's *Come on Over*

19 million: The Beatles' *The Beatles*

17 million: Fleetwood Mac's *Rumours*

17 million: Boston's *Boston*

16 million: Whitney Houston's *The Bodyguard* (soundtrack)

Figures takes from RIAA Statistics (www.riaa.com).

Just remember that the music business is fast and ever-changing, especially in areas relating to record labels and record royalties, advances, and deals. That said, I point out several websites you can regularly check to stay up-to-date on the very latest news.

TYPES OF RECORDING DEALS

Before getting into the finer details of record royalties and advances, it's important to have a basic understanding of the various recording deals that exist.

Among the many record deals available, the most worthy of discussion are the do-it-yourself deal, the independent-label recording deal, the production deal, and the granddaddy of all deals: the major label deal.

The Do-It-Yourself Deal

The do-it-yourself deal (or rather, approach), in which a band funds, releases, and distributes its own recordings, can be anything one wants it to be. If this sounds vague, the general philosophy, distribution methods, and funding/profits discussed below should clarify.

General Philosophy

The general philosophy surrounding the do-it-yourself deal, or rather, the "do-it-yourself*er*" can be summed up in four simple scenarios:

1. I'm an artist who understands that to attract the attention of those who can help me (i.e., managers, labels, etc.), I must first help myself by getting my music to people.
2. I'm an artist whose work is not going to be contingent upon some corporate business-person's view of when and how I can do it, so I'll do it myself.
3. I'm an artist who wants to keep all the profits from my CD sales instead of having a royalty drawn up by a record company (which will ultimately mean a largely reduced fraction of sales) that will only be used to pay back my recording expenses.
4. I'm not an artist, but I just want to release a record like those yo-yos I see on MTV.

Regardless of which scenario depicted above may describe you, the availability of home recording equipment, affordable CD manufacturing, and the abundance of Internet sites to promote new musicians make it is possible nowadays to bypass the record labels altogether and essentially be your own record label—giving you absolute creative freedom without the worries of conforming to a specific music genre, age, or image from a record label.

Budgets/Profits

The method by which you generate funds to record your own music, promote it, and perhaps turn a profit, is totally left up to your creativity. Some artists borrow money from family members, ask their fans to pre-purchase records or donate funds, take out loans from banks, find investors willing to part with their money, ring up personal credit cards (although this approach is certainly not recommended due to high interest rates), or use their own money they've saved working their asses off for years.

While many producers may feel that it takes a minimum budget of $11,000 to record and manufacture a really competitive CD, the average budget I've seen the young do-it-yourselfer get by on to produce and manufacture a CD is about $7,000. This means it takes 1,000 CDs, the amount you probably had pressed (manufactured), to make back your initial investment ($7.00 x 1,000 = $7,000).

Now, let's suppose you sell each CD for $10.00. This means it only takes 700 CDs to recoup your money ($10 x 700 = $7,000). The remaining 300 CDs can be used either as giveaways or to make another $3,000 in sales ($10.00 x 300 = $3,000). With this, you can reorder another 1,000 CDs, pay off some of your marketing expenses, or use it toward buying your own recording equipment so that your profits from your next CD are greater, since your equipment cost will have been already covered. You get the idea!

At the do-it-yourself level, anything is possible. The deals are left to your imagination and to what you reasonably believe you can accomplish. I've even seen some DIY artists really take charge of their career, invest as much as $30,000 into making their own record, and then convince a major record company to

Got CD replication? Besides getting CDs "replicated" (a process involving a glass master of your recording where usually a minimum of a thousand CDs are made), some do-it-yourselfers go so far as buying "CD duplicator" machines and burning minimum runs. Just stack up your CDs, set the number of discs you need, and you're all set. Some models also offer automated printing. Check out Disc Makers (www.discmakers.com).

sign them and buy the master record for three times as much. That is pretty darn cool. The power is in your hands!

Distribution

The traditional brick-and-mortar distributors, those that move product into retail stores across the country, are generally not a first option for the do-it-yourselfer; these distributors typically distribute products that are already in high demand. Therefore, the do-it-yourselfer must rely on more alternative forms of distribution, such as the ones available through consignment deals in local music and non-music stores, live performance venues, personal websites, community websites like MySpace (www.myspace.com) and Music.com, and online retailers sites such as CD Baby (www.cdbaby.com), the Orchard (www.theorchard.com), Amazon (www.amazon.com), Smart Punk

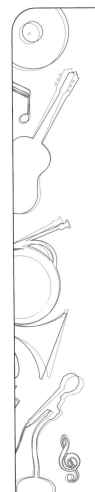

ONLINE RETAILERS: A DO-IT-YOURSELF CALCULATION

Do-it-yourselfers can affiliate with a number of online retailers to sell their original music. One such site, CD Baby (www.cdbaby.com)—which looks like it will be around for a while—sells physical CDs and will also aid in setting up alliances with digital download sites like iTunes (www.itunes.com), Napster (www.napster.com), Rhapsody (www.rhapsody.com), and many others. Using CD Baby and iTunes as a model, let's take a look at what do-it-yourselfers can generally expect to make per physical CD and per download sold. **Note:** There is an initial $35 setup fee with CD Baby that is not factored into the example below.

Per CD:

$10 (your price)
– $4 (CD Baby's flat rate)
= $6.00 (your share per CD)

Per Digital Download (Using iTunes):

$0.99 (standard per-single download price)
– $0.29 (iTunes' cut)
= $0.70
– $0.06 (CD Baby's cut: 0.09 x 0.70)
= $0.64 (your share per single download)

Most digital sites, like iTunes, do not handle direct deals with do-it-yourselfers who are releasing their own one or two album catalogues. Instead, companies called aggregators handle several releases—hence CD Baby's cut. Also keep in mind that companies like CD Baby that handle digital distribution on behalf of artists request "exclusive distribution rights" to your CD, since two companies cannot digitally distribute the same CD on the various download sites. While this is standard practice, always be sure to speak with the proper business professional for advice.

(www.smartpunk.com), It's About Music (www.itsaboutmusic.com), and CD Brickhouse (www.cdbrickhouse.com) to name but a few. All of these methods will be discussed in more detail at the end of this chapter.

> There are many ways to sell your music as a do-it-yourselfer. Using sites like MySpace (www. myspace.com) and Snocap (www.snocap.com) together, you can sell downloads directly from your MySpace page. Strive to find as many methods to sell your CD as possible. For more tips, see "How to Market Your CD and Create a Buzz" at www.bobby borg.com.

The goal for every do-it-yourselfer should be to uncover and take advantage of every sensible distribution method he or she can find. It ain't easy to do it yourself, but whoever said it would be? Bottom line: You gotta work your ass off, and you gotta get your fans to work their asses off for you, too.

The Independent Label Recording Deal

The independent label deal can include many things, depending on the size and experience of the label. Your dad, for example, could start his own independent label out of the tool shed and sign you to the best (or worst) deal ever, or an experienced executive could run a label out of a fancy office and "upstream" you (explained in a moment) to a major label. Regardless of who's running the label, let's look at the general philosophy, royalties/ advances/splits, and distribution deals of independent labels.

General Philosophy

Independent record companies (also called indies) are generally not owned or controlled by the major labels. Instead, their owners and investors finance them. Well, at least this is how the "true indies" like Victory (www.victoryrecords.com), Epitaph (www.epitaph.com), and Boundless Ent/Redemption (www.redemption-records.com) are still run. Many of the larger, more successful indies have been bought by the major labels and are now run more like "major-distributed indies," so the term *indie* is a bit blurry. Oh well.

Unlike major labels that are typically driven by shareholder expectations or by artists whom the major labels feel are most likely to turn a quick profit, independent labels are willing to sign undeveloped musicians and bands whose music is outside the mainstream. Indies were once the breeding ground and lifeline for the punk rock and grunge revolutions in the music industry. Today, they continue their legacy and nourish underground hip-hop, true punk, hardcore, and metal genres—to name a few.

While there is a trend for artists of a variety of styles (even pop) to sign with independent labels with the notion that they'll get more personalized attention, indies usually don't have the same marketing muscle or financial resources that the major labels have. Therefore, they have to rely on a grassroots philosophy. The bottom line: You're not going to see $100,000 MTV videos, billboards on Sunset Blvd, or tour in a forty-five-foot Prevost XLII Entertainer Coach. But you can live without all that, right?

Royalties/Advances/Splits

There are a variety of arrangements by which artists are paid under the independent label deal, including traditional deal structures (for lack of a better title), net profit deals, profit participation deals (often called 360 deals), and digital-only deals. Keep in mind that the deals offered really depend on the business model of the specific company you're dealing with and on what the company feels they want to "put on the table." In other words, what follows is not a shopping list of indie deals but rather an overview of the options your attorney might have when negotiating.

Traditional Deals Recording advances can range from as little as $0 to $100,000, and even more depending on the size of the indie label and the buzz the artist has built over the months or years. The record royalty rate for sales that newer artists (i.e., those who have never been signed or those who have been signed but did not sell thousands of records) can receive from independent labels ranges from 11 to 16 percent, which applies to CDs, digital downloads, master tones (mobile tones), and other sales. Don't worry just yet about what this percent is based on or what the dollar or cents amount works out to be, because it depends on a number of factors, which I will discuss in "Record Royalties, Rates, and Escalations" later in this chapter.

Net Profit Split Deal Like a traditional deal, a net profit deal offers a recording advance ranging from as little as $0 to well up into the $100,000 range, and even more depending on the size of the indie label and the clout of the artist. However, in this type of arrangement, the label and the artist/band *split the profits 50/50* from the sales of CDs, digital downloads, DVDS (and sometimes any merchandise) after deducting expenses. Hence the term *net profit split*. Ryan Kuper, CEO of Redemption Records, explains: "The important thing to understand is exactly what expenses the label deducts before arriving at the net." Attorney Joe Sophio adds: "In addition to the customary expenses, like the recording fund and other advances [see "Advances: Recording Funds and Formulas" later in this chapter], it is not unlikely that a label deducts advertising and promotion costs, distribution fees, and third-party marketing costs (for publicists, street team marketing firms, and independent radio promoters) before arriving at the net and offering you a share. You may never get a split. But if a record is extremely successful, this situation can actually work out quite nicely for everyone."

Profit Participation Deal Like the traditional and net profit deals, a profit participation deal (sometimes called a 360 degree deal) offers a recording advance ranging from as little as $0 to well up into the $100,000 range, and even more depending on the size of the indie label and the clout of the artist. However, with this kind of an agreement, an indie label offers a royalty *or* a split of the net profits, and *it shares in all of your revenue streams* including CDs, digital downloads, mobile tones, merchandising, publishing, touring, and tour sponsorships. Ryan Kuper explains: "The idea here is that the label claims it will work harder for you in other areas to generate more income, and this is what justifies its share or split." Attorney Joe Sophio adds, "If a label is actually set up in areas of music publishing and merchandising to make more money for you, then its share in revenue may be good and fine. However, what often happens is that an indie label is [comprised of] the same two guys in an office who want a piece of these rights to guarantee a few more dollars in their pockets. They then license these rights off to some third-party company, creating yet another middleman. While there may be no other offer on the table for you and this offer is as good as you're going to get, in the best scenario, a label has a staff of people skilled in handling publishing, merchandising, touring, and sponsorships. In any case, profit participation deals may be the deal of the future with indie labels—especially with the majors."

Digital-Only Deal Ryan Kuper notes that there's an increasing number of smaller labels structuring deals that only allow for master exploitation in digital format, generally leaving the rights and profits for physical CD sales to the band. Deals vary considerably, but in many cases the artist supplies the finished masters, and the label either pays a royalty for digital sales similar to the traditional deal we looked at already; or the label splits net profits from digital sales 50/50 with the artist after certain expenses have been covered. We're probably going to be seeing a lot more of these types of deals in the years to come.

Distribution

Independent labels generally rely on regional or national independent distributors to warehouse manufactured CDs, prepare CDs and songs for digital encoding and release, and handle the fulfillment and delivery of orders. They charge the label a fee ranging from 5 to 35 percent.

Distributors will also work directly with stores to arrange retail promotions for which the labels can choose to buy into. Such promotions include listening booths (which provide customers the opportunity to try before they buy), end-cap positioning (which provides the most opportune placement of CDs on stores shelves), bin cards (which are the cards that separate CDs on shelves), and co-op advertising (which is the kind of advertising used among several labels with one store to cut costs (e.g., the full-page ads you see in local newspapers where twenty CDs are on sale at Virgin Megastore).

Examples of successful independent distributors include, Red Eye Music Distribution (www.redeyeusa.com) and Nail Distribution (www.naildistribution.com). Other, even larger independent distributors coincidently owned by major record labels include RED (www.redmusic.com), owned by Sony/BMG; Alternative Distribution Alliance (ADA) (www.ada-music.com) and Ryko Distribution (www.rykodistribution.com), both owned by Warner Bros.; Fontana (www.fontanadistribution.com), owned by UNI; and Caroline (www.carolinedist.com) owned by EMI.

Examples of companies that specialize in working with independent labels to digitally prepare music and to push it out to e-tailers include the Independent Online Distribution Alliance (IODA) (www.iodalliance.com) and IRIS (www.irisdistribution.com).

The Production Company Deal

While the "production company" deal may appear to be much like the independent record deal previously discussed, the difference (for purposes of this discussion) is that it is structured record producers (those who produce physical records) who act as middlemen between you "record companies" (i.e., those who sell records and have marketing staffs, distributors production deal is often viewed in the industry as either being a godsend or a pact with The general philosophy, the royalties/advances/splits, and the distribution associate deals should reveal why.

General Philosophy

Production companies consist of record producers of all levels of skill and clout. The companies consisting of well-respected and seasoned pros may be those with multimillion-dollar studios in beautiful homes or buildings. The companies consisting of less reputable producers may be those with no more than a pro-tool rig in a garage. Of course, sometimes a less reputable producer could also have an incredible studio, but you get the idea.

In a typical production company deal scenario, the production company finds and signs talent ranging from the obscure artist who needs grooming (much like those the independent record companies sign) to the commercially viable pop artists. In either case, the production company develops, produces, and records the artist and in turn enters into a recording agreement with a record company *on behalf of the artist*. In other words, the production company signs to the record label and you sign to the production company. The production company then receives a royalty rate for sales, which is typically split 50/50 between you and the production company. Advance monies left over (if any) after the production company has covered its recording expenses are also split 50/50. So in case it hasn't sunk in, the deal in which the production company enters into with the label is structured, in concept, the same way it would be if you entered into the deal with the label yourself, but only now your deal is essentially cut in half by the production company.

As mentioned in my opening paragraph, production deals can be viewed as either a "godsend" or a "pact with the devil," depending on the finer details of the deal, your stature, and the clout of the producer. Attorneys Shawna Hilleary and Ryan Kuper explain:

> "It's a godsend," says Shawna Hilleary, "when a band, who would otherwise not have the connections to get signed directly to a label on its own, gets picked up and developed by a reputable producer, who by virtue of his or her clout gets signed to a major on behalf of the artist. While I still have a problem with the artist's royalty being cut in half, it's not impossible—with a good attorney—to negotiate a more favorable percentage of 70/30 [artist/production company]. Or, at the very least, it's not unheard of to have the percentage increase in favor of the artist on subsequent recordings. That is, 60/40 split of the royalty rate on the first, and 70/30 on the second."

> "It's a pact with the devil," says Ryan Kuper, "when a band carelessly signs a deal with some small-town producer that locks it into an agreement it can never get out of. That being said, it's important to ask any production company with which you sign to guarantee that it will enter into an agreement with a reputable label on your behalf (a 'major,' not 'Joe Blow' distributors) within a set period of time—say six to nine months—after your CD is recorded, or otherwise the deal is off. Furthermore, make sure that if the production company gets dropped from such label while you're still under contract, you will not be bound by contract to the production company if it doesn't find another reputable label to release you to in an agreed upon time of, say, six to nine months."

Royalty Rates/Advances/Splits

previously stated, record labels oftentimes pay a production company a record royalty rate for typically in the range of 14 to 18 percent, which it then splits with the artist 50/50). This means label credits the production company for record sales at 18 percent per CD, you would receive a royalty rate of 9 percent—half of what the production company receives from the label. What this amounts to in pennies is discussed later in "Record Royalties and Escalations." In any case, your royalty is typically not very high. The rate discussed above applies to CDs, digital downloads, master tones (mobile tones), and other sales.

The production company typically receives a recording fund from the record label in the range of $100,000 to $250,000, sometimes much more—depending on the stature of the record producer and artist and on the offer of the record company, but Kuper says he has seen deals for under $100,000. If there are any monies left after the recording expenses have been paid, the production company will usually split the remainder 50/50 with the artist.

Distribution

The label for which the production company is contracted handles the distribution of music as previously discussed under independent labels. Examples of major distributors include Sony/BMG, EMD, UMG, and Warner Music Group.

The Major Label Deal

As of this writing, the four major record companies are Sony/BMG (www.sonybmg.com), Warner Music Group (www.wmg.com), Universal Music Group (www.universalmusicgroup.com), and EMI (www.emigroup.com). This list could even be further reduced to three labels due to the possibility of yet another merger—or it could even grow to include a few more labels as a result of new entertainment groups rising to power. Stay tuned.

Let's look at the general philosophy, royalties/advances/splits, and distribution methods of the major label deal.

I STREAM, YOU STREAM, WE ALL STREAM FOR UPSTREAM

Los Lonely Boys, Maroon 5, and New Found Glory were all "upstreamed." What's that, you ask? Some deals that independent labels offer new artists contain a clause in which they upstream an artist to a major label once a sales figure is reached. This means that a major label will provide distribution for the independent label, creating a scenario that is a blend between an indie and a production deal. In other words, the artist is signed to the indie label, which is signed to the major label/distributor. The major label typically pays the indie a royalty, which then pays the artist a royalty that is set forth in its independent label deal (usually anywhere in the range of 11 to 16 percent). The good news about upstreaming is that it often allows the band's marketing to continue seamlessly from the indie to the major label, and that there is no interim—as there was in the past—between when a band's deal expired and when they are negotiating to find a new label. However, the downside is that when a band is doing really well, it is already bound to the terms of the preexisting contract they signed when they had less negotiating power. But, as attorney Burgundy Morgan advises, as long as you consider "bumps" in your original agreement at certain sales levels, there will be a commensurate increase in your royalty rate.

General Philosophy

Major labels are called major labels because they are just that: the major league. They are responsible for the majority of commercial recordings sold in the United States.

Each major has large staffs who perform a variety of functions, including A&R, press, promotion, sales, advertising, new media, business and legal, and finance. Perhaps this is why they are often referred to as the "major label machine."

Majors are also part of larger corporations that run a system of distribution channels, regional offices, international divisions, and other music businesses, such as record clubs, music publishing, and merchandising (booking and management divisions will soon follow, if they are not already in place by the time you are reading this).

Since majors are publicly traded, they must report to stockholders and show bottom-line profits. That being said, major labels typically seek more commercially viable artists who show the greatest potential for the quickest return on their investment. Despite this fact, and despite the fact that a label could easily invest a few millions in breaking one artist alone, the odds still weigh heavily against the major succeeding with a new artist and making money. But with as much as forty releases a year (including new and older bands), the general philosophy on which majors were built remains the same: *The hits will eventually pay for the stiffs.*

Royalty Rates/Advances/Splits

There are essentially four structures in play at the majors, which I will call demo deals, traditional deals, multimedia deals, and singles deals. The deals that the majors offer depend on the specific label you're dealing with and, of course, your individual situation.

Demo Deal In this deal, the record label offers a small amount of money to the band to record a few tracks. If the label likes what it hears, it has the first right to negotiate a deal. If a satisfactory deal cannot be reached, it then has the first right to match any deal the band may make with another label. If another label ends up signing the band, it has to pay back the demo money.

Demo deals have been around for a long time and are not as common as they used to be. Essentially, they give the label a chance to see how a band sounds before shelling out a bunch of cash.

Traditional Deal In a traditional deal, the record label pays a new artist a royalty rate for sales in the range of 13 to 16 percent, which applies to CDs, digital downloads, master tones (ring tones), and other sales. Again, don't worry just yet about what this percent is based on or what the dollar or cents amount works out to be, because it depends on a number of factors, which I will discuss in "Record Royalties, Rates, and Escalations" later in this chapter. Advances also depend on a number of factors, but may range from $100,000 to $300,000 and even higher (pop and R&B bands can earn advances far greater, since these genres typically use multiple producers per album). The label signs the artist for perhaps several records (one or two firm record agreements with several single one-record options at the label's discretion). This business model is primarily structured around a label's ability to profit from sales of master recordings through normal retail outlets, digital sites, and mobile carriers.

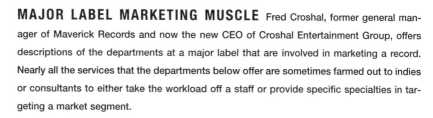

MAJOR LABEL MARKETING MUSCLE Fred Croshal, former general manager of Maverick Records and now the new CEO of Croshal Entertainment Group, offers descriptions of the departments at a major label that are involved in marketing a record. Nearly all the services that the departments below offer are sometimes farmed out to indies or consultants to either take the workload off a staff or provide specific specialties in targeting a market segment.

New media department. Develops the websites for artists or bands and continues to market them by setting up online promotions such as pre-release streaming to entice pre-orders (through sites like Amazon.com), prominent positioning and exclusive tracks and digital CD booklets (through various e-tailer sites like iTunes.com).

Press department. Writes the artist or band's biography and sends out advance copies of its music to various promotional outlets for exposure, such as album reviews, features, and interviews in magazines and newspapers, appearances on TV or radio, or online music sites.

Promotion department. Focuses on getting songs played on radio stations and garnering airplay. This can mean getting a band or artist to play at a special radio station event, organizing contests such as ticket giveaways, fly-aways (a contest that flies the winner to a location to see the artist or band), and other promotions.

Sales department. Works with the distribution companies and retailers to get records in stores, on sale, and in the right positioning on the shelves.

Marketing department. Works with all the departments above to develop a timeline and a marketing plan for an artist or band. The product manager is involved with the marketing tools such as CD samplers, stickers, key chains, etc.

General management department. Brings everyone together to work as a team, including the new media, press, promotion, sales, and marketing departments.

A&R department. Stays in touch with the product manager in the marketing department and the other departments and reports any and all the developments of the artist or band.

Multimedia Deal (360 deal) A multimedia deal (or 360 deal) allows the record company to sign the artist for fewer records and then pays a higher royalty rate than the traditional deal (and perhaps a higher advance); however, it shares in the net income of additional income streams, like publishing, merchandising, sponsorships, and touring. These rights could all be acquired under one agreement at the time of signing or under separate agreements. In essence, the label acts more like a venture capital firm, merging with artist management firms. This business model is primarily structured on declining CD sales in the digital age. Like it or not, some executives predict that the 360 deal may be the business model of the future.

Singles Deal In the singles deal, the record company signs the artist to release one or two singles (sometimes called "clusters") to be promoted via online, mobile, and the radio (and in some cases video) with an option to record a full album should certain sales criteria be met. These deals are not much different than the record industry of the past, when the Beatles would release singles and then the album. The label pays the artist a small advance to record the single and allocates a royalty rate. Candy Hill, a band signed to a singles deal on Universal, says, "Basically, it's a shot at success." In these deals, the record company acquires additional income streams, like publishing, merchandising, touring, and sponsorships.

This model is also structured on the label's need to maximize its budgets and to determine the potential success of an artist before it spends millions. In the realm of maximizing budgets, deals may even be limited to just ring tones at first. For the fans of jazz, classical, and some rock bands (like Tool, Radiohead, etc.) who prefer album-length listening experiences, perhaps the CD may live on. But for the fans of pop, rap, R&B, and country music, whose purchasing decisions are closely tied to the airplay of singles, the album may be entering its twilight. Single deals may be the deal of the future, but only time will tell.

> Independent singles deals also exist. Brian Perera, CEO of Cleopatra Records, is one of the first indies to do singles deals with bands like Motor Head. The indie label Cordless, although it is part of Warner, is another example. They sign artists to deliver songs in clusters of three with options for additional clusters or an album, should sales criteria be met.

Distribution

Major labels own their own wholesale distributors and thus distribute their own recordings, as well as the recordings of a number of sub and independent labels—in both physical and digital forms. The major distributors include Sony/BMG (who distributes Columbia, RCA, and Epic), EMD (who distributes EMI Recordings and Capital), UMG (who distributes Interscope, A&M, and Geffen), and Warner Music Group (who distributes Atlantic, Warner Bros., and Reprise).

RECORD LABELS AS FAN CLUBS Some record companies, including the Warner Music Group and the EMI Group, have been considering a system in which fans would pay a fee, perhaps monthly, to subscribe to their favorite artists and receive a series of recordings, videos, and other products. Executives realize that they must establish more lasting connections with fans who may well lose interest if forced to wait two years or more before their favorite artists release new music. This is not an entirely new idea. Todd Rundgren announced as early as 1997 that he would start a subscription service in which fans could participate in the recording process of an album. When Rundgren's twenty-year-old contract expired with Warner Bros. Records, he was ready to experiment with the idea. For twenty to thirty dollars a month, fans were able to download new tracks and offer feedback. "For the artist, that's fantastic," said Rundgren. "I don't have to write songs and package them into twelve slots. If I write a couple tonight, I can have them online and get feedback by the morning. If you're wrong, you can do a U-turn. That's an instant form of gratification."

ADVANCES: RECORDING FUNDS AND FORMULAS

Now that you have a general understanding of the different types of recording deals that exist, let's focus more closely on the details of recording funds and formulas. While many of the examples and dollar amounts may relate more to a major label model (because the numbers have historically been higher and are also more fun to work with), keep in mind that the broad concepts discussed here generally apply to independent and production deals as well.

Recording Funds

Most record deals today are structured to provide all-inclusive recording funds. The recording fund covers all your recording costs (including the record producer, studio costs, and equipment rentals and purchases), and any money that remains serves as your advance. For example, suppose you are a band that is advanced a recording fund of $250,000 under a traditional deal structure. Two hundred thousand may go to the budget for recording costs, and the remaining $50,000 may go toward your advance. But before getting excited about that whopping fifty grand, you'd better read on.

Out of your $50,000 advance, $12,500 (or 5 percent of the total recording fund) may go to your attorney for negotiating your record deal. Another $10,000 (or 20 percent of your advance) may pay your personal manager's commission. An additional $2,500 (or 5 percent of your advance) may pay your business manager's commission. And, of course, out of the remaining $25,000, $7,500 (approximately 30 percent) will go to Uncle Sam for taxes—although I'm aware that this amount can be reduced with the timely advice of a tax accountant. Nonetheless, the remaining $17,500 may then be split between the four members of your band, which leaves each of you with a grand total of $4,375. Your recording budget will typically provide for a union fee to be paid to you for recording your record, as well as provide a daily allowance for living expenses; but beyond what's budgeted, it's easy to see how there may be very little left over—if anything at all—to split among your band as an advance.

Although the above numbers are only estimates, the concepts outline a pretty accurate picture of recording finances. So be realistic, and don't expect to get rich. And remember that a record deal is not the means to a certain end but only a chance you're given to make your dreams come true. The following equation breaks down the distribution of the recording fund.

$250,000 (recording fund)

− $200,000 (recording cost budget)

= $50,000

− $12,500 (attorney's commission, 5% × $250,000)

− $10,000 (manager's commission, 20% × $50,000)

− $2,500 (business manager's commission, 5% × $50,000)

= $25,000

− $7,500 (Uncle Sam's cut, approximately 30% × $25,000)

= $17,500 (artist's advance)

÷ 4 (number of members in the band)

= **$4,375** (artist's advance per band member)

Formulas

The recording fund for your first album is typically a set amount—as the $250,000 in our example above. However, the recording funds for your subsequent albums are typically based on a percentage, or "formula" (usually 60 to 70 percent), of the royalties credited from prior records sales during a specified period of time—say the first ten months after your record is released. If your formula is 60 percent, and you were credited only $100,000 in royalties for your first record over a ten-month period, then the recording fund for your second record would be $60,000 (60% x $100,000 = $60,000). If, however, your record sells extremely well and you were credited $2,000,000 in royalties, your fund would be as much as $1,200,000 (60% x $2,000,000 = $1,200,000) for your second record. But as you'll see below, there are some variations to this formula, which are generally known as minimum (or floor) and maximum (or ceiling) formulas.

Signing bonus anyone? Although most recording deals are structured to provide all-inclusive recording funds, anything and everything is negotiable. In fact, your attorney may be able to get the record company to give you extra monies in the form of a "signing bonus" (which is usually not recoupable) as an incentive for you to sign with a specific label. This may be more likely in those rare cases in which several record companies negotiate to sign your band in what's known as a bidding war.

Floor/Minimum Formulas

In the previous example, the recording fund for your second record was based on the royalties formula, which was $60,000. But how can you be expected to record an album for as little as $60,000 when the recording fund for your first record was $250,000? Doing so may be difficult, and that's why you should have an attorney negotiate a floor (a minimum amount) for you. For example, no matter how poorly your first record sells, your contract can ensure that your recording fund for your second record will be no less than $275,000. Note that if the recording fund for your first record was $250,000, a $25,000 fund increase between your first record and your second record suggests your attorney may also be able to negotiate a bigger recording fund for subsequent records.

Ceiling/Maximum Formulas

To protect itself from paying huge amounts of money, should your first record sell substantially well, the record company will set a ceiling (maximum) in your contract on the amount of money you may receive for a recording fund. The ceiling is often two times as much as the amount of the floor, but it is negotiable by your attorney. For instance, if you have a floor of $275,000 on your second record, the ceiling for the recording fund may be $550,000. Keep in mind that these numbers are just examples. Also keep in mind that none of this may matter anyway—if your record is extremely successful, your attorney will likely go in and renegotiate all of your terms. If, however, your album is a flop, the label will likely exercise its option to drop you like a hot potato.

RECOUPABLE ADVANCES AND EXPENSES

No matter how big or small your recording fund may be, and no matter what your floor or ceiling formula for subsequent records may be, an extremely important concept to remember about recording funds is that they are *recoupable*. This means that before you see a penny from the sale of your record, you must pay back your recording fund to the record company. In fact, recording agreements may state that *any money spent on behalf of the artist is a recoupable advance, unless the company states in writing*

OPTION! OPTION! READ ALL ABOUT IT! A press release announcing that a band has signed a five-album deal with a total of $20 million in advances leads one to believe that recording deals are like striking it rich. While you may have noticed that these deals typically exist for super-successful bands renegotiating their contracts, you should also know these deals, like most, are based on "option periods," which means the 20 million reflects the total in advances. In other words, the record company may guarantee payment of an advance for two "firm" albums and then will have the option to pay for another three records, one at a time. However, if your first record sells poorly, the record company may choose to exercise its right not to record another album and release you from your recording contract. You would then be free to sign with another record company. By the way, those huge deals are becoming less common, even for the big boys and girls.

that it's not an advance. For this reason, you must be very clear at the time you sign your recording agreement about which monies will be deemed advances, and which will not. At least you'll know the ground rules, so you can cut expenses whenever possible.

The 1990s R&B group TLC, for example, found itself in deep debt after (among several other things) carelessly demanding the most expensive hotels and travel accommodations during promotional trips, all of which were initially charged to the record company. Unbeknownst to TLC, the costs were all recoupable. As a result, although it was selling millions of records, the group was nearly broke. Needless to say, you don't want this to happen to you!

What follows is a brief examination of some of the advances and other expenses that are typically recouped from your future record sales—namely, the recording fund, tour support, video expenses, and independent radio promotion. As you'll see, these expenses can add up quickly.

What else is recoupable? Marketing charges for retail promotion and advertisements in consumer magazines are typically *not* recoupable by the record company. However, as record deals evolve into profit splits, in which labels are becoming more like venture capitalists and dipping into other artist revenue streams like touring and merchandising, it is even more important to be clear as to what will and will not be considered recoupable.

Recording Funds (100 Percent Recoupable)

Recording funds are the monies paid by the record company for the purposes of recording your CD. As shown in our example above, a band may receive $250,000 as its recording fund, which is 100 percent recoupable. So, for purposes of the example given below, let's say your deficit to the label starts at $250,000.

Tour Support (100 Percent Recoupable)

Tour support, the monies advanced by the record company for the purpose of subsidizing a tour, is 100 percent recoupable from future record sales. Record companies are aware that touring costs like hotels, gas, crew, and tolls outweigh the fees a band can earn from performing. To help make up for these losses, a major record company may advance anywhere from $50,000 to $100,000 — depending on the actual tour expenses incurred. But note that the label may only agree to award these funds after a band meets certain requirements. For instance, a band may need to be scheduled to perform before a specific number of people or to be selling a certain number of records per week before it receives tour support funds. Furthermore, the label may stipulate that the tour support fund must only be used for certain tour expenses and that if the monies are used for purposes like buying musical instruments, it will keep this equipment as its property. For purposes of our example, let's say the tour support you receive is $50,000, which now leaves the following deficit owing to the label:

$250,000 (recording fund)

+ $50,000 (tour support)

= $300,000

Video Expenses (50 Percent Recoupable Against Audio Royalties)

The costs of producing promotional videos (such as the ones you may see on MTV, VH1, and local cable shows) are also recoupable. Typically, however, only 50 percent of these expenses are charged against your audio royalties. So, if you have a video budget of $150,000, only $75,000 will be charged against your account. Attorney Dina LaPolt of LaPolt Law says that sometimes the record company may structure its contracts to read that costs in *excess* of a specific dollar amount (say, $75,000) will be 100 percent recoupable, while costs up to that amount are *not* recoupable—which is essentially the same thing as our above example. Overall, though, probably a good rule of thumb is simply to think of video expenses as being 50 percent recoupable. For purposes of our example, let's say that your recoupable video costs are $75,000, which gives us a new amount owed to the label:

$250,000 (recording fund)

+ $50,000 (tour support)

+ $75,000 (50% of the video fund of $150,000)

= $375,000

Independent Radio Promotion (50–100 Percent Recoupable)

The costs of hiring an independent radio promoter to help get your record played on the radio, specifically commercial radio (which includes national networks, regional networks, independent stations, and syndicators), is usually 50 to 100 percent recoupable. A record company's promotion department can create hype for an artist's single, but independent promoters have direct connections and relationships with nationwide consultants who advise radio programmers on what to add to their playlists. Commercial radio stations, and I stress *commercial*, are businesses interested in attracting the greatest number of listeners and advertising dollars by playing music that is guaranteed to be successful (i.e., music that, in part, is viewed as being heavily supported and promoted by the record labels). A record company may spend anywhere from $75,000 to $350,000 per single in independent radio promotion. If this sounds like a lot, labels once spent much more, until New York attorney general Eliot Spitzer launched an examination of record companies for fraudulent practices (payola—the process of bribing radio stations to play your music). But no matter what a label will currently spend, the monies are 50 to 100 percent recoupable against your record royalties—for newer bands it is more likely to be 100 percent recoupable. And finally, for purposes of the last stage of our example, let's say that the independent radio promotion you receive of $100,000 —is also 100 percent recoupable.

Your current deficit to the label would be as follows:

$250,000 (recording fund)

+ $50,000 (tour support)

+ $75,000 (50% of the video fund of $150,000)

+ $100,000 (independent radio promotion)

= $475,000 (your total recoupable expenses to the record label)

NONRETURNABLE ADVANCES

Between the recording fund, tour support, the video budget, and independent radio promotion, you have quite a debt to repay. In the above example, you owe $475,000 to the record company in recoupable expenses. But what happens if you never credited enough royalties to pay back these expenses? Good question. Most advances by the record company are deemed nonreturnable. In other words, advances are only recoupable from record royalties, and not out of your own pockets (or your cousin Vinny's pockets) should you fail to be credited enough in royalties. But note that your debt will then extend to subsequent recordings and royalty earnings in something called "cross-collateralization."

CROSS-COLLATERALIZATION

Cross-collateralization essentially refers to one big pot of expenses in which royalties (whether credited from the first or second record) go toward paying off your total debt. For example, if you have an unrecouped balance of $300,000 from your first record, and your recording fund for your second record is $325,000, you will now have a combined unrecouped balance of $625,000 that you owe the record company before your second record ever hits the store shelves or digital download sites. Scary, isn't it! To make matters worse, the record company will charge interest on all unrecouped balances.

You may wonder, then, why some record companies often give a band a second and third chance to record an album. It's simple—the artist's royalty account bears no resemblance to the actual number of records the record company needs to sell, for instance, to recoup all of its expenses. That's right! The record company starts to make a profit long before you do. While you may be credited about a dollar per CD toward recoupment (you'll see why it may be just a dollar in the next section), remember that the record company is credited with a higher dollar amount. So, if you get a second shot to record an album and you're still a couple hundred thousands dollars in debt, you may not be considered a significant financial success to the record company but, rather, in the words of an anonymous record executive, "One who helps keep the lights on."

What else is subject to cross-collateralization? Publishing monies called mechanical royalties (especially by indie labels), merchandising royalties, and perhaps even touring incomes (as new multimedia, or 360 deals, evolve) may be used by labels to recoup expenses, which is usually not the most favorable arrangement for the artist.

RECORD ROYALTIES, RATES, AND ESCALATIONS

Due to the vast amount of changes in record distribution because of new technology—which is constantly altering record royalties—and due to the fact that record companies each structure their contracts differently, record royalties are a bit tricky to nail down. At the risk of leaving out some finer details, I opt for taking a straight and general approach. Now, let's take a look at record royalties, royalty rates, and escalations.

Record Royalties

Record royalties are percentages (also called points) that the record company pays you for the sale of your record. The term *record* can be defined as "any kind of delivery of music for consumer use, whether it be stand alone or with visuals." This definition, of course, includes physical sales of CDs, audiovisual DVDs, and digital transmissions like digital downloads, master tones (i.e., ring tones and ring backs), and other goodies.

Royalty Rates

The percentage at which a record company will pay you for the sale of your record is known as the "royalty rate." A common royalty rate for newer rock bands signed to a major label under a traditional deal structure, for instance, can range from about 13 to 16 percent. The actual dollars and cents amount this equates to is subject to a number of factors listed below:

+ The price at which records are sold to dealers:
  At a wholesale full price—sometimes called the published price to dealers, or PPD (e.g., $12.05), midprice (between 60 and 80 percent of the full price), budget price (below 60 percent of the full price), or "schlock" (which is a really low price). For years many record labels have based their royalties on the suggested retail list price, but it seems as though the labels' contracts are changing to the published price per dealer as indicated above.

+ How records are sold:
  Through normal retail channels (i.e., record stores), mail-order and television-only packages, or record clubs (which are the clubs you read about in magazines where you can buy ten CDs for one penny).

+ Where the records are sold:
  Are they sold in the United States or in foreign territories?

+ To whom the albums are sold:
  Are they sold to military post exchanges and public libraries?

+ The physical configuration in which records are sold:
  CDs, digital downloads, master tones, and "any other device now and hereafter known that is capable of transmitting sound alone or sound with visual images" (which is essentially a catch-all phrase to pick up any new technology that might come along).

Again, the above factors can all affect the amount you'll be credited in royalties, but don't get bogged down with all these details for the moment. Remember, the aim of this chapter is to give a general idea of how they work. Things are likely to change, so be sure to check the latest news by logging on to the websites that I provide at the end of this chapter.

For the sake of simplicity, let's look at a royalty example for a CD under these four factors:

(1) it sells at a wholesale "full price," or PPD, of $12.05, (2) it sells through normal retail chain outlets, (3) it sells in the United States, and (4) it will be based on 14 percent, because that's the royalty rate the record company gave you in our example. The royalty calculation would be as follows:

> $12.05 (wholesale full price, or PPD, of CD to retailers in the U.S.)
> x 0.14 (your royalty rate)
> = $1.68 (your royalty)

Ta da! Wasn't this exciting! Well, it may get a little depressing as we discuss certain deductions later. Now let's check out another concept, called royalty escalations.

Royalty Escalations

As pointed out, a royalty rate for a newer artist signed, for instance, to a major label under a traditional deal structure can be anywhere from 13 to 16 percent. Regardless of your rate, the record company will usually agree to royalty escalations (or adjustments) based on the success of your record. So, for example, if you're a newer artist with a royalty rate that begins at 14 percent, the rate for your CDs may increase by one-half to one point after 500,000 units have been sold. For sales of over 1,000,000 units, your royalty rate may increase by another one-half to one point. By the way, royalty escalations are only determined by sales of your CDs at a full price in the United States through normal retail chains (USNRC sales). If your attorney negotiates for it, digital downloads, or perhaps more significant, an aggregate of ten or twelve single digital downloads, can equal one unit sale in determining escalations. Take a look at the example below.

> Royalty rate for first album: 14% for sales up to 500,000 units
> 14.5 % for sales after 500,000 units
> 15 % for sales after 1,000,000 units

So, how might your royalties be structured on your second record? Well, if you had a royalty rate beginning at 14 percent for your first recording, your attorney may be able to negotiate for a royalty rate starting at 14.5 percent for your second album, with similar rate increases of one-half to one point when your record reaches predetermined sales figures.

> Royalty rate for second album: 14.5% for sales up to 500,000 units
> 15% for sales after 500,000 units
> 15.5% for sales after 1,000,000 units

As attorney Dina LaPolt reminds us, none of this may really matter anyway. If your record ends up being a huge hit, you'll have the leverage to go back to the record company and renegotiate your deal. As the saying goes, "He who has the gold makes the rules." On the other hand, if your record isn't successful—and unfortunately, the majority of records released aren't—the record company may not want to record another album with you, and you may end up getting dropped. This information is not meant to discourage you; it's just the plain and simple truth.

Now that we've gotten escalations out of the way, let's go back to some basic royalty computations while trying to keep things as simple as possible.

BASIC RECORD ROYALTY COMPUTATION: PART ONE

When discussing record royalty computations as applied to this next segment, we should look at three basic concepts: the wholesale price, the all-in/net royalty rate, and free goods.

Wholesale Price/Published Price per Dealer (PPD)

As previously shown in our example, record royalties are often based on the wholesale published price to dealers, or PPD, which is the price for which retailers purchase CDs from the record companies. As we calculated, a record selling at a wholesale full price of $12.05 to retailers in the United States that is multiplied by an artist royalty of 14 percent equates to a royalty of about $1.68. Just in case you forgot, here it is again:

> $12.05 (the wholesale "full price," or PPD, of your CD to retailers in the U.S.)
> x 0.14 (your royalty rate)
> = $1.68 (your royalty)

Keeping the above calculation in mind, if you sell 100,000 records you'll have a whopping $168,000; a small fortune compared with the low-budget days of eating Top Ramen noodles and mustard sandwiches. Pretty cool, right? Wrong!

Before picking up the phone and telling Mom all the good news about royalties, there are a few more principles you'd better know about and how they're computed.

The All-in/Net Royalty Rate

The standard royalty rate a record company offers you is known as an "all-in rate." Not to anyone's surprise, but this certainly does not mean it's "all in your pocket." Rather, it means that your record producer, who also receives a royalty for all his or her hard work, is allocated a percentage *out of your share*. For example, if you have an all-in royalty rate of 14 percent, and your record producer negotiates a deal that gives him or her 4 percent, you now have what's called a "net royalty rate" of 10 percent (the all-in rate, minus the producer's agreed-upon rate, equals the net royalty rate). As you can see, this is another factor that reduces your royalty per CD.

> $12.05 (wholesale full price, or PPD)
> x 0.10 (10%: 14% – 4% = 10%)
> = $1.20 (your royalty per CD)

You may be wondering whether you can hold onto those extra royalty points by producing your own record. The answer is no. Most new artists will typically be required by contract to hire an experienced studio producer to ensure the best possible product, thus protecting the label's investment in you.

Free Goods

The next royalty deduction that most record companies levy—called free goods or special campaign free goods—is really derived from the actual percentage of sales that the record company agrees to pay you. Typically, most labels will agree to pay you on only 90 to 95 percent of sales (a deduction of 5 to 10 percent it claims is offered as a discount to retailers). For you math geniuses, this deduction in units amounts to the same as if you were to subtract 5 or 10 percent from our wholesale price (let's use 10 percent just for the sake of melodrama). Doing this, we finally arrive at your royalty per CD. Ta da!

    $12.05 (wholesale full price, or PPD)
   – $1.20 (10% free goods)
   = $10.85
   x 0.10 (10% your net royalty rate)
   = $1.08 (finally, your royalty per CD)

Note: In case you're wondering, record labels will try to apply the automatic free goods reduction to digital downloads and mobile tones as well. However, as attorney Shawna Hilleary notes, since free goods is a provision that was theoretically designed to encourage sales of physical product to retail stores, most labels will usually exclude downloads and mobile tones from the free goods provision, as long the artist's attorney is sharp enough to negotiate for this.

BASIC RECORD ROYALTY COMPUTATION: PART TWO

As demonstrated on the previous pages, your record royalty for U.S. sales of your record at a wholesale full price, or PPD, sold through normal retail channels, is $1.08. But it's not quite like the record company multiplies your royalty by the number of units you sell and writes you a big check. This is on account of two reasons: recoupable expenses and reserves.

Recoupable Expenses

Keep in mind that all the royalties credited to your account must go back toward paying all recoupable advances (recording funds, tour support, video expenses, and independent radio promotion—all discussed earlier in this chapter). This means that if you have a $475,000 debt to the record company, you have to sell about 440,000 units (440,000 x $1.08 = $475,200). Let's check out the equation below.

    440,000 (number of CDs sold)
   x $1.08 (your royalty per CD)
   = $475,200 (gross artist royalties credited)
   – $475,000 (recoupable costs)
   = $200 (the money you use to buy your mansion!)

> While record royalties from sales yield you next to nothing, unless you sell tons of records, don't worry just yet. You'll learn about another type of royalty called mechanical royalties in Chapter 11.

Reserves

Once all advances are recouped, the record company holds onto any royalties due to you in something called reserves. You see, record companies generally offer a 100-percent return policy to retailers as an incentive to stock new product. This means that although your album is ordered by retailers and shipped to their stores, it is not yet considered a bona fide sale as far as your royalties are concerned. If retailers can't sell your records, they can send them back to the record company for a refund. Therefore, to ensure that you're not paid a royalty on records that are later returned, the record company will withhold or "reserve" payments due to you of 10 to 50 percent of the payments of your "gross royalties" (i.e., before deducting recoupable expenses—so in the

To help control the number of records returned by retailers, record companies often set a percentage (approximately 20 percent of the total records shipped) that determines the refund to retailers. If over 20 percent of the records are returned, the retailer receives less per unit than what it paid. If less than 20 percent is returned, the retailer often gets more than it paid as a bonus.

above example, you're not going to get that whopping $200 for quite a long time).

The amount in reserves depends on whether you are a newer artist or a more established, successful artist. Royalty statements are sent out two times a year: sixty to ninety days after the close of each six-month period (June 30 and December 31). Reserves are liquidated throughout subsequent statements—typically over the two years following the statements in which the reserves are taken. In other words, the record company is intentionally behind in its payments to you so that they can avoid crediting you for records that are later returned by retailers. By the way, if you're wondering how reserves apply to digital downloads (since iTunes doesn't send back a song to the record company if it doesn't download), attorney Shawna Hilleary of Artist Law Group says that monies for digital transmissions, as ridiculous as it may sound, are also held in reserves. This, however, could change as sales of downloads outsell CDs and physical distribution goes away, or if an artist's attorney is able to successfully negotiate this out of the recording agreement at the time you sign the deal.

Isn't there an easier way to run this whole reserve system than just waiting to see what records are returned? Absolutely! Nielson SoundScan, an information system offered since 1991, tracks the weekly sales of records in retail stores, including Internet retail sites and digital download providers, by monitoring registered bar codes associated with the product. While SoundScan is not 100 percent accurate (a major portion of the retail market is monitored, while the remaining sector is accounted for by extrapolating data), it gives record companies a pretty good idea of which records are selling and how many. Therefore, SoundScan's data often affect the percentage that record companies withhold from artists' payments. SoundScan is also a helpful marketing tool for record companies because it can monitor locations around the country where an album is selling or not selling. Record companies can use these data for pinpoint promotion, thereby focusing their marketing energies in specific regions. By the way, SoundScan's data are what also make up the *Billboard* sales charts.

AREAS THAT AFFECT ARTIST ROYALTIES

Now that we have some of the royalty basics out of the way, let's discuss in more detail the five general areas that affect artist royalties: The price for which records are sold to dealers (full, mid, new and developing artist prices, budget, and "schlock"), how records are sold (normal retail channels, record clubs, and mail-order and television-only packages), where the records are sold (United Sates and foreign territories), to whom the albums are sold (military, and libraries), and the physical configuration in which records are sold (CDs, digital downloads, master tones, and "any other new technology that might come along"). With the exception of how records are sold to libraries and military post exchanges (since these areas aren't especially meaningful right now), let's take a closer look at how your royalties may be affected in the aforementioned categories.

AN ANTIQUATED ROYALTY COMPUTATION For years, most labels used an antiquated system for computing record royalties that consisted of many deductions, and some still use this system today for preexisting contracts. Thankfully, though, labels are changing all this nonsense in their newer agreements, but check out the following anyway:

1. *Suggested Retail List Price (SRLP)* The price a label "suggested" a record be sold at retail

$18.99 (the top-line SRLP for CDs)

x 0.14 (a potential royalty rate paid to a newer band)

= $2.66

2. *Package Cost Deduction* For the "cost" of the plastic cases and artwork

(This deduction usually amounts to much more than the actual costs.)

$18.99 (SRLP)

– 25% (CD packaging cost of $4.74 per unit)

= $14.24 (your new "royalty base" on which your royalty is calculated)

x 0.14 (14% is your band's royalty rate)

= $1.99

3. *The "All-in" Royalty Rate* The artist's royalty, including 3% to 5% to be allocated to the producer

$14.24 (your royalty base)

x 0.10 (14% is your "all-in rate" minus 4%, the producer's rate)

= $1.42

4. *Phony Free Goods* For the so-called purchasing incentive that labels offer retailers; for every 100 records shipped, the label "theoretically" billed for 85 (a difference of 15%)

$14.24 (your royalty base)

– 15% (free goods deduction of $2.14 per unit)

= $12.10 (your new "royalty base" on which your royalty is calculated)

x 0.10 (10% is your "net royalty rate" after deducting 4% for the producer)

= $1.21

5. *CD Reduction* For the pain of adapting to new manufacturing processes of CDs (a deduction of 85%) (Note that CDs were invented circa 1985)

$12.10 (your "royalty base")

x 0.85 (85% CD reduction)

= $10.28 (your new "royalty base" on which your royalty is calculated)

x 0.10 (10% is your net royalty rate)

= $1.03 (your royalty rate per CD)

Algebra Quiz: $1.02 is what percent of $18.99?

$1.02 = x \cdot $18.99

$1.02 = $18.99x

$1.02 \div $18.99 = 0.053 or (round down) = 5%

So then, why didn't they just say this in the *first place*?!

The Price at Which Records Are Sold

Artist royalties are often affected by the cost at which record companies sell records to retailers. These may be divided into five primary categories: full-price records, midprice records, new and developing artist prices, budget records, and schlock/scrap.

Full-Price Records

Full price records are those that are sold to retailers at a wholesale PPD, which is the price on which we've been basing our examples in this chapter. At the time of this writing, a full-price CD sells to retailers at a wholesale PPD of $12.05. Your royalty for records sold at a full price are based on your U.S. royalty rate (or "all-in royalty rate"), which, for newer artists, could be in the range of 13 to 16 percent under a traditional deal structure. Don't forget that you still have to deduct your producer's share for this and everything that follows to arrive at your net rate.

Midprice Records (75% Reduction)

Mid-price records are those that are sold to retailers at a PPD between 60 and 80 percent of the full price. For instance, a midpriced CD may sell at between $7.23 and $9.63, considering a full price of $12.05. Since the record company makes less profit on these records, so do you! Your royalty reduction is typically 75 percent of your U.S. all-in royalty rate. So if you have an all-in royalty rate of 14 points, your all-in royalty for midprice records is 10.5 points (14 points x 75% = 10.5 percent.

New and Developing Artist Prices (75% Reduction)

Labels will often sell the records of "new and developing artists" to retailers at a PPD that is a "mid price" for the purpose of stimulating sales. The idea is that consumers are more likely to try something new if a record is sold at a lower price. Again, since the label makes less on these records, so do you—at the same rate as stated for midprice records above. But note that as your popularity builds as an artist, the label will likely raise the costs to retailers.

Budget Records (50% Reduction)

Budget records are those that are sold to retailers at a PPD that is at or below 60 percent of the full price. For instance, a budget CD may sell for $7.23 (and lower), considering a full price of $12.04. Since the record company receives less per record, you also receive a reduction that is 50 percent of your royalty rate. For example, if you have a U.S. all-in royalty rate of 14 points, your all-in royalty for budget records is 7 points (14 points x 50% = 7 percent).

Schlock/Scrap (100% Reduction)

Schlock refers to the records that are sold to retailers at a record company's cost (or below cost) as a way to get rid of them. Scrap is what ends up happening to your records after they're sold to be broken up and used as parts. To add insult to injury, you receive no royalty on schlock or scrap whatsoever.

Promotional records, such as those given to radio stations to encourage airplay, are always given away free and marked "not for sale," and you will not be paid record royalties for these records.

How Records Are Sold

Artist royalties may also be affected by how records sell. Let's take a look at three major categories: normal retail channels (e.g., record stores), record clubs (which are the clubs you read about in magazines where you can buy ten CDs for one penny), and mail order.

Normal Retail Channels

"Normal retail markets" essentially refers to record stores (which is what we've been using in many of our examples). Your royalty for sales here is your U.S. royalty rate (or "all-in royalty rate") in the range of 13 to 16 percent.

Record Clubs (50% Reduction)

Record clubs are the ones you use to read about it in magazines in which you can "buy ten CDs for the price of one" (for an example, check out BMG's official site at www.bmgmusic.com). Record labels may license your master recordings to record clubs (to manufacture, distribute, and sell) in order to reach consumers who theoretically cannot be reached at normal retail outlets. Typically, your royalty is 50 percent of your U.S. all-in royalty rate. So if you have a U.S. all-in royalty rate of 14 points, your all-in royalty for record clubs is 7 points (14 points x 50% = 7 percent).

By the way, it is probably also significant to note that when computing your royalty, the percentage of free goods that the record company gets away with deducting for record clubs is typically much higher than for normal retail sales—it can be as much as 50 percent, compared with the standard 15 percent. This means that for every 100 records sold by the record club, you're not only receiving an all-in royalty that is 50 percent less than your normal rate, but you're only paid on 50 percent of the total number of records sold through record clubs.

Mail Order and TV-Only Packages (50% Reduction)

Your royalty rate for records that are sold direct by mail order from the record company or through television advertising (everyone's heard of Monster Ballads, One-Hit Wonders, and products of that nature) is typically 50 percent of your U.S. all-in rate. So if you have a U.S. all-in royalty rate of 14 points, your all-in royalty for record clubs is 7 points (14 points x 50% = 7 percent). If, in the case of packaged albums, you are one of many artists, you royalty is prorated based on the number of compositions on the record.

Where Records Are Sold

Artist royalties are often affected by where records are sold. This topic may be divided primarily into two categories: the United States and foreign territories.

The United States

Your royalty rate, the all-in rate between 11 to 16 percent that we've been discussing throughout this chapter, is called the "U.S. basic rate."

Foreign Royalties (50–85% Reduction)

Because record labels' operating costs lead to smaller profit margins, there is a reduced rate for American records sold in Canada at 85 percent of your U.S. basic rate and a reduction for foreign major markets (Japan, the United Kingdom, Germany, Holland, France, and Italy) at typically 75 percent of your U.S. basic rate. For example, if you have a U.S. basic royalty rate of 14 points, your foreign all-in royalty in major markets is 75 percent of this rate (14 points x 75 percent = 10.5). For other territories in the world, your all-in royalty is around 50 percent of the U.S. all-in basic rate, or 7 points.

The Physical Configuration in Which Records Are Sold

An important factor that may affect artist royalties is the configuration in which records are sold. We've already been discussing CDs, for which the record company credits you a U.S. basic rate between 11 to 14 percent and you subtract the producer's share between 3 to 5 percent to arrive at a net royalty rate. But now let's discuss "recordings sold primarily via electronic transmission," like digital downloads, master tones, subscription services, and "any other device now and hereafter known that is capable of transmitting sound alone, or sound with visual images" (which, remember, is essentially a catch-all phrase to pick up any new technology that might come along).

ROYALTIES AND ELECTRONIC TRANSMISSIONS

Electronic transmissions of music by album or single song downloads via sites like iTunes (www.itunes), master tone sales via carriers like Verizon (www.verizon.com), "interactive" streaming audio and video via services like Yahoo! (music.yahoo.com), and "noninteractive" streaming (e.g., webcasting) via XM satellite radio (www.xm.com) and MusicChoice (www.musicchoice.com) all have different payment structures, thereby affecting your royalty.

While many of the prices for which music is sold and the methods by which royalties are computed may slightly change, the important thing to focus on here are the new sources (including some mysterious ones discussed below) of income that are available to you. While a new price base or royalty computation may yield a few more (or less) pennies here and there, remember that all of these monies (with one exception for which I'll note) get thrown into the big pot of recoupment. In case you forgot what this means, until you make enough money to pay back all your recoupable expenses to the record company, everything we discussed in this chapter on royalties would mean zilch to you, because you'd make no profit.

By the way, a list of websites that will help you get the very latest info is provided at the end of this section.

Digital Downloads (i.e., iTunes-Type Royalties)

Digital downloads from online companies like iTunes (www.itunes.com) and eMusic (www.emusic.com) are essentially "untethered downloads." While there may be some restrictions to what the consumer can do with the download, he/she can copy it, burn it, upload into an iPod, and own it. Royalties are credited to you by your label at the same royalty rate you get for CDs, even when considering single-song downloads (which are far more popular than downloads of CDs and therefore our focus). If your U.S. basic rate was 14 points, for instance, and you pay a producer 4 points, your net royalty rate is 10 percent for digital downloads.

Royalties for digital downloads are typically computed by your record company on the price to the consumer, with consideration to a share that goes to the company providing the download and to some other funky computations by the record company that may exist. For instance, as attorney Dina LaPolt tells me, sometimes the record company may do what's called a "wholesale markup of 130 percent before computing your royalty, or less commonly it may deduct music publishing royalties (called mechanical royalties, as discussed in Chapter 11) before computing your royalty, but the difference really amounts to pennies.

For purposes of example, if a single-song download sold on iTunes for 99 cents, 29 cents of this would go to iTunes, leaving 70 cents. The record company then multiplies this amount by 130 percent to create an artificial wholesale markup of 91 cents ($0.70 x 1.30 = $0.91). The label then multiplies this amount by your net royalty rate of, say, 10 percent, arriving at your royalty per single digital download of approximately 9 cents ($0.91 x 0.10 = $0.09).

Let's take a look at the computation below of a single-song download with (1) the record company wholesale markup, and (2) without the record company wholesale markup of 130 percent. Note that I am not factoring in other customary deductions like free goods and reserves, but keep in mind that unless they are negotiated out of the recording agreement, they could also apply here as well.

> Sale versus a license? A hot battle in the music industry between labels and artists has been whether a download actually constitutes a sale, in which case the artist is paid his or her royalty rate (as shown in our examples), or a license, in which case the artist is paid as much as fifty percent. While it looks like the artists are losing this battle, you'll want to stay tuned.

Example 1:

$0.99 (single-song download price to the consumer)

– $0.29 (iTunes share)

= $0.70

x 1.30 (130 percent wholesale markup)

= $0.91

x 0.10 (artist net royalty rate of 10 percent)

= $0.09 (artist royalty per single-song download)

Example 2:

$0.99 (single-song download price to the consumer)

– $0.29 (iTunes share)

= $0.70

x 0.10 (artist net royalty rate of 10 percent)

=$0.07 (artist royalty per single-song download)

> Will there be variable pricing ($0.79, $0.99, $1.29) for downloads that allow you to make unlimited copies versus those that do not, for artists that are considered more successful versus newer artists, and for tracks that are considered a better sound quality? Perhaps there already is. Stay tuned.

Master Tones (aka Mobile Tones)

Master tones, another type of "untethered download," are snippets of songs from your CD downloaded via mobile carriers like Verizon (www.VerizonWireless.com) and used on cell phones—a song alerts a consumer that someone is calling, and a song alerts the caller that the phone is ringing or busy. Royalties are credited to you at the same net royalty rate for CDs. If your U.S. basic rate is 14 points, for instance, and you pay a producer 4 points, your net royalty rate is 10 percent for master tone sales.

For purposes of an example, if a master tone is sold through a carrier like Verizon for an average retail price of $2.49, Verizon receives half of this amount (50%), leaving $1.24 ($2.49 x 0.50 =

> Sale versus a license? Like digital downloads, master tones have been at the center of debate between artists and labels as to whether they constitutes a sale, in which case the artist is paid their royalty rate, or a license, wherein the artist is paid as much as fifty percent. Again, it looks like this is a losing battle for artists, but stay tuned.

$1.24). The record company then deducts music publishing royalties (called mechanical royalties, as discussed in Chapter 11) at about 10 percent of the retail price of $2.49, which is approximately 25 cents (but this could be reduced to as low as 9.1 cents and even lower—so you want to stay tuned), leaving 99 cents ($1.24 – $0.25 = $0.99). The label then multiplies this amount by your net royalty rate of, say, 10 percent, arriving at your royalty per single master tone of approximately 10 cents ($0.99 x 0.10 = $0.099).

Let's take a look at the computation below of a single-song master tone with the record company deducting a mechanical royalty of approximately 10 percent of the average selling price (e.g., $0.25). Again, though, this could change. Note that I am not factoring in other customary deductions like free goods and reserves, but keep in mind that unless they are negotiated out of the recording agreement by your attorney, they could also apply here as well.

Example 1:
$2.49 (average retail price to the consumer)
– $1.25 (carrier split of 50%)
= $1.24
– $0.25 (Music publishers/songwriters share of approx. 10%)
= $0.99 cents
x 0.10 (artist net royalty rate of 10 percent)
= $0.099 (artist royalty per single master tone)

Note: I just want to stress again that the music publisher's rate could change to a statutory rate of somewhere around 9.1, or another penny rate. Nonetheless, giving or taking some change, the above example still shows how everyone gets their cut.

Interactive Streaming Audio/Video

"Interactive" subscription services like Yahoo! (music.yahoo.com), AOL (music.aol.com), MSN (www.music.msn.com), Napster (www.napster.com), and Rhapsody (through RealNetworks' www.rhapsody.com), in which the consumer interacts with the service (streams on-demand, creates personalized play lists, etc.), is a form of "tethered download." This typically means that as long as the consumer pays a subscription fee, he/she can "use" (not own) all the music desired so long as he/she keeps on paying fees. According to attorney Dina LaPolt, when the record company licenses the master recordings of your songs or music videos to these services it will collect a fee per stream (about a penny per stream) and credit you with a split of these earnings at a rate that is likely half a penny—or $0.005 as in our example.

LaPolt continues: "Although permanent royalty rates are still being worked out between the record labels and some of their artists as the industry evolves more into the digital realm, a partial list of interactive digital subscription services and information pertaining to them can be found by logging onto CD Baby (www.cdbaby.net). Once logged on, click on 'Sell Your Music,' then 'Digital Distribution,' and then click on 'Partner Companies' on the right-hand side." Some other websites that are also helpful are www.soundexchange.com, www.ASCAP.com, and www.BMI.com. **Note:** Payment for broadcasts on terrestrial radio may also one day apply, so stay tuned.

Noninteractive Subscription Services

"Noninteractive" subscription services like terrestrial (land) radio stations and fan-based stations that broadcast music to satellite subscription services like XM (www.xm.com) and Sirius (www. sirius.com) to subscription services like MusicChoice (www.music choice.com) via satellite transmission on digital cable television like Dish Network (www.dishnetwork.com) and DirecTV (www. directtv.com), are all sites that *do not* allow consumers to interact (i.e., pick songs as they wish, make set lists, and download music). Nonetheless, when the master recordings on which you performed for your record company are streamed via these mediums, you are due a webcasting royalty by law. Webcasting royalties are collected and paid out to you *directly* by two different agencies: Sound Exchange (www.soundexchange.com) and Royalty Logic (www.royaltylogic.com) — so *these monies do not go toward recoupment of your advances.*

> Isn't there also something called a "performance royalty" due to the songwriters and publishers for interactive and non-interactive streams of compositions over the Internet? You bet, and it's collected by the performing rights organizations ASCAP, BMI, and SESAC. More on music publishing in Chapter 11.

Under the digital Millenium Copyright Act of 1995, Congress provided that 50 percent of these monies are paid to the owner of the sound recordings (i.e., the record label), 5 percent is paid to the unions AFM (www.afm.com) and AFTRA (www.aftra.com) for session players, and the other 45 percent is paid to the featured performers (i.e., you) on the recording. Just be sure to register with either Sound Exchange or Royalty Logic before your record is released.

Podcasts

Podcasts, "shows" including music and interviews that can be downloaded onto a consumers' computer (and to the popular iPod portable device), are usually available for free on websites that earn money through advertising or subscription fees. Therefore, if podcasts really take off from a commercial standpoint, and they may already have by the time you're reading this, your royalty may be based on a percentage of advertising revenue or subscription service fees. Time will only tell how this will all work out.

Fill-up Stations and Kiosks

Kiosks are machines in various stores that allow consumers to burn a song selection onto a disc. Just as people sit at home and buy songs from Apple's iTunes for 99 cents a pop, they can also burn songs in places like Starbucks, bookstores, electronics stores, and record shops for a three-dollar fee to cover the costs of a jewel case, customized labels, and a CD. The machines provide a "virtual inventory," offering a far greater supply of music than the physical CDs that most stores can stock. The software on the machines can recommend artists that a customer might like based on his or her past purchases, which keeps customers burning and also in the stores.

Fill-up stations are like gas stations for your portable listening device (e.g., your iPod) — you pick a song from a machine in a store that downloads it right into your player.

The royalty for both fill-up stations and kiosks will likely be similar to the royalty you get for a digital download. In any case, be sure to check out Donald Passman's book *All You Need to Know about the Music Business*, in which he discusses the fill-up stations and kiosks.

Uranus Streams and Other Stuff

Okay, so the planet Uranus part is a joke, but you can bet that any device now and hereafter that is capable of transmitting sound alone, or sound with visual images, will eventually entitle you to a royalty once everyone scrambles to figure out how to deal with it. And just when they do, a newer technology will be invented to replace it, and everyone will freak out all over again. Donald Passman calls this the "Passman Theory of Technological Cycles." Let's face it, some of us have seen the media of music distribution change from phonograph records, to 8-track tapes, to cassette tapes, to CDs, to MP3s. What makes us think it's not going to change again? It will. So get ready and enjoy the ride. And while we must accept that music is a business, let's hope that with all this new technology the world doesn't forget the most important ingredient of all—THE MUSIC, and even more important, THE REAL MUSICIANS that respect, love, and CREATE IT!

SHOW ME MO' MONEY: MASTER USE, GAMES, AND AUDIOVISUAL DVDS

Let's take a very brief look at some of the other methods by which you are credited an artist royalty for the license or sale of your CD, including film and TV master use licenses, video game master use licenses, and audiovisual DVDs (aka home videos). Once again, keep in mind that all these monies essentially go toward the recoupment of all your recording and other advanced expenses.

Film and TV Master Use Licenses

Master use licenses—where the record company licenses the recorded masters of your music to video games, film, and television—will pay you 50 percent of the monies received. If this sounds simple enough, note that sometimes the label may take what's called a "special markets division" fee off the top (before calculating your percentage) for all its efforts in trying to push your record in these areas.

Isn't there also something called a "synchronization license" due to songwriters and publishers for the licensing of your musical compositions in film, TV, and video games? Sure is! We'll discuss this in Chapter 11.

Video Game Master Use Licenses

Video games like *Grand Theft Auto* by Rockstar Games (www.rockstargames.com), *Guitar Hero* by Red Octane (www.redoctane.com), *Joe Madden Football* by Electronic Arts (www.ea.com), and many others, are yet another medium by which you will receive an artist royalty from the record label for the licensing of your CD. Attorney Dina LaPolt says, "The video game industry has followed the model used by the film industry when it comes to obtaining a license for music on video games. Accordingly, with few exceptions, most game companies license music as a 'buyout' (meaning they don't pay a unit royalty for sales). Buyouts can range from $5,000 to $10,000 per master recording. The record label collects this money and splits it with you 50/50."

HOW TO INCREASE RECORD SALES DOING IT YOURSELF

Do-it-yourself artists can be empowered by all the new tools and technology available today to increase sales and exposure. The idea is to attract the attention of those that can help you by first helping yourself. Here are a few tips:

Establish creative pricing. Establish a "special discount price" or a "package deal incentive" (e.g., sell your CDs for $10, T-shirts for $15, key chains for $2, and all three for $20) for fans that attend shows or visit your website.

Sell at your live performances. Display your CDs and merch in attractive setups at your shows to stimulate healthy sales. Be prepared to take various payment methods, including credit cards (see CD Baby's Swiper program at CDbaby.com).

Sell from your website. Generate sales by signing up with a free and easy-to-use e-commerce service like PayPal (www.paypal.com).

Affiliate with online retailers. Check out CD Baby (www.cdbaby.com), the Orchard (www.theorchard.com), Tune Core (www.tunecore.com), and Amazon.com's Advantage program (www.amazon.com) that all have strong sales and fulfillment services.

Affiliate with community sites. Sites such as MySpace.com (www.myspace.com) and Music.com enable you to sell your music in various ways (downloads, master tones). Check out these and many other sites.

Establish local consignment agreements. Establish local consignment agreements with independent record stores, clothing and sports shops, and even with your fans.

Increase your sales skills. Read books like *Zig Ziglar's Secrets of Closing the Sale* that will help increase your sales, negotiation, and intrapersonal skills.

Promote sales. Post messages on community sites like MySpace and on discussion groups found on Yahoo! (www.yahoogroups.com). Send sales announcements via your e-mail lists and arrange agreements with local bands to have your announcements sent on their e-mail lists. Get your CD reviewed in local magazines and e-zines like *Pitchfork* (www.pitchfork media.com). Seek radio play at local colleges or start a blog to attract attention.

Track sales. Register your bar code (the code on the back of your CD) with Nielson SoundScan (www.soundscan.com) so that sales of your CD can be verified when sold at retail and from digital download sites like iTunes. To help verify sales with SoundScan at your live performances, ask the venue owner if they are registered with SoundScan and if so to provide a "venue verification form."

Find a retail distributor. The main function of a distributor is to fulfill a demand that you've already created. Assuming you have verifiable data that you're making sales, there's a strong buzz about your band, and you can show you have finances to pay into special "marketing programs" arranged by distributors, start getting referrals from local indie artists who have distribution and/or refer to *Billboard's International Buyer's Guide* (www.billboard.biz.com) and make contact.

Check out www.bobbyborg.com for more tips on how to create a buzz and market your CD and on putting together and initiating a marketing plan of attack.

Audiovisual DVDs (aka Home Videos)

Audiovisual DVDs, like "compilations" of individual video clips with other artists, or of one only artist (like *Metallica: The Videos 1989–2004*); documentaries (like *Metallica: Some Kind of Monster*); and live concert videos (like *Metallica with the San Francisco Symphony*) are other media by which you are credited a royalty by the record label. A common royalty rate for sales of your DVD is anywhere from 10 to 20 percent of the wholesale price. If your video(s) is part of a compilation with other bands, then you get paid a prorated amount of your royalty depending on the number of clips you have on the DVD (a band that has a 15 percent royalty rate and one video on a ten-song DVD gets a royalty of 1/10 of 15 percent or 1.5 percent of the wholesale price).

Video production costs are huge: It can cost from $75,000 to $350,000 produce a single high-quality promotional video. These expenses are all paid back to the record company from sales of audiovisual DVDs before you ever see a penny. And if you were paying attention, you should remember that once all video expenses are recouped, your audiovisual DVD royalties are then used to repay all record expenses that have not been recouped, and vice versa for the record royalties (i.e., once record expenses are recouped from record royalties, record royalties are then used to repay unrecouped audiovisual DVD expenses). Typically, only 50 percent of video expenses are charged against record royalties.

STAY UP TO PACE WITH TECHNOLOGY BY LOGGING ON

The music business is fast and ever-changing, making it difficult to keep up with. For the most up-to-date information pertaining to the music industry and the digital space, please visit the following websites:

Sound Exchange (www.soundexhange.com)

Royalty Logic (www.royaltylogic.com)

Billboard magazine (www.billboard.com)

CD Baby (www.cdbaby.net)

Copyright Office (www.copyright.gov)

Recording Artist Coalition (www.recordingartistscoalition.com)

Future of Music (www.futureofmusic.com)

Music Manager's Forum (www.mmfus.com)

Harry Fox Agency (www.harryfoxagency.com)

Recording Industry Association of America (www.riaa.com)

American Federation of Musicians (www.afm.com)

American Federation of Radio and Television Artists (www.aftra.com)

Bobby Borg (www.bobbyborg.com)—look for "revision updates"

Bobby Borg (www.bobbyborg.com/promotion)—look for special offers

CHAPTER 11

Music
Publishing

"Making music is an art. Making a living from it is a business."
—BILLY MITCHELL, Author of *The Gigging Musician*

As Ed Pierson, vice president of business and legal affairs at Warner/Chappell Music aptly says, "Music publishing is the business of songs." It deals with everything from the ownership and control of your compositions to the income generated when your songs are used by record labels, motion picture and television companies, Internet sites, game manufacturers, and print companies. Licenses for the use of your compositions can be issued by you or by a more experienced music publishing company representing you. If all this sounds complicated—guess what? It is. But you're not alone!

Music publishing is perhaps one of the most difficult areas of business for musicians to understand. It's based on complex and ever-changing laws, and as in any other legal setting, there are numerous exceptions to every rule. Covering each of these exceptions might make an interesting read for the sharp-eyed purist, but it would just confuse the hell out of the rest of us. So for the sake of simplicity, we'll take a straightforward approach to this chapter, discussing the "ifs," "ands," or "buts" only when necessary. Additionally, copyright laws differ in foreign territories, so we'll emphasize U.S. laws and focus primarily by example on the copyrights in your words and music. We'll also look at publishing incomes, publishing deals, starting your own publishing company, and tips on pitching your music for film and TV.

Don't be frustrated if it takes a few rereadings before this information sinks in; most industry professionals will admit they had to deal with this stuff for years before getting a grip on it. (Well, at least some will admit it.) But make no mistake—music publishing is one of the most important aspects of your music business education. It's an area in which fortunes have been both lost and found. So take everything you're about to read very seriously.

COPYRIGHT BASICS

The first step to understanding music publishing is to understand the basics of copyright and copyright protection. Why? Well, let's see if it becomes more clear when we break it down for you. The word *music* refers to the compositions you create. That's pretty obvious! The word *publishing* refers to the process of making your compositions available to the public by sale or other means. *Copyrights are the rights that constitute your legal protection against the unauthorized use of your original works.* Make sense? Great! Now you're ready to learn more about copyrights.

According to a myth that exists among musicians, to obtain a copyright for your compositions, you need to fill out a registration form and send it to the Copyright Office in Washington, DC Although copyright registration provides certain benefits under law and is highly recommended (more about this later), *a copyright exists as soon as an original idea is affixed into a tangible form.* In other words, as soon as one of your song ideas is recorded on a cassette tape, CD, hard drive, etc., or the lyrics to one of your compositions are written on a sheet of paper, you automatically have a copyright. It's that's simple! So, in essence, a copyright basically exists when the song itself is transcribed in some form.

As the proud owner of a copyright, you get an exclusive bundle of rights that goes along with it. For instance, as stated in section 106 of the United States Copyright Act, a copyright grants you the exclusive right to reproduce (i.e., copy), distribute (with the intent to sell), and perform your compositions. If so desired, you could sit around creating copyrights for days, only to lock them up in a drawer, never to be used. Although this would hardly be the most efficient way to spend your time, it's your right!

A copyright also grants you the exclusive right to make any "derivative works," which are works based on your composition. For instance, before Weird Al Yankovic recorded his version of Michael Jackson's song "Beat It" and renamed it "Eat It," Yankovic had to first obtain permission from Jackson. Before comedian Cheech Marin recorded a version of Bruce Springsteen's "Born in the USA" and renamed it "Born in East LA," he had to ask The Boss for permission. In fact, when Cheech was asked if it was easy to obtain approval from The Boss, he replied, "I would have an easier time giving birth." In the electronic genre, before DJs can legally record remixes of original songs, they, too, must first obtain permission from the author or owner. You get the idea!

As you can see, without copyright law, there would really be no point in creating anything new at all businesswise, since anyone could conceivably use any piece of work for any purpose for free—and that, needless to say, would suck! In fact, as stated in the Copyright Act, the purpose of a copyright is to promote the progress of useful arts by giving creators exclusive rights to their works for a period of time. So rejoice! You get a lot of mileage out of owning a copyright, and all for simply being the creative person you are.

WORK FOR HIRE

Before you get comfortable, you need to know about a situation called "work for hire." This essentially means that if you create a work under the scope of employment, or if you are commissioned to create a work, *the employer becomes the author and owner of the copyright.* You should get paid an initial fee for the job, and may even be listed as the creator, but the employer gets ownership and all the generated dough (except, perhaps, the writer's share of performance income, which you'll learn about later). A work-for-hire arrangement may exist if you're employed by a jingle house to write songs for television or radio commercials under specific guidelines, or if you're commissioned to write songs for a film under similar guidelines (the laws are actually a bit more defined, but you get the idea). Aside from this one clear distinction under United States copyright law, our good friend Ed Pierson at Warner/Chappell Music says that the general principle underscoring copyright law is as follows: *If you write it, then you own it.* Make sure to understand the conditions of any relationship in which you compose songs, and, of course, make sure you never sign any agreement you don't fully understand.

JOINT WORKS

If what we've discussed about copyrights seems reasonably easy to understand so far, just wait—things get much more complicated when you get into discussing something called "joint works." What's a joint work? It's exactly what it says. When two or more people come together to create a song, and each person makes a lyrical or musical (i.e., melodic or hooky groove or beat) contribution, the resulting composition is considered a joint work. The copyright is jointly owned. Take a look at the vast majority of records released today, and you'll find that there's more than one writer listed next to each song.

As previously mentioned, joint works fall into an area of copyright law in which things get a bit more tricky. Therefore, a few principles regarding joint works must be understood by all of the work's authors. The most important principles have to do with ownership and control.

Ownership of Joint Works

A primary concern regarding joint works is the division of ownership. Let's begin by taking a look at what copyright law says, then explore the exceptions to copyright law per written agreement, and finally consider its "all-for-one, one-for-all" philosophy.

Division of Ownership under Copyright Law

There's a presumption under copyright law that the authors of a joint work are automatically considered equal contributors. This simply means that if a band writes a song, *each writer automatically owns an equal share of the rights—no matter how big or small their musical or lyrical contribution actually was.*

Determining a *musical or lyrical* contribution is less simple. A "lyrical" contribution obviously constitutes the words written as part of a musical composition. What constitutes a "musical" contribution, how-ever, is often the source of great confusion. Neil Gillis, vice president and director of operations at Dimensional Music Publishing, says that a musical contribution includes the melody, as well as any preexisting riff or groove that becomes an integral hook to the song. Take the drum part in the song "Wipe Out," for example, or the bass riff from the song "Come Together." Would these songs be the same if either part were excluded? The answer is no! Nevertheless, Neil Gillis warns that he would never walk out of a writing session without first making it clear among all the writers what percentage of each composition he owned. A simple agreement will suffice. It's not a bad idea to record writing sessions on a small recorder and to keep copies of original lyric sheets in case a dispute between writers ever materializes. Unfortunately, disputes between writers are not uncommon.

Exceptions to Copyright Law Per Written Agreement

Keeping in mind what copyright law says, if the split percentage in ownership of a composition is intended in any way to be something other than equal, there *must* be a written agreement setting forth what that split really is. For instance, if the other members of your band agree that the bass player's contribution in a song should only entitle him to a 10 percent share in ownership rights, this must be put in writing!

You may be wondering whether any musician would carelessly agree to a smaller percentage share than he or she actually deserves. It's been known to happen! In fact, I've known several musicians who, throughout the course of performing with one extremely successful rock singer (who must remain anonymous), signed away 100 percent of their song shares in return for a small sum of money paid up front. Not realizing the potential value of their shares over the long term, the guys felt that it was what they needed to do at the time to keep their positions in the band. Needless to say, they're all kicking themselves now. This is one area in which you want foresight, not hindsight.

> Be clear that a joint work means that each writer owns a piece of the *whole song*. For example, if one writer composes 100 percent of the lyrics and another writer composes 100 percent of the music, each writer owns 50 percent of the entire song. In his book *All You Need to Know about the Music Business*, Donald Passman uses a great metaphor to illustrate this point: "It's like scrambling the white and the yolk of the egg together." The two parts are not easily separable afterward.

The "All-for-One, One-for-All" Philosophy

With all this talk of what's copyrightable and who's entitled to what, you might ask what happened to the "all-for-one, one-for-all" philosophy that most young bands and writers swear to. After all, if a group of writers stuff themselves into a practice room to spend hours of their valuable time experimenting with song ideas and recording demos, is it really fair that the harmonica player gets zero interest in a song just because he wasn't feeling as lyrically or melodically creative as the others that day? And what happens when all the writers make relevant suggestions and have to determine whose chorus idea gets used? Can this potentially turn the writing process into a competitive game of who's getting credit rather than a group attempt to focus on writing the best song possible? I know this all sounds a bit immature, but it's a very real problem. Consequently, many bands have an initial agreement stating that all of its members will receive an equal split in the songs, regardless of who comes up with what.

The all-for-one, one-for-all philosophy makes perfect sense at first and works for many years of a relationship. However, once a group becomes successful and everyone in the industry begins telling the vocalist or guitarist that he or she is the real star and genius of the band—trust me, the divisions in the new songs will quickly change in their favor. This is also when the Jimmy Pages and Robert Plants of the world begin wandering off on their own and creating demos of complete song ideas to bring back to the band. In other words, this is usually when other members get cut out altogether! It may be a harsh reality, but one or two writers in a group dynamic are usually the principal creators, and it takes a great deal of maturity on the part of the other members to recognize this.

Control of Joint Works

The next issue of importance regarding joint works involves how the control of the rights to a song is shared. Let's take a look at your licensing rights under copyright law, then cover exceptions to copyright law per written agreement, and finally focus on the transfer and sale of copyright.

Rights Under Copyright Law

Under U.S. copyright law, each individual writer of a composition can issue as many "nonexclusive" licenses as he or she wants (to record companies, film companies, etc.), as long as he or she accounts to, and pays, all of the other writers their respective shares. For example, if four writers each own 25 percent of a composition, one writer can license (grant permission) the use of the complete song in a film for $4,000, as long as he or she pays each of the other three writers $1,000. The person doing this better also remember to report the payout to Uncle Sam properly so he or she will pay taxes only on the $1,000 and not the $4,000 collected. Nonetheless, as one can only imagine, too much freedom of use of a song among the writers can eventually cause problems. One coauthor might not want to see a composition licensed in a specific film, while the other coauthors may be thrilled by the idea.

To complicate matters even more, suppose the members of a band all collaborate on writing a large repertoire of songs, only to end up separating after a disagreement occurs. If any of the members form new groups, procure recording agreements, and then want to record the same song on their album, each author is technically entitled to the "first use" of the composition. It basically comes down to which writer beats the others to recording first.

Exceptions to Copyright Law per Written Agreement

Clearly, when two or more writers get together to write a song, it's advisable for the coauthors to have a written agreement between them that not only confirms their individual shares in a song (as previously discussed) but also defines *how a composition can and cannot be used, and who can use it first.* Some successful artists are known for going as far as having long-form agreements granting them primary control of a song whenever they collaborate with other writers. This means that if you ever write with such an artist, it's possible you can own a 25 percent share in a composition and have absolutely no say in how the song will be used.

Although written agreements are extremely important and are always the best remedy for avoiding potential misunderstandings or disputes, Ed Pierson at Warner/Chappell Music says you'd be surprised by the number of collaborating writers who never formulate an agreement. And despite what copyright law might say, the standard practice among most companies interested in using your music is to *first and foremost obtain permission from each author individually* anyway. This is in no way meant to undermine the importance of a written agreement. Again, a preliminary understanding among owners as to how a composition can and cannot be used is still the best precaution for all involved.

Note that a license is only a partial and temporary grant of permission. A nonexclusive license means that other licenses (for films, etc.) can be issued simultaneously. When an exclusive license is issued—one with more restrictions, as in a national advertising campaign—no new licenses can be issued while the commercial is being aired. (See "Points of Negotiation" later in this chapter.)

Restrictions to Transfer or Sale of Copyright

Finally, this is one more brief point regarding joint works and the control each writer can or cannot exercise. It deals with transferring or selling copyrights, which happens when you sign a publishing agreement with a publishing company. Remember, according to the principles you have just learned, the joint owners of a composition can technically issue as many nonexclusive licenses as they want, as long as they account for them to the other owners. The exception to this rule is a case in which a written agreement between the writers exists that states otherwise. But note this one important distinction: There's a difference between licensing the rights and selling the rights, *and under no circumstances can the individual writers transfer or sell the rights in the entire composition unless all the writers jointly agree!*

Suppose you co-wrote a song with a friend who was about to release an album with a major label. Since there was a lot of hype generated around the band, your friend decided to seek the assistance of an experienced music publishing company to help issue licenses for the use of his songs, place his songs in films and television, and as an added bonus, pay him a large advance against future royalty earnings. The price for all of this, however, is that he had to transfer copyright ownership in all of his songs on his forthcoming record (as is generally the case when signing most publishing agreements—more on this later). So here's the problem: Your friend is permitted to transfer *his rights* in the song, which you co-wrote, but he cannot transfer the entire song unless you *jointly agree*. In essence, he can sign over his shares in the song to a publishing company, while you retain your rights and sign with a publisher of your choice. If that isn't clear, then compare it to two friends who jointly own real estate. If one owner wants to sell his share, it's his right; however, he cannot sell the entire property without your permission.

THE COMPULSORY LICENSING PROVISION

You've already learned that as soon as you transfer an original idea into a tangible form, you automatically get a copyright. But before you get too comfortable with all of the exclusive rights you get

FIRST USE, NOT MISUSE In practically all situations, despite ego, pride, or any other hangup you can think of, most co-writers of a composition are happy simply to have their song released on phonorecord—regardless of which writer is using the song first. But as Leah Furman illustrates in her book *Korn: Life in The Pit*, when the rock group Korn recorded its debut album, the group used a previously unrecorded song from vocalist Jonathan Davis's former band (SexArt) without notifying or giving proper credits to its co-writer. This, of course, shifted the issue from a matter of first use to one of misuse. Ryan Schuck, also a former member of SexArt and coauthor of "Blind," the song in question, promptly sued Korn for copyright infringement. The case was settled out of court, and Schuck now receives both writer's credit and royalties from the song. And here's the storybook ending: Despite Schuck and Davis's dispute, the former bandmates have buried the hatchet and are now friends. In fact, Schuck's new band, Orgy, ended up signing to Korn's record label, Elementree. But as you'll see later in this chapter, things don't always work out so amicably in infringement cases.

with a copyright, you need to know about an exception to the rule that allows others to use your song under a provision of copyright law called the "compulsory licensing provision." This provision applies in various ways to music licensed for jukeboxes, the public broadcasting system, cable television, digital phonorecord delivery (or DPDs of musical works for sale on sites like iTunes), master tones, ring backs *and* polyphonic ring tones, and phonorecords (i.e., audio-only recordings as opposed to audiovisual DVDs) of musical compositions. Let's take a look at one of the most significant area: licenses for phonorecords of musical compositions.

What else is compulsory? Under the Digital Millennium Copyright Act of 1998, the owners of "master sound recordings" (as are many do-it-yourself artists) must also issue a license to webcasters of noninteractive websites (like Web and satellite radio stations) wishing to broadcast your music, in return for a set fee. For more details, go to the Sound Exchange website (www.sound exchange.com).

Under section 115 of the Copyright Act, the word *compulsory* means "mandatory." In not so many words, the compulsory licensing provision states that (1) As soon as you record a composition for the first time on phonorecord, and (2) as soon as it's distributed for commercial sale to the public, (3) you must license it to any other artist who wants to release it on their record. That's right! As long as the above-noted conditions exist, and the lyric or melodic content is not significantly changed or modified, *anyone who wants to record your song for commercial release on phonorecord has the right to obtain a license by law*. This rule grew out of a concern in Congress that the music business could become a monopoly, and, as a result, the members of Congress wanted to limit your rights as an author. But, don't worry; you'll get paid a fee for the use. In fact, a trio of copyright royalty judges called the Copyright Royalty Board (CRB) sets a fee called a "statutory mechanical royalty." Don't worry about the specifics of mechanical royalties for right now because they are covered in "Mechanical Royalties" later in this chapter (you can also read more at the Copyright Office website, at www.copyright.gov).

Just be assured that mechanicals can add up to a great deal of money if another artist makes your song successful and sells a significant number of CDs or digital downloads. In fact, the artist covering your song may give it a whole new life and allow you to earn mechanicals for years to come (as well as other royalties from the performances of the song on radio and on the Internet and fees from when the song is used in film and TV, which we'll also discuss later).

But there's one downside to all of this—the artist covering your song may make it more famous than you have, and the general public, which generally doesn't understand album liner notes in respect to ownership, will never know that you were the author. Did you know that Fleetwood Mac wrote and recorded "Landslide" before the Smashing Pumpkins covered it, that the Guess Who wrote and recorded "American Woman" before Lenny Kravitz covered it, and that Bob Dylan wrote and recorded "All Along the Watchtower" before Jimi Hendrix covered it? Okay, so you knew this bit of history, but you'd be surprised at the number of people who don't!

COPYRIGHT DURATION

Now that you understand what a copyright is and the bundle of rights you get when you create one of these valuable creatures, you may be wondering how long all this good stuff is going to last you. You may also be wondering whether if you sell your copyrights, as in the case when you sign a deal with a music publishing company, you can ever get them back.

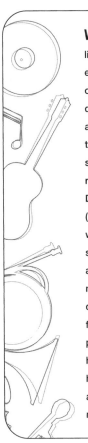

WHEN YOU COVER SOMEONE ELSE'S SONG... Under the compulsory licensing provision in copyright law, you have the legal right to record or "cover" someone else's song (a song which has first been released on record in the U.S. by the legal consent of the owner) and to distribute that recording on either a CD or over the Internet (called a digital phonorecord delivery, or "DPD") as long as you follow proper licensing procedures and compensate the publisher accordingly. At the most complex level, a "notice of intent to obtain a compulsory license" must be sent via certified mail to the writer/publisher of the song containing information like your name and band name, the name and address of your record company, the date of release, and the "configuration" of release (i.e., CD and/or DPD). You are also required to make monthly royalty accountings and statutory payments. (For detailed information, please see www.copyright.gov or www.cdbaby.com. Search for writer/publishers through www.ascap.com, www.bmi.com, or www.sesac.com.) At the simplest level, a "mechanical license" can be issued and less onerous accounting terms and lower royalty rates be negotiated by either the writer/publisher or by representatives—namely the Harry Fox Agency (www.harryfox. com)—or at www.songfile.com. Britt Draska, director of royalties at Lakeshore Entertainment Group, says you may be able to prepay a flat fee if you are only pressing a limited run from 250 to 2,500 CDs or creating 150 to 2,500 permanent downloads of a song from a server located within the U.S., so that you don't have to deal with accounting and statements. In any case, by covering a popular song or hit, you can generate interest in your own band and entice sales of your CDs, merchandise, and live performance tickets. As long as your version rocks and you take care of all business matters properly, everyone wins!

The Copyright Term

When discussing the term of a copyright (or copyright "duration") you should know that the law has undergone significant changes dating as far back as 1909. But all you really need to know for now (and yes, I'm really simplifying this) is that according to the U.S. Copyright Act of 1976, all compositions written on or after January 1, 1978, receive a copyright term for *life of the author plus fifty years*. In 1998, the late, great Sonny Bono (the musician who was married to Cher and was half of the Sonny and Cher duo) successfully lobbied to extend the copyright term by twenty years. Therefore, when you compose your original smash hit in your bedroom tonight, the current *copyright term lasts for the life of the author plus seventy years*. I know you can't take your prize possessions with you when you die, but your family (for instance) can enjoy the fruits of your labor for another seventy years after you pass—as long as you properly manage your affairs and will these rights over to them.

As for joint works, the copyright term currently lasts for *seventy years after the death of the last surviving author*.

When a work is created under a work-for-hire condition (remember that this a situation in which the employer gets ownership), the current copyright term lasts for ninety-five years from publication and one hundred and twenty years from creation, whichever comes sooner.

After the copyright term has ended, the composition falls into something called the "public domain," which essentially means that anyone can use the composition free of licensing fees. But don't worry, by that time, you won't mind too much, because you'll be long gone. Okay, enough of this morbid stuff. I suggest you get around to reading more about the copyright term at www.copyright.gov, but let's move on for now.

Reversion of Copyright

So what happens when you transfer or sell your copyrights, as in the case when you sign a publishing agreement? Are you permanently signing over your publishing rights to the song? The answer is yes! Well, sort of. You see, in most publishing contracts, especially when you have a little negotiating power, there's usually a clause incorporated into your agreement called "reversion of copyright." The reversion of copyright clause stipulates that your copyrights will revert to you at a predetermined time in the future (say, about ten years after your contract expires). That's great news, right? Let me emphasize, however, that reversion of copyright is not part of actual copyright law; *it's a clause that must be negotiated into your publishing agreement*. Absent this clause, you do have another crack at getting back partial ownership. However, you will have to wait quite some time.

Thirty-Five-Year Statutory Right of Termination

In the worst-case scenario, if you were unwise to not negotiate a reversion clause in your agreement with a music publisher, copyright law provides that *all original copyright owners (or their heirs) will have a chance to reacquire ownership after thirty-five years of the date of copyright transfer*. This "right of termination" only applies within the United States and to licenses issued *after* the termination date (that is, assuming you successfully complete a number of legal formalities—which are way too confusing to deal with given the scope of this book and the time allotted). The music publisher still keeps all foreign rights and has the right to continue to collect on any licenses already issued (this is a big deal if the original license includes future media language). What I'm saying is that you should fight damn hard to get reversionary language negotiated into your publishing agreement, because it is ultimately much better than termination. You simply can't get the same results by just relying on the copyright termination laws, but you should at least know they exisit.

As always, there's an exception to the right of termination law that falls under a work-for-hire relationship. Once again, a work-for-hire is when you're hired to compose under the scope of very specific guidelines, or when you sign a written agreement that clearly states a work-for-hire relationship. And since the employer in that arrangement retains the rights of ownership in all of the compositions you create, *you can never get your copyrights back,* despite the right of termination law! Why? Because you never owned them in the first place. Again, it's vital you be clear about the terms under which you compose for or with anyone.

COPYRIGHT REGISTRATION

As previously mentioned, as soon as you affix an original idea into a tangible form, such as recording your song idea on a cassette tape, CD, hard drive, etc., or a lyric onto a sheet of paper, you automatically have a copyright. When and how is it best to register? What are the benefits of copyright registration?

The Benefits of Copyright Registration

Registering your compositions with the Copyright Office in Washington, DC, provides you with three major benefits:

1. You get the "rebuttable presumption" that you're the original author and owner of a composition. But you must register a work within five years of its first publication. Note the word *presumption*. If you randomly register the next Madonna single, you won't get very far in a court of law when valuable evidence indicates you're lying.

2. You get the right to file an infringement case in a court of law should someone intentionally use one of your compositions without your permission, knowledge, and/or payment. In case you didn't get this, *you cannot file an infringement case until you register your compositions.*

3. You qualify to (potentially) receive court fees as well as "statutory damages." Statutory damages are a determined fee set by a judge when the "actual damages" of an infringement are difficult to prove. To qualify for statutory damages, registration of your copyright has to have occurred before the initial *act* of infringement (i.e., before the defendant committed his or her first action to screw you) or within three months of the *publication* of the work (i.e., before the release date of the first CD containing the composition). Kyle Staggs, vice president of business and legal affairs at BugMusic (www.bugmusic.com), adds, "Since you can never know when someone is going to start screwing you over, the most prudent course of action is to register all of your copyrights either (1) as unpublished works prior to the initial release date or (2) within three months of the initial release date. Should you fail to do this, you may find it difficult to even hire an attorney to represent you should someone infringe your rights."

The Poor Man's Copyright

If you've just completed your first week of guitar lessons and are still hacking away in the tool shed, it's probably not necessary to register every song you write—or, in fact, any song at all! But don't fret; practice makes perfect, and, hopefully, in no time you'll have written a few number-one hits that you'll feel compelled to register. Does this mean you should begin shelling out your hard-earned money to the Copyright Office in Washington? Probably not. In fact, as an alternative, you can save a couple bucks by mailing yourself a copy of your works by certified mail; have the post clerk stamp dates on the seals of the envelope, and *don't open the package when it arrives*. This procedure is a "poor man's copyright"; it may help establish the date a composition was originally created, though this is not really an effective method. But note that this does not provide the same benefits as registering your composition with the Copyright Office. At this stage in your career, however, a poor man's copyright should suffice.

The Copyright Office

When the big day comes for your songs to be commercially distributed to the public, such as when you decide to press your own CDs and sell them at your shows, I highly recommend that you officially register your compositions with the Copyright Office. You'll be required to file a performing arts form (PA) and send in a deposit copy of the published works (such as a CD or tape) along with a whopping $45 fee per song for paper registrations and $35 for online registration (rates subject to change). As you can imagine, this can quickly add up.

To save money, you can register all of your compositions on one PA form under a "collection of works," as long as all the songs are written by the same author(s). For instance, you can register a batch of ten songs under the title "John and Jane Doe's Summer Songs of Love" (sappy, but you get the point). However, since all of the compositions will be listed under one title, this form of registration is not quite as effective, because individual songs will be more difficult to locate if someone is searching for them. However, Kyle Staggs notes that you can submit a supplementary registration (Form CA) to the Copyright Office listing all of the separate titles of the collection, allowing any third party to easily locate them. But this can only be done after the initial collection is registered, and the fee is $100. This is a business decision, but it may be worth it. For example, instead of registering ten titles separately and incurring a total fee of $450, you could register the collection for $45 bucks and then follow with a supplementary registration for $100 for an aggregate fee of $145, with the same results.

> For registration forms, call the Copyright Office at (800) 688-9889, or go online to www. copyright.gov

If the $145 is still too much for you, you can make one registration under a collection of works, and once you get signed to a record or publishing company and it looks like you're actually going to have a crack at a long-term career, you can go back and register each song separately at a later date. In fact, upon signing a publishing deal with a publishing company, they'll customarily go back and re-register each song anyway. So you're covered!

THE COPYRIGHT NOTICE

When you create a copyright, is it really necessary to include a notice (for example, Copyright © 2010 John and Jane Doe Music) on each and every finished work you create? Well, copyright law has always said that since it's impossible to put a notice on something you can't see, such as a song, it's not necessary. So why do you see the copyright notice on so many of your favorite albums? Well, sometimes the lyrics are printed on the inside booklet, which you can see. Or, in some cases, the creator of the artwork in which your music is packaged is indicating his or her copyright. Lastly, since the actual CD in which your music is embodied is considered a tangible form, the record company (which could be you, if you're a do-it-yourself artist) uses a different copyright symbol, represented by the letter *P* in a circle to indicate its rights in the actual sound recording (which is an entirely separate copyright from your music and one that is filed on form SR with the Copyright Office). In any case, as of the United States' official entry into the "Berne Convention" (an international copyright treaty), which occurred with the Berne Convention Implementation Act on March 1, 1989, a copyright notice is no longer necessary. However, it's still the most prudent approach, since it clearly indicates to others you're serious about protecting the work you so proudly create.

COPYRIGHT INFRINGEMENT

A "copyright infringement" occurs when someone uses the material you create without your permission, knowledge, or payment. But now that you've taken all the steps we've discussed to ensure the maximum protection of your songs, you shouldn't have anything to worry about—right? Wrong! *No matter what precautions you take, you can't stop anyone from attempting to infringe your copyrights.* With that said, worrying whether you're getting ripped off by every co-writer, band member, group you open for, or record company you send a package to is only going to drive you insane. And even if you discover that someone is infringing on your rights, you must first determine what the damage really is. Of course, in principle it's wrong (how dare someone steal your art), but for any attorney or judge

CRIME DOESN'T PAY, BUT INFRINGERS EVENTUALLY DO

In the early 1990s, a small, unsigned band sued a successful major-label recording artist for copyright infringement (sorry, the names must remain anonymous here). The band claimed that the artist's hit song contained a chorus that was an exact replica of one of their own. Not only did the band show that they were the first to register the song with the Copyright Office, but they were able to prove a variety of other aspects necessary to resolving the case. First, the band was able to prove the likelihood that the artist could have stolen its composition. This is called "proving access"—the local band opened for the artist on several occasions. Second, the band was able to show that the artist's chorus was "substantially similar" to their own. Third, the band was able to show that their chorus was so unique in character, it undoubtedly was not copied unintentionally. In other words, the infringement was "willful." Fourth, the band brought in a witness whose life the lyrics documented. Finally, the band exhibited newspaper clippings showing performance dates of the song long before the artist's band even formed. Needless to say, there was mounting evidence in the band's favor. The case was settled out of the court, and the band received an undisclosed sum of money.

In another well-known case, 2 Live Crew re-recorded both the guitar intro and first line of lyrics to Roy Orbison's song "Pretty Woman" and used it in one of their songs. Was using such a small part considered an infringement? Before addressing this question, perhaps it's a good time to clear up a common myth among musicians: The rule that you can borrow up to four bars of music without it being a copyright infringement is a fallacy. The issue is not over the amount used, but over the "significance" to the original song. For example, a hooky guitar riff, even just two bars, would probably be considered a significant part of the original song, while perhaps a section of the bridge might not. It depends on the particulars of each individual case.

There is one exception to this rule that is worth mentioning, which brings us back to our friends 2 Live Crew. Although the parts they used in their song were significant to Orbison's original, the judge ruled that it fell under something in U.S. copyright law called "fair use." Basically, this means that small amounts of copyrighted material can be reproduced for the purposes of critical review, parody, news reporting, teaching, etc. Since 2 Live Crew's version contained social criticism and parody of Orbison's original, they got off without owing Orbison a dime.

to take an infringement case seriously, you need to have suffered a substantial loss. For instance, if you hear your song played on the radio or on MTV, or in a television commercial, or in a movie, you've probably suffered a loss of income as a result. Unfortunately, until a significant event like this occurs, someone using your song is essentially like a tree falling in the forest—it doesn't make a loud enough noise for anyone to really care. The best course of action is to simply understand as much as you can about your copyrights, handle your business at all times in as prudent a manner as you know how, and try to work with as many quality people in your career as possible. That's really all anyone can do! (See the box "Crime Doesn't Pay, but Infringers Eventually Do.")

PUBLISHING YOUR MUSIC

Congratulations! You've come a long way. And now that you understand a little bit about copyrights, we can begin discussing more about music publishing. In fact, after reading this chapter, you may even have to run out and get yourself some new business cards. Why? Because *by virtue of creating a copyright, you inherit not only the rights as the author and owner of a composition but also the rights as the music publisher!* I bet you didn't know that.

In fact, when you publish your music by making it available to the public by sale or other means, the monies taken in are theoretically divided into two separate and equal categories: the writer's share and the publisher's share. So, if one dollar is earned, fifty cents goes to the writer (which is you), and fifty cents goes to the publisher (which is also you). If this sounds absolutely crazy, it is, but it's just the way the publishing system works. Even crazier, it's the publisher who takes on most of the responsibilities, like ownership of the copyright, making sure the songs are being used and earning money, collecting all the generated incomes, and paying the writers their respective shares. It's like having dual personalities making good use of both sides of the brain; the right side, or creative side, is the writer, and the left side, or analytical side, is the music publisher—but there's still one brain! You may ask, Can't you contact a more experienced music publisher to take on the publishing side of the responsibilities for you so that you can simply concentrate more on being the writer? Absolutely! In fact, in our following discussion, the word *publisher* can mean you or an outside publisher. But once again, before going into detail about publishing deals, I'm going to leave you in suspense just a little bit longer while we take a minute to discuss some of the income you might earn when your songs are released to your adoring public.

"Samples" have probably crossed your mind, since they are frequently the source of infringement. Samples are song snippets (either re-recorded or lifted from an existing sound recording) to enhance a musical track. They require the permission of, and compensation to, the copyright holders of the music and/or the copyright holders of the sound recording (which are often two separate entities). By not properly "clearing" a sample use before releasing a project, you are accepting the risk of having to either (1) clear the rights at a later date for a much higher fee/split or (2) defend yourself in an infringement lawsuit.

The Song

Writer's Share

Publisher's Share

SOURCES OF PUBLISHING INCOME

There are several types of income derived from music publishing: mechanical royalties, performance royalties, synchronization fees, print royalties, electronic transmissions, and foreign subpublishing incomes. Each is discussed in detail below.

MECHANICAL ROYALTIES

Mechanical royalties are a major source of income that can be derived from music publishing. As defined by the United States Copyright Act and established by provisions set in law, mechanical royalties are licensing fees paid by the record company for the use of your songs on "phonorecord" (i.e., audio-only recordings, whether that be in the form of CDs, digital downloads, or mobile tones). Attorney Burgundy Morgan clarifies that the use of your songs in film, TV, or video games (i.e., audio-visual recordings) requires entirely different licenses and fees, which are discussed later under Synchronization Royalties. Don't confuse mechanical royalties with record royalties (discussed in Chapter 10). Record royalties are percentages that are usually based on the wholesale published price per dealer (and in some cases on the suggested retail price), subject to the recoupment of numerous recording and other expenses. *Mechanical royalties are mandatory by law and should not be* (unless you agree to it) *subject to recoupment of recording costs by the record company*. In fact, mechanical royalties are one of the more immediate incomes you derive from sales of your record. For that matter, mechanicals may be the only income you get for a long while, since it will probably take quite some time before you begin earning monies from other revenue streams discussed in this book, such as touring (as you'll see in Chapter 12). So make sure to pay close attention to every detail below.

A Brief History

Mechanical royalties have quite a long and interesting history. The word *mechanical* refers back to the old days when music was mechanically fixed or copied to devices such as piano rolls—you know the ones you see in western movies when the piano plays by itself? Although piano rolls are long gone, the name has never been changed, but rest assured the mechanical rates surely have.

Dating back to 1909, the statutory mechanical rate was $.02 per composition. This rate existed until the new Copyright Act of 1976 (effective January 1, 1978), when it was finally changed to $.0275 per composition. There have been a number of increases since then, but in 2006, the statutory mechanical rate was changed to $.091 (9.1 cents) for compositions "less than five minutes in length" (which is the rate sometimes referred to as the "minimum statutory rate"). A statutory rate also exists for songs written "above five minutes in length" (which is the rate sometimes referred to as the "maximum statutory rate"), and in 2006, this rate was also changed to 1.75 cents for every minute or a fraction of a minute thereof. For example, if a composition is just ten seconds over five minutes, the mechanical royalty payable by law is the per minute rate rounded up to six (1.75 x 6 minutes = 10.5 cents). Nevertheless, it is the minimum statutory rate that is key to our discussion. A group of three copyright royalty judges (CRJ), often referred to as the Copyright Royalty Board (CRB), now adjusts the statutory rates, so keep your eyes open for changes by logging on to the Copyright Office website (www.copyright.gov) or by logging on to the Harry Fox Agency (www.harryfox.com).

One last thing: As defined by the United States Copyright Act, you're paid a statutory mechanical licensing fee for all records *made and distributed*. So according to law, even when records are manufactured and not sold, you still get paid. Sounds cool! Sure does, but there's one major exception that you'd better make sure you understand. If you're either a signed recording artist or you're writing songs for or with a signed recording artist, a great deal of what we have just covered is all subject to change. Why? You'll see in a minute. But I'll give you a hint, it's called the "controlled composition clause." You won't want to miss this!

The Harry Fox Agency

When a record company wants to use your composition on a phonorecord, a license must first be issued by the music publisher. The license most commonly used, as discussed above, is the mechanical license. The music publisher then monitors the record company to make sure the proper mechanical royalties are paid according to the number of records that are sold. In the United States, there's a major mechanical rights society called the Harry Fox Agency, which is more than happy to take care of these responsibilities on behalf of music publishers.

Founded in 1927 by the National Publishers Association (NMPA), the Fox Agency represents well over 17,000 music publishers. In fact, Ed Pierson at Warner/Chappell Music notes that most publishers, both big and small, use Harry Fox's services. It's especially cost effective for the music publisher representing a huge repertoire of songs, since they would otherwise have to employ their own staff just to keep up with the work. Another advantage of Harry Fox's services is that the company periodically audits record companies, which can otherwise be extremely expensive for music publishers. Audits can cost as much as $30,000. Although you may think audits are unnecessary, you might find it very disturbing to know that most record companies audited by the Fox Agency show an underpayment of royalties to music publishers. The truth is that record companies are known to get sloppy.

Lastly, Harry Fox Agency will issue mechanical licenses and collect royalties for a fee of approximately 6.75 percent of the gross mechanicals collected. This fee is known to change, so keep your eyes open for the latest news.

The Controlled Composition Clause

Okay, as promised, now comes the really juicy stuff, called the "controlled composition clause," mentioned above. There are a few very important things you need to know about mechanical royalties and recording contracts. Remember, mechanical royalties are licensing fees defined by the United States Copyright Act and set by provisions of law. Unlike the rest of the world, the United States has something called "the right to contract." This means that although the rate is set in law, it can be modified by contract. Therefore, in most recording agreements, *the record company will insist on taking a number of limitations and deductions, which could reduce your mechanical royalty dramatically*. These limitations are stipulated in your recording agreement under something called the "controlled composition clause." This clause applies to all "controlled compositions."

A controlled composition is any song written or co-written by the artist or otherwise owned and controlled by the artist. To clarify, this means that no matter what copyright law says, the record company will want you to agree to a reduced mechanical fee, or they may be unwilling to do business with you. Seriously! In fact, for all you composers out there who are co-writing songs with signed artists, and for those composers who write complete compositions for signed artists, the record company will want you to agree to this clause as well—even though you're not directly signed to them. Of course, it's your right to decline, but as a result, the song may simply not get cut. Let's take a look at some of those limitations and deductions.

The Controlled Rate

For new or midlevel artists, the record company will typically negotiate a royalty that is 75 percent of the minimum statutory mechanical rate (e.g., .75 x $.091). The resulting rate, $.068 (6.8 cents), per composition is known as something called the "controlled rate" or the "three-quarter rate." **Note:** According to the Digital Performance Right in Sound Recordings Act of 1995, this reduction should not apply to digital downloads (i.e., iTunes-type royalties or mobile tones).

The Cap

Whether you have ten songs on your record or fourteen, the controlled rate per composition discussed above usually only applies to a maximum, or "cap," of ten (e.g., the controlled rate per song of $0.068 x the cap per record of 10 songs = $.68, or 68 cents). If this sounds completely unfair, Los Angeles–based attorney Jeffrey Light offered the following encouragement in a lecture he delivered at UCLA: "The best way to look at the cap is that you're getting a flat penny rate per record, period! Don't think you're not getting paid on the eleventh or twelfth songs. Make the record you need to make creatively; if that means recording twelve or fourteen songs, do it."

> Escalations at predetermined sales can be negotiated. For instance, at 500,000 album units, the rate might increase to 85 percent of the minimum statutory rate (e.g., .85 x $.091 = $0.077, or 7.7 cents per composition). It's something to work toward. Note that twelve individual song downloads typically equal one album unit.

Now let's take a look at two examples, A and B, below to see how your royalty has already been dramatically lowered by the record company—and we're just getting started! Assume that you have written fourteen songs for release on a physical CD and that we are using the statutory rate established in 2006 for our computation. (It wouldn't matter if we used the 2002, 2000, or 1998 rate. The point is that we want to see the reduction. Observe with care!)

Example A: By provision set in United States copyright law:
    $.091 (statutory mechanical rate per song)
    x 14 (number of songs written by the artist)
    = $1.27 (your mechanical rate payable per record made
    and distributed)

Example B: Under the controlled composition clause:
    $.091 (statutory mechanical rate)
    x .75 (75 % reduction under the controlled
    composition clause)
    = $.068 (controlled rate per composition)
    x 10 (maximum, or cap, the label will pay)
    = $0.68 (total amount in mechanicals the label pays
    per record)

> A double album's worth of material (e.g., twenty songs on one CD) is still subject to the ten-song cap, since the label doesn't charge stores much more for these records. But for double albums, you may get an increase on the cap. If so, it's usually based in proportionately to the record company's increase of the wholesale published price per dealer.

Now, to find the new per-song rate:
    $ 0.68 (total amount in mechanicals the label pays per record)
    ÷ 14 (number of songs on the record)
    = $0.049 (per-song mechanical rate of 4.9 cents)

Note: These deductions are standard and are usually difficult to negotiate for newer artists. However, in the words of Jeffrey Light, "anything is possible." It's not unlikely that a savvy attorney may be able to successfully negotiate for the full minimum stat rate (i.e., $ .091, if staying with our example above) with a cap of as much as twelve songs. Although the $ .091 rate (or five-minute-or-less rate) we used in our example is technically called the minimum statutory rate, it's sometimes called the maximum, or "full stat rate," because it's usually the most any record company is willing to pay. Got it? Good.

Changing Rates

As illustrated in the example above, the record company gets away with lowering your royalty by nearly 50 percent, and it'll want to make sure it stays that low, too! Since the statutory mechanical rate changes frequently (usually every two years), the record company will usually lock in the rate on the day your record is delivered or released. For example, if the label released your record on December 31, 2005, when the statutory rate was $0.085, you would be paid a percentage of that rate (i.e., .75 of $0.085 cents per composition), even though the rate rose to $0.091 on Jan 1, 2006.

The Minimum Statutory Rate

As you already know, the statutory mechanical rate also provides a higher royalty for songs over five minutes. For instance, in 2006, the increase changed to 1.75 cents for every minute or a fraction of a minute thereof. Under the controlled composition clause, however, your royalty will always be based on the "minimum statutory rate" (i.e., the five-minutes-or-less rate). I wouldn't worry about this deduction, though. Unless you're doing something really wrong, most compositions will be less than four minutes, because that's just the way most radio station formats like them!

Free Goods

By statute, mechanical royalties are paid on all records made and distributed. But, for every hundred records distributed, the record company will contractually deem 15 percent as "standard free goods"—a so-called incentive to entice retailers to purchase your record. (A similar concept was also discussed in reference to record royalties in Chapter 10. Free goods may apply to digital downloads and mobile tones as well, unless your attorney is successful at negotiating this out of your recording agreement.) In theory, for every hundred records shipped, fifteen are theoretically given away for free, and behold—you're not paid a royalty for them either. This may be indicated in your recording contract as payment on only 85 percent of all records sold. If you have negotiating power, the record company may agree to pay mechanicals on 50 percent of standard free goods (i.e., 92.5 percent of all records sold). Now, let's use a cap per the change in 2006 as an example; but remember, it doesn't matter what rate we use for our computation—the concept is the same.

Example A: Mechanicals payable factoring in free goods:
    50,000 (records made and distributed)
    x 0.85 (85 % free goods factor)
    = 42,500 (royalty bearing records payable)
    x $0.68 (maximum, or cap, the label will pay per record sold)
    = $28,900 (mechanical royalty payable)

Note: Again, do not confuse mechanical royalties with record or artist royalties. Mechanical royalties are typically not used by the record company for recoupment of recording funds or other costs! Therefore, in the above example, even when the band sells a minimum of 50,000 records (which would be considered a flop by most commercial standards), the group is still credited $28,900 in mechanical royalties. "This is why mechanicals and making sure to negotiate the right controlled composition clause are so important to artists," says Los Angeles–based attorney Stacy Fass.

Reserves

Remember that by statute, mechanical royalties are paid *on all records made and distributed*. However, the record company pays you on a reduced percentage of all records made and distributed and makes another little adjustment in their contracts to pay you only for *records that are sold and not returned*. And to make sure they make no mistakes, they'll take something called a "reserve." You see, most record companies send out royalty statements to music publishers four times a year. In these statements, record companies typically withhold 50 to 75 percent of mechanicals as a reserve, which protects a company from overpaying in case records are returned by retailers. (I know it is hard to imagine a digital download returned from iTunes if it doesn't sell, but don't apply logic here. Until this changes, expect a reserve on digital phonograph deliveries as well. "Even so," notes attorney Burgundy Morgan, "it is worth trying to carve out a reserve on digital downloads in your contract.") Monies held in reserves are liquidated throughout subsequent statements, up to eight quarters (two years) after the reserves were first taken.

Midprice Records, Record Clubs, and Budget Records

Further deductions in your mechanical royalties are taken by your record company for "midprice records" (i.e., records marked down to between 60 and 80 percent of the full price), which amounts to 75 percent of the rate (e.g., .75 x $.068 = $.051, or 5.1 cents). For records sold in "record clubs," like the ones listed in magazines that offer ten CDs for one penny, and for "budget records" (i.e., records sold to retailers at a PPD that is at or below 60 percent of the full price), your record company pays mechanicals 50 percent of the normal rate (e.g., .50 x $.068 = 3.4 cents).

Promotional Records

You will not receive a mechanical royalty on records shipped by the record company to retailers during special promotions or on those free "promotional records" given to radio stations and disc jockeys that are marked "not for sale."

Video Limitations

Also found in most controlled composition clauses, the record company will want to use your compositions free of licensing fees in promotional (MTV and VHI videos) and home videos (like concert videos, documentaries, a collection of videos). Mark Goldstein, former vice president of legal affairs at Warner Bros. Records, notes that the licensing fee the record company is referring to here is generally what's called a synchronization fee (which you'll learn about later in this chapter). However, the language under the video limitation clause is often kept broad enough to cover *any other* kind of fee that might possibly come up.

Outside Songs

When you want to cover another artist's song (what's often referred to as an "outside song"), you must obtain a mechanical license and pay the publisher a mechanical licensing fee. Note that the publisher does not have to issue a license lower than the statutory rate—after all, he isn't signed to your recording agreement. Either way, just keep in mind that the fee paid to the publisher to cover a song comes out of your cap per record, which ultimately reduces the mechanical royalties paid to you.

PERFORMANCE ROYALTIES

If you've been paying attention throughout this chapter, you already know that under copyright law one of the many rights you get as author and owner of a composition is something called a "performing right." This not only gives you the right to offer your compositions to the public but also obligates anyone who wants to perform your music in public to ask permission and pay a licensing fee. This includes radio stations and television networks, cable stations (such as HBO, MTV, and VH1), Internet sites, mobile carriers, nightclubs, concert halls, shopping malls, bars, in-flight radio stations, hotels, colleges and universities, "some" stores and restaurants (stores under 2,000 square feet and bars and restaurants under 3,750 square feet are exempt), and virtually any other venue open to the public where music is played. A list of licenses and parameters can be found by logging on to ASCAP.com, BMI.com, and SESAC.com.

But unlike a mechanical royalty, where there's an established fee for the use of your songs on phonorecord, the system in the performing rights area is much more intricate than simply saying you get x amount of monies for the performance of one of your compositions. Additionally, if you think about the number of radio stations that exists in the United States alone (over ten thousand), it would appear impossible for music publishers (even the larger companies) to individually issue licenses to each and every one, collect royalty payments, and police the world to make sure that all other music users are paying licensing fees. With the amount of music performed each day on one radio station, can you imagine how much paperwork would be involved in seeking licenses from each and every music publisher? Out of a general concern to deal with performing rights in an efficient manner, something called a "performing rights organization" (PRO) was born.

Performing Rights Organizations

The three performing rights organizations (PROs) in the United States are, the American Society of Authors, Composers and Publishers (ASCAP), Broadcast Music Inc. (BMI), and SESAC (formerly known as the Society of European Stage Authors and Composers). Although each of these organizations conducts its business differently, they have similar functions and one general principle: *to protect the performing rights of songwriters and publishers*. Here's a very general overview of how they operate.

Blanket Licenses

The performing rights societies issue "blanket licenses" to music users, including radio stations, television networks, nightclubs, some restaurants, concert halls, airlines, shopping malls, and Internet sites for a negotiated fee that covers all of the compositions registered to a society by thousands of different writers and publishers. The fees paid by these music users are dependent on a number of variables. For instance, a radio station's broadcast range and/or yearly advertising revenue may count as factors that determine its licensing fees. If you're really interested, each of the organizations provides schedules of available licensing fees. In any case, all of the monies are collected by the societies and then divided up and paid accordingly to writers and publishers based on the number of performances per quarter. Statements are generally sent out four times each year. But how do the societies keep track of the use of your compositions?

Monitoring Songs

The PROs conduct research to give them a representation of the copyright titles broadcast during each royalty period. Although there is quite a variety of licenses issued by the PROs, royalty payments are based primarily on the number of radio and television performances each quarter, since these are the primary sources of license proceeds and easiest to keep track of. Monies collected from "general licenses," such as through restaurants, nightclubs, and hotels, are distributed based on the allocation from the television and radio pool. Therefore, it makes sense to concentrate on the various monitoring methods used for radio and television. These are just the basics, so be sure to check out each PRO's website for more specific information.

Radio There are generally two methods of monitoring used for radio performances: digital monitoring and random radio "logs."

Digital Monitoring Digital monitoring by services like Mediaguide used by ASCAP, Nielsen Broadcast Data Systems (BDS) used by SESAC, Mediabase used by BMI, and BlueArrow[SM] by Landmark Digital Services[SM] used by BMI are all different technologies, but they generally work on the principle of encoding songs with some sort of recognition technology and monitoring and uploading data into a centralized database where it can be retrieved.

Logs Logs are a part of a sample survey used by the performing rights organizations whereby a diverse array of radio stations are asked to list every song they play over a two- to three-day reporting period each quarter. These playlists, including titles, artists, and the respective performing rights society, are then uploaded (or they can be sent in by e-mail) into a mainframe database, where the information is used to calculate the frequency and selection of songs being used on all other radio stations.

Television The monitoring of television stations, cable, etc., is generally accomplished primarily by one method: using "cue sheets" and comparing them to broadcast schedules.

Cue Sheets A cue sheet is a producer or editor's instruction detailing what song was used, the composer and publisher of each song, and how, when, and where music is used. Information also includes whether the use was for a feature, background, or theme. According to music attorney Steve Winogradsky, in some ways, the cue sheet serves as an "invoice" for the publishers and writers, advising the PROs on who needs to be paid for the music in any particular program.

Just How Accurate Are the PROs?

Since there are only so many hours of research performing rights organizations can conduct in a cost-effective manner, it's more likely that only frequently played songs on the radio get picked up through monitoring. Does this mean the system basically favors hit songs? I hate to say it, but generally, yes. In fact, it really dispels the myth among musicians that every time your song is played on the radio, it's an automatic "cha ching"—money in the bank. But with new developments in technology, this is likely to get better. In fact, the Internet is an area that is more accurate with regard to monitoring and royalty distribution.

As far as television is concerned, monitoring by cue sheets has been far more accurate than for radio. Therefore, if your song is performed in this medium, it's likely you will receive payment.

And as an additional note, another area the PROs monitor is that of the top two hundred grossing tours as reported in the magazine *Pollstar*. Basically, the PROs review a band's set lists sent in by its managers. Note that SESAC, being the smallest of the three PROs in the United States, is known to receive the set lists of bands playing in even smaller venues than those featuring the top gross tours.

> One hit song can easily generate a total (combined writer/publisher earnings) of anywhere from $500,000 to $1 million a year. A theme song on a prime-time network television show can generate an average of $150,000 a year.

Separate Writer Affiliation

The payment of performance royalties is quite different from the income derived through your songs. When the PROs collect licensing fees, allocate them, and send out the appropriate shares to those who have earned performance credits, they send the writer's share (50 percent) automatically to the writers and the publisher's share (the other 50 percent) to the publishers. Supposedly this system was created to protect writers from the big, bad publishers who could potentially rip them off. In any case, regardless of whether you self-publish or enter into an agreement with an established music publisher, you must affiliate with a PRO as the writer. Of course, there's an individual publisher affiliation that's also necessary for publishers. But keep in mind, the writer and publisher have to affiliate with the same organization. In other words, for songs written by one person, both 100 percent of the writer's share of a song and 100 percent of the publisher's share must be affiliated with ASCAP. On the other hand, if two writers compose a song together, one writer and publisher can affiliate their shares with one organization, while the other writer and publisher can be affiliated with another.

Which Performing Rights Organization Should You Join?

There's an ongoing debate about which PRO is better at doing its job. Within the industry it's said that the same song would be paid an equal amount in royalties, whether the writer and/or publisher was with ASCAP, BMI, or SESAC. Of course, a representative from any of these organizations would argue this point. It's best to look at the issue this way: *The PROs were set up to protect you, not screw you over!* They are, for the most part, nonprofit organizations (except SESAC; more in a minute), which basically means that all of the money they collect gets allocated to their members after an operating charge is taken off the top to keep their lights on and pay employee salaries. And as mentioned earlier, until your songs are being played regularly on major radio stations (or aired on television), the bottom line is that you won't receive much, if any, in performance royalties anyway. In other words, perhaps you shouldn't be losing sleep on this matter right now.

The best option is to speak with a representative from each office when you're about to have a song published. Base your decision on the information that seems the most reasonable to you and

PERFORMING RIGHTS ORGANIZATIONS AT A GLANCE

HISTORY

ASCAP. ASCAP is a nonprofit organization established in 1914 and is run by writers and publishers.

BMI. BMI has been operated as a nonprofit organization since 1940. BMI was founded by broadcasters, but its "day to day" decisions are made by management.

SESAC. SESAC is a "for profit" organization founded in 1930. SESAC is a much smaller organization than ASCAP and BMI, representing only 5 percent of all the licensed music out there. As a private organization, SESAC is not monitored by the Justice Department, and it can conduct its business as it wishes.

JOINING

ASCAP. ASCAP members must have a song that's about to be published. It's free for both writers and publishers.

BMI. BMI affiliates must also have a song about to be published. It's free for writers to join, and publishers pay a one-time fee of $150 (for an independently owned company) or $250 (for a partnership or corporation). But keep your eyes and ears open, for this fee may soon be eliminated altogether.

SESAC. SESAC members must be selected by a referral process. Since SESAC is a much smaller organization, it has precious resources that must be utilized carefully. It prides itself on giving the best individual attention.

CONTRACT TERMS

ASCAP. ASCAP has a one-year contract for both writers and publishers, which can be terminated by a three-month advance written notice.

BMI. BMI has a two-year contract for writers and a five-year contract for publishers. Termination notices must be sent within a time frame of no sooner than six months and no later than sixty to ninety days prior to end of contract.

SESAC. SESAC has a three-year contract for both writers and publishers. Termination notices must be sent within a time frame of no sooner than nine months and no later than six months prior to end of contract.

CONTACT INFORMATION

ASCAP: (800) 95-ASCAP or www.ascap.com

BMI: (212) 586-2000, (310) 659-9109, or www.bmi.com

SESAC: (212) 586-3450, (310) 393-9671, or www.sesac.com

Note: Rates are subject to change.

on the organization that seems as though it will give you the most personalized treatment when you need it. This could mean that there's a representative at one of the organizations you really like, or simply that the vibe you got when you went into their offices was good. Keep in mind that if you ever want to switch organizations down the road, it's not difficult to do so—although switching can cause you to lose money in the process as a result of PRO policies or can cause general confusion as to which PRO is collecting your share of income. Be sure to ask each organization for membership details.

SYNCHRONIZATION FEES

Like mechanical and performance royalties, synchronization fees, sometimes called "synch fees," are yet another source of income derived from music publishing. Synchronization refers to the art of synching your music with visual images in motion pictures, television, CD-ROMs, DVDs, the Internet, video games, and other audiovisual media. Unlike mechanical royalties, there are no statutory fees for the use of your compositions in these types of reproduction. Nor is there a compulsory license, which means that a publisher has the authority to grant (or deny) permission for any uses of this type. Synch fees are completely negotiable and are based on a number of factors that will be discussed in detail in a moment. But first, you should know that, generally, there are two types of income to be derived from the use of your compositions:

◆ The actual "synch fee" (or up-front fee) which, again, is negotiable.
◆ The performance royalty income generated by the use of your songs on the back end (i.e., as a result of the initial synch use). Remember that performance royalties are paid to you by your registered performing rights society (ASCAP, BMI, or SESAC). According to music attorney Steve Winogradsky, emerging artists with little negotiating leverage should know that "these performance royalties can actually exceed the amount of the synch fees."

Note: In addition to the income mentioned above, if the recording of your song is also being used, anyone requesting a license for your music will technically have to negotiate a second fee to the owner of the actual master recording. This is called a "master use" fee, which is traditionally negotiated on a "most favored nations" basis (i.e., the master use fee is the same as what is paid for the composition, or what is paid for the composition is traditionally the same fee as what is paid for the master—whichever is negotiated first). Typically, do-it-yourself artists and bands will own both the rights to their compositions and the master tapes, entitling them to both fees, or what is called the "all in" fee. On the other hand, artists or bands who are part of a signed recording act will typically not own the master rights. Therefore, it's the record label that collects the master use fee for the actual sound recording, while the publisher collects the synch fee for the music embodied on the masters. For practical purposes, the following discussion will emphasize the scenario in which you are the artist/songwriter signed to an independent or major record company, but what follows really applies to either situation.

Points of Negotiation

As previously mentioned, there are no statutory fees for the use of your music in audiovisual projects. Synch fees and permissions are 100 percent negotiable. In the words of Michael Eames, president of PEN Music Group, "Synch fees are the Wild Wild West."

Below are a few points and questions that publishers typically take into consideration when negotiating synch fees.

Licensee/Type of Use

If your music is going to be licensed in a film, is it being licensed by a major motion picture studio or by an independent film company? You can charge more money for a major motion picture use than you could if your song was going to be used in an independent film. In fact, deals for independent films are often structured as "step deals," in which a smaller sum of money may be negotiated upfront with additional payments made later should certain criteria be met (such as the film achieving distribution or certain box office receipts levels). If your music is being licensed for use in a television show, is it being licensed by a major network for use on free, cable, or satellite subscription services or as a paid extra channel like HBO? You can usually negotiate a higher fee when it is used on pay television stations. However, Michael Eames of PEN music says that the rights for all TV uses these days are typically negotiated in one agreement and not usually separated anymore. If your music is being licensed in a video game, is it a popular game by a leading company, or a lesser-known game by a lesser-established company? The more popular the video game and company, such as Electronic Arts, Activision, and Sony, the higher the fee you can charge. Keep in mind, though, that there aren't hundreds of companies out there, and fees tend to cap at high four figures for video games. Finally, if your music is going to be licensed in a television commercial, is it being licensed by the company of a well-known and established brand?

Context

If your music is going to be "featured" in the scene of a movie or television program (meaning your music and lyrics are carrying a scene and the actors *are not talking*), you can generally charge more than if your song is used as a "background" (in which your music features in a scene coming from a "source" like a car radio or jukebox, and the actors *are* talking). If your music is going to be used over the "main title" (opening credits) or "end title" (closing credits) of a film or a television program, you can generally charge more than if your song is used just in the main body of the work; this is most significantly the case with opening titles. If your music is going to be used "out of context" in the trailer for a film or in the commercial for a television show, you may be entitled to an additional fee than were it just used in the film or TV program. And finally, if your music is going to be used as the theme song of a television show, rather than just in the context of a scene, the fees will also be higher.

Other Media

Will the use of your music be limited to a film or television program? Or will the film or television program eventually be released on home video or distributed via wireless services like cell phones, iPods, the Internet, and any other means "now known and hereafter devised"? Michael Eames says, "While most film and TV licenses these days are drafted for 'all media' and 'all media excluding theatrical,' respectively, keep in mind that the more rights you give, the more you can ask for."

Timing

For how many minutes and/or seconds is your music being used? The longer the use, the more you can charge.

Term

For how long will your music be licensed? For instance, your song may be requested for as short a period as one year and as long as perpetuity (forever). The longer you license your rights, the higher the fee you should receive. It's important to understand that most synch uses are nonexclusive; you will still be able to license your music to other projects. If someone wants exclusivity to your music (which often occurs in the case of TV commercials), there's a premium that must be paid. Since you will not be able to use your composition in whatever areas the exclusivity covers, you are potentially losing income and must be compensated well.

Territory

Where will your music be used? In the United States or the entire world? While most film and TV licenses these days are drafted for "rights to the entire world," keep in mind that your compositions should command a higher price than when your rights are acquired solely for the U.S.

Stature of the Song

How successful is the song? The more popular the song is, the more you can charge. You can be sure Bob Seger is receiving hundreds of thousands of dollars (if not millions) for the use of his hit song "Like a Rock" in the Chevrolet commercials that have been airing for years.

Credits

Will you receive credit for the use of your song over the beginning or end titles of a movie? If so, you must consider that the exposure in a prominent film can lead to other uses of your compositions. This holds true for credits you receive at the end of television programs as well or on the TV series' website. The exposure in these two instances alone can make up for a situation in which you are not receiving adequate income due, for example, to poor negotiations or to the lack of an adequate budget.

More Than You Bargained For

The initial synch fees negotiated for the use of your compositions are not the only monies that can be generated. In fact, the use of your song in a film can snowball into a number of potential revenue streams. Let's take a look at three examples:

> If the record label that holds the rights to release the film's soundtrack album wants to use your song, you earn a mechanical royalty per record or download of your song sold.

> If your song then gets played on the radio to promote the film or soundtrack, you earn a performance royalty as well.

> And if the film ever makes it into theaters outside of the United States—you guessed it—you also earn a performance royalty for the public performance of your composition (note that theater performances in the United States for some boring political reason are not payable, but don't worry about why).

As you can see, the use of your song in just one film can often generate monies that are more than you ever bargained for. Not bad at all for a single day of songwriting!

PRINT ROYALTIES

Print royalties are the monies you make when your compositions are sold in sheet music and music books. In what is coined the Tin Pan Alley era (1911 through the 1940s), print represented a significant income to publishers and songwriters since it was essentially the predominate form of distributing and selling music. By the way, Tin Pan Alley referred to concentrated areas in New York City and London where music publishers' offices were located—the name Tin Pan Alley was derived from the noise created by the sound of pianos playing while the writers worked on their next big hits.

Print today represents only an extremely small percentage of the overall income derived from your songs. In fact, unless you have a hit song or album, or at least some sales success, it's not likely your songs will ever make it into a primary source of print. Nevertheless, print is worth mentioning, so here's a brief—and I mean *brief*—overview.

Print Uses

There are four primary uses of your songs in print music form: single sheet, folios, matching folios, and mixed folios.

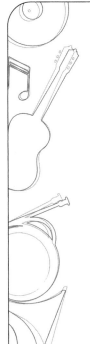

EXAMPLES OF FEES FOR ACTUAL SYNCH USES

For songs that are either well known or current hits:

Television. $10,000 to $40,000 per song per use (for all media excluding theatrical). For use over the main or end title credits, or as the theme of a television program, fees can be as much as $80,000 and more per use per song.

Film. $10,000 to $75,000 per use per song. For use of your compositions over the main or end title credits of a film, fees can be as much as $100,000 and even more per use per song. Can you believe the techno band Prodigy was offered $500,000 for the use of just one of their songs in a film? If a director really wants your music, the money here is big.

Video games. $5,000 to $10,000 as a flat buyout for the song (note that there are no per-unit royalties typically offered like for that of a CD to the artist). However, if the music from the game is released as an audio-only DVD, you should negotiate for a mechanical royalty payment.

For songs that are unknown or noncharting:

Television. $250 to $2,500 per use per song.

Film. $500 to $5,000 per use per song.

Video games. Free to $10,000 per use per song.

Single Sheet

Single sheet music, often called piano sheet music, is just what it sounds like: individual sheets sold in music stores. Sheet music can be a big seller for currently popular or classic songs, especially ballads. Examples include "Wind Beneath My Wings" by Larry Henley and Jeff Silbar, "What a Wonderful World" by George David Weiss and Bob Thiele, and "At Last" by Mark Gordon and Harry Warren.

Folios

Folios are music books that contain a complete library of music by one artist. Examples include *Led Zeppelin Complete* (Alfred Publishing), *The Best of the Police* (Hal Leonard), and *The Best of KISS* (Hal Leonard).

Matching Folios

Matching folios are music books that match a particular record by an artist. The album cover is also the cover of the folio, and there are usually pictures of the artist inside. Examples include *The Jimi Hendrix Experience* (Cherry Lane Music), *Master of Puppets* by Metallica (Hal Leonard), and *The Wall* by Pink Floyd (Pink Floyd Music Publishing, Ltd.).

Mixed Folios

Mixed folios are music books that contain works by a variety of different artists. Examples include *The Gigantic Guitar Songbook* (Hal Leonard), featuring songs like "Come Together" by the Beatles, "Hey Joe" by Jimi Hendrix, and "Radar Love" by Golden Earring. Another example is *The Motown Anthology* (Hal Leonard), featuring songs like "My Girl" by the Temptations, "I'll Be There" by the Jackson 5, and "Let's Get It On" by Marvin Gaye. Mixed folios are probably the most popular of the three folios because they contain so much variety.

Division of Income

Things get a little weird when discussing the payment structure for print music. Unlike other sources of income, such as mechanicals, performances, and synchronization, whereby the publisher receives a sum of money and essentially divides it in some way between the writer and the publisher (i.e., the writer's share and the publisher's share), *print music is the only domestic source of publishing income derived from a royalty system based on the suggested retail price or wholesale price.* Remember when reading the following information that the word *publisher* can mean you or an outside publisher. Here's a quick breakdown of royalties for print.

Sheet Music

The music printer (the company that transcribes the music and makes the books) pays the music publisher a royalty of 20 percent of the retail price. The current retail price is approximately $4 for a single sheet of music, so the publisher receives around 80 cents ($4.00 x .20 = 80 cents). Of this 80 cents, the publisher then pays the writer a flat rate of around 10 to 12 cents. Why is this so low? Because that's just the way it's always been, and no one has thought to change it. If you publish your own music, you don't have anything to worry about because you're both the writer and the publisher. However, if you enter into a deal with an established music publisher, don't expect much from single-sheet music sales.

Folios

The printer pays the publisher a royalty of 10 to 12.5 percent of the retail selling price. The current retail price ranges from $25, so if the publisher has a 10 percent royalty, it receives around $2.50 per folio sold. Of the $2.50, the publisher also pays the writer a royalty of about 10 percent, but it's only based on the wholesale price—the price for which the printer apparently sells the book to retailers (which is basically half of the retail price of $25: $12.50). If the writer has a 10 percent royalty, he or she receives about $1.25 per folio sold ($12.50 × .10 = $1.25—which is basically half of what the publisher gets).

Matching Folios

Royalties for matching folios are generally treated the same way as plain folios. (God forbid we should have to repeat this.)

Mixed Folios

Royalties for mixed folios are the same as for folios as well, but different. Confused? It'll make sense in a minute. The printer pays the publisher a royalty of around 10 to 12.5 percent of the retail selling price (which is the same as the other folios), but the royalty for mixed folios is *prorated based on the number of royalty-bearing works in the book*. Remember, a mixed folio contains the compositions of a number of artists, not just yours. For example, if there are twenty compositions in a folio and you've written five of them, the publisher collects the prorated amount of 5/20ths (one-fourth, or 25%) of the standard 10 to 12.5 percent royalty rate. So, to plug in some real numbers, let's say the retail selling price of a mixed folio is $25 and the publisher has a 10 percent royalty rate. The publisher then collects about 62.5 cents per mixed folio sold ($25 × .025 [one-fourth, or 25%, of the publisher's royalty rate] = 62.5 cents). Now, of the 62.5 cents, the publisher typically pays the writer a royalty in the range of 10 percent (also prorated based on the number of works in the book), but only if it's based on the wholesale price of the mixed folio, which is about half of the retail selling price quoted above. Therefore, the writer receives about 31 cents per mixed folio sold ($12.50 × .025 = 31 cents).

ELECTRONIC TRANSMISSIONS: DOWNLOADS AND MORE

Electronic transmissions of music by album or single song downloads via sites like iTunes (itunes.com), master tone sales via mobile carriers like Verizon (www.verizon.com), interactive streaming audio and video via services like Yahoo! (music.yahoo.com), and noninteractive streaming (e.g., webcasting) via XM satellite radio (www.xmradio.com) and MusicChoice (www.musicchoice.com) are not a totally new type of income in itself (except, perhaps, for interactive streaming) but rather a source that encompasses the various incomes previously discussed. Why, then, is it necessary to have a separate categorization? Well, as we'll see, electronic transmissions are a new and exciting category!

It's important to keep in mind that since many of these royalties are still being worked out, and since new technology is being created seemingly every day, it is important to read up on all of the trades and keep posted to useful sites like those of the National Music Publishers' Association (www.nmpa.org), *Billboard* magazine (www.billboard.com), and the Future of Music (www.future ofmusic.com).

Digital Downloads (i.e., iTunes-Type Royalties)

Digital downloads from online companies like iTunes and eMusic (www.emusic.com) are basically "untethered" downloads (at least, this is how they are essentially treated). The term *untethered* means that a consumer can copy it, burn it, upload into his or her iPod, and, for argument's sake, basically own it. (We're all aware of how iTunes has restrictions on what you can do with the download, but they are now introducing iTunes Plus, which is an MP3 format with no digital rights management). In any case, digital download income is typically collected by the record companies, who pay the music publishers at the full statutory mechanical rate (one that should not be subject to the controlled composition clause), who then pay the writers.

The Digital Performance Right in Sound Recordings Act of 1995 provides that privately negotiated contracts entered into after June 22, 1995, between a recording company and a recording artist who is the author of the musical work cannot include a rate for the making and distribution of the musical work below that established by law. (In plain language, digital phonorecord delivery is not subject to a decrease by the controlled composition clause.)

Master Tones (aka Mobile Tones)

Master tones, another type of "untethered download," are snippets of your songs that are downloaded via mobile carriers like Verizon and used on cell phones—a song alerts you that someone is calling, and a song alerts the caller that the phone is ringing or busy.

In any case, master tone income is typically paid by the mobile carriers at about 10 percent of the retail selling price to the consumer. So if the retail selling price is about $2.49, the publisher receives $0.25 ($2.49 x .10 = $0.25), who then pays the writers. **Note**: Due to changing laws, the royalty publishers could receive for mobile tones may be reduced to as low as 9.1 cents—or even lower! So you will want to stay tuned for updates. By the way, there is also a performing right element involved with mobile tones, which means, in theory, a performance royalty should be due to the publishers (and writers) via their appropriate performing rights organizations.

Interactive Streaming Audio/Video

Interactive subscription services like Yahoo! (music.yahoo.com), AOL (music.aol.com), MSN (www.msn.com), Napster (www.napster.com), and Rhapsody (through RealNetworks .com), in which the consumer can "interact" with the service (stream on-demand, create personalized play lists, etc.), is a form of "tethered" download. This typically means that as long as the consumer pays a subscription fee, he/she can "use" (not own) all the music desired so long as he/she keeps on paying a fee. In any case, the royalty that interactive streaming sites must pay to publishers—who, of course, then pay the writers—is still being determined as of this writing. It might be based on a website's subscription service rate or on its advertising revenue. Again, stay tuned. Also, the performing rights organizations issue licenses to interactive streaming sites as well, so publishers (and writers) should, in theory, earn a performance royalty for performances.

Noninteractive Streaming (e.g., Webcasting)

Noninteractive subscription services like terrestrial (land) radio stations and fan-based stations broadcast music to satellite subscription services like XM (www.xm.com) and Sirius (www.sirius.com), and to subscription services like MusicChoice, via satellite transmission on digital cable television like Dish Network (www.dishnetwork.com) and DirecTV; all these sites *do not* allow consumers to interact (pick songs as they wish, make set lists, etc.) but to just listen instead. In any case, the performing rights organizations issue licenses to noninteractive streaming sites as well, so publishes (and writers) should, in theory, earn a performance royalty for performances.

Podcasts

Podcasts, "shows" including music and interviews that can be downloaded onto a computer (and onto the popular iPod portable devices), are usually available for free to consumers via websites that earn money through advertising or subscription fees. Therefore, if podcasts really take off from a commercial standpoint—and they may have already by the time you're reading this—a royalty may be paid to publishers (who will then pay the writers) based on a percentage of the advertising revenue or subscription fees. Time will tell how all this will play out, so once again stay tuned.

Planet Uranus Streams and Other Stuff

Okay, so the planet Uranus part is a joke, but rest assured you'll eventually receive a royalty of some kind for anything new that has been developed since the revision of this book. That is, you'll eventually get a royalty once everyone is done scrambling to figure out how to deal with it. Technology has a way of getting ahead of all of us at times.

Here's what Neil Gillis, president and chief operating officer of Dimensional Music Publishing had to say on the matter of new technologies:

"Every time a new technology is created, the industry scrambles to figure out how to deal with it, and things can get so complicated. But, as I see it, things can be simplified if traditional laws and practices are used by all parties involved when considering in what way a new technology allows a piece of music to be utilized. For instance:

✦ Is there a performance of the song, based on what we believe the law and business practice states is performance, where a license must be granted?

✦ Is there a mechanical reproduction of the song (i.e., is the song being copied) in a way that a mechanical license is needed?

✦ Is there a visual media relationship whereby a synchronization license must be obtained?

✦ Is there an embedded lyric somewhere in the song whereby a lyric reprint of some kind needs to be involved?

Surely there are going to be new technologies invented that take into consideration other factors that I haven't mentioned above, but for the moment, the aforementioned takes the mystery out of the 'Oh my God, what is this new technology and what is it capable of doing?' dilemma, and it brings everything back to more simple terms. If everyone can only see technology as this, then maybe we can more easily begin to formulate pricing around that technology."

FOREIGN SUBPUBLISHING INCOME

Foreign subpublishing income are the monies earned when your music is published overseas. It's not a type of income itself, but rather it encompasses the various incomes previously discussed. Why is it necessary for a separate categorization? Because the monies in foreign territories are handled much differently than they are in the United States. In fact, U.S. publishers need to seek the assistance of "subpublishers" (publishers in foreign territories) to help with the collection of these monies. Let's first take a close look at how the two primary sources of income (mechanical and performance royalties) are handled, then discuss something called "black box monies," and finally talk briefly about subpublishers.

Foreign Mechanicals

Remember when we discussed mechanical royalties earlier in this chapter and how you get so many pennies per composition per record? This system only applies to the United States and Canada for the most part. In foreign territories, mechanical royalties are calculated differently. Foreign mechanicals are payable on a percentage of either the retail selling price (RSP) of the record or the price per dealer (PPD)—which is basically an equivalent to our wholesale prices. Percentages differ from territory to territory but are generally in the range of 6 to 10 percent, covering all the compositions on a record. For instance, mechanicals in Japan are currently based on 6 percent (RSP), in Germany 9.03 percent (PPD), and in the United Kingdom 8.5 percent (PPD). These rates are unaffected by either the length of the compositions or the number of songs per album. In other words, unlike in the United States and Canada, *writers and publishers cannot be asked to waive their rights to mechanical payments under a system similar to the controlled composition clause.* I bet that makes you happy!

Also much different than in the United States and Canada is the method by which foreign mechanical royalties are collected and paid to publishers. In the United States and Canada, publishers can choose to have the record companies send mechanical royalties directly to them, or they can have an agency such as Harry Fox (for the U.S.) collect on their behalf and CMRRA (for Canada). However, in foreign territories, mechanical royalties are collected by "mandatory mechanical rights collection societies." For instance, in Japan, mechanical royalties are collected by a society called JASRAC, in Germany it's GEMA, and in Great Britain it's MCPS.

So, with all this talk of mandatory stuff, one might ask, "How the heck do I get my money?" That's a very good question. Essentially, the Harry Fox Agency can collect foreign mechanicals through reciprocal representation agreements with affiliated foreign collecting societies and the territories they represent, but I'm told the Fox Agency overall is not the most effective means by which to handle your foreign business affairs. Instead, U.S. publishers typically seek the help of what are known as local subpublishers (or publishers) in foreign territories who will collect mechanicals on your behalf for a fee (more in a moment). *If you don't have a subpublisher representing you, then your monies may go uncollected and often end up in what's known as the "black box."* Sounds ominous, doesn't it? Hold that thought. We'll discuss subpublishers and the black box in detail in a minute.

Foreign Performance Royalties

Foreign performance royalties aren't as complex as mechanical royalties, but there are a few things you need to know. Your performing rights organization in the U.S. (ASCAP, BMI, or SESAC) has reciprocal agreements with all of the performing rights societies around the world for licensing and royalty collections, and all of the performing rights societies have agreements with them as well. The performing rights society in Japan and Germany are as listed above for mechanical rights, and in Great Britain it's PRS. (JASRAC and GEMA collect both mechanicals and performance royalties.) In any case, the foreign performing rights societies send the writer's share of performance royalties to the U.S. organizations (remember the "writer's share" of performances always gets paid to the writer, even for foreign performances), and then the U.S. society pays the writer directly. That's pretty straightforward, right?

However, the "publisher's share" of performance royalties is usually handled a bit differently. So again, the U.S. publisher will want to contract with a subpublisher and pay out a fee (I promise, more on the fee in a minute) to collect the publisher's share of performance monies. If you don't get a foreign subpublisher to represent you, the publisher's share of performance royalties will theoretically make its way back to you via your U.S. performing rights society. This method may take much longer than contracting a subpublisher, though, and is not an effective means of ensuring that all your performance income is collected. Like mechanicals, these monies are also subject to falling into the "black box."

Black Box Monies

When the foreign rights societies collect royalties earned by a song, they hold onto them and identify to whom the monies belong by checking registrations made by local subpublishers. *If the societies are unable to identify where the money should be sent, they forward it to an escrow account known as the black box.* Every society has one of these infamous black boxes holding unclaimed monies. After a certain period of time (usually about three to six years), if no claimant has come forth, the monies are deemed unclaimed or unidentified and are then divided among all of the local publishers in the territory pro rata based on their income. Successful writers who are contracted with a subpublisher, and who also have negotiating power, sometimes share in a percentage of the black box fund. This means that if you do not have a subpublisher in a foreign territory representing you, *other artists will gladly take your hard earned money instead.* But this can be prevented.

Foreign Subpublishers

Now let's take a closer look at these heroes of your foreign monies. As briefly mentioned before, a subpublisher is essentially a publisher in a foreign territory who's more than happy to collect monies for U.S. publishers, among other duties. Subpublishers first make sure that all of the U.S. publisher's works are properly registered with the foreign collection agencies mentioned above. When the foreign agencies collect royalties earned from your songs, they acknowledge the subpublisher's registration and forward the monies onward to it. The subpublisher then takes its share, ranging from 10 to 25 percent of what it collects, and remits the net receipts to the U.S. publisher, which then divides the monies with the writers accordingly. Other functions of subpublishers include seeking uses of your songs in synchronization, printed music, and covers (note that foreign covers may involve a translation royalty to the lyricist adapting his/her native language). The subpublisher makes sure that all these sources of income are collected properly and then sends them back to the U.S. publisher.

At-Source Royalty Collections

There's one more thing that you should know about subpublishers, and it concerns something called "at-source royalty collections." As you already know, when the subpublisher collects monies earned from your songs, it takes a share and sends the net receipts to the U.S. publisher, which then divides it with the writers. If you're both the publisher and the writer, what I'm about to say may not matter. However, if you enter into a publishing deal with a U.S. publisher to represent your works worldwide, and that publisher enters into a subpublishing deal or already has its own foreign affiliates, you may be able to get your share of the income calculated in the territory where the original dollar was earned, before the subpublisher takes its cut and sends the net receipts to the U.S. publisher to be divided with you.

Let me try to clarify this for you. When you enter into a publishing deal with a U.S. publisher, the monies are theoretically divided equally between the writer and the publisher 50/50. But if one dollar is earned in Germany, and the U.S. publisher has a deal with a subpublisher who takes its share of, say, 15 percent (remember, the subpublisher's fee ranges from 10 to 25 percent), then the subpublisher sends the U.S. publisher the net receipts of 85 cents. From this 85 cents, the publisher keeps 50 percent, or 42.5 cents, and sends the other 42.5 cents to you, the writer. But on an "at source" deal, your writer's share is based on the original dollar earned. So, if one dollar is collected in Germany, you will earn 50 cents rather than 42.5 cents. Got it? I'm aware we're only talking about a small difference in change, and there are no "dollars" in Germany, but *the point is that when your foreign royalties are calculated at source, you'll make more money as the writer!* **Note:** At-source agreements are negotiable and are not standard.

WHAT ESTABLISHED MUSIC PUBLISHERS CAN DO FOR YOUR CAREER

You already know that by virtue of creating a copyright, you inherit the rights as music publisher. You also know that there are several sources of income derived from music publishing, including mechanical royalties, performance royalties, print royalties, synch fees, sample use fees, and monies from interactive streaming audio and video sites. You might ask, "Why should I sign over my copyright ownership and a percentage of future earnings to an experienced music publisher?" First of all, don't be misled that publishing deals are being handed out on every corner. They aren't. The information that follows will give you a better sense of what publishers look for, as well as of what they can do for your career. The five major services usually provided by a music publisher include song plugging, securing recording agreements, paying advances, distributing marketing funds, and handling administrative duties.

Song Plugging

For many years, one of the primary roles of a music publisher was to "plug," or place, songs with other artists for commercial release on phonorecord. Most writers didn't perform their own music, and most performers didn't write. Someone needed to bring these two parties together, and music publishers were just the people to do it. But today, song plugging in the traditional sense has changed dramatically. Most artists both write and perform their own music and are therefore self-contained and less reliant on the music publisher. So the conventional role of the publisher as song plugger still exists to a lesser degree, but it has also evolved into what is now an emerging growth area called synchronization. We've already discussed this source of income, but to refresh your memory, it refers to synching your music with visual images. Synchronization is not a new concept; it's been around for a long time, but the thought of merging music with commercial products, television shows, and even movies was once considered selling out by most artists, that is until recently. Today you can hear Sting publicizing Jaguar cars with his song "Desert Rose," Led Zeppelin promoting GM with their classic song "Rock and Roll," and British rockers Oasis endorsing AT&T with its song "All Around the World."

It's not just the successful artists who are "in synch" (pardon the pun); you can also hear newly signed artists on network television shows and even in movies. When you think of how difficult it is for newly signed artists to get airplay on radio stations, you understand that the right exposure on, say, a television show can be an alternative method to breaking new artists into the mainstream. The group Sixpence None the Richer achieved a substantial amount of film and TV exposure for their song "Kiss Me." Singer Lisa Loeb can credit her success to the initial exposure she received from the movie *Reality Bites*, both from the movie itself and from the soundtrack album. Publishing companies also try getting game manufacturers to use your music, artists in foreign territories to cover your songs, and print companies to use your music in sheet music and folios. Print is a less significant source of income and exposure by far than film and TV exposure, but it all adds up!

Securing Recording Agreements

Publishing companies are also known to help unsigned writers/performers procure recording agreements with record companies. The publisher may team you up with seasoned writers to help you compose a collection of well-crafted songs and will then strive to place your songs in television shows and other media to create as much excitement about your career as possible. Basically, an artist's affiliation with a reputable publishing company can be an attractive feature in and of itself to a record label. It sends a message throughout the music industry that a credible establishment stands behind your career. Unfortunately, A&R representatives aren't always able to determine the worthiness of an artist. The more players you can get in your court, the better chance you have at getting a label interested in you.

A LITTLE HELP FROM HER FRIENDS Singer/songwriter Alanis Morissette was signed to MCA Music Publishing when a company representative introduced her to producer/writer Glen Ballard, who was also signed to MCA. Together, Morrisette and Ballard crafted songs that not only helped land Morrisette a major recording deal but also constituted an album called *Jagged Little Pill*, which sold over 30 million copies worldwide. And as if that weren't enough, *Jagged Little Pill* landed Morrisette a Grammy for Best Album of the Year. With a little help from her friends at MCA, Morrisette was able to put all the right pieces of her career together.

Paying Advances

Music publishing companies are often willing to advance money against your projected future earnings. Note the word *projected* here. The truth is that no one really knows whether your songs are ever going to make money (including you), but as long as you're willing to enter into a publishing deal, publishers are typically willing to take the gamble and give you an advance. Essentially, the advance is another source of income. The question then is, How much money can you get the music publisher to give you up front in return for entering into a deal? If you get a large advance and your record ends up failing, you'll have made out like a bandit on the publishing deal itself (the advance is nonreturnable). On the other hand, if your record is extremely successful, then you gave up your copyright ownership and a very hefty piece of your earnings in exchange for the advance. It really comes down to how badly you need money up front and how convinced you are that your publisher is going to be responsible for your future stardom. This is the gamble, and essentially you're gambling against yourself to a degree. Remember, your advance is really your money paid up front—it's recoupable against your share of future earnings (except from your writer's share of performance royalties).

Since advances can range anywhere from a few thousand dollars to in some cases as much as $1 million, publishers must be extremely cautious about whom they sign and what they decide to pay. The publisher looks at a few variables:

+ *Songs.* Is there hit song potential?
+ *Live performance.* Do you have an energetic live performance, and does the audience seem to respond well to your music?
+ *Placement resources.* Are you a writer/producer with resources to place your songs with top artists?
+ *Signed/unsigned.* Are you a writer/performer who has already signed a recording agreement?
+ *What record label.* If you're already a signed artist, then which record company holds your contract?
+ *Clout of A&R.* What's your A&R representative's success rate at the label?
+ *Enthusiasm of label.* How enthusiastic and supportive is the record company about your future?
+ *Radio play.* If the record company already released your first single, is it getting played on the radio?
+ *Sales.* Is your record selling well in stores?
+ *Tours.* Are you booked on any upcoming major tours?

Simply put, the more value the publisher sees in your compositions, the more money they may be willing to pay you up front. So in fact, the longer you can hold on to your publishing rights before signing a deal, the more money a publishing company may advance you. Again, it all depends on how badly you need the advance. Even the smallest advance can be exactly what you need to keep you or your band up and running in the early stages of your career. In any case, it's nice to know that the publishing advance is essentially another source of income available for the taking—if and when you need it.

WHEN THE ADVANCE REALLY COUNTS In the early 1990s, the band D-A-D (an abbreviation for Disneyland After Dark) entered into a publishing agreement with Warner/Chappell Music and received a $1 million advance. The buzz in the industry was that D-A-D was sure to be the next big band. Warner/Chappell Music took a big gamble by offering such a large advance, but as it turned out, D-A-D's album was DOA: "dead on arrival." According to one source at Warner/Chappell Music (who wishes to remain anonymous), sales figures reached a whopping 606 units—perhaps an exaggeration, but you get the point. You might say that D-A-D made out like bandits on the initial publishing deal and advance, but that depends on how you look at it. Their record failed, and they were never to be heard from again, but imagine how much worse off they would have been if their record failed and they hadn't had the publishing agreement at all.

Distributing Marketing Funds

Publishing companies are also known to specifically earmark advance dollars that go toward a "marketing fund," which is a wise move. When a publisher signs a writer/artist who's also signed to a record label, they'll want to have a "plan B" just in case your record company all of a sudden loses interest in your band—which, by the way, could happen under certain circumstances. According to the terms of your contract, the marketing monies may go toward buying a van or perhaps musical equipment so that you can hit the road and build a fan base. *This money can be what saves your failing career if the record company decides to fade out on you.*

It doesn't stop there. Some publishers have even been known to continue supporting a band above and beyond the allotted marketing fund. For instance, Warner/Chappell Music continued to offer the band Remy Zero small advances even after they were dropped from Capitol Records. The band used the advance money to cover living expenses while they looked for a new record deal. Eventually, the band signed to UMG and made a great record, but it was dropped once again. Nevertheless, Warner/Chappell Music stuck by the band and continued offering support and the occasional small advance. Finally, Remy Zero signed with Elektra and enjoyed moderate success with their single "Save Me," which was used regularly on the television show *Dawson's Creek*. The moral of the story here is clear: The record business is based on a one-shot, do-or-die philosophy. Since enormous odds are stacked against you, the question then becomes whether or not you want the major muscle of an established music publisher helping to promote your band. Remember, the more people you can get in your court, the better off you'll probably be!

Handling Administrative Duties

Last but definitely not least, the core function of a music publisher beyond the creative and financial components previously mentioned is administrative business, whose importance cannot be underestimated. Administrative duties include a number of things, as follows:

- Registering your compositions with the Copyright Office in Washington, DC
- Making sure your songs are properly registered with one of the three performing rights organizations (ASCAP, BMI, or SESAC)
- Issuing all types of licenses for the use of your songs, including mechanical, synch, and print licenses
- Negotiating the proper compensation for synch and sample uses (publishers understand proper rates)
- Making sure all generated income is collected worldwide (enlisting foreign sub-publishers to collect on your behalf)
- Keeping a watchful eye out for unauthorized uses of your songs
- Filing infringement claims
- Filing the occasional audit to be sure you're getting every last dime from the use of your songs

As you can see, administrative duties would be a handful for anyone to handle by him- or herself. Because established publishers don't have to be artists like you, they can concentrate on tasks like this all day long. It also just so happens that established music publishers are pretty good at it.

TYPES OF PUBLISHING DEALS

Now let's take a close look at the various types of publishing deals that exist. We'll concentrate specifically on how these deals have evolved throughout the years in regard to transfer of copyright ownership and sharing of income. Remember that until you enter into a deal with a *publisher*, you own 100 percent of all income that is divided into two separate and equal categories: the writer's share and the publisher's share. But with this said, note that a common scenario when entering into a recording agreement with a *record label*, like with an indie (and quite possibly with a major as new deals, like 360 deals, evolve), is that you will be asked to sign over your publishing rights. Handle these situations with extreme care! Consider whether the label is really going to be handling your publishing and bringing value to your songs, or if it is just acting as a middleman for a cut of the dough and using your share of publishing incomes to pay back recording expenses. These are important considerations! Always speak with your attorney, and never sign anything you don't understand.

Now let's take a look at exclusive songwriter agreements, co-publishing agreements, administration agreements, subpublishing deals, and finally, self-publishing.

Exclusive Songwriter Agreements

For years, music publishers served as the mighty middlemen between writers who needed their songs placed and artists who needed songs to record. Even as more artists began writing their own material, music publishers retained a tremendous amount of leverage in the industry. Publishing was simply a mysterious concept to everyone, and you can bet that music publishers liked it that way. In traditional publishing deals, such as "single song" and "exclusive songwriter agreements," publishing companies acquired 100 percent of the copyrights in a composition for the duration of the copyright term. This means they received 100 percent of the publisher's share of income, which essentially amounted to 50 percent of the gross song income (see pie diagram). Needless to say, this was a big piece of the pie, and arguably a bigger piece than publishers really may have deserved. So, for essentially every $100,000 the publishing company collected in earnings, the songwriters earned $50,000, and the publishing company earned the other $50,000. Keep in mind that with the exception of your writer's share of performance royalties, which is always paid to you directly by your performing rights society (ASCAP, BMI, or SESAC), your share of earnings is always charged against the initial advance. It's like your credit card company receiving a payment of a dollar and only crediting fifty cents of that payment to your account. If the advance sounds more like a high-interest loan, it is, but this is basically how all publishing deals work. Once the advance is recouped, you start collecting your allotted share for subsequent earnings. The Beatles and Bob Dylan are examples of artists who signed exclusive publishing agreements, which was the standard practice then. For all the money they made, they gave half of it away. In the words of Ed Pierson at Warner/Chappell Music, "These types of one-sided deals made publishing companies huge cash cows."

> In some cases, the publishing company may further reduce the writer's share of income by taking an additional fee of up to 10 percent for administration charges, but this is negotiable.

EXCLUSIVE SONGWRITER AGREEMENTS

The Song

Writer's Share

Publisher's Share

Copublishing Agreements

Rumor has it that after Brian Lane (the manager of Yes) balked at the idea of relinquishing 100 percent of the band's copyright to its songs and 50 percent of its earnings (by about 1975), publishing deals finally began to change for the better. Enter the concept of "copublishing." Copublishing deals (also called co-pub deals) have become the most common arrangements today for the writer/performer, especially for those who have already procured a recording deal. In fact, the co-pub deal has become the norm for many individual writers as well.

In co-publishing agreements, the publishing company still administers the entire copyright for the full term; however, the writer now gets some benefit by transferring only 50 percent of copyright ownership. Therefore, the sharing of income in copublishing deals is essentially 75 percent to the writer, 25 percent to the publisher. The writer receives not only the 100 percent of the writer's share, which is 50 percent of the whole, but 50 percent of the publisher's share, which is 25 percent of the whole. This essentially means that for every $100,000 in monies collected by the publishing company, the writer is now credited $75,000, and the publishing company takes in the remaining $25,000 (as opposed to the 50/50 income split I discussed in songwriter exclusive agreements above). This is by far more advantageous for the writer than the single-song and exclusive songwriter agreements.

COPUBLISHING AREEMENTS

The Song

Writer's Share

Publisher's Share

Administration Agreements

There are alternatives to the aforementioned agreements. Rather than receiving a substantial advance for the transfer of copyrights, as with the above agreements, the writer can retain 100 percent ownership (acting as a self-publisher) and pay a fee to a publishing company to specifically handle administrative duties (see pie diagram). These types of arrangements, known as "administration agreements" (also called admin deals) have become increasingly popular these days for the artist who writes and performs his or her own music or otherwise has a means to place songs. The term of most admin deals ranges from only one to seven years and may automatically renew. Fees range from 10 to 20 percent of the gross income collected but are more commonly 15 percent. For a slightly higher fee, some administrators may even be willing to offer placement services. If an artist ends up being successful, his or her willingness to receive either a small advance or no advance in exchange for retaining ownership and a greater share of the profits really pays off. Hey, it worked

for both R.E.M. and Prince, artists who signed administration deals early in their careers. They bet on themselves and hit the jackpot.

Note: While advances for admin deals are typically lower than, say, a co-pub deal, Kyle Staggs of BugMusic says, "Substantial advances are sometimes offered for admin deals. When this is done, the advance is based on (1) so-called pipeline income (i.e., income that is verifiable as collectable by the administrator immediately upon execution of the deal) and (2) the songwriter's/publisher's proven past income. The advance may be $35,000 on the high range, but I saw one for $500,000, which admittedly was extremely a rare case."

Subpublishing Agreements

Subpublishing agreements (also called sub-pub deals) are very similar to administration deals, except that they relate specifically to foreign territories. In fact, subpublishing deals are often described as "limited territory administration agreements." Keep in mind that most of the agreements mentioned above cover both the territories of the United States and those overseas (contractually known as "the world"). Therefore, it's not necessary to enter into a subpublishing agreement yourself unless you choose to handle business by self-publishing (which I'll discuss in a moment).

In sub-pub deals, the writer/self-publisher retains 100 percent of the copyrights and assigns the rights to the foreign subpublisher to handle all administrative duties. Subpublisher's fees generally range from 10 to 25 percent of the monies collected. Advances against your future earnings are not uncommon. The term of most subpublishing agreements ranges from three to seven years. Remember that the collection of income in foreign territories is far more complex than it is in the United States, so the services of a subpublisher are absolutely necessary when your music is going to be released in foreign territories (that is, if you don't want your money to go uncollected and ultimately be lost).

Self-Publishing

To take the concept of retaining 100 percent ownership and control of copyrights to its furthest extreme, the writer can act as a self-publisher by directly becoming a member of the various collection organizations in the

United States, such as ASCAP, BMI, or SESAC (to collect performance royalties), and perhaps the Harry Fox Agency (to collect mechanical royalties). As the writer/self-publisher, you could also collect mechanicals in the U.S. yourself directly from the record labels. A subpublisher can then be established to handle foreign administration. Fees will run at around 6.75 percent for Harry Fox in the U.S. and from 10 to 25 percent for a foreign subpublisher. In this scenario, the writer/self-publisher now maintains a greater level of control and a larger share of the profits than he or she does in the various publishing options discussed in this chapter but *does not receive an advance or the various services provided by an experienced music publisher.* (See the self-publishing pie diagram.)

Writers may choose to become self-publishers for a number of reasons:

◆ They were not offered a publishing deal (very common).
◆ They were not offered a large enough advance to entice them into making the deals mentioned above (also extremely common).
◆ They write and perform their own songs, or otherwise have resources to place songs, and choose to hold on to their publishing rights and gamble on the big payoff down the road (also very common).
◆ They were not asked to sign over their publishing rights at the time of signing a record deal, which is something indie labels often ask of artists and is quite possibly what the major labels will be insisting on as new deals, like 360 deals, evolve.

Ed Pierson at Warner/Chappell Music reminds us that "If you hold onto your rights, then you'd better be prepared to do the work. Assuming you already have a means to publish your works, it's absolutely essential that you make sure your monies are properly collected, especially in foreign territories, or otherwise you will lose money. Many artists start off as self-publishers, but with the good fortune of even moderate success, they eventually see the advantages of entering into an admin or co-pub deal."

Michael Eames of PEN Music Group adds:

"Deciding on what to do with your publishing rights is always a matter of doing the math and weighing the pros and cons. If you were to be hugely successful, it [would be] quite lucrative to hold onto your publishing. Paul Simon, Bruce Springsteen, and Diane Warren are all successful writers who own their own publishing. But a publishing deal can also bring opportunities to the table that wouldn't otherwise exist. The decision at hand is whether you feel it is worth giving up partial or complete ownership in your songs to get access to these contacts and opportunities. Also, if an advance is being offered, does it make sense to accept? Any advance is just your own money that you will have to pay back, and sometimes at a high cost compared to a typical bank loan. If the success you achieve is due to the publisher's efforts, however, then it makes sense to have done the deal. If you're responsible for the success and the publisher has done nothing, you've given up ownership and control in your creations to someone you wish you hadn't. Just find people who believe in you and [who] will work with you over the long term. That is invaluable."

SELF-PUBLISHING: STARTING YOUR OWN PUBLISHING COMPANY

Self-publishing becomes an option for writers who weren't offered a publishing deal, who weren't offered the "right" publishing deal, who chose to hold onto their publishing rights to gamble on the big payoff with a greater share of the earnings, or who weren't asked to sign over their publishing rights at the time of signing a record deal. In any case, here's a very brief overview of the bare minimum you have to accomplish to get started.

Affiliate with ASCAP or BMI

The first step in starting your own publishing company is to contact one of the two performing rights organizations (ASCAP or BMI), affiliate yourself as a writer and a publisher, and fill out the necessary clearance forms. Yes, I'm aware I'm leaving SESAC out of this discussion, but that's only because you need to be asked by SESAC to join. SESAC is a smaller organization and is selective in choosing its members. Unless you're a fairly established writer, or you feel you're going to be the next Diane Warren (who, for those of you who don't know, is an extremely successful songwriter), it's not likely you're going to start with this organization.

Publisher Affiliation

As a self-publisher, you're required to affiliate with one of the performing rights organizations and to pick a name for your music publishing company—for instance, "Uncommon Name Songs Unlimited." You're also asked to include two more alternate titles (three names total) in case your first choice is already being used by another music publisher. The less common the name you choose, the better chance you'll have of no one else using it. As of 2007, the fee for affiliating with ASCAP as a publisher is free. BMI charges a one-time fee of $150 if you're an individually owned company and $250 if you're a partnership or corporation (although this may change soon). Contact ASCAP (www.ascap.com) and BMI (www.bmi.com) for details.

Writer Affiliation

Writers are required to have a separate writer affiliation with the performing rights organizations. Remember that the performing rights organizations always send the "writer's share" of earnings directly to the writer, regardless of who the music publisher is—even if it's you. So again, whether you self-publish or not, you must always register as a composition's writer. Oh, and in case you're wondering, you cannot affiliate as a writer with two performing rights organizations at the same time. However, should you be the joint writer of a song, your partner can affiliate with one organization while you affiliate with the other, as long as song percentages are cross-registered to match. In other words, an ASCAP writer can register as 50 percent writer of one song, while a BMI writer can register as 50 percent writer of the same song. There is no fee for affiliating with either ASCAP or BMI.

Clearance Forms

As both the writer and publisher of your songs, it's absolutely essential that you provide your performing rights society with detailed information for every composition so that you can be entered into their system and paid. More important, because a song is divided into two separate and equal categories—the writer's share and the publisher's share—you must indicate the percentages in the compositions you own. If you're the sole writer of a composition, you own 100 percent of the writer's share and 100 percent of the publisher's share. However, if you write a composition with your four-member band and you're dividing the credit equally, then each member owns both 25 percent of the writer's share (4 x 25 = 100), as well as 25 percent of the publisher's share (4 x 25 = 100). It's not uncommon for bands to form one publishing company under a partnership agreement or corporation. Under these circumstances, all of the songs are registered to that company as the sole publisher. Incomes are then divided under the terms of the partnership.

Filing a DBA or FBN

The next thing you have to do to become a self-publisher is to file for a DBA statement with your county clerk's office (see your local yellow pages). A DBA, or "doing business as" statement, is sometimes called a "fictitious business name," or FBN, statement. The reason you need one of these lovely pieces of paper is to enable you to cash checks made out to that clever publishing company name you've come up with. Can you imagine the headaches you'd have in the bank when you try to cash a check made out to John Doe Song Works without one piece of identification proving the connection? That's what a DBA is for.

Getting a DBA is easy. After filling out specific forms furnished by your county clerk, paying a fee ranging from around $45 to $60 dollars (fees vary from place to place), and submitting the contents of the form to a local newspaper for printing (a procedure for which your county clerk will provide assistance), you'll receive your certificate soon after.

One more thing: Since your bank won't allow you to deposit money into an account with a different name (such as one under your personal name), you also need to set up a bank account under the name of your publishing company. When opening a bank account, you may need to provide a Social Security number or a federal tax identification number (which, for a business, is basically the equivalent of an individual Social Security number). A tax identification number can be obtained through applications filed with the IRS. (Contact the Internal Revenue Service at 800-829-1040 or www.irs.gov.)

> Sole proprietor, partnership, corporation, S corporation, or LLC? Another important aspect of starting your own publishing company may be the formation of a business entity. See the interview with attorney Jeff Cohen in Chapter 2 for more information.

Filing Copyright Forms

Remember when we discussed filing copyright registration forms earlier in this chapter? Well, if you have already filled out and sent in forms in your own name only, then you have to refile them using your publishing company's name as the copyright claimant, or file an assignment transferring the rights to your company. Again, if you have any questions regarding how to fill out a copyright form, the Copyright Office will be more than happy to assist you. The copyright registration fee is currently $45. Online registration is $35. (Call the Copyright Public Information Office at 202-707-3000 or log on to www.copyright.gov.)

Other Administrative Duties

Okay, you've finally got your publishing company set up. You've registered with ASCAP and BMI, so you know you can start receiving performance statements, but how do you ensure the proper collection of other incomes derived from your songs, such as mechanical royalties, synchronization fees, print royalties, and subpublishing monies?

Mechanical Royalties

As previously discussed in the "Mechanical Royalties" section of this chapter, when a record company wants to use one of your songs on phonorecord (CDs, digital downloads, etc.), they'll ask you to sign a mechanical license. In any case, record companies can then send you your mechanical royalty statements directly, or if you choose you can have a major mechanical rights collection society such as the Harry Fox Agency both issue mechanical licenses and collect royalties for you. The Harry Fox Agency charges a percentage of your gross earnings, which is currently 6.75 percent, but this is subject to change, so keep posted to their site.

Synchronization Fees

When someone wants to use one of your songs in a film, television commercial, television show, video game, etc., they'll contact you and ask you to agree to a synch license. But unless you're banging on advertising agencies' doors, schmoozing with directors at parties, and generally being a salesman, it's not likely your phone is going to be ringing off the hook whether you're a signed artist or not—unless, of course, you have a hit song and your label's film and TV department is on the hunt for you. Furthermore, unless you have some experience negotiating licenses, it's not easy to know what you should charge for synch fees—there are a lot of factors involved, so be sure to see our discussion of synchronization fees earlier in this chapter, and check out the tips on the next page on pitching your music.

Print Royalties

Unless you have a hit song, it's not likely print companies are going to be tracking you down. There are really only a few print companies in the United States anyway; the most important are Cherry Lane, Hal Leonard, Alfred Publishing, and Mel Bay. If you're aggressive enough, you might have a chance at striking a deal. Anything's possible.

Subpublishing Income

Remember that to collect subpublishing income, you must find a subpublisher in the territory in which your music is to be published. You can ask the record or film company releasing your music overseas to recommend a subpublisher. You can also contact one of the performing rights or mechanical rights agencies (such as GEMA in Germany or JASRAC in Japan) and ask them for a list of their registered local publishers. (If you have a song being released in a foreign territory, most subpublishers will at least be happy to collect money on your behalf.) And last but not least, a far easier approach

HOW TO PITCH YOUR OWN MUSIC IN FILM, TV, AND GAMES

Choosing to self-publish and pitch your own music is no easy task. Here's a few basic tips to help:

Have great songs. Your music must have memorable hooks and clear lyric subjects. It must evoke strong feeling and be applicable to specific moods and scenes.

Have broadcast-quality recordings. Your recordings must embody strong vocal and instrumental performances, the instrumentation and mixes must be current, and any "unauthorized" samples of other artists' music must be cleared or edited out. Have "clean" (no profanities) and instrumental versions of your music available.

Know your music. Be ready to describe the vibe and mood of your music in as few words possible, and understand what television shows or films—as well as what types of scenes (car chase, love scene, etc.)—are best suited for your songs.

Conduct research. Utilize the *Hollywood Reporter* to find films and TV shows in production. Utilize *The Film & Television Music Guide* (www.musicregistry.com) and/or the Internet Movie Database Pro to find contact information of music supervisors, producers, production companies, and music publishers.

Seek placements in student films. Today's film students are tomorrow's festival winners and successful directors. Research institutions with film, video, and/or game art and design departments and get in touch.

Network at film festivals. Film directors and TV/film music supervisors attending festivals can lead you to future work! Put together a list of festivals and start hanging.

Utilize placement services. Taxi (www.taxi.com), Pump Audio (www.pumpaudio.com), and Smashtrax Music (www.smashtrax.com) may provide licensing opportunities in television shows, films, and video games. Check them out.

Approach "music libraries." Ad agencies, film directors, and game companies look to music libraries for music. If you have the goods, check out Opus1MuiscLibrary (www.opus1musiclibrary.com), Rip Tide Music (www.riptidemusic.com), and Master Source (www.mastersource.com).

Be professional. If you're able to get in contact with Joe Placement, be professional, be concise, and be nice. Remember, this is a business of relationships.

Represent with authority. The person(s) you call don't need to know you are the artist/writer. Introduce yourself as the representative/owner of your own company.

Be ready to audition. Be ready to send a CD of your music and/or to e-mail a link where supervisors can preview your music online. MySpace (www.myspace.com) is popular for this.

Be patient. Remember that other independent musicians have been trying to place their music in film, TV, and games for years before you. Hang in there.

Be smart. Certain music users *may* request that you give up certain rights to your songs. Never sign anything you don't understand!

Become an intern. Want to make contacts in the publishing world? Volunteer to work at a music publishing company for free. How sneaky of you!

Note: Remember that there is a separate copyright in a sound recording, for which use, if you are not owner, you have no right to authorize permission.

to the subpublishing game is to seek one U.S. publishing company that has worldwide conglomerates (e.g., Warner/Chappell Music, EMI Music Publishing, Universal Music Publishing Group, and Sony/ATV Publishing, or you can use a smaller independent publisher like Bug Music or PEN Music Group that has a worldwide subpublishing network), rather than setting up individual subpublishing deals in several foreign territories. If they think representing you is worth their time from an economic standpoint, a deal can be established to cover "the world," except for the United States and Canada. Considering the time differences and language barriers involved when doing business abroad, among other things, this approach to administering foreign territories makes doing business much easier.

Q & A WITH MUSIC PUBLISHER NEIL GILLIS

Neil Gillis is president and chief operating officer of Dimensional Music Publishing. In the following interview, he discusses the contract terms with song pluggers and music libraries and the finer points of publishing deals with established music publishers and briefly comments on record companies that demand your music publishing rights.

Q: For do-it-yourself artists who record their own music, what types of deals might be arranged with "song pluggers" and "music libraries" that pitch to film and TV?

N.G.: The deals are really all over the place, but I'll give you one example that is somewhat common. The artist negotiates with a music exploitation company on a "nonexclusive" basis, giving it the right to pitch his songs (or group of songs, such as an album) in film and television for a period of one to three years. When the exploitation company gets a placement, it takes a fee ranging from 25 to 50 percent of the generated incomes, which could include both synchronization and performance monies.

The artist is still free to do whatever he wants with his songs: sell records at shows, get placements in film and TV via his own efforts or through the efforts of another exploitation company, or get the music played on Internet sites and on the radio.

To help differentiate between the performance incomes that are generated by the exploitation company and the performance incomes generated by the artist, there is a common practice of re-titling (or renaming) a song. In other words, the exploitation company will register a work with its appropriate performing rights organization under a completely different title. And at the same time, the artist will register (or will have already registered) the very same song under the title he gave the song upon creation. Note that re-titling is not something that all exploitation companies practice—and in fact, it's actually frowned upon by the copyright office, but it does happen in the real world.

And just to be absolutely sure, the artist—by simply allowing the exploitation company to re-title the song and create a so-called new work or "derivative work"—*does not* transfer copyright ownership in the song. *The artist continues to own the song.*

Q: Do any other deal scenarios exist for do-it-yourself artists?

N.G.: The artist would negotiate with the music exploitation company on an "exclusive" basis (meaning that no one else can pitch the songs in film and television at the same time), but he is still free to do whatever he wants with his songs in other areas, like selling CDs at shows, getting music on the radio, etc.

To help differentiate incomes generated by the different parties, the song is re-titled, but the exploitation company *does take* ownership in 100 percent of the so-called new or derivative work.

This essentially means that the exploitation company has the right to collect the incomes it generates from the re-titled work for the full life of copyright. This scenario is not uncommon of music libraries.

But again, deals are really all over the place and subject to individual terms. I strongly advise your readers to consult with the proper business professional before signing anything.

Q: Stepping things up a notch, what about the contract terms in publishing agreements with established music publishers? What's most important?

N.G.: While the publishing advance (the amount the writer gets up front) is often treated as being the most important, there are other deal points that can be equally, if not more, important. The two that come to mind are "reversion of copyright" and "prior approvals." While there are many more, these are two quality examples.

First, reversion of copyright is commonplace in deals today. Simply put, it's a point in time after the termination of the deal when your rights return to you. That can be very important in terms of how your career moves forward. Upon getting your copyrights back, assuming you had any success, you can renegotiate for a larger advance or benefit by earning a greater share of monies by virtue of owning 100 percent of the songs.

Second, prior approvals are vital in that they are your control factor in terms of how a publisher can and cannot utilize your works.

On a side note, one must consider the objective of managers and attorneys who often advise their clients to hold out for the largest advance. Although most artists' managers and attorneys in the business are straightforward and have the best interests of their clients in mind, there are some folks out there who may simply wish to bring in a large front-loaded advance because it could have ramifications for how they're paid for their services (i.e., the greater the advance, the greater their commission). If your representative is capable of negotiating quality deal points on a majority of the important issues mentioned above, and they get you a large up-front advance, then you have the best of both worlds. Just be sure to understand that one does not always accompany the other, and it is in your best interest to have both issues met.

Q: Can you clarify "term of agreement" and "term of copyright"?

N.G.: The best course here might be to simply define each of the terms you mention.

"Agreement term" is language found in publishing agreements that specifically relates to how long the publishing deal will last. (It has nothing to do with copyright duration, as you'll see in a moment.) Agreement terms are usually based on a certain number of years, or in many cases, a certain number of records.

"Copyright duration" is different from the agreement term. It deals with language found in publishing agreements that specifically relates to the amount of time the publisher will continue to own your songs—that were created during the term—after your agreement term has expired. For instance, the publisher may continue to hold on to your songs after the agreement term for the full life of copyright (LOC), or in the case you've negotiated a reversion of copyright clause into your agreement, the publisher may have to revert the rights back to you at a specified period of time (say, ten years after the agreement term expires). It all depends on the finer points of your agreement and what you're able to negotiate.

Q: What about "option periods" found in publishing contacts?

N.G.: "Option periods" is language in publishing agreements that deals with the publisher's choice or "option" to extend the term of your deal upon it expiring. For instance, if your publishing agreement is time based, your publisher may exercise its option (or multiple options) to continue the agreement for another year(s). If your agreement is record-delivery based, your publisher may exercise its option (or multiple options) to continue your agreement for another record.

Q: What about a "delivery commitment" found in publishing contacts?

N.G.: "Delivery commitments" is language in publishing agreements that defines what you're responsible for delivering to your publisher during the term of your agreement. For instance, your agreement may require you to write a certain number of "commercially acceptable" songs, or it may require you to write a certain number of songs that get recorded and released by you or by other artists who desire to use your songs. This language is extremely important for artists to consider when negotiating their deals, since they can end up getting stuck in a deal that theoretically never ends.

Q: Any comments about record labels that ask for an artist's publishing rights in new recording deals?

N.G.: Many independent labels have historically been known to ask their artists to sign over their publishing rights. Now, in recent deal structures [like 360 deals], a number of labels, including majors, are trying to do the same. It is not a new concept by any means. It is an old practice that meets a need in the current climate. That need is for a label to diversify its holdings so that it can try and cut its risk on just being a record label. Publishing helps fortify those assets that traditionally come in a record deal.

If you choose to consider this as an option for you as the artist/writer, then you have to ask yourself a few basic questions. First, is this label really going to bring anything to the table and add value as a publisher? Does this label truly understand publishing and have a legitimate business in that regard, or are they just going to pass this off to a third party to do the business for them but they still gain the benefit of this revenue share? Second, does this label and its publishing entity want to cross your income from either deal against each other? You want to keep your royalty flow on each of these deals as distinct as possible, as you can be negatively affected by crossing.

If a young band should feel that it has to sign with a record company that wants publishing, they need their attorney and their management team around them to make sure that the deal is at least a fair deal from both an economic and creative standpoint.

CHAPTER 12

Live Performing
and Touring

"Without a plan, the road is just the road to nowhere."
–CHRIS ARNSTEIN (Tour manager, Agent, Promoter)

Live performing and touring is one of the most basic ways for artists to introduce their music to the marketplace. By performing before vast audiences, interviewing with radio stations and the press, visiting record stores, and connecting with the fans and other bands, a new group can build a grassroots following of music lovers that will loyally support them for years to come. A classic example of this is Guns N' Roses, which was playing locally in Los Angeles for years before getting signed and eventually hitting the road to support its first record *Appetite for Destruction*. With a great live show and unique brand of raw "in your face" rock, the band slowly, but surely, won over more and more fans, which subsequently led to increased record sales, to radio stations and MTV playing their single, and to concert audiences growing into the thousands. The rest, as they say, is history.

On the surface, live performing and touring may appear to most people as being fun, glamorous, sexy, adventurous, incredibly lucrative, a nonstop party, or an escape from reality. However, when looking deeper, there's much more to live performing and touring than what may initially meet the eye.

In this chapter we'll take a behind-the-scenes look at the costs and realities of live performing and touring, how to get the right gigs and tours, how you're paid for live performance deals, how live performance deals are negotiated, and at live performance contracts and riders.

THE COSTS AND REALITIES OF LIVE PERFORMING AND TOURING

Every year we read stories in magazines and newspapers about artists who sell thousands of tickets to their live performances at costs above $50 to $100 a pop and more. It's no wonder most people think there are millions of dollars to be made from performing live. Although major artists have earned substantial sums of money through touring, do not be deceived! The truth is that it usually takes a long time before a new group can expect to turn large profits from performing live—if it ever happens at all!

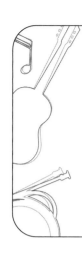

THE VENUES YOU MAY PLAY

✦ Coffeehouses and bars: approximate capacity 20–100 people

✦ Colleges (lounges, quads, arts centers): approximate capacity 200–600 people

✦ Youth centers: approximate capacity 50–500 people

✦ Clubs: approximate capacity 100–2,000 people

✦ Amphitheaters: approximate capacity 3,500–20,000 people

✦ Sheds (or outdoor theaters): approximate capacity 3,500–20,000 people

✦ Arenas: approximate capacity 10,000–35,000 people

✦ Stadiums: approximate capacity 35,000–300,000 people

Whether you're a singer/songwriter with hopes of getting paid for playing local clubs or a new group already signed (or close to it) with dreams of getting the big bucks playing the largest venues, what you're about to read will intrigue you.

Your Local Club Scene

"A journey of a thousand miles begins with a single step." —*Lao-tzu*

In the early stages of most artists' careers, they'll book their own gigs and play local coffeehouses, bars, and small clubs early in the week for no pay (read: FREE), and may even have to buy their own tickets and sell them to friends and family (a concept known as "paying to play," discussed later in this chapter). As a group's local following builds, they'll play weekend gigs and may earn a door percentage (ranging from 50 to 100 percent) of the amount people pay to see them. If the group really starts packing people in and proving themselves to local promoters, they may even receive a flat guaranteed fee (from $50 to $125). At this level of performing, really any payment agreement can exist. Just keep in mind that no matter what amount, or method, a band is paid for its performance, the money will typically go back toward covering expenses for the gig. In other words, in the early stages of most artists' careers, they're likely making zero profit or taking a loss. Your live performance expenses might include the following:

✦ Advertising for the promotional postcards and CDs
✦ Van rental to haul your equipment to the venue for the night
✦ Parking
✦ Tips to the sound and light personnel at the venue
✦ Side musicians (especially if you're a solo artist)
✦ Complimentary drinks for industry folks you might invite
✦ Bribes to get your friends and family to come see you (just kidding)

Just remember one thing: playing your local market is a necessary part of developing your career—from finding your target demographic audience, to establishing your identity or "brand," to

TAKING CHARGE As the old saying goes, "You can't save souls in an empty church," and Linkin Park was definitely not playing empty clubs before getting signed. Andreas Wettstein, who worked with the band while VP of new media and marketing at Warner Records says, "When we signed Linkin Park, I was impressed by how much they took charge of their own success. That confidence really generated a lot of excitement at the label. The band was already paying so much attention to their image and their fan base, and [they] came through the door with a rock-solid demo that sounded as good as their album. I'll never forget seeing them live at Roseland in NYC. The album wasn't out yet, and already everyone in the crowd knew all the words. That was powerful. And keep in mind it was before iPods, LimeWire, etc. They worked incredibly hard, and it paid off."

building a buzz around your group. The more your band can develop on its own at a local and regional level, the more chance you'll have at one day making a living, attracting investors, and/or negotiating a favorable recording deal and getting the support you deserve.

The Early Stages of Touring

"A record release is the flagship on which a tour is launched." —Richard Bishop, Henry Rollins' manager

The first time many bands hit the road for any significant period of time is after they've pressed a record and have a record company (or some other financial backer) willing to promote them. With a record in hand, a band can simultaneously establish its name in the press, on the radio, and on the Internet, and in retail stores across the country, which will lead to more and more fans attending its live shows. But this is not as easy as it sounds, and without the marketing expertise as well as the financial support of someone like a record label to set up such promotional events, hitting the road *may* otherwise make no sense. Why? Momentum is everything; everything has to hit at once if you expect to make an impact on a national level. Bottom line: A new band will only last on the road for so long before it simply can't afford to tour any longer. Let's take a look.

New groups with a record deal can only command nightly fees in the range of $250 to $600 (*maybe* more) as the opening act in clubs. If this money sounds like a lot compared to what you're used to getting paid for performing locally, after budgeting in tour expenses, this equation usually doesn't add up to making a profit nor to breaking even. Tour expenses may include the following:

- ✦ Transportation, such as a passenger van and a trailer to haul your musical gear
- ✦ Fuel to get your vehicle from point A to point B
- ✦ Tolls for the state highways on which you travel
- ✦ Hotels to provide you with a decent night's rest and a hot shower
- ✦ Food for nourishment—and to relieve hangovers
- ✦ Insurance for theft or damage to your instruments and vehicle
- ✦ Crew members (respectfully known as roadies) to help set up the gear
  and drive your band and equipment from gig to gig

ROAD DOGS The Swedish rock group the Hives was known for relentlessly working hard and building its buzz in its early years, which is what inevitably led to its current success. The band released their first record on a Swedish independent label in 1997. Over the following years, they toured around Sweden and Europe, steadily growing their audience with each show. In 2001, Alan McGee (famous for signing Oasis and Primal Scream) saw a video the Hives' had out on a local Swedish cable station and instantly signed the band to his newly formed Poptones label. McGee re-released the Hives' first album and kept the band out on the road touring over the next two years. Eventually, the Hives caught the attention of a major label, Universal Music, who offered them a multimillion-dollar deal. In 2004, Universal released the Hives' third recording, entitled *Tyrannosaurus Hives*, which quickly sold millions across the world. Needless to say, all of the Hives' hard work on the road paid off.

Minimizing tour expenses can help. Traveling in a van with one crew member, sleeping five to a hotel room, and allowing for salaries or allowances that are just enough for everyone to eat at fast food salad bars are all sacrifices your band can make to save money (and to go insane. I know. Just ask me about the $5-a-day diet). But even then, a new group signed to a label can easily return home from a tour owing money. If you're lucky, the record company pays expenses in the form of something called tour support (an additional advance to help subsidize a tour), but nonetheless, these monies must be paid back. As I explained in Chapter 10, tour support is 100 percent recoupable from the band's future record sales. That's right! Tour support is basically monies fronted by the label in exchange for the opportunity to go out and promote your band and record. So, your time on the road must be spent wisely. In the words of manager Tom Atensio, who has worked with artists such as No Doubt and Perry Farrell, "It's not enough for artists to play and look cool. They also have to work their asses off. If a band is not signing autographs and collecting names for its e-mail list, they're not working."

> Merchandising (e.g., the sale of T-shirts, hats, stickers, etc.) is a common means by which a band can help subsidize expenses while out on a tour. For major artists, merchandising can even generate substantial profits. Merchandising is discussed in detail in Chapter 13.

Midlevel Touring

"Watch the pennies, and the dollars take care of themselves." —Danny Goldberg, Music Industry Executive

Once a group reaches the level where its record is starting to sell well, it's getting great reviews and stories in the press, its single is getting played on the radio, it's drawing an increasingly large number of fans at concerts, and it's headlining large clubs or theaters, the fees it can receive for a live performance will be much higher. Let's call this stage in your career "midlevel touring." Midlevel bands may receive guaranteed fees in the range of $5,000 to $30,000 for headlining larger clubs or small theaters. In some cases, a group may even earn a percentage of income based on the total number of tickets sold (which will be discussed in detail under "How You're Paid for Live Performance Deals").

Yet, despite these increases in fees, a band might only break even by the end of a tour or, if they are careful with handling finances, earn a small profit at best. This is due to the inevitable increase in expenses at this level of touring. Additional tour costs may include the following:

- ◆ A tour bus (complete with a bus driver) for a more comfortable and sane means of travel
- ◆ A trailer to haul the band's equipment
- ◆ A larger crew to set up and break down the band's equipment
- ◆ A live-sound engineer to help replicate the nuances of the band's studio recording
- ◆ A tour manager to ensure that day-to-day business matters are run smoothly, to collect the money at the end of the night, to make sure the artists get on and off stage on time, and to coordinate press interviews
- ◆ Additional hotel accommodations for the bus driver, crew, and tour manager
- ◆ A business manager to help put together the tour budget and ensure that all finances are in order and that everyone is paid
- ◆ A talent agent to coordinate tour dates, determine the pricing of tickets, negotiate performance fees, and collect deposits from the concert promoter in advance of the show (typically 50 percent)
- ◆ A personal manager (whom you've already had for a long time at this stage of your career) to hire touring personnel, inform the record company of the tour dates so that it can set up press and radio interviews for the band, and help the talent agent coordinate tour dates and negotiate performance dates

As you can see, although the band may begin earning more money per performance, it can also incur many more expenses. You may have already been subjected to some of these expenses at lower levels of touring. Nevertheless, in case it hasn't sunk in already, keep one thing in mind: *You pay for it all!*

> The more a band tours, the more efficient it should become at minimizing expenses and profiting from the road.

The Big Leagues of Touring

"It's hard to make money by touring. Managers make money, the people in the service organizations make money, the crews make money, but there are so many times when a band spends six or seven months on the road and ends up with very little to show for it, even when a tour is grossing millions of dollars."
— *Bud Prager, manager for classic rock bands Foreigner and Cream*

If a group can work hard, overcome incredible odds, have all its prayers answered, and make it to the level at which it's headlining larger venues like amphitheaters, sheds, arenas, and stadiums, the guarantees it can earn are now much greater. Bands whose records are selling upward into the hundreds of thousands of units may earn guarantees in the range of $30,000 or more for playing smaller amphitheaters or sheds and often as much as $200,000 or more when progressing to playing large arenas or stadiums. (I'm told that Sting was offered a guarantee of $1 million for an expected sellout New Year's performance.)

Sometimes a group may receive a guaranteed fee *versus* a percentage of ticket sales (which I promise to discuss later in "How You're Paid for Live Performance Deals"). Nevertheless, while it may appear as though a group can now earn substantial profits on the road, it must still be very careful with its expenses. Additional expenses may include the following:

+ Massive stage set designs
+ Special effects
+ Pyrotechnic explosions to add a bang to the band's presentation
+ Sound and lighting systems (which groups must rent at this level of touring)
+ Trucks (complete with drivers) to haul the sound, lights, and staging
+ Loaders, who unload and load the trucks
+ Lighting crews, who operate the lights during a performance
+ Lighting directors, who ensure the artistic quality of the light show
+ Riggers, who climb above the stage and hang the sound and light gear
+ Monitor engineers to ensure the best quality sound on stage and to assist the sound engineer
+ Elaborate stage costumes in order to look outrageous or glamorous for the fans
+ Dancers to enhance the presentation of the live performances
+ Wardrobe personnel to take care of the elaborate costumes

As if those expenses weren't enough, when factoring in five-star-hotel accommodations, rented limousines, and perhaps even Learjets as an extravagant means of transportation for the band, tour costs can reach into the millions of dollars. Some bands may even get into "hubbing," in which they centralize themselves in one major city, settle into one hotel, and fly back and forth between performances. Although hubbing is more comfortable for the band because they don't have to unpack and pack their suitcases every day, it gets expensive, since they incur round-trip costs for each gig. When all is said and done, although the guarantees for playing larger venues are high, costs can quickly eat up profits.

As one way to minimize expenses, some major artists choose to play smaller venues (such as theaters) for two or three consecutive performances in one city rather than performing in a larger venue such as a stadium for a single night. Not only does this create excitement, since tickets are more likely to sell out quickly, but a band can save money by keeping the equipment set up. Tearing down equipment, traveling to the next city, and setting it up again can be very expensive. Playing consecutive nights in one venue also spreads out the band's exposure in a particular market and increases its availability for press and promotion. For example, rather than booking Sting at the Staples Center (a large venue in Los Angeles) for one night, agent Ian Copeland booked the artist at a smaller venue called The Greek Theater for three consecutive nights. The shows were an incredible success.

The challenge for any artist putting on a live performance is to make it exciting, to deliver a statement, and to return home from a tour with a profit. *Rolling Stone* magazine reported that Britney Spears grossed over $23.7 million on one of her concert tours. But due to inflated costs, sources say she netted less than 8 percent. Still not bad, but this gives one an idea of the tremendous expenses. Custom stages and risers, a climactic rainstorm, costume changes, dancers, and eighteen tractor-trailer trucks sure added up.

Corporate-Sponsored Touring

"With public opinion on its side, nothing can fail." —Abraham Lincoln

If a group is able to reach the level at which corporate sponsors are willing to exclusively underwrite world tours, its profit potential is considerably greater. In fact, the potential is huge. Corporations have paid fees as high as $15 million for the rights to advertise their products in conjunction with an artist's tour. For example, Pepsi Cola worked exclusively with Michael Jackson, Sears Corporation sponsored Phil Collins, Jovan worked with the Rolling Stones, Trojan worked with Ozzy Osbourne, and Honda Civic sponsored Maroon 5, Incubus, and Fall Out Boy. Corporations can increase their sales base and profit margins by targeting audiences in the concert industry. Keep in mind, though, that an artist must decide whether he or she wants to be branded with a specific product. What will the effects be in the long run? It may be, for instance, damaging to a band's career to be sponsored by cigarette or alcohol companies, regardless of the amount of money they may have offered.

Full Circle: Back to Where We Started

"The distance isn't important; it is only the first step that is difficult." —Marquise du Deffand

Before getting too excited about headlining stadiums, receiving guarantees into the hundreds of thousands of dollars, and attracting corporate sponsorships worth millions, you should also know that only a few groups ever make it to this level of touring. In fact, to zap you back to reality, should a newly signed band be refused tour support funds to cover road expenses by its record label (which often happens), a band may be unable to hit the road for any significant amount of time. The band may not be deemed a priority by its label, which inevitably leads to it getting dropped. So the next time you think of live performing and touring as merely fun, glamorous, sexy, adventurous, and lucrative, you'll understand some very important facts:

- ✦ Never underestimate the importance of performing locally and building a strong following. There is a lot you can accomplish right in your home region. Put together a strategic plan of attack and get to work.
- ✦ Touring is not a sightseeing trip or vacation you take to fulfill your rock star fantasies. You must always determine the return on the investment time, money, and resources before hopping in the van.
- ✦ Touring requires a lot of hard work, sacrifices, and tenacity. In other words, you better be prepared to pay a lot of dues and live off a very limited budget.
- ✦ While it can appear that you're making substantial profits from touring, remember that every expense on the road essentially comes out of your pocket. And while on the topic of pockets and expenses, let's not forget your personal expenses at home (i.e., rent, car, phone, credit cards, and mortgage). They just don't disappear, you know!
- ✦ If you're conservative with your finances and if you can use your valuable time on the road to promote your band and help sell records, the rest, as they say, just might be gravy.

GETTING THE RIGHT GIGS AND TOURS

A band, in the early stages of its career, is responsible for working hard and getting gigs on its own, DIY style. As the band progresses, a personal manager may come aboard and aid a group in its performing needs. When a group can command fees for its performances or has created a monster buzz, a licensed talent agency usually comes aboard to procure employment.

Do-It-Yourself (DIY) Style

A band can end up on the right gigs or tours by simply acting as its own personal management, publicity, and booking team by (1) seeking contacts and recommendations from local "like" bands, (2) impressing the hell out of local promoters, (3) considering performances in colleges, (4) forming alliances with other like bands, (5) keeping its eyes open on corporate-sponsored sites, and (6) watching for unsigned artist openings on festival tours.

Seek Contacts and Recommendations from Local Like Bands

Probably the quickest way to getting gigs and becoming part of your local music market is to seek contacts and recommendations from local like bands that have playing the circuit long before you. With these referrals, call the club promoter, tell him or her that so-and-so sent you, and then direct him or her to your website, where MP3s, video clips, and bios can be reviewed. Remember to follow up in a week so as to ask for a night to play, and always be pleasantly patient. To be sure, getting gigs really isn't rocket science at this stage of the game. You just have to be a businessperson and sell yourself.

Impress the Hell out of Local Promoters

Once you've received a booking to perform, understand that the fastest way to move up in your club scene and to get better gigs is to impress the hell out of local promoters. Consider the following tips as only a partial list of things to do.

Promote the Hell out of Each Gig Utilize your e-mail lists, hand out CDs at like venues, get other bands to announce your shows and to wear your merchandise on stage, contact college radio and local press, post messages on community sites and online message boards, and utilize free gig calendars in hometown papers and websites.

Make Each Gig an Event to Be Remembered Invite a celebrity in your city (actor, athlete, radio DJ, musician) to MC your show, make the performance a benefit concert for your favorite charity, align with corporate sponsors like Red Bull (www.redbull.com) or Jagermeister (www.jagermeister.com), make your live show visually stunning (e.g., incorporate special lighting), sound amazing (hire a personal soundman if needed), play your asses off (be super well rehearsed), and then throw a wild party after the gig.

Presell Tons of Tickets If a club requires you to sell tickets in advance (which I'll soon discuss), make sure to sell more than any other band ever has. Utilize e-commerce systems like PayPal (www.paypal.com) to sell tickets from your website, get your fans selling tickets for you around town, and even arrange free transportation for fans that purchase a ticket (you can have a few "pick-up points" where fans can catch a ride if needed). The more tickets you sell, the more you are sure to impress a promoter.

Consider Performances at Colleges

Colleges are a great way to make new fans, expand your territory, and make a few bucks in the process. The best part about all of this is that colleges usually have budgets ranging from $150 to $750 for new music every week. This means that you just might get paid! Sounds like the right gig to me. Chris Fletcher of Coast to Coast Music Booking advises, "Get an updated phone list for colleges in your area, by either conducting an online search or asking another local band to share its list with you, and contact the student activities department. Tell them you would like to be considered as part of their weekly entertainment concerts or "nooners" (colleges often have regular "noontime" concerts). Also try contacting NACA (National Association for Campus Activities—www.naca.org) and ask about its events that would be perfect for getting you connected with college bookers nationwide."

Form Alliances with Other Like Bands

Get out and see other bands play live, surf the Web and contact cool artists in your hometown and surrounding cities, and show your support by posting their website links on your site. Bottom line: *Bands help bands.* If one group has a weekend date, they might be able to pull you in as the opener and vice versa. And better yet, if one group gets signed, they just might tell its label about you and even ask you to go out on tour. For instance, Papa Roach took a friend's band, Alien Ant Farm, on tour not too long ago. Never underestimate the value of forming band alliances. This is important!

Keep Your Eyes on Corporate Sponsors

Companies like Jagermeister (www.jagermeister.com), Zippo lighters (www.zippohottour.com), Jim Beam (www.jimbeam.com), and Ernie Ball (www.ernieball.com) have long reputations for supporting up-and-coming bands. They provide opportunities to compete in "battle of the bands" competitions and to perform on sponsored tours. Although sponsors usually reserve these opportunities for artists that are already creating a small buzz in their community, create a list of corporations whose products are associated with your target fans. Use the Internet to gather each company's name, marketing director, address, phone number, and its submission policies. Get in touch and tell them about how you share a similar demographic audience and about how excited you are about promoting their products.

You can also try referring to *The IEG Complete Guide to Sponsorships* and the *IEG Source Book* (www.sponsorship.com). These are two helpful resources that list strategies for obtaining sponsorships.

Watch for Unsigned Artist Openings on Festival Tours

Promoters of major festivals like Bonnaroo/Vegoose (www.superflypresents.com), Vans Warped Tour (www.warpedtour.com), and Voodoo Music Festival (www.voodoomusicfest.com) are usually more than willing to give deserving local bands (i.e., bands that are already busting their asses locally and are generating a buzz) a shot at an opening slot. This could lead to a lot of exposure for a young band. However, if a group isn't ready to capitalize on this exposure, it could turn out to be a waste of time and money. Promoters accept packages, but since they receive so many, it is better to get different credible sources to send promoters your packages. You might also encourage your fans to get on the festivals' websites and spread some love in their forums. Another way to get on a festival is to check out the string manufacturer Ernie Ball (www.ernieball.com). Ernie Ball hosts an impressive battle of the bands, with the prize being a week of dates on the Vans Warped Tour.

A Personal Manager Comes Aboard

As a group generates a buzz and progresses in its career, a personal manager may come aboard to aid a group in its performing needs by doing the following: (1) finding a reputable talent agent, (2) pulling favors from people in the business he knows (such as from other managers), (3) using connections at the record label and publishing company (assuming you've signed to these companies), (4) enticing the record company to guarantee "ticket buys," and perhaps even by (5) arranging "buy-ons" to get on certain festivals.

Find a Reputable Talent Agent

First and foremost, managers will try to secure a licensed talent agent to procure employment for their artists and negotiate live performance deals. A talent agent also helps route a tour, price the artist, and collect deposits. We'll discuss talent agents more in a minute.

Pull Favors

A new band often lacks a draw when venturing from its hometown region and therefore may not be an attractive item to concert promoters (understand that promoters are in the "putting asses in the seats business" first and foremost). That being said, managers will pull favors from friends in the business (managers, agents, promoters, etc.) to hook you up with successful bands with whom you can tour. Andy Gould of AGM Management commented that his smash band Linkin Park could not understand why they initially could not take their friends' bands out on the road with them. Andy argued, "They couldn't take their friends because I have favors to repay to others that have helped me throughout the years. It's the way the music business works."

Use Connections at the Record or Publishing Company

Managers may also use the connections of a band's A&R representative at its record label or a representative at a publishing company to get a group on tour. These professionals usually have numerous connections with other bands, managers, promoters, and agents.

Inspire Ticket Buys

Managers may "inspire" the record label to use marketing dollars for ticket buys to get an artist on a tour. In other words, the label will purchase a certain number of tickets in various markets. Since headlining acts want opening acts that can help sell tickets, ticket buys guarantee sales and therefore opening slots. The tickets can then be used for giveaways and contests promoted on radio stations and Internet sites.

Arrange Buy-ins

Sometimes a manager may even find ways to arrange money to buy you into certain festival tours. In other words, the value of getting you on a specific tour and in front of a certain number of people can perhaps be made to look like a valued marketing expense. Perhaps he will convince the record company to front this money, or maybe it will be handled in some other way. All I know is that buy-ins do exist. I've seen them.

A Talent Agency Comes Aboard

Once your group is generating substantial live performance fees, drawing large local crowds, or getting attention from labels and publishers, a talent agent of national clout may become interested. A talent agent will work together with your manager to formulate your tour strategies, package you with other bands, determine whether you should open or headline, route a tour, price your tickets, determine when to put your tickets on sale, negotiate live performance deals, collect deposits, and monitor show publicity. Bottom line: Your talent agent's business is live performances and touring, and when an agent gets behind you, you're probably further along the way to getting on the right gigs and tours than you ever were. (Be sure to read Chapter 9.)

HOW YOU'RE PAID FOR LIVE PERFORMANCE DEALS

There are a number of methods used to compute how you're paid (or not paid) for a live performance. The most common are as follows:

+ Nothing (aka free)
+ Pay to play
+ A straight percentage
+ A flat guaranteed fee
+ A guaranteed fee versus a percentage

A number of factors determine which of these payment methods is used, including the stature of the artist, the size of the production, the size of the venue, whether the band is an opening act or a headliner, and the reputation of the talent agency (if there is one) negotiating on the band's behalf. The concert promoter wants to pay as little as possible, and the band wants to make as much as it can. This makes the deals, as well as the sums of money negotiated, difficult to nail down. The truth is, anything goes.

Nothing (aka Free)

In the "nothing" or free deal, a situation that usually exists at the very beginning stages of your career when you're starting to play in small clubs and bars (or anywhere you can twist people's arms to let you), the booker offers zero monetary compensation. But don't despair. Money isn't everything. You can always put out the tip jar and think of all the other benefits and opportunities you get. The "nothing deal" helps you to . . .

+ Get your musical ya-yas off
+ Socialize
+ Get tighter performing before large audiences
+ Define your target audience

- ✦ Hone your songs and figure out what people respond to
- ✦ Develop the theatrics and visuals of a great live show (i.e., your branding)
- ✦ Connect with fans and build e-mail lists
- ✦ Build a "community" buzz (with press, college radio, and local stores)
- ✦ Meet other bands and develop invaluable connections
- ✦ Prove yourself to promoters so as to get better gigs
- ✦ Sell CDs and merchandise (get your name out there and maybe cover expenses)
- ✦ Get one step closer to making a living playing music
- ✦ Get discovered and signed

You see, the free deal doesn't sound so bad after all, does it? And the best part is, if you can hang in there long enough and maintain a great attitude, you just might move along to the other methods of payment discussed next. Let's take a look.

Pay to Play

The pay-to-play arrangement is yet another situation—when, for example, you're just starting to play at clubs in your hometown—in which a club promoter essentially contracts you to buy tickets in advance, leaving any profit you make to go in your pocket.

Here's generally how the pay-to-play system works: A promoter prints up x number of tickets with your name, date, and time, under a written contract that says you will return $100 to him or her on the date of the show. If you sell 20 tickets at $5 each (20 × $5 = $100), you break even. If you sell 40 tickets at $5 each (40 × $5 = $200), you make $100.

The pay-to-play arrangement doesn't sound too difficult, right? Manager Dionney Sepulveda tells me his band Pennywise did it for years when they were just starting out, as did tons of other bands. The challenge, however, is when you're booked to play the most popular clubs in your home-town and the promoters ask you to pay as much as $900 (and up) on the night of the show. My advice: Stick to smaller bars or alternative venues (like house parties and cellars) until you build up some fans first.

To understand how the pay-to-play system evolved, you have to see it from the club pro-moter's and owner's side of it: They're providing you a place to showcase your talent and to throw a pretty happening party. In their minds, they're doing you a favor to let you perform.

Understand that running a club costs a crapload of money. First you have to scout out a loca-tion, renovate and remodel, get a liquor license, put in a stage with lights and sound system, hire and pay personnel (bartenders, security guards, and waitresses), pay for insurance, and cover rent and electricity. This adds up, and promoters need to cover "basic nut" (general expenses). And since there are so many bands out there that talk up a big game about how great they are and then draw no more than four people (Mom, Dad, Grandma, and Granddad), and because there are so many other ven-ues competing for customers on a given night, promoters ask bands for a guaranteed payment until each band can prove they can pack the place. You see, that's all promoters care about: putting asses in seats, whether it takes you farting the alphabet or shredding the *Star-Spangled Banner*. This is just business. So until you buy your own club, get used to it. Just remember: If you're an entrepreneur and know how to sell, you will prevail.

Straight Percentage

In a straight percentage deal, an arrangement that also usually exists in the early stages of your career at the club level, a promoter pays you a percentage of the total money taken in at the door. Percentages can range from 100 percent of the door money down to 50 percent and may be arranged to kick in after a certain number of people walk up and pay.

A common arrangement for a young band in L.A. might be an amount of 50 percent of the door after twenty people pay entrance. Obviously, the harder you promote your show and the more people you can bring in, the more money you make. "But just make sure to have your own people counting heads at the door so that you always get the fair end of the deal," cautions tour professional Chris Arnstein, who has worked with the Eagles, Madonna, and Julio Iglesias. "Promoters are not always to be trusted."

John Pantel, of The Agency Group Ltd. (www.theagencygroup.com), tells me that percentage deals aren't only reserved for local bands just starting out. If a group knows that it has a big draw with the potential of selling out a club, a straight percentage can work out quite nicely. Reverend Horton Heat, a popular band on the national club circuit, often plays the House of Blues in Los Angeles and asks for a straight percentage deal. The band usually sells the venue out and makes good money, while the venue profits from selling liquor inside and parking spaces outside. Everyone's happy.

Typically, though, once a band hits the road and depends on earning a certain amount of dollars to meet its expenses to get from one city to the next, percentage deals can turn a tour into a nightmare if shows are poorly attended. For this reason, the following forms of payment are typically used.

Flat Guarantee

A flat guarantee deal—an arrangement that usually exists once a band can draw a crowd in clubs or after they've latched onto a talent agency or record label—is one in which a promoter pays you a guaranteed sum of money for your performance. This amount can range anywhere from $50 to $125 or substantially much more, depending on the stature of the artists and the capacity of the venue. For a new band touring in unfamiliar territory where its fan base is questionable, a guarantee (even a small one) can help ensure that you'll at least be able to cover your estimated costs. For the more established artist, a flat guarantee can also be advantageous if it is negotiated so that it's reasonably high. The maximum amount, however, usually depends in part on the risks the concert promoter is willing to take. If the promoter pays a high fee and ticket sales are low, he or she could potentially lose his or her ass. Therefore, in order to split the risks between the promoter and the artist, the two parties usually agree upon deals like the "versus" deal discussed below.

Guarantee versus Percentage

A "guarantee versus percentage" deal—an arrangement that is usually reserved for more established artists playing at larger venues (theaters, amphitheaters, sheds, arenas, or stadiums)—is one in which a promoter pays you a negotiated guaranteed fee *or* a negotiated split of 80 to 90 percent of the adjusted gross receipts, or *whichever is higher*. Adjusted gross receipts are the sum of all tickets sold, minus all expenses. Some expenses may include the following:

- ✦ Hall rentals for the venue in which you perform
- ✦ Opening act fees for the bands that play before you

- Insurance for theft and damage to your equipment and for personal injury
- Police to make sure fans behave, to control traffic outside the venue, etc.
- Security guards to keep fans from climbing onstage or getting out of control and for watching buses and trucks parked around the venue
- Barricades to keep fans from climbing onstage and entering unauthorized areas within the venue
- Medical personnel and supplies, in case of injuries at the venue
- Advertising (including radio, TV, Internet, and print) to ensure that people show up for the event
- Telephone usage backstage for the road manager and production crew
- Power, sound, and lights to ensure the sound and look of the show is top quality
- Electricians to make sure the wiring for the lights and sound is functioning properly
- Stagehands to set up and break down equipment
- Box office personnel to sell tickets and take tickets from fans as they pass through the venue gates
- Clean-up crews to remove garbage from the night's performance
- Dressing room facilities (which include everything from the furniture and phone lines to towels)
- Catering (which includes everything from snacks, beer, and pizza to cooked meals)
- Runners (people on-call to run around taking care of last-minute business matters such as making sure all of the band's catering requests are met)

After the promoter deducts all of his or her expenses from the gross receipts, what's left over is multiplied by a negotiated percentage ranging from 80 to 90 percent to determine how the band is paid: the guarantee or the percentage. So if a successful band's negotiated guarantee was $125,000, the gross receipts from a sold-out concert were $500,000, and the promoter's total expenses were $300,000, the balance of $200,000 would be multiplied by, say, 90 percent to get $180,000. Since $180,000 is more than $125,000, the band's pay for the night is $180,000.

Here's a breakdown of how the band's pay for the night may look:
  $500,000 (gross ticket sales)
– $300,000 (promoter's expenses)
= $200,000
x 0.90 (90%: the band's negotiated percentage split)
= $180,000

  $180,000 (adjusted gross receipts) > $125,000 (the band's negotiated guarantee)
= $180,000 (the band's pay for the night)

In percentage deals, promoters are known to drum up false receipts, exaggerate expenses, and lie by underestimating the number of people who actually paid to attend a concert, all with the intention of pocketing that money and reducing the adjusted gross receipts and therefore the split. For these reasons, a tour manager must be scrupulous in reviewing all expenses when "closing out" a show with a promoter. Mark Goldstein, former vice president of business affairs at Warner Bros. Music, puts it strongly, but fairly: "It's not that promoters are lying, cheating scumbags, but there's a good chance that they are, and you have to assume the worst."

Chris Arnstein adds these final words of wisdom: "In general, settlement is a game of hide-and-seek. The promoter's job is to hide from you anything they can and to deny any expenses they feel they are not contractually obligated to pay. The job of the person settling the show for the act is to play seek and grab. Figure out how the promoter will try to work the system. Find the hidden or amortized expenses. Demand the contractually agreed-upon expenditures. Destroy any inflated or created expenses on behalf of the promoter. Seasoned settlers know the tricks of the trade and recognize the game. They enter into the negotiations with some level of respect between them, like poker players, so that compromises can be reached in a businesslike manner and not based on ego."

HOW LIVE PERFORMANCE DEALS ARE NEGOTIATED

Early in an artist's career, when he or she is performing for free or even paying to play, live performance deals are often dictated by the set terms of the venue promoter. However, as an artist's career begins to grow in stature and his or her audience size increases, the venue capacities get larger and the methods by which deals are negotiated can be more systematic and sophisticated. Let's first take a closer look at something called the gross potential and then at deals that are negotiated on a per-show versus a per-tour basis. Finally, we'll look at co-headlining.

The Gross Potential

As mentioned in Chapter 8, it's the job of the talent agent to negotiate performance agreements on behalf of the artist. One way they do this is to first consider the seating capacity of the venue in which the artist will be performing, as well to consider the ticket price that is most acceptable to charge. Keep in mind that there are usually several ticket prices within a venue depending on the proximity of the seats to the stage. The capacity of the venue is then multiplied by these ticket prices to result in a figure called the "gross potential," which is the total amount of admissions that could be earned for the night.

For simplicity, say the seating capacity of a venue is 25,000 and the average ticket price is $20. Twenty-five thousand seats multiplied by twenty dollars results in a gross potential of $500,000.

Another factor that must now be considered is the promoter's estimated basic expenses. If his or her expenses are, for instance, $300,000 (and considered reasonable by all parties), they are subtracted from the gross potential. In keeping with our example above, that's a difference of $200,000 ($500,000 − 300,000 = $200,000). Negotiations are then worked downward from there to a point at which both sides believe it is a reasonable risk to put on a show.

Now let's take a look at the equation.

25,000	(The capacity of the venue)
x $20	(The average ticket price)
= $500,000	(The gross potential)
- $300,000	(Promoter's estimated expenses)
= $200,000	(Amount at which negotiations work backward)

Note that if the promoter is also the owner of the venue, he will count on the money taken in from food, alcohol sales, parking, etc., for a reasonable profit. But, if a promoter is simply renting the venue and does not share in these ancillary revenues, he must always consider the possibility of the venue selling under capacity (below the gross potential), or he could otherwise lose his butt.

Per-Show versus Per-Tour Negotiations

Another factor that may affect the amount of what an artist earns from a live performance is whether deals are negotiated on a per-show or a per-tour basis.

When booking U.S. tours, talent agents individually negotiate performance deals with a variety of promoters across the country. However, there are also mega-promoters (such as Live Nation—a spinoff of Clear Channel Entertainment—which also acquired HOB Entertainment, another mega-promoter) that own a variety of large venues across the United States and Europe. In essence, the talent agent negotiating on behalf of the band is negotiated for an entire tour or a package deal. Business manager Jeff Hinkle of Gudvi, Sussman & Oppenhiem explains:

Live Nation (a spinoff of Clear Channel Entertainment) owns, operates, and/or exclusively books, 135 live entertainment venues, including 29 in Europe. It also produces concerts such as Ozzfest and the Jägermeister Music Tour. Furthermore, it acquired HOB Entertainment, a mega-promoter in its own right, being the operator of the House of Blues chain. Live Nation subsidiaries are located all over the world.

"These per-tour package deals basically work the same as the single-show 'guarantee versus percentage deals.' But rather than the artist receiving the greater of a negotiated fee or a percentage of the net profits for just one night, the artist earns the greater of his or her negotiated guarantees for the entire tour or a percentage of a 'pool,' which is the net profits from all of the shows added together. For instance, let's say the artist's guarantee is $150,000 per show for a total of twenty shows on a tour. That's a total of $3 million in guarantees for the entire tour (20 x 150,000 = $3 million). And let's say that the pool or net profits from all of the shows added together is $5 million. Being that the artist receives the greater of the total negotiated guarantee or a percentage—typically 90 percent—of the pool, the artist would receive a percentage of the pool totaling $4.5 million (0.90 x $5 million = $4.5 million in net profits > $3 million in guarantees)."

Co-Headlining Tour Negotiations

If understanding how a single band negotiates live performance deals was simple enough, perhaps you've raised the question about what happens when there is more than one headliner on a bill. Jeff Hinkle explains:

"In a co-headlining tour, each co-headlining artist will negotiate his or her respective guarantees with the promoter. If there is a stronger artist on the bill [one that will usually close the show], the artist will usually get a higher guarantee and also a higher percentage of any overages. To make it easier, sometimes the promoter will pay the closing artist 100 percent of any overage that is due. The closing artist then settles up with the other artists for their share of the overage. So basically a settlement with co-headliners works the same as it does with just one, except the money gets divvied up among all of the artists."

LIVE PERFORMANCE CONTRACTS AND RIDERS

The first page(s) of a contract between an artist and concert promoter include basic terms such as payment, percentage splits, dates, times, and load-in of equipment. Attached to this contract, however, is a separate document called a "rider."

A rider outlines the specifics of what a band needs for a performance. It can run in length in excess of twenty or more pages, depending on whether a group is at the beginning stages of its career and playing locally or at more established venues.

In the Beginning: Local Gigs to the Early Stages of Touring

For groups that are just starting out and playing locally, your rider is probably not going to be any more than one page that says you'll get "one warm glass of shut the hell up" (a phrase from the movie *Happy Gilmore*). In other words, you can make several requests for beer backstage, warm towels, and other stuff, but you're probably not going to get many of these requests fulfilled until you start generating some money for promoters. Even then, your rider in the early stages of touring may provide for no more than, for instance, a case of beer and a few other small requests.

At the Midlevel to Big Leagues of Touring

For more established artists, which can mean the midlevel to big leagues of touring, a group's rider might include personal requests for dressing rooms and catering, sound and lighting, and legal issues like cancellation policies and anti-bootlegging provisions.

In percentage-based deals, where the artist either gets a guarantee or a split of the profits (i.e., the total ticket sales minus all the promoter's expenses), remember that every expense listed on the band's rider potentially reduces the money the group will take in at the end of the night. Therefore, to ensure maximum profits per performance, close attention must be paid by the group's attorney, talent agent, and personal manager when establishing an agreement with the promoter.

Below is a brief discussion of just a few of the items that may be listed on a group's rider, including dressing room accommodations, catering requests, free tickets, security, internal transportation, cancellation provisions, and video- and audiotaping restrictions.

Dressing Room Accommodations

Some groups may have more elaborate dressing room needs, beyond the basic requests for a clean room, ample chairs, a mirror, a toilet, and a sink with running water. A group may want a specific room or even multiple rooms. The Black Crows, for example, were known to request specific carpeting, black lights, lava lamps, incense, and throw pillows in their dressing room.

Catering

Most bands make specific requests for the food and drink they want backstage. In addition, there are requirements for breakfast, lunch, dinner, and tour bus supplies. Some groups may have simple requests, while other artists require lavish spreads. All kinds of food, including pretzels, candies, gum, pizza, soda, bottled water, beer, hard alcohol, potato chips, cheese and crackers, deli meats, roast beef dinners, vegetarian pasta, baked or broiled fish, and even lobster, can be found on a group's catering rider. Most bands leave a lot of the food uneaten backstage, which is then usually devoured by the guests, so a group can actually limit its expenses by making prudent catering requests.

Free Tickets

Language stipulating the number of free tickets to be allocated to both the band and the promoter can typically be found on a rider. Here are the details.

A band may have a specific number of free tickets it wishes to give away to family and friends. Just remember, though, that when a group is working to collect a percentage basis of the net profits, each ticket given away potentially reduces the income that the band can earn at the end of the night. By the way, Elvis Presley is said to have given away no free tickets to his performances.

A promoter may also receive a number of free tickets to give away to radio and television stations in an effort to promote a show. This amount must be stipulated in the rider. In fact, the promoter is also typically required to provide the group with a statement that details to whom each ticket was given. This is to prevent the promoter from engaging in unscrupulous activity. At a concert featuring Hootie & the Blowfish, for example, the show's promoter sold his share of free tickets to scalpers for a large profit rather than using them as he should have for promotion. According to agent Ian Copeland, this kind of thing happens all the time.

"Papering the house" is a procedure that is not necessarily discussed in a rider, but it certainly has something to do with promoters and free tickets. If ticket sales for an event are low and the promoter is unable to meet all of his or her expenses (the band's guarantee being one of those expenses), that promoter may ask the group for the rights to "paper the house." This means that the promoter will give a large number of tickets away in the hopes of packing the venue with thirsty bodies. If a promoter owns the building, at least he or she will take in money from alcohol sales and parking fees. Papering the house also benefits the artist by creating the illusion for the fans and press that the artist has sold a substantial number of tickets. That way the band at least takes home its guarantee that night and is also spared the embarrassment of playing to empty seats.

Security

Although we've all heard the lead singer of a band cuss out security guards for not letting the fans start a mosh pit or get closer to the stage, the band essentially hires and pays security to be there as indicated in the rider. Security ensures the safety of the band and the band's staff and also protects the equipment and touring vehicles. Security costs are yet another expense deducted from the gross receipts before the artist receives a split of the profits.

Internal Transportation

A group may request that a passenger van and a responsible driver be available on the day of the performance. Some groups may even request that multiple vehicles or limousines be available to them at all times of the day.

Sound and Lights

A band may also make specific requests on the rider for sound and lighting, along with the requirements for power. In the event that the venue cannot meet the power requirements, a generator may be supplied.

Insurance

The rider must include provisions that require a venue to have general liability insurance. This will protect the band in case of personal injury or damage to the group's equipment. On several occasions, the Doors had their equipment trampled and destroyed after fans rushed the stage, although Jim Morrison himself usually incited this behavior.

Cancellation Provisions

A group, upon cancellation of a performance by the promoter, may ask for 100 percent of the agreed payment with two weeks' notice, or for 50 percent with one month's notice.

By the way, should a group miss a show due to health, sickness, death, or an act of God (e.g., a hurricane or earthquake), it cannot be held responsible for loss or damages the promoter may incur as the result of a cancellation. This clause in live performance agreements is called "force majeure."

Video- and Audiotaping

Many groups prohibit the recording or filming of their live performances to prevent the unauthorized reproduction and sale of their music. The Grateful Dead, however, allowed its fans to both tape and film their live performances. The venues in which the group performed often looked like a sea of telephone poles, with thousands of microphones affixed to boom stands pointing toward the stage. Quite impressive!

THE TOP TEN RIDER REQUEST COUNTDOWN
Most bands treat rider requests very seriously; specific items can bring peace of mind to certain artists while out on the road for several weeks. However, other requests are just downright silly and perhaps frivolous, made to prove that, after being mistreated for so many years, one can now make other people jump through hoops. In any case, here is the top ten rider countdown:

10. Christina Aguilera requested police escorts that had the authority to route the vehicles in which she was traveling through any potential traffic delays to and from the venues.

9. Cher requested one "wig room" backstage to store her wigs.

8. Marilyn Manson requested Cristal champagne and beef jerky.

7. Mariah Carey requested Cristal champagne with bendable straws.

6. The Killers requested Maker's Mark and Absolute vodka on Mondays, Wednesdays, and Fridays; Jack Daniel's and gin on Tuesdays, Thursdays, and Saturdays; Jameson Irish whisky and tequila on Sundays, and Coors Light, Corona, and red wine every day.

5. Axl Rose requested Dom Perignon, Wonder Bread, cigarettes, and pornography.

4. Prince and Willie Nelson each requested one physician to administer B-12 vitamin shots before their performance.

3. Iggy Pop requested a Bob Hope impersonator backstage.

2. Diddy requested that all food and ice be inspected for hair and insisted that catering personnel wear nets on their heads.

And the drum roll, please. The number one rider request of all time . . .

1. Van Halen requested M&M candies be provided backstage with all of the brown ones taken out.

Note: For more wacky rider demands, check out the Smoking Gun (www.smokinggun.com).

CHAPTER 13

Merchandising

"When a person is in fashion, all they do is right."
—LORD CHESTERFIELD

Merchandising refers to the process of selling merchandise—T-shirts, hats, stickers, programs, posters, and other goods—that bears an artist's name and often his or her likeness. When these products are sold in conjunction with a concert tour, they can generate substantial sums of money. Merchandising monies may also be useful in helping new artists subsidize expenses when the money they're earning for a live performance is minimal. Furthermore, merchandising may be helpful to certain artists who are already signed, should their record companies fail to provide adequate tour support funds. In any case, it's important to have a basic knowledge of how merchandising works and to have a broad understanding of everything from your merchandising rights to making merchandising deals to handling your own merchandising independently.

MERCHANDISING RIGHTS

The first step to understanding how the merchandising business works is to understand a simple law called the "right of publicity." This refers to an individual's rights to grant or not grant the use of his or her name and/or likeness for commercial purposes. In other words, you have the right to decide who, if anyone, can use your name and likeness on T-shirts, hats, posters, or other products for commercial sales. When considering your legal rights to a fictitious name, such as your stage or band name, you should register the trademark or service mark with the federal government. This is especially important when you reach the point in your career at which you will be exposed on a national level. Federal trademark and service mark registration makes it easier for you to successfully sue anyone who attempts to use your band name or logo without your permission. To avoid lawsuits, choose a distinctive name that is not confusingly similar to that of other bands or entertainment-related companies, and then conduct a trademark search to make sure no one else has already claimed the name.

When your name is going to be promoted at the international level, foreign registration may also be necessary. (For more information on trademark registration, see the interview with attorney Jeff Cohen in Chapter 2.)

Now that you know something about your merchandising rights, let's discuss a few options for using them.

GRANTS OF RIGHTS

There are three typical scenarios that apply to using your merchandising rights. They are as follows: the grant of rights to your record company, the grant of rights directly to a merchandiser, and handling your merchandising independently.

> The term *service mark* and the word *trademark* are sometimes used interchangeably; however, the two have different meanings. A service mark identifies a service, such as your live performances. A trademark identifies products that are bought and sold, such as your records and merchandise.

Grant of Rights to Your Record Company

When signing a recording agreement, your record label typically wants to secure your exclusive merchandising rights. This is especially true when you are a new artist signing with a small independent record label or when you have little or no negotiating power when dealing with a major label. (Another instance may be when you sign on with a record company, or "multimedia entertainment group," using a new and evolving business model called a 360 deal that acquires all your revenue streams.) Traditionally, your record company then licenses these rights to a third-party merchandising company to manufacture product and oversee sales. The merchandiser pays the record company a merchandising royalty, and the label in turn splits it with the artist 50/50.

This arrangement could put you at a disadvantage for two reasons. First, you make less money than you would if you were able to hold on to your own merchandising rights and make a deal directly with a merchandiser. Second, your record company will typically want to cross-collateralize your merchandising royalties with your record royalties. In other words, *any monies that would otherwise be payable to you from merchandising sales go toward paying back all the outstanding expenses for which you still owe your record label.* In this instance, it could be a long time before you ever see any money from merchandising sales. Needless to say, it's best to try to avoid giving up your merchandising rights if at all possible. However, if you're in a "take it or leave it" position in your negotiations, weigh the pros and cons before making any decision. (See Chapter 10 for more on record royalties, recoupable expenses, and cross-collateralization.)

> "Multimedia entertainment group" is a term many record companies are using lately, and, coincidently, they are arranging new deals, like 360 deals, whereby they acquire a number of revenue streams like publishing, touring, and merchandising. Hillary Duff is one artist who signed this type of deal, and perhaps, as you're reading this, there'll be many more artists who follow.

Grant of Rights to a Merchandiser

If you're able to secure the rights upon signing a record deal, you can enter into a merchandising deal directly with a merchandising company. The merchandiser agrees to manufacture products and oversee sales and then pay you a royalty and an advance against projected earnings.

Merchandising monies, particularly in the form of a merchandising advance, are often a much-needed source of income for bands in that they can help subsidize expenses. Rehearsals, van rentals, techs, hotels, airfares—and at the more advanced level, tour buses, trucks, and production—can add up. An advance is especially helpful if you're a new band and the fees you're receiving for live performances are small and/or if you're a band whose record company is no longer providing you with tour support funds to cover expenses. In any case, securing merchandising rights and entering into an agreement directly with a merchandiser is more advantageous for you than is our first scenario because you not only keep a bigger percentage of royalties since there is no middleman, but you have more control to negotiate the deal you want, or not make a deal at all and handle your merchandising independently.

Handling Merchandising Independently (Doing It Yourself)

The last option for merchandising is retaining your merchandising rights and handling your merchandising independently (i.e., doing it yourself). In other words, rather than licensing your rights to a merchandising company, you simply hire a printer (preferably one who is experienced in handling merchandising for touring performances) to supply you with the product and then handle the merchandising sales on your own. This way you will make more profit per T-shirt or item, although you'll forgo a merchandising advance and other benefits of a merchandiser.

> Don't confuse exclusive merchandising rights with promotional rights. A record company typically has the promotional rights to manufacture products using your name and likeness in connection with records, videos, and biographical information. A label may also give away T-shirts, stickers, and posters via record stores, websites, or radio stations to promote record sales. Furthermore, a label may want your rights to "digital merchandising," such as wallpaper for cell phones and computer desktops and "voice tones" (i.e., non-musical performances where you might be asked to record messages like, "Hey this is the band John Doe, and the person you called is not home right now").

This scenario is usually applicable to the beginning of an artist's career when playing small venues in which handling the merchandising is still manageable; or when a merchandising deal has not yet been offered, or when the artist fails to negotiate the type of deal he or she wants (such as a higher royalty or larger advance) with a merchandiser and chooses not to make a deal. However, once an artist progresses to a point in his or her career where he or she is signed with a record label and is packing fans into much larger venues, the burden of ordering product, shipping, accounting, and sales may not be practical. Hence, the merchandising deal with a merchandiser becomes necessary.

Since, at the time of this writing, it may still be possible for you to successfully negotiate to maintain your merchandising rights at the time of signing a recording deal, and since this is traditionally what made the most sense to shoot for anyway, the next part of our discussion deals with entering directly into an agreement with a merchandising company. Following this discussion, Bob Fierro, president of Zebra Marketing (www.zebramarketing.com), discusses his views in a Q & A on independent merchandising and doing it yourself.

MERCHANDISING COMPANIES

As of 2008, a few major merchandising companies control most of the merchandising business. These are Bravado International Group (www.bravado.com—representing artists like Christina

Aguilera, Eminem, 50 Cent, Hilary Duff, Beyoncé, Iron Maiden, and Led Zeppelin), Cinderblock (www.cinderblock.com—representing artists like the Killers, the Strokes, Green Day, Rise Against, Dixie Chicks, Misfits, and Yellow Card), Giant Merchandising, Inc. (www.giantmerchandising.com—representing artists like Korn, Disturbed, Def Tones, Rage against the Machine, Marilyn Manson, Nine Inch Nails, and No Doubt), and Signatures Network (www.signaturesnetwork.com—representing artists like Incubus, System of a Down, Justin Timberlake, Usher, Enrique Iglesias, Gloria Estefan, and Coldplay). All of these companies are divisions of larger corporations and, with some discretion, can afford to pay their artists substantial merchandising advances. As you can see, most of these companies tend to work with established artists in the pop, R&B, and rock idioms.

Bob Fierro says it's important to note that in addition to the major companies mentioned above, there are several smaller companies like BandMerch (www.bandmerch.com) and Zebra Marketing that are perfectly capable of taking care of your business. "You shouldn't be attracted to a company primarily because of the size of the advance it can offer, or even if it can offer one at all, but on the basis of whether it shares your ideas about what you want to do with the merchandising. It's also about relationships," says Fierro. "How excited the company is about signing your band, the types of designs and products they're interested in manufacturing for you, and the quality of services they provide are equally important factors to consider before entering into a merchandising agreement with a merchandiser."

TYPES OF MERCHANDISING DEALS

Merchandising deals typically fall into two different categories: tour merchandising and retail merchandising (the latter includes sublicensing and Internet, as well as retail stores).

Tour Merchandising

Tour merchandising refers to the sale of merchandise at your live performances. Since most concert-goers are usually pumped up for months before a show and are ready to take home a souvenir of the event, the money generated from tour merchandising can be substantially more than that from retail sales. Fans already know to bring enough money to cover the costs of a T-shirt, hat, or tour program, plus a little extra cash for food and drink (but that's another story). In fact, have you ever noticed how the merchandising booths are strategically placed at the venue's entrance? That's not coincidental. It's done to ensure that fans make a purchase just as they're coming through the main door. The merchandising company hires its own personnel (often referred to as a "merch guy" or "merch girl") to travel with, or to follow, your band on the road, check in product with the venue, set it up in the booths, return to count the number of items sold at the end of the night, check out the merchandising with the venue, and then move on to the next city to do it all over again. If this seems like a great deal of effort just for the sake of selling a few measly T-shirts and buttons, note that major stars like Garth Brooks and Madonna can gross well over $100,000 in merchandising sales alone in just a single night. Needless to say, *that's not small potatoes!*

Retail Merchandising

Retail merchandising refers to selling products through department stores, T-shirt shops, record stores, Internet sites, mail-order operations, and sublicensing agreements. Sublicensing occurs when your merchandiser grants the rights to a specialty company to manufacture items such as dolls, trash cans, telephones, napkins, lunch boxes, and stationery products—anything beyond the manufacturing capabilities of your primary merchandiser. Note that marketing items at the retail level requires a slightly different approach than marketing them on concert tours. For instance, merchandisers know that it's more likely for fans to purchase more obscure items (such as a KISS lunch box) at retail outlets than at live concerts, so merchandisers push novelty items at retail. Merchandisers also know that fans will want to buy T-shirts unique to the live performances they see, so they may also work at designing shirts exclusively for sale at retail outlets. (You may be able to get a KISS T-shirt at a retail store that's unavailable at one of the band's shows.) But in any case, even though artists such as Michael Jackson, the Rolling Stones, Guns N' Roses, KISS, and My Chemical Romance have all earned substantial sums of money through retail sales, tour merchandising is still, by far, more lucrative. The excitement generated by a live concert performance is nearly impossible to duplicate at a retail venue. Unless, of course, you decide to tour the malls across America.

KEY TERMS IN MERCHANDISING CONTRACTS

When signing a merchandising deal, it may be possible to separate your rights and sign with two different merchandisers—one to handle tour merchandising and one to handle retail sales (which typically includes sales in retail stores as well as through sublicenses and on the Internet). Jake Versluis, formerly of BandMerch (www.bandmerch.com) adds that it may further be possible to separate your Internet rights as well. But it really depends on your clout. Typically, your merchandiser uses one contract form to acquire all your rights: both tour and retail. Our discussion will emphasize touring, since the legal and business issues of merchandising agreements deal primarily with that. Important issues in a merchandising deal include the royalties, hall fees, advances, performance guarantees, agreement term, creative issues, territory, exclusivity, and the sell-off period.

At one time, the band System of a Down had merch available online through BandMerch while it had merch available on tour and in retail stores through Sony Signatures. While it is not necessarily the norm for various rights to be separated in merch deals, sometimes one company can prove its strength in areas over another company and acquire these rights.

Royalty Rates: Tour Merchandising

Let's take a look at two different royalty structures for touring: U.S. tour royalties and foreign tour royalties.

U.S. Tour Royalties

Merchandising royalties for products sold on tour, such as T-shirts, sweatshirts, and baseball caps, are based on your gross merchandising sales (the money the fans pay) less taxes and credit card fees. That's generally it! The royalty rate for sales in the United States ranges anywhere from 25 percent to 35 percent, with 30 percent being the norm for new artists. So a T-shirt selling at $25 (note that superstars like Madonna might charge up to $40) multiplied by a royalty rate of 30 percent equals $7.50 (I left out sales taxes and credit card fees for the sake of simplicity, but you get the idea.) In some cases, merchandisers pay a higher royalty, of up to 65 percent, but only when reducing this royalty by an additional expense, known as a "hall fee," which we will discuss in a moment.

Foreign Tour Royalties

The merchandising royalty rate for sales in foreign territories is usually less than the U.S. rate—generally, it's around 80 percent of your domestic rate. For example, if your U.S. royalty rate is 30 percent for merchandise sold at live performances, your royalty for sales in foreign territories is 24 percent ($0.30 \times 0.80 = 0.24$ or 24%). Sometimes deals are arranged on a net split at 75/25 merchandiser/artist (net, meaning the money the fan's pay, minus credit card fees and taxes, minus the costs of manufacturing and design). Your foreign royalty is lower because the profit margin to the merchandiser is reduced by higher taxes, customs duties, and other costs of doing business abroad. Just keep in mind that any royalties due to you must first go back toward paying off your advance (advances will be discussed shortly).

> Royalties for sales of tour programs, which are still a fairly popular item at concerts, are on a different basis than T-shirts and hats since tour programs are generally more expensive to manufacture. Sales are based on the "net" profits received by the merchandiser at splits of 75/25 merchandiser/artist.

Hall Fees

You already know that your merchandiser pays you a royalty based on the gross sales less taxes and credit card fees. You also know that a common royalty rate for a new band is around 30 percent. However, sometimes your merchandiser will agree to pay you a higher royalty of 65 percent (sometimes more) but will reduce this rate by an additional expense known as a "hall fee." So, you might ask, what the heck are hall fees?

Each of the venues where you perform hires its own personnel (or an outside concession company) to handle all of the merchandising sales within the building. In return, the venue takes a percentage of your merchandising sales, ranging anywhere from 30 to 40 percent. This is standard procedure. Your merchandiser sends out its own personnel to show up at every gig, check in the right amount of merchandising, make sure all the displays are set up properly, and then return back at the end of the night to check out the merchandising and pay the hall a percentage.

Again, since your merchandiser typically pays you a royalty on the gross sales (*before* deducting hall fees), artists were traditionally not affected by the percentage the merchandiser paid the hall each night. But, as more and more artists began negotiating with merchandisers over the years for higher royalty rates, and because hall fees can vary from one venue to the next, merchandisers started to reduce artists' royalties by the amount of the hall fee. So now, a T-shirt selling for $25, in a venue with a 35 percent hall fee, subtracted from a 65 percent royalty (65% − 35% = 30%), yields an artist royalty of approximately $7.50 per shirt ($25 \times 0.30 = \$7.50$—again, for simplicity, note that I left out the sales tax and credit card fees). The resulting figure usually works out to be the same as it would have been if you had a lower royalty computed before the hall fees. However, the higher the hall fee, the less you'll make from merchandising sales. Therefore, because it's your talent agent's responsibility to call promoters across the country and negotiate your live performance fees and other expenses (see Chapter 8 for more on talent agents), you might go as far as telling your agent to include a clause in a section of your contract (a rider) that says you'll agree to pay only a certain amount for the hall fees. Again, the standard hall fee is about 35 percent, but it can range anywhere from 30 percent to 40 percent. Whether you can get the venue to budge on its percentage is based on your band's success and negotiating power, as well as on your agent's incentive or motivation to fight for you. But just keep in mind that your agent only gets paid a percentage of your live performance fees and not a percentage of your merchandising revenue.

Advances

The merchandising advance is perhaps the key reason why most bands first enter into a merchandising agreement with a merchandiser, but one of the biggest misconceptions they have is that it is based on an arbitrary figure. On the contrary, merchandising advances are essentially projected based on a band's gross merchandising sales over the course of a tour, multiplied by the band's negotiated royalty rate. For instance, if you have a royalty rate of 30%, and a merchandiser projects that you will gross $120,000 in merchandising sales on a tour, your merchandising advance may be $36,000 ($120,000 X .30 = $36,000). But how does the merchandiser know what you'll gross over the course of a tour? This is where things get a bit more involved.

The merchandiser may take the following factors into consideration when determining the gross merchandising sales: (1) the number of performances on a tour, (2) the capacity of the venues in which a band is performing, (3) the number of paid attendees, (4) the price for which the merch can be sold, (5) the target demographic audience a band appeals to (fans of hard rock music are known to buy a lot of merchandise), and most important, (6) what other "like" bands under similar circumstances have grossed over the course of a tour.

Bob Fierro says merchandisers have actually gotten really good over the years at guesstimating the amount a band may gross down to something called a per-head or per cap (per capita) figure. The per cap figure is the projected amount spent on merchandising by *each fan* who sees you perform over the course of a concert tour. While this is really more "merchandiser speak," let's take a closer look at this so-called per cap figure.

For simplicity, say a rock band is scheduled to play for thirty nights in 1,000-seat capacity clubs (making the projected total number of people in which they perform before 30,000) and it is projected to sell 200 shirts per night at $20 (making the total projected gross in merchandising $4,000 per night, or $120,000 over the course of the tour). This means that the band will meet a per cap figure of $4 ($120,000 in gross merch sales ÷ 30,000 paid attendees = $4 per fan). Depending on the circumstances, bands can do anywhere from 50 cents to $12 (and higher) per cap. Metal bands tend to do $7 to $10 per cap since their audiences tend to be more fanatic. The English pop band Depeche Mode actually hit an all-time high of $25 a head at one time. Now that's pretty impressive!

You may be wondering how your merchandiser estimates a per-head count when you're playing festivals with other bands. How can you tell which band the fans actually paid to see? The answer is, you can't. Therefore, the merchandiser makes an adjustment in its calculations by reducing the number of paid attendees, for example, by half.

Performance Guarantees

Since merchandising advances are based on an estimate of the total number of paid attendees at your show, plus the average amount of money each paid attendee is expected to spend on T-shirts and other items, it's easy to understand why your merchandiser will want you to agree to something called a "performance guarantee." This means that when accepting a merchandising advance, you're also agreeing to play a specific number of live performances in front of a specific number of people *or, otherwise, as your guarantee stipulates, you must automatically repay the total unrecovered balance of your advance with accrued interest.* Before you freak out, you should know that this usually happens only in the unfortunate circumstance that your band breaks up in the middle of a tour or if someone suffers an untimely injury or death and the merchandiser is afraid it will never be able to recoup its advance from sales. If you've already spent the advance, merchandisers have been known to sue if necessary to get it back.

If you fall short of meeting your performance guarantee, the merchandiser will—usually—let the advance repayment ride and wait to recoup the advance on your next tour, or on the tours that band members may book as solo artists or as members of other bands. And as you'll see in a moment, the merchandiser will not be required to pay you another advance until he or she makes back every last dime with interest!

The Agreement Term

The term of most merchandising agreements is based on one or two "album tour cycles" (the period of time between one album release and the next, including all touring done in connection with the first recording). One reason the agreement term is structured this way is that all of the images, designs, and logos used in promoting an album may be used when creating merchandising products. For instance, your album title, cover artwork, or special logo may all be replicated in T-shirt designs, baseball caps, and/or bumper stickers. Since each album release projects a new vibe and image, an album tour cycle is a logical milestone at which to evaluate your relationship with your merchandiser.

The term of merchandising agreements may seem like a simple concept, but it can actually get quite complicated. The agreement term is also structured to continue until the merchandiser recoups all advances it has paid to you. Clearly, if your advance is recouped at the end of your album tour cycle, then you're free to renegotiate your contract for better terms and another advance. However, if your advance is unrecovered at the end of your cycle, *your merchandiser automatically gets the rights to your next tour without having to renegotiate anything at all*. Even if you recouped all but $10,000 of a $100,000 advance, you could still be locked into your original agreement. This is obviously not the ideal situation to be in, since the terms you negotiated at the beginning of your career may become less favorable as you become a more established artist. You may need another advance as well to survive while writing and recording your next album or to help cover the start-up cost for your next tour. Plus, it's possible that you may have been unhappy with the service your merchandiser provided and you may simply want out of your agreement—something an agreement term may not allow.

For all of the above reasons, your attorney may be able to negotiate for something called buy-out rights. In this scenario, you can get a competing merchandising company to actually pay your unrecovered balance and buy you out of your existing contract. You can be sure, however, that your attorney is going to have to fight for this clause. Why would your merchandiser take a chance on investing in your career when you're just getting started, only to give you the opportunity to shift allegiances to a competing company later? The company will at least want to have the opportunity to reap the benefits of the relationship as you develop into a more successful artist.

If your merchandiser agrees to a buyout clause, you can count on a number of stipulations being attached to it. For instance, you may be required to pay back the unrecovered balance with added interest. Or, you may even have to pay back an amount greater than 100 percent of the unrecovered balance. And finally, the merchandiser may insist on the "rights of last refusal," which means that if a competing company makes you an offer, your merchandiser has the right to either match the offer or let you out of your deal.

Creative Issues

Most artists are given creative control over and the right to approve all merchandising designs on products to be sold. In fact, the merchandiser sometimes asks the artist to supply them with a series of photographs and designs. Your name and likeness, your album artwork, and the dates and cities of your upcoming tour are typical elements incorporated into designs included on products such as T-shirts, hats, and posters. But Bob Fierro notes that artists are often unsure of what they want and end up holding up production as a result. "The artist has to trust the people with whom they get into bed, so to speak. Keep in mind that as merchandisers, we have years of experience in the business and know what sells and doesn't sell. You'd be surprised at the number of artists who purposely go out of their way to design a really bad shirt [laughing]. And these artists are very serious. I heard of one artist who wanted his name printed upside down, and another who didn't want both his name and logo on the shirt at all. I understand that these guys were trying to make an anticapitalistic statement to their fans, but isn't this a bit hypocritical after they just pocketed a large advance? Remember, merchandising is a very calculated business where hundreds of thousands of dollars can be made. There's a science behind designing that catchphrase, logo, and design, and then putting it all together in just the right way [so] that a product sells like hotcakes."

A large advance isn't always desirable. If your merchandiser doesn't earn it back, it could mean that the term of your agreement never ends; worse yet, you may be asked to repay the advance immediately. Therefore, it may be better to take a smaller advance to ensure that you'll be a free agent at the end of your agreed-upon number of album tour cycles. You may then be in a position in your career to renegotiate for a deal with better terms.

The Rolling Stones' tongue logo and the Misfits' skull are both great examples of hugely successful merchandising designs.

Moving on to the legal aspects of creative issues, you should know that all artists are responsible for getting permission from and paying fees to the owners of any outside designs used in connection with the merchandising. While you may be set on using a special design or a unique photograph from a book, to get the rights to use it, you may either be asked to pay a fee or a royalty from the sale of any merchandise that features that artwork; and *the cost will come out of your pocket.* In cases where the artwork from your forthcoming album is used in connection with the merchandising, your record label usually owns the rights to it and may ask for compensation for the costs of producing the applicable artwork. "But in most cases," notes Bob Fierro, "the record company is usually willing to let this one slide."

Territory

The designated territory for most merchandising deals is *the world.* However, once you're an established artist and have some negotiating power, you may be able to limit your agreement to certain territories, such as North America. This way you can negotiate with companies in foreign territories for an additional merchandising advance. Promoters in Japan are especially eager to acquire merchandising rights when you venture into their country on tour, and in some cases they're willing to pay large advances to get them. Therefore, even if you're a new artist, you might try limiting the territory with your U.S. merchandiser to "the world, except Japan." Whether they agree to this, of course, is subject to the individual situation.

Exclusivity

When you're a new group entering into an agreement with a merchandiser, remember that you're signing over the *exclusive* rights to utilize your name, likeness, and logo in connection with the manufacture, advertisement, distribution, and sale of products. In plain English, this means that you cannot enter into another agreement with another merchandiser during your contract term. It's also important to note that merchandising companies want to secure not only the rights to your band as a unit but also the rights to each individual band member. So, as pointed out earlier in the section "Performance Guarantees," if you leave the group and start your own solo project, you may still be obligated to the preexisting terms of the contract.

The exclusivity clause may also restrict radio stations and sponsors from giving away promotional materials (such as T-shirts, stickers, and hats) within a twenty-mile radius of your live performance, and within a forty-eight-hour period before the event. However, nothing should preclude the record label or its distributors from standard record promotion in connection with the sales of your album.

Sell-Off Period

After the term of your merchandiser agreement has ended, you will be free to license your rights to manufacture, advertise, distribute, and sell products to a new company; these products can be similar or even identical to previously licensed items. In other words, if you had a particular style of products that sold well, such as a long-sleeve, black shirt with your name in white lettering down the sleeves, you have the right to authorize your new merchandiser to manufacture this very same item. Your former merchandiser can no longer continue to manufacture products but will have the rights to sell off any leftover stock it may have. Your attorney, however, can attempt to negotiate a few restrictions with the merchandiser:

+ The merchandiser's sell-off period will only last for a limited period of time, such as 90 to 120 days after the agreement term.
+ The merchandiser will only have nonexclusive rights during the sell-off period. In this way, you can enter into a new deal with another merchandiser and negotiate for a new advance.
+ The merchandiser will only sell off product at wholesale prices through department stores, T-shirt shops, and mail-order companies and will pay you a royalty set forth in your agreement for retail sales (which will be discussed in a moment). Your merchandiser, however, cannot sell products, at drastically reduced (or distressed) prices just to get rid of them; this would obviously put your new merchandiser in direct competition with your former merchandiser for sales.
+ The merchandiser will be unable to mass-manufacture product (known as stockpiling) for a period of 120 days before the end of your agreement term. The merchandiser does, however, have the right to manufacture product to meet any reasonable demands during the remainder of the term.
+ The merchandiser will notify you of the quantity of unsold product after the sell-off period. At this time, you or your new merchandiser have the right to buy the existing product at cost.

MORE KEY TERMS IN MERCHANDISING CONTRACTS

Okay, as previously stated, the key terms in merchandising agreements deal with touring, but it's a good idea to understand a few things about how you'll be paid for retail merchandising sales as well.

Royalty Rates: Retail Merchandising

Let's take a look at a few different royalty structures under the category of retail: retail stores and Internet, sublicenses, and foreign royalties.

Retail Stores & Internet

Merchandising royalties for sales in retail stores (i.e., for sales in department stores, T-shirt shops, and record stores) as well as for sales on the Internet (i.e., sales on sites like ARTISTdirect and MusicToday) are computed differently than they are for live performance sales. Rather than being computed on the total gross income less taxes and fees, royalties for retail sales are based on *the wholesale price*, which is the price at which your merchandiser sells products in bulk to distributors and retailers. So, you might ask, what's a typical wholesale price for a T-shirt sold to retailers?

Although a typical wholesale price is really impossible to nail down, let's use $10 as a guesstimate. The retailer then marks up this price as much as 150 percent (even 200 percent at times), which means the $10 shirt sells to consumers for $25 (the wholesale price of $10, marked up 150 percent). Your merchandiser then pays you a royalty rate ranging from 7.5 to 25 percent of the wholesale price in the United States, depending on the type of store (such as top-line stores like Hot Topic, midlevel like stores Sears, and mass-market stores like K-Mart) and on the stature of your band. For the sake of this example, let's take a band at top-line retail stores earning a 15 percent royalty. Therefore, your royalty for a T-shirt selling at $25 is $1.50 (the wholesale price of $10, multiplied by your royalty rate of 15 percent = $1.50). This is a far cry from what you can make for a similarly priced T-shirt selling at one of your live performances; if you remember our example above, you can make an average of $7.50 per shirt in sales at one of your concerts. This isn't to say that substantial sums of money can't be made via retail sales. Remember, artists such as Guns N' Roses and Michael Jackson have made millions. But those examples definitely do not reflect the norm.

> Sites such as ARTISTdirect (www.artistdirect.com) are essentially online resellers of merch. They buy manufactured product directly from the merchandiser at a wholesale price and then sell it to the public. Therefore, royalties are treated like retail store sales.

Sublicenses

Retail sales include sublicensing licensing agreements your merchandiser enters into with third-party companies to manufacture specialty products like lunch boxes, trash cans, bumper stickers, trading cards, dolls, condoms, stationery products, and any other product that's beyond the manufacturing capabilities of your primary merchandiser. (Your merchandiser should always be willing to give you the final approval on the sublicenses into which it enters.) The sublicensor then ships these products into retail stores, monitors sales, and pays your primary merchandiser a royalty. Your merchandiser keeps a 20 to 30 percent share of these monies and remits the balance of 70 to 80

> According to *Rolling Stone* magazine, KISS made over $2 million in just one year from more than 130 merchandising licenses. Among the most notable were a KISS coffin and a Sterling Marlin collectable car.

percent to you. Essentially, your merchandiser does nothing more than act as the middleman. And until you're in a megastar band, like KISS, and choose to negotiate a variety of licenses and handle the accounting yourself, you might as well get used to having a middleman. In fact, if it's any consolation, I'm told the merchandiser is actually well worth the fees it takes for acting as a middleman. The profit margin from sublicenses is only minimal in the early stages of your career, and trying to deal with a number of companies all at once can be a royal pain in the butt!

Foreign

Foreign royalties for retail sales, just as with foreign royalties for touring, are usually 80 percent of your U.S. royalty rates. Once again, just keep in mind that any royalties due to you must first go back toward paying off your advances.

Cross-Collateralization

Finally, it's important to note that your royalties from both retail-merchandising sales and tour-merchandising sales are cross-collateralized. In other words, if the same merchandising company has the rights to both your tour merchandising and retail merchandising (which is usually the case), all royalties go toward paying back any advance monies paid to you by the merchandiser. Thus, if you are paid a large advance by your merchandiser before one of your concert tours, the royalties from both your tour merchandising and your retail merchandising go toward paying back that advance. (For more information on cross-collateralization, see Chapter 10.)

Q & A WITH INDEPENDENT MERCHANDISER BOB FIERRO

Zebra Marketing is an entertainment merchandising company that handles custom screen-printing and production, licensing, concessions, and wholesale distribution. Its clients past and present include Henry Rollins, the Red Hot Chili Peppers, Crystal Method, Mötorhead, Prodigy, Paul Oakenfold, and Brian McKnight (to name a few), as well a number of local do-it-yourself artists in Southern California. Zebra Marketing has been in business for over twenty-five years.

In the following Q & A, Zebra's president, Bob Fierro, discusses the process of independent merchandising, from artwork and printing to selling merchandise on the road.

Q: Are " merch deals," in the traditional sense, reserved for the big boys?
B.F.: Well, first let's take a look at the three basic levels of merchandisers in which a "merchandising deal" might be contracted: major merchandisers, midlevel to small merchandisers, and smaller Internet-based companies.

Major merchandisers, like Giant, Signatures Network, Bravado, and Cinderblock, just like the major record companies, have to report a profit; and despite their substantial cash flow, the net profit margin from merchandising sales can often be too small for them to stay in business. Therefore, they must focus on artists most likely to turn substantial profits, like Christina Aguilera, Eminem, 50 Cent, Green Day, System of a Down, Korn, and Disturbed. You get the idea.

Midlevel to small merchandisers are those more than able to work with bands that are perhaps just signed and have a good buzz happening, etc., but can't compete with the large advances of the majors— that is, if they even offer advances at all. But as I said earlier, while the advance is the first thing a band and its manager will look for, it shouldn't always be the most important consideration.

Finally, smaller Internet-based companies are those that are seemingly everywhere on the Web, ready and eager to work with young bands. Some of these companies are even signing young bands, offering merchandise up front for them to take out on the road—and nothing more, but tying them into long-term agreements. The problem with these deals is that, if all of a sudden the band starts to take off, it's stuck in an agreement with some small company that quite possibly offered it a one-sided deal.

The truth is that a band at the beginning stages of its career can easily handle the merchandising on its own, by following a few simple steps.

Q: What are the various steps to doing it yourself?
B.F.: There are generally four preliminary steps to getting started: (1) selecting the company, (2) submitting artwork and design, (3) selecting the T-shirts and other products, and (4) deciding on the quantity.

Q: Could you please elaborate on selecting the company?
B.F.: Selecting the company can be as simple as opening up the yellow pages in your city or getting on Google and finding a shop like Zebra Marketing (www.zebramarketing.com) and using the key words *screen printing* and *promotional items*. Or, you can always ask other indie bands in your area for personal recommendations. No matter where you live, you can usually always find someone local to you so that you can avoid spending the extra money in shipping charges.

Big 10 Productions (www.bigten. productions), Fat Rat Press (www.fatratprinting.com), Sticker Junkie (www.stickerjunkie.com), and Sticker Guy (www.sticker-guy.com) are just a few Web-based companies that are pretty well known for helping do-it-yourselfers get merch printed and shipped out to them relatively for cheap. Cafe Press (www.cafe-press.com) allows you to set up an on-demand homepage where you don't have to manufacture any merch up front. Check them all out for yourself.

If your band is at the level where you are going to be hitting the road, it's best to work with a company that has actual tour experience. A company must understand the necessity of getting merchandise to the band on time and into the specific city where they need it. This requires much more planning and experience on the part of the company than you may expect. If the merchandise arrives one day late, the band will have already moved on to the next city.

Q: What do we need to know about submitting artwork and designs?
B.F.: Most indie bands are pretty creative about designing their own logos and coming up with T-shirts designs. I'm often blown away by some of the stuff I see—with designs down the sleeves and logos front and back, the use of lyrics or catchy slogans, album titles—it is often more specialized than the majors would do. Bands can always get their art school or graphic design buddies to set up their artwork using Adobe Photoshop [www.adobe.com], which is what we typically require for submitting artwork.

In some cases, where artists really have no clue about designing shirts, they can always work together with the print company to help them get the artwork designed and in the proper format for printing.

Q: Can you discuss picking the products? T-shirts, stickers, or patches?
B.F.: T-shirts and tour programs are the number-one sellers. Other products I've seen work well for

bands include laminated lanyards (the tour passes that artists wear around their necks), stickers, patches, hats, bandannas, hoodies, and rock art silk-screen posters. Just be creative.

Q: What about the quantity?

B.F.: Price breaks begin after twelve dozen, or 144, shirts, with increased savings per shirt at twenty-four dozen. Despite these savings, it's usually better to order a smaller line of items at a smaller quantity first. Once you've determined what products are selling the best, you can have a larger quantity printed up.

Q: Moving on from the preliminary steps, what is the average cost per shirt?

B.F.: The cost depends on how elaborate the artwork is, the number of colors used, and the quantity of shirts to be printed. But on average, colored shirts printed on both the front and back usually run between $4 and $4.50.

Q: What is the potential profit margin for the artist per shirt?

B.F.: There are about five different things to consider:

1. You must consider the cost of the shirts to the fans. Indie bands are known to sell T-shirts anywhere from $5 to $25, but let's go to the higher end of $20.

2. You must consider sales tax. Check your local state and city taxes. In Los Angeles, sales tax as of this writing is 8.25% or $1.65 [$20 x 8.25% or 0.825 = $1.65].

3. You must remember that venues typically require around a 35 percent cut or $6.42 [$18.35 x 35% or 0.35 = $6.42].

4. You have to factor in the cost for the shirts (known as the "cost of goods") at an average of about 20 percent or $4 [$20 x 5% or 0.05 = $4.00].

5. You must consider miscellaneous expenses for freight and shipping charges and/or for the staff you pay for selling the shirts at around four percent or $0.80 [$20 x 4% or 0.04 =$0.80].

Once you deduct all these expenses, the average profit margin per shirt for the artist who is handling his or her merchandising is around $7.13. Remember that this figure can vary depending on what you charge per shirt, whether you're responsible enough to deal with tax, whether the venue in which you are performing enforces a hall fee, and whether you pay someone to help you sell merch.

Now, let's take a look at the equation:

$20.00 (cost of shirt to consumer)

- $1.65_ (8.25% *Los Angeles sales tax: $20 x .0825)

= $18.35

- $6.42_ (35% hall fee: $18.35 x 0.35)

= $11.93

- $4.00_ (20% cost of goods: $20 x 0.20)

= $7.93

- $ 0.80_ (4% miscellaneous: $20 x 0.04)

= $ 7.13   (profit to the artist)

*Check your sales tax per state/city

Q: Any tips for selling merch on the Internet?

B.F.: As long as a band is responsible in fulfilling orders and drawing hits on their site, they can always sell products from their website using e-commerce solutions like PayPal [www.paypal.com].

A band can use its website to sell limited items such as shot glasses or mugs that may not be the best-selling items at a live performance. If anything, it's a good way to test the market to see what you should manufacture in volume and potentially even take out with you on the road.

Q: Any tips for live performance sales?

B.F.: There are a number of important things artists can do that I'll attempt to briefly list.

1. Make sure to set up an attractive merch booth that is going to get people to come over and check out the products.

2. Announce that your products are on sale during your band set.

3. Be able to accept various forms of payment: cash, check, and credit cards. I understand that CD Baby [www.cdbaby.com] offers a credit card swiper program, or you can look into opening your own merchant account. Speak with your CPA or local bank.

4. Get someone who knows how to sell. On the local level, you can probably use someone that's attractive, personable, and fairly responsible. However, when you hit the road, you should really think about getting someone more experienced.

Q: Who do you recommend to handle sales on the road?

B.F.: Sometimes your road manager may even be willing to do the merchandising in addition to his regular duties, or he'll phone ahead to each of the venues, making sure that a local experienced merchandiser will sell for you.

Q: Sales tax: How is it handled when traveling from state to state?

B.F.: In smaller clubs and ballrooms, the club will ask for its hall fee and then ask you to fill out a receipt saying that you will pay the state and local taxes yourself. Larger venues usually have inside concession companies that take out the local state sales tax and pay it for you. Before the venue takes its hall percentage, the state sales tax gets taken off the top. It is important to make sure that you leave with a signed receipt and a copy of the hall's contract stating that they are responsible for the tax.

AFTERWORD: THE FUTURE OF THE MUSIC BUSINESS

I hope my book has inspired and given you the beginning tools you need to get up, jump into the music world, and start living your passion. As you've learned, the music industry is a tough one, but at the end of the day it's much more satisfying to know that you are living what you love instead of living with a lot of "What if?" regrets.

Lastly, I would like to share with you a couple of insightful predictions that various leading music industry professionals—including attorneys, music publishers, managers, producers, and music business educators—shared with me regarding the future of the music business. Obviously, no one can know for sure what awaits the music industry in the near future—especially after witnessing how quickly new technology has changed the traditional music business in just the past five years—but I think you, too, will find it interesting to see what the industry professionals below had to say about the music business in the year 2013. Until the next revision, I bid you farewell.

Music will become a service, not a product. Like the current model for television, people will have access to music for free if they are willing to listen to commercials. For a small fee, the music is delivered commercial-free. Either way, revenue is generated to compensate creators and artists. And through wireless technology, consumers will be able to hear anything they want, anytime they want, anywhere they want. —Steven Winogradsky, *attorney*

I don't think record companies in the traditional sense are even going to exist anymore. Rather, larger brand companies like Coca-Cola will have entertainment divisions that sponsor artists and sell music, as just one of the things they do. We already see this with Starbucks and Hear Music. There will be many more that follow this model.

—Joseph Sofio, *attorney*

What's wrong with the music business today is the record business. By 2013, the postmodern record industry will have been cut to its knees, and the Music Renaissance, carved by the same double-edged sword of the Internet, will be in full bloom. Instead of record success generating box office strength, live performance will dictate the value of an act. Merchandising will become a high art form. The music will probably be free.

—John Hartmann, *former manager of Peter, Paul & Mary;*
Crosby, Stills & Nash; America; Poco; the Eagles; and others

Music publishing, as always, will be the solid rock of the foundation of the music business. Music will continue to play a major role in everyday life and in every environment via means we cannot even dream of today. Music will have been so accessible for so many years that more and more people will be in the business of making music. Music will be so pervasive that schools—yes, even public schools—will have begun new programs, embracing all kinds of music. Music education will be thriving everywhere. Start being a mentor now!

—Neil J. Gillis, *president & CEO of Dimensional Music Publishing*
(formerly DreamWorks Music Publishing)

By 2013, vying for consumers' attention will become more and more difficult. As the younger generation matures, they will increase the amount of disposable income they have to spend and decrease the amount of time they have to surf around finding the music they like. Obviously, as the pipeline of the Internet expands, legal downloading will flourish. However, matching individuals to the music they desire will become key. They will spend more downtime viewing Web broadcasts, TV shows, and films. The trend of marketing emerging ditties via the aforementioned mediums will provide an increasingly powerful platform for songs and bands. Music supervisors will be better termed "music marketers."

—John Charlillo, *music producer*

Whether it's downloaded, productized, or delivered as an all-you-can-eat service, music will have to be delivered to consumers by methods that make it easy for them to consume it. While high school and college kids might have the time and the will to spend hours per week surfing the Internet to find and filter what they want, the other 50 percent of the market will not. I can't see my mother-in-law working that hard to get her Barry Manilow fix. I'd place my bet on the company that makes it easy and convenient for grown-ups to consume music. They've got the most disposable income and a strong love of music. The kids are just going to steal the music anyway—so why bother? Unfortunately for the music industry, it has traditionally been transfixed on the youth market (the very people stealing music today) and has completely overlooked the baby boomer market. —Michael Laskow, *CEO of TAXI*

The future? Yes, we will go much deeper into digital, and the CD may well disappear; but the music will still come from the same sources: the musician, songwriter, and artist. I'm less concerned about how the music will be delivered and more concerned about its creation. With seemingly every second person writing songs and producing them in his or her living room, I still don't see anything that will musically blow us away. Even the "good stuff" and the "latest trend" aren't very exciting. When rap arrived, it was new, controversial, and exciting. When rock arrived, it was new, controversial, and exciting. When hip-hop showed up, it was new, controversial, and exciting. Going back even further, jazz caused the same stir as did the blues, etc. So did the Beatles, Rolling Stones, and punk music. What's new now? What's controversial? What is being played that really causes headlines and shakes the world? That is what is scary. Forget about downloads and the latest technical trend. We'll always get our music—some way, somehow. But give me some music that is so exciting they are talking about it on the streets. Good music is the future.

—Mike Gormley, *LA Personal Management;*
former manager of the Bangles, Oingo Boingo, and Danny Elfman

Music will be sold primarily via downloads and Internet delivery. CD packaging, too, will be delivered by the Internet.... Viral databasing of fans and music consumers will be a primary sales tool. Additionally, your computer will be able to track your music interests and turn you on to new tunes, in the manner that www.last.fm is currently pioneering. Instead of using only radio as a promo task, labels (big and small) will promote, via fan databases, social networking sites by "seeding" the blogosphere. There will be portable music players on various sites to play music and link to sales sites (similar to how you currently find Google access on various websites). All artists will have their websites offering their content as their central operation. Being successful in the music biz will mean that one can quit his or her day job and pursue music full-time. In general, there will be more folks attaining this important threshold, thus democratizing the industry and taking back the power of creating the music culture from the large multinational conglomerates.

—Andrew Frances, *music industry consultant*

Melody is the salvation of the music industry! It is a 2,500 plus year truism, and so it shall be in 2013. Understand and learn from the past, for therein lies your future. We human beings are hard-wired for music—and always will be. The only thing that has changed since Bach's Well-Tempered Clavier in 1722 is the delivery system of this twelve-note thing we call music. And just as hard-wired for music as we are, we are also hard-wired for melody. When the music industry collectively decides to get off this "it has to be edgy" jag and returns to moving millions of people with strong songs comprised of hummable melodies with great lyrics, rhythms, and beats, millions of people's dollars will once again flow back into the coffers of the music industry. It's that simple. Rock 'n' roll began to die (lose market shares) the day the melody did; the same happened with R&B and even hip-hop. Only country music numbers have remained consistent, because their melodies and lyrics have stayed strong. Song is king in country, and our human emotional connection will always lie with melodies. Melodically accessible songs that the majority of the buying public can hum and sing—which has been proven over and over around the world, irrespective of culture or language—will always be the salvation and profitability of the industry, not just "edgy" music. So let it be written; and so let it—hopefully—be done and sung.

—Samm Brown III, *award-winning record producer, songwriter, arranger, orchestrator, and conductor*

INDEX

Investment strategies and planning, 124–125. *See also* Finances

J

Joint works, 52, 197–200, 202, 235

K

Key person clauses, 115–116, 145, 148–149
Kiosks, 191–192

L

Label deals. *See* Major label deals
Label shopping percentages, 98, 99
Leaving-member clauses, 88–89
Legal considerations. *See also* Agreements;
  Attorneys; Copyrights; Negotiating agreements;
  Royalties references
    business entity options, 58–60, 128
    contract employment vs. self-employment,
      62–63, 83–84, 92
    indemnity provisions, 91
    solo artists as employers, 89–91
Levine, Michael, 39–41
Lifestyle
    drugs, alcohol and, 38–39, 43, 111
    staying balanced, 38–39
Limitations, knowing, 19
Live performing and touring, 242–261
    big leagues, 246–248, 258–261
    business manager responsibilities, 125–126
    cancellation provisions, 260
    catering considerations, 258
    co-headlining tour negotiations, 257–258
    collecting deposits, 141
    contracts and riders, 258–261
    corporate-sponsored tours, 248
    costs and realities of, 242–249
    doing it yourself, 249–251
    dressing room accommodations, 258
    early touring stages, 245–246, 258
    financial matters, 125–126
    flat guarantees, 243, 254
    free performances, 252–253
    free tickets, 259
    getting right gigs/tours, 249–252

gross potential, 256–257
guarantee vs. percentage deals, 254–256
hall fees, 141
insurance, 260
internal transportation, 259
local gigs, 243–244, 248–249, 258
manager assistance with, 107–108, 251–252
merchandising, 265, 276
midlevel touring, 245–246, 258–261
monies from, 51
negotiating, 140, 256–261
negotiating deals, 140
paying to play, 253–254
payment options, 252–256
per-show vs. per-tour negotiations, 257
pricing artists, 139–140
routing tours, 138–139
security, 259
sound and lights, 259
straight percentage deals, 254
talent agent roles and responsibilities, 136–141,
  252
top ten riders requested, 261
tour support monies, 177–178
video- and audiotaping, 261
when to sell tickets, 140
LLCs, 58, 59, 60, 128
Location considerations, 19
Lodging and travel, 75–76

M

Major label deals, 153, 171–174
Managers. *See* Business managers; Personal managers
Marketing. *See also* Marketing yourself; Talent agents and agencies
    of electronic transmissions, 288–292
    funds, publishing companies distributing, 230
    major label muscle, 173
    personal manager role, 106, 251–252
    of records, 186–188
Marketing yourself. *See also* Press kits
    adopting sales approach, 21–22
    branding and, 22–23
    defining audience (market) and, 22–23

"The information in *The Musician's Handbook* is worth its weight in gold; it can mean the difference between succeeding or failing in the new music business. In his second life, Bobby will be reincarnated as a music attorney. This book is a must-read!"

—*DINA LaPOLT*, entertainment attorney at Lapolt Law, P.C.

"*The Musician's Handbook* provides a solid foundation for understanding the business at large, yet it comes at you from an everyman's perspective. If you want to learn more about the new basics from someone who's survived and thrived the biz, this book is a great read."

—*NEIL GILLIS*, president, North America and Global Head Creative

"It would take years of personal experience to acquire the knowledge and wisdom provided in *The Musician's Handbook*; a must-read for anyone interested in a thorough yet concise overview of the new music industry."   —*DIONY SEPULVEDA*, manager of Pennywise

"The wisdom to be gained by reading this comprehensive, easy-to-understand book will help musicians, and so many others, position themselves to have a successful career in the new music business. Knowledge is power, and that's why this book is so important."

—*GERRY BRYANT*, secretary of the Board of Directors of California Lawyers for the Arts

"There are many books out there dealing with the music business, but *The Musician's Handbook* has a special and important perspective—that of the working musician.

—*MARK GOLDSTEIN*, former senior vice president of business affairs at Warner Bros. Records

"*The Musician's Handbook* is an artist's first ally; it lifts the fog and lights the path to a successful career in the music industry."

—*JOHN HARTMANN*, former manager of Peter, Paul & Mary;
Crosby, Stills & Nash; America; Poco; Eagles; and others

"If you can read this sentence, you are already more than qualified to be an international rock superstar. If you can read this book, you might even get your music into the marketplace with a price tag on it; and actually make a couple of bucks in the process, too."

—*MIKE INEZ*, Alice In Chains

"Thoughtful, insightful, sobering, and—above all—useful insights and advice for anyone in need of a roadmap through the tangled jungle that is the *new* music industry."

—*MARK NARDONE*, senior editor, *Music Connection* magazine

"Kudos to Bobby! I'm impressed with how readable and understandable this book is; a valuable tool for anyone interested in a serious career in the new music business!"

—*BURGUNDY MORGAN, ESQ*

"I'm not saying that you'll fail miserably and die penniless and alone if you don't read Bobby's book, but why take the chance?"

—*DAVID DARLING,* producer for Boxing Gandhis, Brian Setzer, and Meredith Brooks

"*The Musician's Handbook* is the layman's guide to understanding the music industry."

—*RANDY CASTILLO,* drummer for Ozzy Osbourne and Mötley Crüe

"If you're even thinking about pursuing a career in music (or wondering why it hasn't turned out as expected), *The Musician's Handbook* is an important book."

—*JEN FRISVOLD,* former managing editor of *Performing Songwriter* magazine

"There's only so much information about the music business that you can absorb at one time. *The Musician's Handbook* does a great job of summing it up clearly and concisely."

—*IAN COPELAND,* talent agent to Sting, The Police, and No Doubt

"*The Musician's Handbook* is an easy read. It gives a synopsis of our business today— a great quick reference guide for anyone interested in the new business of music."

—*FRED CROSHAL,* CEO of Croshal Entertainment Group
and former general manager of Maverick Records

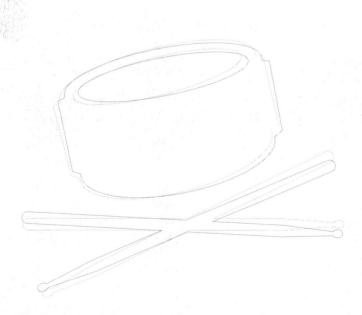